Fictions of Whiteness

NEW WORLD STUDIES
Marlene L. Daut, Editor

Fictions of Whiteness

IMAGINING THE PLANTER CASTE IN
THE FRENCH CARIBBEAN NOVEL

Maeve McCusker

University of Virginia Press
Charlottesville and London

University of Virginia Press
© 2021 by the Rector and Visitors of the University of Virginia
All rights reserved
Printed in the United States of America on acid-free paper

First published 2021

9 8 7 6 5 4 3 2 1

Library of Congress Cataloging-in-Publication Data
Names: McCusker, Maeve, author.
Title: Fictions of whiteness : imagining the planter caste in the French Caribbean novel / Maeve McCusker.
Description: Charlottesville : University of Virginia Press, 2021. | Series: New world studies | Includes bibliographical references and index.
Identifiers: LCCN 2021023922 (print) | LCCN 2021023923 (ebook) | ISBN 9780813946771 (hardcover ; acid-free paper) | ISBN 9780813946788 (paperback ; acid-free paper) | ISBN 9780813946795 (ebook)
Subjects: LCSH: Caribbean fiction (French)—History and criticism. | Whites in literature. | Creoles in literature. | Race in literature. | Plantation owners in literature. | Plantation life in literature. | LCGFT: Literary criticism.
Classification: LCC PQ3944 .M38 2021 (print) | LCC PQ3944 (ebook) | DDC 843.009/35872976—dc23
LC record available at https://lccn.loc.gov/2021023922
LC ebook record available at https://lccn.loc.gov/2021023923

Cover art: Engraving from *De planter brunel en zijne slaven asa en neno* by Henderikus Christophorus Schetsberg, 1858. (iStock/duncan1890)

To Emer, Patrick, and Kieran

Contents

Preface: A Note about Race	ix
Acknowledgments	xv
Introduction	1
1. "A Certain Uncertain Writing": Anxiety and Ambivalence in Traversay's *Les amours de Zémédare et Carina et description de l'île de la Martinique*	31
2. Unsettling the Pigmentocracy: Levilloux's *Les créoles* and Maynard's *Outre-mer*	49
3. Sympathy for the *Béké*?: Glissant and Chamoiseau	74
4. Empathy and Estrangement: Vincent Placoly's *Frères volcans*	110
5. "Here, It's Black or White": Marie-Reine de Jaham's *La grande béké* and the Unbearable Whiteness of Being	138
6. Killing the *Béké:* Crime, Fiction, and White Death	160
Conclusion	189
Notes	199
Bibliography	223
Index	241

Preface
A Note about Race

> Race is the persistent legacy [...]. No one born and nurtured in this soil has escaped its scars, and everyone—whatever their ancestral origin—is endowed with an acute racial consciousness.
> —George Lamming, *Coming, Coming Home*

EARLY IN *Texaco* (1992), Patrick Chamoiseau's heroine Marie-Sophie attempts to describe her father's master, a figure known in the Antilles as the *béké*. She has often tried to imagine this "bugger," but her father, Esternome, who claimed to know neither "his name nor his history," refused to describe him, "fearing he would come back to haunt his old age." She continues, "I like to think that his lip was thin, and that he had the dull eyes of those big cats who no longer walk man's earth. [...] Today the young *békés* in import-export have that same lip, the same eyes, and are moved more easily by a number than by the most beautiful poem."[1] This quotation, drawn from a novel in which the white master is a marginal but structuring presence, nicely encapsulates the position of the *béké* in the Antillean imaginary. Esternome, in one of a series of what we might call "un-rememberings," flatly refuses to recall his master. Such willed forgetting is a way of taking control of his own history, a history that is being radically rewritten in this epic novel to privilege the experience of Black characters rather than white. It is also, crucially, an attempt by Esternome to prevent his old age, and more significantly his daughter's youth, from being contaminated by the traumas of the slave past.[2] This forgetting causes Marie-Sophie to construct and even to relish—"I like to think"—an imagined version of the master. For both father and daughter, the *béké* is at once a source of dread—the dull-eyed, extinct felines of Marie-Sophie's imagination are uncanny, zombie-like specters drawn from the horror repertoire—and the subject of an active and willed amnesia. But he is also a figure of fascination for both, therefore as much a projection or a fantasy, or indeed a product, for the daughter at least, of what contemporary theorists might call "post-memory," as a known entity.³

The French colonized the Antilles over two hundred years before "the scramble for Africa" had even begun. The islands of the Caribbean were therefore laboratories in which colonial ideologies emerged and took shape; their history is crucial to understanding subsequent colonialisms and to the evolution of race and racism in the modern world. Coercive sexual relationships ensured immediate and intense interracial mixing on the plantation; but *békés* increasingly, as time went on, self-identified as "white" to distinguish themselves from "Blacks"—to whom they were genetically and culturally connected—and to ensure that property and capital remained in "white" hands. Race and skin color continue to occupy a fraught and painful place in the contemporary Antilles (throughout this book I use this term to denote the French Caribbean islands of Martinique and Guadeloupe: Haiti's 1804 revolution ensured a very different fate for that island's white population). These islands, as *départements d'outre-mer,* sit in turn, however uneasily, within a Republican context where whiteness remains silenced, undertheorized, and often dismissed as an Anglo-Saxon preoccupation.

I discuss the usefulness and limitations of whiteness theory in more detail in the introduction, but here I simply wish to explain my approach to the concepts of race and skin color in this book. Skin color is a marker that may trigger race-based responses, but is of course only one of a number of racial cues. One is deemed visibly white because of a complex network of visual signifiers, including the shape of the nose, eyes, and lips; the color and texture of hair. The range of phenotypes identified in the Antilles, discussed in my introduction with reference to Moreau de Saint-Méry's infamous typology, breaks apart any binary Black/white racial model. These phenotypes also reflect a pigmentocratic structure in which proximity to a "pure," unitary, and absolute whiteness (there are many ways of being Black, but only one way of being white) is indelibly associated with privilege. Richard Dyer suggests that it would be preferable to use other terms, like pink, olive, and gray, precisely to break up the monolithic nature of whiteness. But, as he argues, in our use of this one term, white, "its loading and its designation of a group not ineluctably tied to geographical origin are crucial to our understanding of white people's hold on privilege and power."⁴ The Antilles offer a spectacularly apposite example of both the supernal idealism of whiteness, and the continuing imbrication of whiteness and privilege.

Critical skepticism toward any biological concept of race, and the absurdity of racial phenotypes, are well established, and have been ably articulated by a range of voices, from the progressive to the conservative. Poststructuralist and postmodernist theorists have insisted over the last decades that *all* identity is a construct or a performance, what Judith Butler famously describes as a "stylized repetition of acts."[5] "Racial" identity is therefore as unstable, as unknowable, as all other categories (gender, sexuality, class), less a property of skin than a set of historically conditioned and sanctioned practices. Whiteness is, according to these perspectives, a performative iteration rather than a biological essence; it can be a convention, even a conviction, rather than an intrinsic condition.[6] Such resonances are captured in the title of this monograph, with its emphasis on the fictional quality of race. But critical discussions of race, as Dawn Fulton usefully reminds us, are enmeshed in "a forbidding array of conceptual and discursive double binds" that revolve around two key linguistic functions: the implication of the language of race in description (exposing the real-life experience of prejudice) and prescription (validation of the operation of this prejudice). Fulton summarizes what is at stake when we talk about a category as highly contested as race: "While exposing the fallacy of biological groundings for the concept of race has established its constructed status, the persistent and concrete effects of racism necessarily temper the impulse to debilitate the term unilaterally, and critiques of racism confront the catch-22 of discussing a paradigm whose discursive impact they seek to eliminate." Hence, as she argues, "to reject out of hand the continued invocation of this 'floating signifier' resembles too closely a dismissal of its historical, cultural, and socioeconomic incidence."[7]

This highly polarizing debate around race, a debate that is longstanding, but that has been painfully and spectacularly reignited during the months in which I was finishing this monograph,[8] has been more muted in France than in other postcolonial nations. This is because of the French nation's commitment to universalism, and its unique (among Western nations) relationship with the concept of race: the state recognizes no racial or ethnic differences among its citizens, meaning that race is invisible as an identitarian category in terms of, for example, census statistics. And yet in recent years these debates, very familiar to those working in Anglophone cultures, had begun to make an impression in France too, even before the fissile force of Black Lives Matter in spring–summer 2020 would reanimate the subject of colonialism, race, and racism in Europe and the French Republic. The unanimous decision, taken in summer 2018 by the French National Assembly, to remove the word "race" from the first article of the Republican constitution, had already polarized opinion on race in France. Whereas, in its 1946 iteration, the constitution promised equality before the law for all citizens, "without distinction of race or religion," the revised version ensures equality "without distinction of sex, origin, or religion." Responses to this controversial modification, which saw race erased and gender inserted, have crystallized precisely around *the* central debate of critical race theory. Those who approve of the word's removal argue that modern science has discredited any biological basis for racial categories, and that race cannot therefore be considered as an objective fact but rather as a concept or a social construction; the word is embroiled, they argue, in a value system that perpetuates the inequities of racism. Those who wish to maintain the word (this camp includes the leading French historian of race, Pap Ndiaye)[9] argue that the signifier forms part of a crucial critical vocabulary, and that removing the term, rather than protecting people, can only weaken the fight against racism by pushing race and racism even further under the national radar. Proponents and opponents of the change have therefore formed, as Lia Brozgal explains, into "the same ideological camps that have come to typify attitudes toward France's famous policy of colorblindness."[10]

The deconstruction of race has also left us, as Paul Warmington has shown, "buckling under the weight of scare quotes, prefixes, suffixes, qualifiers, and euphemisms."[11] If I do not use, beyond this preface, the scare quotes that are so ubiquitous in academic discussions around concepts such as whiteness, blackness, *métissage,* and other markers that seek to name racial identity, it is not only because their use in a book so centrally concerned with the color of skin would become laborious. Their absence is also a way for me to signal the continued pertinence of race and skin color generally, and the particular relevance of such concepts in a society still held to be a pigmentocracy, a society in which white Creoles continue to own vast quantities of the land, and in which infinite gradations of skin color apply.[12] It should be possible, moreover, to recognize "race" (the word and the concept) without condoning the nefarious uses to which it has been put. Race is of course a social construct, but it is also something that has much more concrete lived effects than an ideological illusion.

Writing in 2006, in one of the earliest, and still rare, discussions of whiteness in France, Tony S. Jugé and Michael Perez commence their analysis with an extraordinary statement: "While there is no blatantly racist discourse among the French political class per se, the modern politics of citizenship in France is rooted in France's racialized colonial legacy."[13] Their opening clause, already problematic in 2006, is unthinkable today, in a contemporary context marked by the intensification of racist discourse in France, the Antilles, and elsewhere (notably in the United States), a racism legitimized within and by political discourse itself.[14] This book is written against this backdrop. In my discussion of a very particular intersection between privilege and skin color in the French Caribbean, an intersection that developed under slavery and that endures in post-departmentalization Martinique and Guadeloupe, I run the risk of reinforcing the very concept I seek to critique: in other words, by naming and framing the concept of whiteness as being at the core of the project, the book might be seen to give credence to the very notion of racial phenotypes, validating well-established critiques of the legitimacy of race as a biological category even as it seeks to undermine them. Worse, the focus on the figure of the master or mistress might be seen to privilege the experience the colonizer to the detriment of the experience of the enslaved and their descendants, a project that could be seen as a kind of intellectual bad faith, a manifestation of the cruder excesses of victimology, or even as being complicit with reactionary and ideologically dubious reflexes, typified most recently in the "All Lives Matter" movement that gained traction in the wake of George Floyd's death and this event's reanimation of the Black Lives Matter movement. But race continues to matter, in institutions, in imaginations, in literature. Moreover, the master's voice in early nineteenth-century novels, but also in the work of later writers such as Marie-Reine de Jaham, is a vital presence in attempts to construct the full story of plantation and post-plantation life and literature. Attending to this voice, while also engaging with and seeking to understand the narratives produced by Black Antillean writers, will help us to deepen and complicate our understanding of Antillean fiction more generally, and notably the way in which race has been constructed and imagined. As Jacques Coursil puts it in the epigraph to my introduction, every chain has two ends, and the stories of master and enslaved are inexorably tethered together, indissociable, fundamentally imbricated with each other, and indeed often complement rather than contradict each other. In affording a privileged place to whiteness in this monograph, and in putting it under scrutiny in terms of its construction by *béké* and non-*béké* writers alike, I endorse Alfred J. López's hope that "Once the authority and superiority of whiteness reveals itself to be a fiction, the revoking of its privileges cannot be far behind."[15]

Acknowledgments

IN WRITING this book I've been privileged to work among a community of scholars who have provided friendship and support along the way. Celia Britton and Patrick Crowley were kind enough to offer comments on draft chapters, and they, along with Charles Forsdick, Mary Gallagher, Roger Little, Lorna Milne, Martin Munro, David Murphy, and Aedín Ní Loingsigh have been sources of encouragement, excellent counsel, and good humor. Michael Dash enthusiastically commissioned the book and sadly did not live to see its completion. Closer to home, I've had tremendous support from colleagues in the Languages Department in Queen's University Belfast: particular thanks to Janice Carruthers, Dominique Jeannerod, and Isabel Torres for their readings of proposals, funding applications, and draft chapters, and to Claire Moran, Steven Wilson, and Ashley Harris, who offered hands-on and unquestioning help at key moments in the final stages. Gordon Anthony, Lorraine Browne, Debbie Lisle, Mícheál Ó'Mainnín, Maria Meehan, Denise Toner, and Anna Tristram have been sources of friendship, kindness, and fun. Undergraduate students on my Caribbean Cultures final year module have shared my passion for this area over many years, and postgraduate students—in particular Laura McGinnis, Maéva McComb, and Margaret Cunningham—have offered intellectual companionship and practical help. I'd also like to thank Claire Campbell, Derval Conroy, Jill Cush, Nicolas Fève, and Brian Hollywood for their longstanding friendship.

The ideas explored here were tested and refined in papers presented in various institutions: my thanks to Claire Launchbury, Louise Hardwick, Sara-Louise Cooper, Charles Forsdick, Martin Munro, Mairéad Hanrahan, Kate Marsh (RIP), and Aedín Ní Loingsigh for invitations to speak. I owe an enormous debt of gratitude to colleagues working in the Bibliothèque Schœlcher, Fort-de-France, Martinique. Patrick Bredas over the last fifteen years has welcomed me and postgraduate students from QUB to the treasure trove that is the *Fonds local* and took a genuine interest in the various projects on which we were engaged. Claude Misat cheerfully helped me put together a program of outreach activities in Martinique in 2019, and at every turn embodied the Creole proverb "pa ni pwoblem"; he and his colleagues Dominique Catherine, Manuella Marie-Sainte, and Hugues Atine were wonderful hosts and generous, constructive interlocutors. In Paris, I'm grateful to Valérie Bouissou, Pap Ndiaye, Isabel Hollis-Touré, John McIlduff, Alessandra Celesia, and Romain Bolzinger for the interest they showed in the project and for all sorts of practical help. Eric Brandt, Charlie Bailey, and Morgan Myers at the University of Virginia Press, and freelancer Marilyn Campbell, have been supportive and scrupulous editors; and the judicious suggestions of the anonymous readers of proposal and manuscript greatly improved the book. I owe a special debt to the British Academy for the award of a research fellowship at a key point in this project: this bought me time that would otherwise have been impossible to carve out, and provided funding for me to take part in a series of rewarding research activities in Martinique. I'm also grateful to Queen's University Belfast who granted study leave at a crucial time.

This book was completed against the backdrop of Covid-19, which produced a plethora of domestic as well as professional challenges. My sister Siobhán, in particular, moved mountains to be able to help with childcare, and with anything else she possibly could, when the going got tough. My mother, Eunice, and sister Mairéad were unstinting in their support, as were the McEvoy family: Eileen, Morrigan, Órlaith, and Thérèse. Thanks too to Ciara Brennan and to the other Saint Michael's mums—you know who you are!

I am especially grateful to Kieran, who has lived with this project for a long time. His love, encouragement, and interest in the project never wavered, nor did his willingness to shoulder domestic duties, to help with various technical issues, and to select judicious Netflix offerings: all of this lightened the load considerably. I was blessed by frequent visits to my study from Patrick and Emer, whose disappointment that there were so few pictures in this book was balanced by the hope that I would eventually reach "the last page."

An earlier version of chapter 1 was published in a special issue of *French Studies*, "Towards a Postcolonial Nineteenth Century," edited by Charles Forsdick and Jennifer Yee (Maeve McCusker, "'We Were All Strangers Here': Time, Space, and Postcolonial Anxiety in Traversay's *Les amours de Zémédare et Carina et description de l'île de la Martinique*," *French Studies* 72, no. 2 [April 2018]: 209–24). Updated and reprinted by permission of Oxford University Press on behalf of the Society for French Studies. Some of the ideas developed in chapter 5 and in my conclusion were first explored in my article "All Creoles Now? *Béké* Identity and the *Éloge de la créolité*," published in a special issue of *Small Axe* titled "Eulogizing Creoleness? Rereading *Éloge de la créolité*," edited by Celia Britton and Martin Munro (*Small Axe* 21, no. 1, 220–32; © 2017, *Small Axe*, Inc., republished by permission of the rightsholder and present publisher, Duke University Press, www.dukeupress.edu).

Fictions of Whiteness

Introduction

Every chain has two ends.
—Jacques Coursil, "Édouard Glissant et *Le discours antillais*"

ON 26 JULY 2020, as work on this book neared completion, a statue of Martinican-born Joséphine de Beauharnais, which had graced the Savannah of Fort-de-France since 1859, was torn down and smashed to smithereens by sledgehammer-carrying protesters who proceeded to dance on the shattered icon. The daughter of plantation owners and first wife of Napoléon Bonaparte, Joséphine is in the Antillean imagination indelibly associated with slavery. Indeed, slavery was inscribed even on her body. Her famously wry smile, "broad and beguiling but with her teeth resolutely covered," was the result of her front left incisor having rotted from sucking on cane in her father's fields.[1] Joséphine is especially reviled because of the (unevidenced) view that she encouraged her husband to reinstate slavery in Martinique in 1802, following a first abolition in 1794, an intervention supposedly designed to reverse her family's ailing fortunes. Her statue had already in 1991 been the victim of a spectacular beheading. More recently, in the wake of the murder of George Floyd in May 2020, and as the global assault on statues and memorials celebrating colonialism gathered pace, it was further assailed. On the night of 16 July, along with the statue of Governor d'Esnambuc, the trader who first established a colony in Martinique in 1635, and whose effigy also stood on the Savannah, she was the victim of a bonfire, although her excessive height ensured that damage was restricted mainly to her plinth. Her definitive toppling, along with d'Esnambuc's, was undoubtedly inevitable, then, and indeed curiously belated.[2] What is perhaps more remarkable than her eventual removal was precisely her endurance and prominence in the Martinican cityscape since 1859.

In September 1991, Joséphine had famously been decapitated and daubed with flashes of red paint that resembled streaks of blood. Her plinth was inscribed in Creole: "Respe ba Matinik/Respe ba 22 me"

(Respect for Martinique/Respect for 22 May), the former slogan an indictment of the unequal neocolonial relationship that endures between metropole and department, the latter naming the date preferred locally to the officially sanctioned commemoration of Abolition on 10 May. The act of vandalism, attributed by some to local students, has only recently been claimed, in a remarkable 2018 television news interview with one of the assailants. The speaker recalls that the group who carried out the beheading, apparently unaffiliated with any political movement, had just left the wake of legendary Martinican musician Eugène Mona.[3] But the most immediately striking feature of the interview—and in conspicuous contrast to the manner in which Josephine was finally toppled—is the care taken to conceal the speaker's identity: he sits with his back to camera and his voice has been disguised. For all that the wounded statue (the most visited tourist site on the island) stood for almost thirty years as a symbol of postcolonial resistance to, and reappropriation of, white power, and the graffiti as a very literal "writing back" to a (still) overwhelmingly present colonial center, this historic decapitation clearly remained, even in 2018, a politically and culturally sensitive act. Meanwhile, the replica head that was subsequently recast was never reinstated, some say because the wounded and defaced icon was a more potent symbol for a defiant ex-colony, others because of fears of inciting tension in a society in which anxieties around race are never far from the surface, and which would radically resurface three decades later.[4]

The white Creole planter, known colloquially as the *béké* (and a term I privilege because of its less gendered connotations than master, planter, or *colon*), belongs to a remarkably slight demographic minority in the French Antilles. Arriving in the Caribbean at roughly the same time as the enslaved peoples over whom they would rule, *békés* historically constituted a demographic maximum of between 10 and 15 percent of the Antillean population, and today account for approximately 1 percent of the Martinican population.[5] Although marginal, as we shall see, in fiction, theory, and literary scholarship,[6] the *béké* is a foundational presence in the collective Antillean imaginary: a reviled character associated with both the trauma of slavery and with continuing economic domination, s/he is at the same time a fantasized and fetishized figure. The extent and complexity of these issues of fantasy and fetish are encoded, not just in Joséphine's maiming and more recent destruction, but also in the statue's longer history, a history that tells us much about the perennial anxieties attaching to race and skin color on the islands today, and which provides a resonant way into the issues dealt with in this book. Other icons of whiteness have been vandalized in the modern Antilles; abolitionist Victor Schœlcher has been subjected to repeated—if, until very recently, less audacious or spectacular—assaults.[7] Joséphine, too, had already been assailed many times before her decapitation while, in a strictly fictional desecration, Édouard Parépou's *Atipa roman guyanais* (Atipa, a Guyanese novel, 1885) features a Black man defecating on the statue on the day of its inauguration. In a much later piece of performance art, a naked (white) woman artist, Sarah Trouche, her body painted in a red dye associated with the Carib population, proceeded to whip the statue.[8] But Joséphine's headless (re)incarnation was for almost thirty years to speak, in a particularly suggestive way, to the complex history and highly symbolic afterlives not only of this white Creole celebrity, but also of the *blanc créole,* known as the *béké* or the *blanc pays,* in the Antillean imaginary more generally. The act of decapitation was especially symbolic, recalling the guillotining of hundreds of white Creoles in Guadeloupe during the French Revolution, a fact that helps explain the smaller proportion of white Creoles living on that island (and a fate that Joséphine herself had narrowly escaped in France).[9] Her injured, unrestored, and marginally decentered,[10] yet, until very recently, dominant, position at the center of the Martinican capital encapsulates the paradoxes and tensions that characterize a caste described, in the title of the only other monograph devoted to them, as a "dominant minority,"[11] and whose identity and self-image are intrinsically and anxiously bound up with the conflicting notions of power, vulnerability, and resilience captured in the statue.

In its original, pristine form, the sculpture also captured many of the virtues that white Creoles identified with Joséphine, and by extension themselves, their wives, and their ethnocaste more generally. She wears the classic empire-waisted dress in which she was crowned, is bedecked in chiffon, lace, and gauze, and holds a picture of Napoléon; her carefully constructed femininity emphasizes her virtue, and softens and disguises "an essentially masculine and patriarchal power: that of the white plantation owner and slave owner, that of Imperial France."[12] Femininity, piety, fidelity, and empire combine, apparently unproblematically, in this icon of white beauty and power.[13] Yet even at its inception, the statue had less to do with any triumphant celebration of untrammeled white power than with the shoring up of an already fatally weakened plantocracy. This tension can be seen even in the choice of materials used. Bronze was identified early in the planning process as the most resilient material, given the ravages of the island climate and the position of the statue so close to the seafront. However, Louis Henri de Gueydon, the governor of

Martinique who had commissioned the statue, insisted on white marble. As Laurence Brown argues, "Beyond aesthetic or practical considerations, the representation of Joséphine as a dark figure would conflict with the racial hierarchy of the colony."[14] Joséphine of necessity had to be cast in a whiter than white material because, as the governor wrote to the minister of the navy and colonies, "the somber color of bronze [. . .] will give rise to suggestions amongst the population that his Excellency can imagine without my having to suggest them here."[15] While bronze was indisputably the more durable material (and questions of durability and endurance, as we shall see, go right to the heart of white Creole anxieties), an untrammeled whiteness was held to be of yet more significance. Even then, the statue was not white enough to please all: a contemporary commentator noted the "black vein unfortunately imprinted in the marble."[16] Like so many New World manifestations of a seemingly triumphant whiteness, then, the statue is itself a work of canny construction, a performance, even a fiction, and also the site of profound unease.

During the ceremonial laying of the first stone of the statue, Jean Catel, then mayor of Fort-de-France, alluded to the "revolutionary hurricane which struck Martinique in 1848," which meant that it was only in 1852, when "calm had succeeded the storm, and tranquility restored under the reparative government of H.M. Napoléon III," that the work of commemorating Joséphine could begin. Catel's euphemistic dismissal of the 1848 revolution, which brought with it the second and definitive Abolition of slavery, as a passing tempest, a temporary interruption in the ongoing narrative of white dominance, is an act of profound denial.[17] The statue, commissioned a mere four years after this cataclysmic event, is therefore inseparable from the traumatic (for the white plantocracy) historical context in which it was commissioned and produced, and was always a marker of the end of empire rather than an icon of its endurance. Indeed, so worried were those responsible for commissioning the monument about potential attacks on it in the 1850s that a hugely expensive railing had to be imported from France to protect it from assault. In other words, the celebration of strength, power, and dominance that was ostensibly inscribed in the excessive size of the monument (five meters high), her classic empire attire, and the pristine white marble in which she was sculpted was always inextricably linked to anxieties around that very dominance. The statue therefore testifies to an early and ongoing desire on the part of white Creoles to cast themselves (literally, in classical statuary and portraiture, but also discursively and metaphorically in literature and other cultural production) as the ancient, indomitable, and legitimate owners of land only recently, and shamefully acquired, cleansed of native peoples, planted and populated with enslaved Africans.

The original statue's exaggerated assertion of legitimacy, longevity, and nobility can thus be read as an attempt to occlude both the horror of the plantocracy's foundations and the shakiness of its tenure. And her vandalized, desacralized, headless, and, more recently, anonymized state[18] showed her to be a figure of resilience as well as fragility, looming large in the Martinican cityscape, in the white Creole imaginary, and in collective memory more generally. Joséphine continued for decades to stand, at once broken *and* unbowed. Her immense but anonymous form towered over a disdainful, often hostile, populace, just as the stranglehold of her caste over the Antillean economy remained pervasive but curiously faceless. In perhaps the only fictional portrayal of those who carried out the decapitation (and in marked contrast to Aimé Césaire's synecdoche of the "malevolent or zealous hands" which had maimed the statue),[19] Édouard Glissant in *Tout-monde* describes Joséphine's beheaders as intrepid "décabosseurs," dent removers. As Kylie Sago notes, the term gestures toward the idea that the beheading "restored the statue to its original contours," and evocatively suggests that the statue's head was itself "the dent in need of repair."[20] Glissant intimates, in a way that directly resonates with the concerns of this book, that the wounded icon had an integrity and a specific iconic resonance to which the original statue could only aspire. The tensions between omnipotence and persecution, between dominance and muteness, or at the very least the uneasy relationships among supremacy, vulnerability, victimhood, and anonymity that characterize the post-Abolition, and especially perhaps the post-departmentalization plantocracy, were captured in the wounded memorial, itself as we saw a fiction of triumphant whiteness, a "postcolonial performance,"[21] and a site of ambivalent and even traumatized power. These same tropes and motifs permeate the fiction analyzed in this study.

Joséphine's removal in 2020 was effected not under cover of night as her decapitation had been, but on a busy Sunday morning, by a large group of mostly unmasked (even as Covid-19 raged) activists. Many sang, chanted, and brandished the Martinican flag, and were defiantly filmed by a jubilant crowd. The highly public nature of this act, and the exuberance of the actors, reveals a radical transformation in Antillean "memory wars" over slavery, and points to an assertion of a local identity that confidently rejects the legacies of colonization and slavery captured in the statues of d'Esnambuc and Joséphine. It remains to be seen whether the statue's removal signals a more fundamental repositioning of the *béké* caste in Antillean society more generally.

The Invention of Whiteness

From the beginning of colonization in the early seventeenth century, the Antillean plantation, known locally as the *habitation,* was characterized by the extreme proximity in which masters and slaves coexisted. Coercive sexual relationships ensured intense intercaste mixing, amplifying, much more than on the huge plantations of the US Deep South, the interactions within and between its occupants.[22] Racial designations, always unreliable, acquired an especially unstable character in this context. Frédéric Régent's examination of early census data in Guadeloupe and Martinique concludes that for the first half century of the colonial enterprise the term "white" was not used at all as a substantive, European settlers being referred to simply as "French."[23] The emergence of a category of "whites" was, then, belated, and propelled by the emergence of the mulatto caste; this triggered the desire for segregation and therefore the interdiction of marriage between Blacks and whites. The designation "white," first used in a census in 1694, became a means to construct a judicial and social order, and from its earliest usage was, as Régent shows, a fiction, or what he calls a "fabrication." Régent gives the example of the parish of Anse Bertrand in Guadeloupe where, out of sixty-nine plantation owners who qualified as white in the census of 1797–98, twenty-eight had a Black ancestor. This 40 percent was, he states, a minimum proportion, given that the ancestry of many whites could not be guaranteed to be 100 percent European. He quotes Victor Schœlcher who, in 1842, noted that a mixed population in La Désirade and Les Saintes (dependencies of Guadeloupe) had been declared white almost a century earlier by a Supreme Court judgment. When Schœlcher queries this, he is told that "they must have needed whites at that time!" (for the defense of the colonies, or for managing the enslaved, for example). Moreover, these "mixed whites" ("ces réputés blancs issus du métissage") were the first to participate in the exclusion of peoples of mixed blood who found themselves on the wrong side of the color line. The success of the category of "white," as Régent notes, came therefore from the mixed race themselves.[24]

Once the French presence was secured, and the dominant caste judged itself to be sufficiently numerous to protect itself, the white population closed in on itself in order to exclude others from its ranks. Individuals of mixed race who had not been recognized as white found themselves relegated to the category of "free person of color." This moment is held to be around 1700.[25] Régent distinguishes this reflex to categorize and to separate races in the Caribbean from the scientific racism that would emerge in the nineteenth century; when arguments in favor of discrimination were made by Antillean planters, it was always in the context of morals and the social order, rather than physical difference. Between 1625 and 1848, any essentialist racism was unthinkable because it contravened observable and lived social realities. On the other hand, the invention of the "white" category had a strong social utility: the maintenance of the domination of this class over all others. It was wealth and reputation, as well as color, that created the white individual. In other words, the relationship between skin color and race was and remains a slippery one. It was only in 1835, on the cusp of Abolition, that the terms "white" and "race" became entwined in the dictionary of the Académie Française.[26]

And yet, beyond their linguistic conjoining in an official dictionary, race and skin color were already interconnected in the colonial imagination, an uneasy intimacy most notoriously delineated in Moreau de Saint-Méry's *Description topographique, physique, civile, politique et historique de la partie française de l'isle Saint-Domingue* (Topographical, physical, civil, political, and historical description of the French part of the island of Saint-Domingue, written between 1776 and 1789 and published in 1797).[27] In what Joan Dayan describes as "the first attempt to theorize color as part of a peculiarly colonial enlightenment,"[28] this Martinican-born white Creole slave-owner (1750–1819), who also claimed common ancestry with Joséphine,[29] produced an infamously detailed typology, based on arithmetical theory, of the various permutations of skin color possible in the French colony of Saint-Domingue (now Haiti). Moreau hierarchizes 128 possible combinations of Black–white miscegenation emerging from nine categories (the *sacatra*, the *griffe*, the *marabout*, the *mulâtre*, the *quarteron*, the *métis*, the *mamelouk*, the *quarteronné*, and the *sang-mêlé*) and establishes white colonists as constituting a supreme epidermal aristocracy. As Dayan observes, no matter "how many kinds of blackness can be named and claimed, whiteness remains a supernal ideal."[30] Unsurprisingly, this colonial encyclopedia has been roundly exposed as "one of the more remarkable legalistic fantasies of the New World," a work that is "stranger than any supernatural fiction."[31] Critics have ridiculed its classificatory paranoia, dismissed the absurdity of its ambition to account for all possible phenotypes, and critiqued the gender politics that underlie Moreau's vision of racial mixing. But in general terms, the study responds, as Doris Garraway explains, to two basic dilemmas: first, how to "rationalize the release of white libidinal energies across the colonial color spectrum while at the same time marking the limits of white purity." Secondly, and more importantly for the white elite, it represents an early attempt to "manage the biological reproduction of colonial society so as to ensure its own survival within it."[32] The question that lies at the heart of Moreau's work, of just how to protect whiteness, was contemporaneous with the increase in property ownership and prosperity among free people of color in the late eighteenth century.

The slave-owning class, then, would progressively and self-protectively identify as white, to mark their difference from the "mixed" populations to whom they were genetically and culturally connected and, crucially, to ensure that property and capital remained concentrated within clans rather than dissipated. The more pressure that was brought to bear on whiteness in these laboratories of *métissage,* the more the white Creole community insisted on its separateness. This community remains today an intensely self-segregating and secretive one, bound by its own internal codes. *Békés,* who constitute today approximately 1 percent of the population, are willfully disconnected from the majority population, send their children to private schools, socialize among their own caste, frequent their own beaches, and, most importantly of all, operate a system of endogamy designed to ensure that wealth remains within the caste. For most Antilleans, they are "quasi-mythical beings, more talked about than seen, and social relations between white Creoles and other categories of the local population remain a rarity, though it is often said that the *békés* are less racist than in the past—at least they now marry metropolitans."[33] The Antilles remains a society obsessed with gradations of skin color, and with the social hierarchies that largely reflect, or are determined by, racial identity.

The pathological desire among nonwhite Antilleans to "blanchir la race" (whiten the race) or to "chapè sa peau" (escape one's skin), by marrying "whiter," or to acquire "la peau sauvée" (saved skin) by being born lighter than one's parents, is well attested in literary, sociological, and psychoanalytic material. If, as Claudia Benthien notes in her study *Skin,* language retains "the close relationship among identity, self-consciousness, and one's own skin" through colloquial expressions such as "to get under someone's skin,"[34] these everyday Antillean expressions register the prevalence and intimacy of racial hierarchies in the Antilles, and the imbrication of social mobility and skin color. Skin is a key marker of status. The elusive drive to "absolute" whiteness is poignantly encapsulated in the title of Laurette Mas-Camille's collection of short stories *Quand je serai béké . . . et autres nouvelles plus probables* (When I'm a *béké* . . . and other more likely stories, 2013). These various impulses are counterbalanced by the *béké* desire to "preserve the race," a historic dictum that remains a watchword of contemporary society, and which was used to such incendiary effect by *béké* Alain Huyghues Despointes in the 2009 documentary *Les derniers maîtres de la Martinique* (The last masters of Martinique), discussed in my conclusion. All of this is complicated by the islands' anomalous political position: ex-plantation colonies, Guadeloupe and Martinique have since 1946 been *départements d'outre-mer* (DROMs, overseas departments and regions). Their inhabitants are full French citizens, therefore members of the avowedly "colorblind" French Republic. They live in a society in which sensitivities to race and skin color are determining features of everyday life, and yet are subject to a Republican constitution that refuses to recognize race or skin color as an identitarian variable. The minority status of *blancs créoles,* meanwhile, means that their skin color is experienced less as an unquestioned norm or as a "noncolor"—the starting point for critical whiteness studies—than as a highly marked and visible condition. This has inoculated them from what we might call the banality of racial privilege, or from what Richard Dyer describes as the naturalization of whiteness as "not a color."[35] Even when asserting their own "lack" of color, fictional characters repeatedly betray anxiety rather than security, not just in relation to the Black population but, more worryingly for them, the mulatto. As a character in Raphaël Tardon's novel *La caldeira* asserts, "We have no color [. . .]. My son, don't involve yourself any more with this Perrier. He's a mulatto. Cultivate your own prestige."[36]

Régis Antoine notes that the fraught historical position of the French Caribbean planter is reflected even in the vexed nomenclature of the plantation; the profusion of names by which he was known suggests that he was a "figure who made and reinvented himself according to historical vicissitudes."[37] As Antoine notes, "l'habitué" and "l'habitant" (the habituated and the inhabitant) were early designations that have fallen largely out of use, but that endure in toponyms and other expressions: he cites the example of local crabs, known as "crabes zhabitants." (That the Antillean plantation is much more commonly known as the *habitation* amplifies, as Mary Gallagher suggests, the "quasi-ontological category of dwelling [. . .] rather than a provisional economic arrangement," replacing the harsh realities of labor with the "more clement and congenial connotations of residence.")[38] The figure was also known as the "colon" and as the "Américain," a term particularly common in France in the eighteenth century, and one that authors such as Traversay, Louis de Maynard, and much later, Daniel de Grandmaison, will claim as their own. Other designations identified by Antoine include "le maître d'esclaves," "le Blanc créole" and "le Béké." This last term, *béké*, is perhaps the most common, and the most politically charged, of all those used to describe the white Creole in the Antilles today.

In the opening pages of Glissant's *Tout-monde*, set in 1788, the narrator (introducing La Roche, whom we shall meet again in chapter 3 of this book) wonders whether "they were already called *békés* at this point" (11), a moment that registers the historical instability of the word. While Lambert-Félix Prudent has identified an instance of the term as early as 1755,[39] it was only in the 1820s and 1830s that it gained currency.[40] Deborah Jenson identifies an early usage by Marceline Desbordes-Valmore in a letter of 1833,[41] and its first fictional appearance, as *béquet*, was in Louis de Maynard's *Outre-mer* in 1835.[42] One of the earliest local usages that I have identified is in an 1823 letter written by planter Pierre Dessalles, an example already embedded in a context of sexual exploitation. The letter refers to the presumed impregnation of a slave, Trop (whose very name bespeaks the egregious inequalities of plantation life) by an elderly *béqué*.[43] The entry of the neologism *béké* into general parlance in the 1820s and 1830s exactly parallels the entry of the terms "white" and "race" into the dictionary of the Académie Française as we saw above, suggesting a particularly heightened anxiety around race in the period between the Haitian Revolution and the Abolition of 1848, a point to which we frequently return in the first three chapters of this book.

Commentators have suggested wildly varying etymological histories for the term. Some claim that it is a distortion of the command to hoe ("béchez"), others that it derives from the initials of "blancs kréols," others still that it originated in the name of Scottish explorer William Balfour Baikie (1825–1864), who spent significant time in Nigeria, and whose name was supposedly used by Ibos to describe whites. (This last explanation, which has a certain currency as the one offered by Wikipedia,[44] is implausible, given that Baikie was only ten when Maynard's *Outre-mer* was published.) Andrea Stuart also connects the word to the Ibos, but claims that it derives from the phrase "whites found under the leaves," which has "derogatory connotations of low or illegitimate birth."[45] It is probable that Stuart conflates the substantive with a term commonly used to name a lower-class *béké*, a "béké en bas feuille." Others suggest that it derives from oral French, whether "Eh bé qui?" or to describe the *blancs des quais*,[46] quay-side whites. Deborah Jenson writes that the term comes from an African loan word, *buckra,* present as early as 1688 in Aphra Behn's *Oroonoko* as "backeary," and which was adapted into French Creole as *béké*.[47] In keeping with the animalistic origins of other racial designations (mulatto from mule; *chabin,* a sheep-goat hybrid), Chantal Maignan argues that *béquet* comes from *biquet,* a young goat,[48] although her thesis is dismissed by Raphaël Confiant on the basis that such a bestial association is unlikely in a name used to designate the master.[49] Not only, then, does the French planter and his descendants go under a wide number of aliases, but the origins of his most commonly used sobriquet—which either does, or does not, derive from the racial designation *blanc*—vary quite wildly. Often said to be an exclusively Martinican term, it is current in Guadeloupe, where the designation "blanc pays" is also used. Although it is commonly used by white Creoles themselves (and in a novel such as Jaham's *La grande béké* acquires a totemic status as the protagonist's privileged mode of self-address in her interior monologues), the word *béké* nonetheless carries a strongly political, and sometimes pejorative, charge. The term remains embedded in the psycholinguistic structure of the contemporary Antilles ("What do you do for the *béké?*" is a common way to ascertain someone's job) and was notably mobilized to highly polemical effect in the slogan "békés dewo" (Out with *békés*) during the 2009 strikes. And, as Michael Giraud reminds us, racialized terminology easily slides into class; the term can simply designate "a boss, or a rich man, regardless of the color of the individual concerned."[50]

The history of white Creoles since Abolition remains conditioned by slavery, and societal stratification along race and class lines remains deeply entrenched. Land and business assets are still controlled by a tiny white economic elite. In Guadeloupe the plantocracy, already more fragile than in Martinique due to the temporary abolition of slavery in 1794, lost its economic dominance and by 1802, when slavery was reinstated, "had been superseded by metropolitan and Martinican companies,"[51] although Yarimar Bonilla makes clear that the *béké* remains to this day an economically powerful figure in that island too. In Martinique, however, the *béké* caste, in an unbroken narrative of dominance and exploitation stretching back to the time of slavery, retained much of its stranglehold on the local economy. The profound inequalities between local landowners and former slaves persisted: throughout the nineteenth and early twentieth centuries, local whites remained firmly in control of the political landscape and managed to retain their economic supremacy. Planters, who had been compensated by government for the loss of their slaves, continued to control labor laws and paid paltry wages.

Part of the rationale for departmentalization had been to wrest power away from the white elite. Bonilla argues that the fear that independence from France would consolidate *béké* wealth "led many in the region, including intellectuals like Aimé Césaire, to turn to the political project of French incorporation."[52] Politicians of Césaire's generation considered the promises of political and economic equality embodied in the French Republic as being ideologically incompatible with the racial and social hierarchies operating in the Antilles. Therefore, as Justin Daniel suggests, "obtaining rights from the state was the path followed by these classes to take revenge and to struggle against the *békés* (white creole class) and their hegemony."[53] Yet, post-1946, as Glissant reminds us, *békés* were "salvaged and promoted" in an economy now based on tertiary rather than primary or secondary products.[54] The caste has adapted to changing economic patterns, transitioning "from a production-based plantation model to a consumption-driven import, tourist, and service dominated economy";[55] they have also, for example, launched a strikingly successful business around the production and export of prestige rum. More generally, as Bonilla explains, "*békés* continue to be synonymous with the 'owning class'—they have successfully morphed from planters into businessmen by continuing to control the shifting means of production in the French Antilles."[56] Today the caste controls the export-import and agri-food industries, and dominates the hotel business and most major wholesale and retail operations. They have progressively distanced themselves from the rest of the Martinican population, and constitute an elusive, reclusive, and exclusive minority, who frequently present themselves as victims in contemporary society.

Let's (Not) Talk about Race: Whiteness in a Minority Context

The remarkable rise of critical whiteness studies in Anglophone scholarship over the last twenty-five years (notably in the US, the UK, South Africa, and Australia) reflects a growing attentiveness to the supposedly dominant, but invisible norms that structure power relations. Just as masculinity studies evolved as an outworking of, and a complement to, feminist criticism, so scholars of ethnicity and race, working in a range of fields from psychoanalysis to anthropology, from social sciences to literary studies, would from the 1990s gravitate to another dominant identity, whiteness. Indeed, some have argued that whiteness is not just another unexamined norm, like masculinity, but is in many ways the overarching norm from which all others derive. For Ross Chambers, for example, whiteness is so prevalent in Western discourse that it should be seen not as a classificatory identity, but rather as synonymous with being human. Chambers argues that "there are plenty of unmarked categories (maleness, heterosexuality, and middleclassness being obvious ones), but whiteness is perhaps *the* primary unmarked and so unexamined—let's say 'blank'—category."[57] In the attempt to theorize this "blank" category, and to better understand how the so-called center constructs and imagines itself, a dazzling and diverse range of studies have appeared, from Richard Dyer's classic study, *White*, through titles such as *Desiring Whiteness; Displacing Whiteness; Undoing Whiteness; Imagining Whiteness; Deconstructing Whiteness; Performing Whiteness; Revealing Whiteness; Postcolonial Whiteness; Habits of Whiteness*. All start from the position that whiteness is based on no epidermal or biological reality. Critics have instead asserted the slipperiness of race, its scientific invalidity, and its constructed or imagined status; these almost universal caveats, which necessarily de-essentialize whiteness in order to emphasize rather the spurious, metaphorical, or fictional quality of the topic under discussion, are perhaps most pithily summarized in Gerry Turcotte's observation that the very idea of "an isolated and pure whiteness" has always been "a pigment of the white imagination."[58]

In Anglophone criticism, the field is now a well-established subject of enquiry, as attested by dedicated research networks (the Critical Whiteness Studies Group in the University of Illinois at Urbana–Champaign; the Australian Critical Race and Whiteness Association), academic conferences, special issues of journals, dedicated bibliographies—Engles's "Towards a Bibliography of Critical Whiteness Studies" dates from as early as 2006—and a growing visibility in journalism and writing beyond the academic community. Indeed, so rapid has the rise of whiteness studies been that already in 2011, the editors of a landmark collection could identify three distinct waves in the field's development, in a parallel to the accepted metaphor for feminist criticism.[59] Although the field is strikingly interdisciplinary, and is today arguably dominated by research emanating from the social sciences, most commentators locate its origins in literary studies, and specifically in Toni Morrison's exhortation in *Playing in the Dark* to "discover, through a close look at literary 'blackness,' the nature—even the cause—of literary 'whiteness.'"[60] Morrison's call has been answered by the numerous studies devoted to the construction and representation of whiteness in varying literary and historical contexts, from Shakespeare's to Victoria's to Thatcher's England, and from contemporary Latino cultures to contemporary South Africa.[61] The vast bulk of literary analyses sparked by her call have, however, focused on postslavery cultures in the United States, with some extending to the Anglophone Caribbean. Morrison's own work has been approached via this critical angle, as has writing by other writers from plantation cultures, both Black and white.[62]

Given this energetic and rapidly expanding field of study, it may seem surprising that critics and theorists of French Caribbean literature have all but ignored whiteness as a structuring motif in culture and society.[63] While the English word "whiteness" generates 313 hits in the catalog of France's National Library, "blancheur" gives only 150, less than half its Anglophone equivalent, almost all of which qualify nonhuman things, mostly flowers, stars, or snow. Meanwhile whiteness as a search item in the British Library catalog produces 6,641 results.[64] If these admittedly crude indicators reveal anything, it is perhaps both the lack of traction that whiteness studies has garnered in France, and the semantic oddity of the French substantive when applied to skin color. While whiteness passes easily in English, "blancheur" (although used by Morrison's French translator and conspicuously deployed by Fanon throughout his first book) sounds a rather odd note in French.[65] Other nonstandard lexemes such as *blanchité* or *blanchitude* are also marginal. If "blanchité" is the term preferred by scholars such as Maxime Cervulle, Judith Ezekiel, and Laurent Dornel, it too has gained little momentum as a theoretical term: it figures only twice in the catalog of France's National Library (as a thematic keyword: it is strikingly absent as a titular term). Only four doctoral theses, across all disciplines, have to date ever used the term *blanchité* in their title, all from social sciences, only one of which was completed before 2018.[66]

Several factors might be adduced to explain this invisibility, or the blanking out, of whiteness studies in French-language criticism. First, the model is undoubtedly considered to be part of an Anglo-Saxon cultural studies agenda, to which the French academy has been notoriously resistant.[67] As Sylvie Laurent and Thierry Leclère sardonically observe, this "sad racial qualification" is largely associated with "American communitarianism," while for whites living in the supposedly colorblind Republic of France, "we are all blue-white-red."[68] Moreover, in the specific Antillean context, theoretical movements initially privileged the other pole of the color spectrum (*négritude*) and, more recently, celebrated racial and cultural mixing (*créolité*), the latter movement notoriously privileging some Antillean phenotypes above others, despite the rallying cry of *Lettres créoles*, which claimed to celebrate the "open range of the Antillean color palette."[69] Most importantly, though, there are good empirical reasons why the starting premise of whiteness studies—the ubiquity and consequent "invisibility" of whiteness, or as Chambers puts it, its status as a "blank" category—is not especially illuminating in the Antilles. While most US citizens self-identify as white (77% in a 2010 census), whites have always been a tiny minority of the Caribbean population. If white privilege in the West, as Shannon Sullivan argues, is "unseen, invisible, even seemingly non-existent," and therefore operates as a "set of unconscious psychical and somatic habits,"[70] it could be argued that Martinique and Guadeloupe challenge, and in many respects invert, this paradigm. The numerical paucity of whites on these islands, to say nothing of the divisions between French-born and Creole whites (the latter split between *petits* and *grands blancs*) has ensured that any sense of monolithic whiteness has been fractured. *Békés* have always been a tiny, self-segregating minority of already small populations, who therefore experience a heightened visibility and an accentuated sense of their own color(less) status. Peggy McIntosh's evocative image of white privilege, replete with the "invisible weightless knapsack of special provisions, assurances, tools, maps, guides, codebooks, passports, visas, clothes, compass, emergency gear, and blank checks,"[71] is only part of the story of the Antillean *béké*, for whom white privilege is highly marked and often appears to weigh heavily. Unable to portray itself as either benign or "normal" (in the sense of constituting a norm), whiteness in the Antilles has always had to reckon, even subconsciously, with its own history of violence and illegitimate hegemony.

For all of its invisibility in French academic discourse, 2013 saw the publication in France of two major studies which, for the first time, put whiteness at the center of their analysis, explicitly engaging with critical whiteness studies, and specifically interrogating the uneasy position of France's by now notorious claims to institutional colorblindness.[72] Maxime Cervulle's monograph *Dans le blanc des yeux* (In the white of the eyes) announces its intention to "interrogate the social construction of *blanchité*," and to attend to the ways in which, in former colonies, whiteness comes to "occupy a hegemonic position in the context of a racist ideology which seeks to associate whiteness of skin with purity, neutrality, or universality."[73] Cervulle links the origins of his project to the riots that took hold of France in 2005, a year that also saw the founding of the MIR (Mouvement International pour les Réparations—the International Movement for Reparations) and the CRAN (Conseil représentatif des associations noires de France—the Representative Council for Black Associations in France), and a period that he describes as a turning point during which tensions around race and privilege came to the forefront of French society in an especially violent way. In the same year, Sylvie Laurent's and Thierry Leclère's major edited collection *De quelle couleur sont les blancs?* (What color are whites?) brought together a diverse range of commentators and critics, who historicize and theorize whiteness in the French-speaking world. Both publications are theoretically sophisticated works that, in their engagement with conceptual innovations in the Anglophone world, seek to illuminate the construction and sanctification of whiteness in a wide range of francophone contexts, in the metropole and beyond. Rather than heralding an epistemological turning point, however, they can be seen as isolated academic exceptions that prove the more general rule of disengagement; these excellent studies have not in themselves generated any sustained or significant critical interest and crucially have not inspired other scholars to engage with whiteness.

But it would be wrong to caricature the French academy as being *uniquely* resistant to the study of race and whiteness. Francophone postcolonial studies, a subfield that might at first appear the natural home for reflection on race, whiteness, and privilege, has been surprisingly muted when it comes to discussion of precisely these issues. It can be said as a discipline to fall especially heavily between several theoretical stools. In other words, the marginalization of discussions of whiteness is linked, ironically, to the second term of the field's putative title (postcolonial) as much as to the first. Alfred J. López notes that, with the exception of Bhabha and Fanon, postcolonial studies, "with its accompanying aversion to any seemingly oppositional logic and affinity for linguistic and literary, as opposed to sociological, critique," has side-stepped the study of race, and in particular, of whiteness. López continues, "conversely, the under-theorization of colonial whiteness may be the product of a simple conflation; that is, whiteness in this context may be so closely associated with colonial domination that no further distinction seems necessary or desirable."[74] While there is a great deal of scholarship in postcolonial and whiteness studies individually, relatively little addresses the particular intersections of race and power, what López describes as an "undertheorized convergence."[75]

White Writing, Writing White

Antillean colonists, who have throughout history been overwhelmingly outnumbered by the nonwhite, enslaved population, were always acutely aware of the fragility of their tenure and of their minority status. From their earliest writings, the planter class exhibited signs of what Roger Toumson characterized as the "siege mentality" of the colonizer (the original French expression "complexe obsidionale" has a more strongly pathological charge, referring as it does to a collective psychosis).[76] The literary output of white Creoles is admittedly a belated and an uneven one, to say nothing of its questionable literary quality. Eighteenth-century Creole poets such as Parny and Léonard were mostly in denial of their Caribbean origins, and eager to pass as entirely French; as Jack Corzani argues, "indifference to local conditions characterizes almost all the poetry produced by white Creoles during the entire eighteenth century. This poetry is mostly linked to emigration."[77] Although history and ethnography by and about Antilleans was already grappling, however problematically, with issues of race and color, it was only during the nineteenth century that a properly Creole literary tradition emerges, one in which the Antilles are front and center in terms of setting, plot, and themes, and in which the white ethnocaste begins to consider its own history and social status through fiction.[78] The period between the loss of Saint-Domingue in 1804 and the abolition of slavery in 1848 saw a marked intensification in cultural activity: substantial novels were published, important journals and periodicals founded, and the first histories of the islands were produced. This "boom" has been directly linked to the political and social upheavals that beset the white oligarchy,[79] upheavals that created an acute sense of anxiety in the planter caste; it is surely for this very reason that writers such as Glissant and Chamoiseau, in the few novels in which they put planter characters at the heart of narrative (and which are discussed in chapter 3), revert to this period as well. But very quickly Abolition, and the attendant collapse of the economic and ideological system on which the colonists depended, ensured that the concerns of white Creoles came to appear highly anachronistic and reactionary, not to say politically incorrect. This was a short-lived efflorescence, then, which was curtailed by history and had little momentum. Small wonder that by the 1840s we witness a striking reduction in the number of texts published by a group faced with much more pressing challenges,[80] leading one recent commentator to the not unjustified observation that the "white aristocracy on the islands produced a lot of sugar and very few writers."[81]

Only two *béké* writers, at opposite ends of the literary value spectrum, can be said to have any recognition value in the contemporary Antilles: Saint-John Perse, the Nobel-winning Guadeloupean poet often considered as French; and Marie-Reine de Jaham, a prolific and populist novelist whose entire fictional universe is steeped in the French Caribbean and who is discussed in chapter 5 of this book. While other *béké* novelists (for example Daniel de Grandmaison), along with writers wrongly assumed to belong to this caste (Drasta Houël), would emerge sporadically in the twentieth century, and are referred to in passing in this study, their works—society novels that turn on romance, familial intrigue and often murder—can be characterized as "minor." The French Caribbean islands have no white novelist of the stature of a Jean Rhys, for example. White Creoles have been, at least since the mid-nineteenth century and with few exceptions, reticent in culture and politics. As David Macey notes, "the voice of the *béké* is rarely heard" in contemporary Antillean culture.[82] Roger de Jaham's Tous Créoles! movement (discussed in my conclusion), founded in 2007 and an exception to this general rule of silence, might be considered something of a pale imitation of the *créolité* movement and is in any case more engaged in local history and politics than in literature.

Early Creole writers have in turn been marginal in scholarship on the French Caribbean. The nineteenth-century novelists considered here (Traversay, Levilloux, and Maynard) were all one-hit fictional wonders whose output bore many of the hallmarks of literary immaturity. More significant, undoubtedly, are the interrelated issues of ideology and literary value. Although postcolonial literary studies is ostensibly a "margin-hugging field," it is, as Chris Bongie has argued, nonetheless deeply invested in hierarchies of literary taste.[83] Early novels, in their excessive melodrama, sentimentality, and length, often negatively reviewed even in their own time, are particularly inimical to contemporary tastes, especially given the textualist turn of much postcolonial criticism. They are also ideologically at odds with the notions of resistance, subversion, and contestation that are the privileged modes of postcolonial writing. Inclusion in the postcolonial canon, as Martin Munro has suggested, has often "been based on veneration," in the sense that Black authors writing against colonialism and repression have "quite rightly been praised and promoted."[84] The literature produced by white Creoles almost invariably testifies to a self-obsessive gaze, is profoundly committed to the maintenance of the status quo, and tends to be nostalgic for an earlier golden age in which the values of the plantocracy were more secure. This writing, which was never likely to be in the vanguard of literary or ideological innovation, occupies, therefore, an anxious liminal space within the emergent canon of francophone postcolonial studies,[85] a discipline characterized by "the subtle mainstreaming of ostensibly subversive postcolonial discourses by the Euro-North American academy and critical machine."[86]

The invaluable groundwork done by Corzani and others in the 1970s and 1980s, to exhume precursor texts and to make some available to modern readers through reissues, either restricted itself to excavation (Joyau's reprints, for example, have scant introductions and no critical apparatus), or tended toward the encyclopedic, the wide-ranging, and the descriptive. Critical works such as Toumson's *Le nègre romantique* and Antoine's *Les écrivains français et les Antilles* deal with hundreds of primary sources, consider Antillean writers alongside their metropolitan counterparts (often to the detriment of the former), offer plot summaries, and sketch key themes. As Jacqueline Couti suggests, the negative appraisals brought to bear in these early studies may well have acted as a disincentive to subsequent critics.[87] Another, no doubt greater, deterrent to continuing and deepening the work of these early critics was the strong gravitational pull toward Black Antillean writing that we see from the 1980s onward. For literary critics interested in such subjects as slavery, colonialism, and the ghosts of the past, the remarkable outpouring of world-class writing that characterized the French Caribbean in recent decades offered a fertile, highly self-aware, and intellectually rewarding terrain. And in this writing, the *colon* is usually diegetically marginal, or figures as a powerful absent presence. Often, he is literally an absentee, as in Joseph Zobel's *La rue cases-nègres;* occasionally he has been relegated to a position off the narrative register, responsible for primal crimes of rape that have led to characters' conception, but long-disappeared.

Author-driven work on now canonical writers—Glissant, Chamoiseau, Condé—has been complemented by thematic studies that have focused on such topics as gender, place, childhood, memory, and time, all contextualized within the metanarrative of slavery. In parallel, readings privileging a particular theoretical prism (postcolonialism, poststructuralism, feminism, ecocriticism) have ensured that a voluminous and highly sophisticated body of critical work exists to help us better understand the rich complexity of a vibrant, and often demanding or even difficult literary production.[88] The field today, however, reflects the presentist and politically resistant bias that characterizes postcolonial studies more generally, privileging work by Black writers from the 1940s onward to the detriment of earlier texts authored mainly by white Creoles. Moreover, while certain tropes (opacity, creolization, trauma, resistance) and types (the maroon, the storyteller, the authorial double) have been heavily scrutinized, a key structural figure in the plantation chronotope has been almost entirely neglected: the *béké*, the white Creole master and his/her descendants. The *béké* therefore figures as an absence in fiction, criticism, and theory relating to the Caribbean: on the theoretical level, a mask concealing black skin for Fanon, or one element among many for more recent theorists of *métissage, créolité, relation*.

Histories, sociological analyses, and literary studies of the *béké* are also thin on the ground. Edith Kováts Beaudoux's monograph, *Les blancs créoles de la Martinique*, was published in 2002, but the fieldwork on which it is based dates from 1965–66. General histories of the islands have often steered clear of the caste altogether or discussed it only in passing. Rebecca Hartkopf Schloss's *Sweet Liberty* stands as an exception to this rule, although it deals only with the years 1802–48. More recently Kathryn E. Browne, in a seemingly counterintuitive assertion framing her study of Creole economics, declares that "I have included almost no discussion of the relationship of *békés* [. . .] to Creole economics. I leave them out for the simple reason that, almost without exception, they were not willing to be interviewed for this research."[89] In the end Browne's exclusion cannot hold; perhaps inevitably, she devotes significant space to the *béké*, who has roughly as many index entries as Abolition, the Catholic Church, and creolization. But the very fact that a monograph devoted to Antillean economics can reasonably claim to exclude the most powerful actors in that very economy gives a sense of the remoteness and inaccessibility of the caste. Other sporadic articles have been published, often in response to isolated historical incidents. Notably the cost-of-living strikes that paralyzed the islands in 2009 generated a small but significant number of publications.[90] These strikes, coupled with the fallout from the controversial documentary *Les derniers maîtres de la Martinique*, confirmed that the outworkings of Martinique and Guadeloupe's slave past continue to fuel friction between the Black and white inhabitants of the islands, and undoubtedly intensified *béké* reluctance to speak to academics and journalists.

Scholarship on the caste, in the fields of anthropology, sociology, history, and ethnography, has therefore been sparse and fragmentary. In literary studies, less dependent on interview data and thus, in theory, less hampered by the caste's reticence, it is surprisingly almost nonexistent. No full-length study devoted to the literature produced by the caste exists. The story is also, with one or two notable exceptions, one of almost systematic exclusion in studies of the islands' literary output more generally. Sam Haigh's *An Introduction to Caribbean Francophone Writing* (1999) includes a single essay on Saint-John Perse, while an overview collection such as *Elles écrivent des Antilles*, lauded in its preface as "the first exhaustive work devoted exclusively to Antillean francophone women," finds no place for a writer such as Marie-Reine de Jaham.[91] Monographs exclusively focused on fiction, such as Bonnie Thomas's *Connecting Histories* and her *Breadfruit or Chestnut?* tend to omit *béké* writers. If Mary Gallagher's work on Saint-John Perse has been invaluable in teasing out the Creole resonances in the work of the Guadeloupean poet, her monumental *Soundings in French Caribbean Writing*, focused as it is on the second half of the twentieth century and mostly on fiction, concentrates almost exclusively on Black writers. Chris Bongie in *Friends and Enemies* devotes some space to Marie-Reine de Jaham, but her fiction functions primarily as a launchpad for his sociological reading of the hierarchies of taste in the contemporary Antilles, and in postcolonial studies more generally, and the critic concentrates on paratextual factors to the detriment of the text itself. Jacqueline Couti's *Dangerous Creole Liaisons* therefore marks a welcome development in the attention it pays to early writers such as Traversay and Maynard, although her emphasis is on sexuality and nationalism, and her discussion ends in the late nineteenth century.

This book attempts, therefore, to fill a surprisingly empty space in the heavily mined field of French Caribbean literary studies, by examining the figure of the *béké* as represented, throughout history, by writers both from within the caste, and by authors who bring an external gaze to bear on this figure. In a sense, this latter gaze can be seen to bring the scopic regime of colonialism, in which it was the prerogative of the master to look on the enslaved, full circle. Glissant observes that the colonial subject's desire is not to escape the master's gaze but to participate in the scopic exchange on equal terms. He writes, "We hate ethnography [. . .]. The distrust that we feel is not caused by our displeasure at being looked at, but rather by our obscure resentment at not having our turn at seeing."[92] In taking their turn at seeing white, and even at being white, these writers attempt to reverse the intrinsic inequality, and lack of reciprocity, in a relationship in which, historically, those who were seen could not themselves "see" those who see them.

My approach denies the value, and indeed the possibility, of considering writings by *békés* and non-*békés* as entirely separate entities. Indeed, to segregate writers along color lines would be foolhardy, given not only the instability of biographical data,[93] but also taking account of the well-established critiques of the legitimacy of racial categories, critiques that should be taken as axiomatic for this study. And it would be misleading, indeed perverse, to overstate the commonalities in work by *békés* and non-*békés* in terms of ideology, contexts of production, and, indeed, literary quality. Yet what is remarkable is the extent to which shared tropes, topoi, figures, and themes (ambivalence and anxiety; melancholia; nostalgia; topophilia; temporal and spatial insecurity; a rhetoric of victimization and persecution; female dis-ease, illness and disability; what Bhabha calls "the twin figures of narcissism and paranoia"[94]) characterize, with differing emphases and to various effect, representations of the *béké* across the entirety of the corpus. To take a concrete example, while the ridiculousness of slave names endowed by white masters and administrators is a longstanding motif in plantation literature, *béké* names are also mocked in many Antillean novels, by both Black and white authors. Raphaël Confiant, predictably enough, derides the pomposity of white Creole names: *Bal masqué* centers on the family of François-Marie-Joseph Dupin de Flessac de Laverdière, while the Beauchamp de Chastaigné family are similarly over-endowed with names that register their landed wealth and property. Drasta Houël, too, mocks her *béké* characters through pleonasm and word play: one of the characters in *Amours et tendresses* is called Béké de la Békesserie. What is perhaps more surprising is that *béké* writers themselves ridicule the naming strategies of their own caste. This can be seen as early as 1835, in the character of Deshauteurs-Desvallons in Levilloux's *Les créoles,* whose "ridiculous obsession with nobility" causes him to add to his lowly sounding surname a second, loftier moniker (67).

More profound tonal convergences between *béké* and non-*béké* writing abound. Jacqueline Couti observes that "while the objectives of *béké* writers frequently differ from those of Black authors, their visions of femininity and female bodies, and the national implications of those visions, mirror each other."[95] This insight can easily be extended to a range of other tropes, themes, and diegetic details. Many fictional *békés* regret the debasement of the present (and this present can be located anywhere from the nineteenth to the twenty-first century) and romanticize the strength, courage, and singlemindedness of the first *colons:* loving mantras describing their physical work of clearing, planting, and building are threaded through *béké* discourse in the fiction of Maynard, Jaham, Chamoiseau, Glissant, and others. Antillean fiction, through time and across all contexts of production, registers a sense of mourning for a prerevolutionary golden age era, in which the values of the plantocracy were (apparently) more secure. The postrevolutionary plantation in such novels is a space under threat from outside and from within. Notably, incest casts an oblique shadow over writing by and about *békés* and will be a frequent reference point in this study. It acquires significance, and takes on a particular charge, early in the Antillean literary tradition, in the figure of Monsieur Nicole, Flora's father in Maynard's *Outre-mer* (Overseas): this monstrous *petit blanc,* clearly distinguished from the noble Longuefort in the vulgarity of his tastes and his petty jealousy (and also by the fact that the latter is born in France), is the perverted patriarch of a plantation devoid of *nègres,* peopled by mixed-race slaves who interbreed with each other, and whose primordial father was Nicole himself. In a much more contemporary example, Maryse Condé's *La colonie du nouveau monde* (The Colony of the New World) features a (not unsympathetic) *béké* who lives in a claustrophobic and incestuous relationship with his daughter in whose very name, Opale, paleness is inscribed: "the youngest, the blondest, who never left the house without a hat so as not to spoil her white skin" (39). But more generally, it is a story repressed and even denied in contemporary fiction: Marie-Reine de Jaham's *La grande béké* is an especially flagrant example of a narrative that works hard not to contain the threat of incest, but rather to recast it as a version of *métissage* and productive mixing. And in many novels, this threat from within is both generational and gendered. The enlightened young white daughters of Maynard, writing in 1835, and Micaux, in 2011, like, perhaps, Condé's Loraine, when in her prime before *La belle créole* begins in 2001, can be seen as especially powerful challenges to the peculiar nexus of patriarchy, paternalism, and privilege that are the structuring principles of the plantocracy. That so many of these women end up dead testifies also to the enduring power of this structure, a structure experienced as especially "unhomely" by many fictional white Creole women.[96]

Every monograph emerges from a process of inclusion and exclusion, and the potential vastness of the present topic has required difficult strategic choices to be made with regards to the corpus analyzed. Faced with such a rich, and continually burgeoning, literary field, the decisions I have been obliged to take around inclusion have been primarily genealogical, generic, diegetic, and thematic. By genealogical, I mean that my focus is squarely on the *béké,* the descendant of the first planters on the islands, rather than on whiteness in general. Being white in the Antilles is not synonymous with being *béké: petits blancs* (poorer whites who came to the colonies to make their fortune), colonial administrators, and religious, and latterly a whole host of incomers (engineers, businesspeople, and civil servants) have been resident on the islands almost since the start of the colonial enterprise. As Macey explains, the *béké,* in contrast to the "pied noir" in Algeria, for example, is not just a white settler: "there were no *békés* outside the Caribbean [. . .]. A *béké* is as much a native of Martinique as any mulatto or Black."[97] The peculiar status of the *colon* is frequently underscored in fiction: Confiant's *Bal masqué* features the following exchange between the detective hero and his lover: "'Who was that old white man you were talking to?' 'It's a ... béké.' The lover jumped slightly."[98] Not all whites are *békés,* but *békes,* in theory at least, are all white.

This unusual status has implications for my use of critical whiteness theory, discussed above in terms of its problematic "fit" for the islands studied here. Although theories of whiteness will be implicitly, and often explicitly, present in each chapter, other theoretical models and analytical tools will also be brought to bear where they can illuminate the peculiar anxiety and paranoia with which whiteness is freighted in Antillean fiction. This means, for example, that Bhabha's concept of ambivalence will be the primary theoretical prism through which I analyze Traversay's *Les amours,* a novel that seeks to repress and contain the presence of nonwhites, and whose historical setting registers a nostalgia for a more secure (if historically nonexistent) period of uncontested white power. Chapter 4 deploys a discrete strand of critical whiteness theory, the "whitelife novel," to interrogate Vincent Placoly's anonymous *béké*-narrator, a one-off in French Caribbean writing, in a chapter that also puts language at its analytical core. In more recent Antillean fiction the performative nature of whiteness, the starting point of much critical whiteness theory, is asserted through references to iconic embodiments of various modes of being "white": Charles Bronson, Lady Gaga, and Catherine Deneuve (Confiant); Gloria Swanson and Glenn Close (Condé); and implicitly, perhaps, in the intertextual dialogue staged between *La grande béké* and *Gone with the Wind.* Throughout this book, theories of whiteness will intersect flexibly with, or will be overlaid by, theories deriving from psychoanalysis, narratology, or gender studies.

Second, I focus exclusively on the Caribbean *départements et régions d'outre-mer,* and when I use the term Antilles or Antillean it is to designate the islands of Guadeloupe and Martinique. Haiti, invoked frequently by the novelists discussed here, would have provided a fascinating point of comparison. Attending to this other island would have allowed a contrapuntal examination, almost along the lines of a controlled experiment, of the emergence, operation, and imagination of whiteness in contexts shaped by intensely similar, and then radically divergent, political histories. Similarly, works by writers of the Indian Ocean would productively interact with the experience of Antillean writers. Pressures of space have meant that this work must be left for another time. Third, I have limited myself to the novel form. This is the form in which a properly Antillean literary tradition emerged, and it remains, to a remarkable extent, the dominant, and most creatively vibrant, genre today. It is also without doubt the form in which the condition and construction of whiteness (and of identity *tout court*) has been most intimately and extensively explored in the Antilles, the poetry of Saint-John Perse standing as a conspicuous exception to this rule. The novel, axiomatically, with its extended temporal canvas, is a privileged platform for the discussion of history and collective memory, and this explains to a significant extent why the form has been so privileged by Caribbean writers. Although several of the works discussed here might be characterized as historical fiction (Maynard's *Outre-mer,* Levilloux's *Les créoles,* Placoly's *Frères volcans*) their inclusion in this discussion is not primarily because of what they tell us about the Antillean past. More relevant is the peculiar capacity of the novel to shine a spotlight on social and cultural phenomena, and to give voice to a unique range of voices and perspectives. All these novels attempt to produce meaningful knowledge about fraught and contested histories in line with Fredric Jameson's definition of the genre: "The production of aesthetic or narrative form is to be seen as an ideological act in its own right, with the function of inventing imaginary or formal 'solutions' to unresolvable social contradictions."[99] The solutions offered in the novels discussed, mostly (self) destructive and often apocalyptic, are in themselves revealing, gesturing to the capacity of the novel, through the stories of love and death that it so often prioritizes, to explore fantasy, desire, and repression. Moreover, as Glissant says, the novel "is an attempt at totalizing reality, in all its details, with the goal of attaining complete understanding":[100] the Caribbean novel form accommodates subjects, types, and identities that would struggle to find space in more constrained forms.

But above all, it is the peculiar power of narrative, at precisely those moments of disjunction between diegesis and metaphorical or imagistic undertow, or in the space that opens up between the perspective of author, narrator, and character, or in the polyphony or cacophony of narrative voices in play, that the form has most power in (de)constructing a racial imaginary and, specifically, in inventing, undermining, or destabilizing whiteness. Most of these novels, which span a generic range from historical to sentimental to crime fiction, depart from the experimental, avant-garde, and "difficult" modes that have characterized the (Black) Antillean novel over the last fifty years. With the exception of Chamoiseau's two hallucinatory novels, *Slave Old Man* and *Un dimanche au cachot* (Sunday in the dungeon)—the former grants interiority to a dog, the latter includes melding characters, dialogue between reader and writer, and sees the ghosts of Perse and Faulkner intrude into the diegetic space—the works discussed here sit within the generic frame of realism and seek to produce culturally contextualized and referential fictional worlds. Some, such as Jaham's *La grande béké* (The grand *béké*), Cabort-Masson's *Qui a tué le béké de Trinité?* (Who killed the Trinité *béké?*), and Confiant's *Bal masqué à Békéland* (Masked ball in Békéland), could even be considered populist fiction. And yet even in these texts, the possibilities of fiction, for example the use of free indirect discourse, authorial irony, or the disconnect between paratext and text, open up a space, simultaneously, for two or more interpretative possibilities. At other moments, one truth is held in tension with another, voices interact, disagree, contradict each other, or simply fail to intervene at all. At such moments, the reader is enabled to read against the grain to become an active co-producer of meaning. I advocate here, above all, rigorous close analysis of the language of the novels, and scrutiny of their thematic and stylistic tendencies, to expose the tensions, contradictions, processes of containment, and the gestures of refusal at work in these texts.

Even within the genealogical, geographical, and generic parameters that I have set myself here, this study has no pretension to be an all-inclusive account of fiction by and about *békés;* it is intended to be neither encyclopedic nor comprehensive. Rather, the novels to which I devote most space are those that seem, to this reader at least, to have most to tell us about the experience of being, and the experience of imagining, white Creoleness. Bluntly put, the diegetic prominence of the *béké,* or the thematic significance of whiteness, has been the crucial criterion of inclusion. Through a close reading of (admittedly very select) texts of narrative fiction, and in going deeper (rather than broader), the challenge is to see what narrative reveals, wittingly and unwittingly, about the characters and situations at the center of its diegesis. The unconventional linkages that this book makes between radically different historical contexts, and differently raced and gendered writers, make for the delineation of a Caribbean cultural history where the blind spots of the field become visible. In this way I hope to shed new light on major novels by some of the most significant Antillean authors of recent years, while at the same time expanding the "disturbingly fixed roster of writer-intellectuals who have thus far interested theorists of postcolonial (francophone) literature."[101]

Of the eleven writers considered in detail here, four belong to the *béké* caste, three of whom were writing in the nineteenth century. This reflects my commitment to deepening our historical understanding of the French Caribbean novel by attending to precursor texts that have been largely neglected, and that deal primarily, from "inside the whale," with *béké* identity. In terms of geographical origins, only two of the eleven are Guadeloupean (Maryse Condé and Henri Micaux). While this might seem to replicate an entrenched critical bias toward Martinique, there is legitimate historical justification for privileging this latter island. Guadeloupe has a much smaller and significantly less powerful *béké* population than Martinique, and its white elite is often composed of minor branches of Martinican *béké* families.[102] More tendentious, perhaps, is the fact that only two of my key novelists, Condé and Jaham, are women. Antillean women novelists have a long history of engagement with skin color, and specifically with whiteness, in their fiction. But the dramas of racial self-loathing explored in such novels as Mayotte Capécia's totemic *Je suis martiniquaise* (*I Am a Martinican Woman*, 1948) and *La négresse blanche* (*The White Negress*, 1950); in Michèle Lacrosil's *Sapotille et le serein d'argile* (Sapotille and the clay canary, 1960) and *Cajou* (Cashew, 1961); and in Warner-Vieira's *Le quimboiseur l'avait dit* (*As the Sorcerer Said*, 1980), play out largely against a metropolitan French backdrop. The racial inferiority complexes that underlie these fictions are fermented in the Antilles and are intrinsically linked to slavery. But these narratives of alienation are often rooted in the false promises and white lies of departmentalization and assimilation, rather than exposing the egregious and damaging racial hierarchies that operate in the Antilles. More recent women writers (Simone Schwarz-Bart, Gisèle Pineau, Suzanne Dracius, Mérine Céco) privilege heroic stories of female strength and survival in the islands or explore the traumatic legacies of slavery by showing how intergenerational dysfunction plays out almost exclusively *within* Black families. That Maryse Condé, *the* major Antillean female novelist, devotes a novel to the relationship between a *béké* mistress and her gardener is surely an exception to a more general fictional rule of marginalization, and necessitates inclusion of *La belle créole*. And Jaham, whose entire fictional output revolves around her caste, falling somewhere between ethnography, history, and hagiography, is a necessary, illuminating, and often provocative inclusion in any literary study of the *béké*.

The novels discussed here will be treated in broadly chronological order. The inaugural work of Antillean fiction, Traversay's *Les amours de Zémédare et Carina* (The loves of Zémédare and Carina, 1806), is the subject of my opening chapter. This novel, which until recently had been almost entirely ignored, is a white-on-white love story (although the flaws of the white Creole woman in many ways undermine the conventional romance plot), which exhibits a highly fraught relationship to space and time. This can be seen in the very fact that Traversay projects back in history, setting the novel in the 1770s rather than contemporaneously. Drawing on Homi Bhabha's concept of ambivalence, and homing in on such strategies as prolepsis, I show how slavery is made to function in the novel as a strategic exclusion: it is afforded remarkably minimal diegetic space, the enslaved are euphemistically described as "cultivators," and the happiness of their condition is persistently emphasized. But this attempt to contain the threat to the plantocracy, and the striking absence of racial mixing (its assimilated *métis* characters are vocal advocates against their own condition) register a profound ambivalence around the sustainability of the plantocracy.

Traversay's *Les amours* is shot through with anxiety and ambivalence, but issues in a happy marriage and, most significantly, in the production of that rarest and most valuable of commodities in plantation fiction: healthy children who will themselves procreate. The novel's almost exclusively white narrative world is unimaginable for the writers discussed in chapter 2, Levilloux and Maynard, as is the sense of familial regeneration and secure genealogical moorings. These novels of the mid-1830s, produced as the pigmentocracy was fragmenting and as the inevitability of Abolition was becoming clearer, put mixed-race protagonists at the front of the fictional stage: their stories are prioritized, and their psychological responses showcased. In the characters of the honest Estève O'Reilly and the conniving Marius, the former able to pass as white, the latter recognizably of mixed heritage, we see two divergent versions of the threat posed by the mulatto or the *métis*. The tragic destinies of both young men, and the apocalyptic endings of their respective entourages, point most obviously to the ferocious threat that *métissage* poses to the plantocracy.

Chapter 3 brings us from early, and still relatively obscure, Creole writers to two literary titans of the twentieth and twenty-first century, Édouard Glissant and Patrick Chamoiseau. In many ways this chapter forms the central analytical pillar of the monograph, dealing as it does with the work of the two most significant novelists to emerge from the French Caribbean, and bridging the gap between early and modern writing. It also marks a historical, if not a diegetic, leap: the crucial period of the 1830s remains privileged by Glissant in *The Fourth Century* (1964) and, most strikingly, provides the exclusive historical setting for Chamoiseau's novels *Slave Old Man* (1997) and *Un dimanche au cachot* (Sunday in the dungeon, 2007). Both novelists seek to sound out and excavate this anxious pre-Abolition period: while Glissant's two male planters in *The Fourth Century* embody different ways of being "white," the plantation mistress, Marie-Nathalie, is depicted in a more ambivalent manner, and her racial grounding, like that of Charlotte Brontë's Bertha Mason, is less secure. For Chamoiseau, meanwhile, the threat of incest that remains implicit in his 1997 novel becomes explicitly incorporated into *Un dimanche au cachot,* a much more disturbing treatment of the *béké* than the often-sympathetic *Slave Old Man*. But both novelists, through the interplay of intimacy and irony afforded by free indirect discourse, allow the reader privileged access to the stories of the master.

If the resources of free indirect discourse allow for empathy and distance, chapter 4, devoted to a single short novel, Vincent Placoly's *Frères volcans* (Volcano brothers, 1983), is almost entirely relayed through the intimacy of the first person, and specifically through the diary form. This novel warrants detailed attention because of its unique status in Antillean letters; here we have a Black author writing, via a frame narrator (a historian), in the voice of a sympathetic white narrator who is recording his thoughts on the Abolition period (the novel is set during the uprising of 1848, which saw the abolition of slavery). While the frame narrative allows for both proximity and distance, the claustrophobic sense of interiority generated by this intensely introspective narrative draws the reader, in an often vertiginous way, into the world of the white male, an enlightened *béké* who supports Abolition and who has already liberated his slaves. Drawing on critical work on the "white-life novel," a US genre which involves Black writers adopting an exclusively white narrative perspective, I show how, through the interplay of intimacy and estrangement, Placoly has new and often quite radical ways of representing white subjectivity. And yet the novel remains embedded in a very questionable approach to gender politics, one that is all too familiar a feature of male-authored French Caribbean fiction.

Chapter 5 is devoted to the contemporary author who has most assiduously and exhaustively interrogated the identity of the *béké* ethnocaste: Marie-Reine de Jaham. I focus on her first, and most controversial novel, a publishing phenomenon and a *succès de scandale, La grande béké* (The grand *béké*, 1989). The novel embodies an extraordinary, and in many ways entirely anachronistic, example of what Chris Bongie has called "creolist discourse."[103] Jaham's fiction of genetic exhaustion and corruption (the "infected vat" is a metaphor used repeatedly to describe her clan) seems to resonate with narratives by Glissant and Chamoiseau. But the protagonist's solution to this dissipation (Jameson's description of fiction, above, is especially resonant) is in fact to transplant her grandson, a Parisian with no cultural experience of the plantation but deeply (genetically) connected to it. In other words, a maneuver that is presented as opening the "line" to otherness and difference is in fact a reinsertion, and reassertion, of sameness. In the last section of this chapter I move beyond the strictly literary, to contrast Jaham's novel with the TV film of the novel made almost a decade later. The radical diegetic and tonal changes made in the film, while themselves not unproblematic, speak to the dubious ideological underpinning of Jaham's novel, and suggest a declining tolerance for such "white on white" fictional universes.

My final chapter examines a subgenre of Antillean fiction, one which has recently attracted both mainstream and more obscure authors, and which revolves around the violent death of *béké* characters. Here, I analyze four very different crime novels, which range from the police procedural to a reworking of the courtroom drama. Guy Cabort-Masson's *Qui a tué le béké de Trinité?* (1991), Condé's *La belle créole* (2001), Henri Micaux's *De nègres et de békés* (Of Blacks and *békés,* 2011) and Confiant's *Bal masqué à Békéland* (Masked ball in Békéland, 2013) all stage violent, often gory, *béké* deaths. And in the end, reflecting perhaps the extent to which the Antillean crime fiction subverts the codes of the genre, but also registering the extent to which police, detectives, and the legal system generally remain invested in the myth of white innocence, justice (and even secure identification of the culprit) proves impossible in each story. But all four novels are less about the fatal confrontation *between* castes in the Antilles than about a pronounced tendency toward self-destruction (alcoholism, suicide, infanticide, mariticide) *within* white Creole culture itself, via the family, the couple, even the individual.

The journey plotted in this structure, from origins to violent endings, and from love (*Les amours*) to death (*Qui a tué le béké de Trinité?*), should not be read as a *mise en abyme* of white Creole destiny, nor as a mapping of any teleological progression from birth to extinction. As with whiteness itself, rumors of the demise of the *béké* have been greatly exaggerated, and the plantocracy continues to enjoy excellent economic health. As we saw above, Yarimar Bonilla argues that since departmentalization, white Creoles have proven to be "surprisingly resilient."[104] By closing with a chapter on white murder, I draw attention instead to a strand of writing by Black writers that suggests a self-destructive capacity in white Creole culture. In most of these texts, *béké* characters act as victim and perpetrator, monster and prey. The killings explored in this final chapter are in fact perpetrated from within the caste, the clan, and even the self, and register the vulnerability of the caste, perpetually aware of the threat from outside and insufficiently attentive, perhaps, to the threat from within.

1 "A Certain Uncertain Writing"

Anxiety and Ambivalence in Traversay's *Les amours de Zémédare et Carina et description de l'île de la Martinique*

IN *THE Location of Culture*, Homi Bhabha identifies ambivalence as a core condition of the colonial narrative, a condition that destabilizes any claim to absolute monological authority. Writing in reaction to Edward Said's suggestion that colonial power is uniquely and entirely possessed by the colonizer (held to be a historical and theoretical simplification), Bhabha argues instead that "the language of culture and community is poised on the fissures of the present becoming the rhetorical figures of a national past." Thus, the colonist, whose present is always already fractured, is bleakly aware of the precariousness and transience of his own position. As Bhabha suggests, the "desperate acknowledgement of an aporia in the inscription of empire [leads to the] performance of a *certain uncertain writing* in the anomalous discourse of the present of colonial governmentality."[1] This "certain uncertain writing," which at once reveals, and attempts to cover up, the gaps, slippages, and indeterminacies in colonial power, suggests the extent to which colonial discourse is founded on anxiety, and, as Robert Young puts it, points to the manner in which "colonial power itself is subject to the effects of a conflictual economy."[2] For Auguste-Jean Prévost de Sansac, count of Traversay, author of the first known French Antillean novel, *Les amours de Zémédare et Carina et description de l'île de la Martinique* (1806),[3] representative of a liminal group neither comfortably within, nor wholly outside, the French nation, and member of a minority population in the islands, such ambivalence is perhaps to be expected. Traversay (1762–1849) was born into one of the most influential *béké* families of Martinique. The clan was well connected to local government, and the Sansac de Traversay family had a long association, on both the maternal and the paternal side, with the French navy and cavalry. Moreover, like many subsequent planter clans (including that of Marie-Reine de Jaham), the Traversay family claimed common ancestry with the most famous Creole of them all, Joséphine de Beauharnais, who herself graces the story with two appearances.[4]

Despite the inaugural status of Traversay's novel in French Caribbean fiction, and in view of its relatively easy availability (it was republished in 1977 in Joyau's series of nineteenth-century Antillean novels), it has elicited even less attention than later nineteenth-century Creole fiction. With the notable but very recent exceptions of Jacqueline Couti's monograph (2016) and critical edition (2017), the novel has been afforded little more than a casual (and often distorting) reference by successive critics. Léon-François Hoffmann lumps *Les amours* unceremoniously together with contemporaneous works of metropolitan melodrama set in the colonies by authors such as Victor Hugo and Jean-Baptiste Picquenard, whose complicated plots are "rich in *coups de théâtre*, more or less gratuitous coincidences, and in the twists and turns of melodrama."[5] Régis Antoine passes over the novel entirely, to mention one of its appendices.[6] Dominique Chancé attributes an erroneous publication date (1841) to the novel and suggests, anachronistically, that it explores Antillean society "in the second half of the nineteenth century."[7] For Roger Toumson, the work is representative of a strand of Creole writing dealing with "conflictual interracial relations,"[8] a somewhat misleading observation given the striking marginalization of such conflict in the story. More faithful, at the level of plot at least, is Joyau's claim that Traversay "considered slavery as well as color prejudice as a given fact and that it was out of the question to contest the foundations of both."[9] Jack Corzani, meanwhile, claims that *Les amours* shares the literary mediocrity of early Creole works such as *Les créoles* and *Outre-mer;* for him it is a novel of sensibility, belonging to the "mawkish" current of eighteenth-century literature rather than to the Gothic strand to which Maynard and Levilloux's works belong.[10] This is an assessment of literary style, but it also intimates a political judgment: while the Gothic is concerned with that which is troubling and disturbing (in the cases of *Outre-mer* and *Les créoles,* the troubling of racial boundaries, which leads inexorably to the apocalyptic endings of both novels), Traversay's "black and white" certainties in *Les amours* appear resolutely intact. To this extent Joyau's categorical diagnosis of Traversay's conservative politics, contrary to Toumson's analysis, is at the level of the novel's plot, at least, entirely justified.

Of course, none of the early novels mentioned by the above critics—by French and Antillean writers alike—can be read as resistant in any straightforward postcolonial way. Traversay's forgotten novel, however, whose insistent evocations of the excellence of the white colonizing caste and the superiority of plantation slavery over other forms of social organization, seems at first not so much to reject such postcolonial tropes as hybridity, in-betweenness, and the contact zone as to propose a world in which such positions are unthinkable. Such (apparent) lack of ideological tension, ambivalence, and complexity perhaps explains the novel's neglect. This chapter will argue, however, that by reading the novel against its own rhetorical and diegetic grain, we can discern the prevalence of that most classic postcolonial preoccupation: a sharp anxiety in space and time, an anxiety that points above all to a sense of the ephemerality of ownership. This in turn produces a fundamental anxiety and ambivalence at the core of the novel—an ambivalence often directed toward the Creole woman in particular—which ensures that the text is a privileged site through which the white Antillean subject is invented (it is, after all, the first of its kind) and celebrated, and at the same time problematized and undermined. Very often this ambivalence operates as a kind of damning with faint praise, through a narrative voice that undermines, or at the very least cannot sustain, its own apparent rhetoric at crucial junctures in the text. At other points, this ambivalence is manifest in a "highly charged relation to time and space,"[11] a trope identified by Mary Gallagher as inflecting twentieth-century (Black) writing in its quest for legitimacy, but which can be seen to permeate the writings of the plantation-owning caste too, right from the beginning of white Creole Antillean literature.

Traversay's only novel was conceived, as we are told in his preface, on the advice of an unnamed *homme de lettres,* with a twofold purpose: it alternates between discrete, self-contained descriptions of the colony and chapters detailing the love story of the eponymous couple, allowing the reader to choose "fact" or "fiction" (3), "according to the disposition of his mind or his heart" (4). Thus, the project is systematically framed as a dual one, to "make known the colony of Martinique, and to make the two lovers loved" (31)—in other words as having both a pedagogical and a sentimental function, appealing to both head and heart. Published within a decade of Moreau de Saint-Méry's *Description topographique* and echoing its title, the descriptions of the island that intersperse the romance plot can be seen in some respects as a similar attempt to classify, order, hierarchize, and typologize.[12] Drawing on botany, zoology, archaeology, and the natural sciences, these passages attempt, like earlier travel narratives and like many subsequent Creole novels, to impose an orderly, purposeful, and rational grid on an alien and unpredictable territory. These sections also act as a foil to the vagaries and excesses of the romance plot, which progressively overtakes the descriptive passages in the overall economy of the text.

The novel opens in the 1740s. Carina, the long-awaited and only child of M. and Mme Sainprale, is a beautiful and obedient girl, the epitome of white Creole virtue; saintliness is conspicuously suggested in the patronymic. She is destined to marry her cousin, the valiant Zémédare, whose heroism is established by his helping to quash an English invasion in 1758.[13] On her mother's death, which marks the end of the first part of the novel, Carina begins to embrace worldly pleasures and frivolity and, under the influence of an unsuitable lady in waiting, falls in love with and agrees to marry the malevolent French libertine Mélidore. Zémédare, broken-hearted, falls ill and travels to Brittany to recuperate on his uncle's farm. Meanwhile Mélidore, nephew of the French minister for war, is posted to France, and a still besotted Carina and her father decide to accompany him there. During the sailing, Mélidore's true dastardly character becomes evident to all, and he dies of smallpox. A storm causes the ship to wreck on the shores of Brittany, and Zémédare, in one of those credibility-stretching coincidences so beloved of novelists of the time, happens upon the scene. He rescues father and daughter, Carina having held M. de Sainprale afloat (Traversay's assertion that Carina, like most Creole women, can swim is according to Couti a "final jab at [Bernardin de Saint-Pierre]"),[14] but he is too weak to survive. Carina retires to a convent but is eventually won over by Zémédare's loyalty and persistence. The couple marry and have several children in France (the number is unspecified, but we are told that the eldest, a girl, is called Carina), and eventually make a triumphant return to Martinique. The novel ends with the death of the protagonists, whose continuation is assured by the marriage of one of their unnamed children.

Traversay acknowledges in his preface that the love story at the center of his novel may or may not be true; but he claims that his firsthand experiential knowledge of the colonies confers a literary and an ideological advantage over his great model, the "elegant" author of *Paul et Virginie*. In the first of several back-handed compliments, he declares that he knows his island better than Bernardin knew the Île de France, and therefore that "his pictures must be more multiple and even truer to life" (3). It is a self-conscious, and self-confident, statement of purpose. The author claims to speak with insider authority, even though Traversay himself, like Bernardin, was born in France. Traversay's characters are "drawn from nature" (3) and some of the plantation owners named in the text are still living on the island. If the story doesn't have the exactitude that one might demand from a historian, "truth is only very slightly altered there" (3). This means above all that "the slavery of blacks and their liberation" will be presented in this novel, for the first time, "according to their true nature" (3). In addition to this self-justifying preface, an almost axiomatic inclusion in novels of the time, the text's two original volumes are each succeeded by a heterogeneous range of explicitly didactic documents relating to various aspects of colonial life in Martinique. These texts are disparate in terms of authorship, genre, and length, ranging from a substantial 1777 report (a "mémoire") signed by King Louis XVI in Versailles, to a tract outlining a code of practice for the Capuchin nuns in the colony, to a number of brief essays presumably written by the author himself, on a range of subjects close to his heart, and destined for churchmen, military, politicians, and administrators.[15] Traversay makes no mention of these various documents in the preface or novel; they appear without comment or contextualization, forming a documentary supplement to the fiction, and appear to anchor the text in an authoritative, authentic, politically informed, and verifiable reality. The novel's appeal to authenticity and truth in its fictional narrative and in its detailed topographical descriptions, combined with the documentary authority of its paratextual materials, means that it attempts to impart a clear pedagogical message to the reader. By celebrating the eponymous couple, by presenting the island in exhaustive detail, and by giving the reader privileged access to the challenges facing colonial administrators, religious orders, and even the king, it will justify and even glorify Creole culture more generally.

In keeping with this appeal to authenticity and authority, the text appears on the diegetic level (and in contradistinction to later works by Maynard and Levilloux) to shore up an unproblematized and relatively secure white Creole identity. The plantocracy's future appears at the end of the novel to be assured by the reproductive success of the eponymous characters, so that a new generation is ushered in in the closing pages (although it is significant that the child who marries at the novel's end, and the only one identified in terms of gender, is female: this feminization of Creole culture, and the sense of an ebbing patriarchy, are themes that haunt fiction by and about white Creoles). Moreover, what is most striking about the treatment of slavery in *Les amours,* especially given its prominence in the preface, is the extent to which it is contained, marginalized, or euphemistically displaced. The enslaved are almost invisible, their contact with white Creoles minimal; when they appear, they are systematically segregated, structurally and diegetically. Resistance to white power is minor and easily contained, and the specter of racial mixing that haunts later texts is notably absent. The infant Carina is breastfed by her mother rather than by a *da,* a domestic slave (12),[16] and slaves are forbidden to "speak black in front of her" to prevent corporeal and linguistic contamination (15). In a scene notably devoid of enslaved Black bodies, the young girl is shown around the plantation, "to teach her how sugar was made"—the passive voice and use of the impersonal pronoun ("comment *on* fabriquait," 16, my italics) further obscuring the conditions of production. Slave-owners are euphemistically described as farmers ("cultivateurs," 20), and their slaves are submissive and calm, and work with zeal and pleasure (42). The plantation is consistently figured as a benign and happy space, in which pregnant women are protected from hard labor, children are required to work only from the ages of twelve, fifteen, or later, and the sick are cared for at the master's expense.

More generally, the text rehearses arguments common in the press of the time about slavery's ancient forms justifying its contemporary use, and the fact that Caribbean slaves are happier than warring Africans and more content than laborers and serfs in Europe (43, 69). The single episode of slave resistance, a poisoning campaign directed by an overseer, Artaban, is diegetically displaced—the episode occurs not on the Sainprale plantation but rather on that of (an equally benign) neighbor, the widow Mme Flaméau—and rendered outlandish by the excessive evil of the perpetrator. Artaban is presented as an aberration rather than as a typical slave. He is "the most treacherous and perverse of all Blacks" (38) and is so monstrous that, with his wife's help, he kills his four youngest children in the process (39). Meanwhile, the novel's (token) *homme de couleur,* Eugène Dérima, is a passionate advocate for the continuation of slavery, rather than an agent of its destruction. Over five pages of monologue, he defends the plantation regime better than any planter could, declaring that he owes his happiness to the generosity of white men, and asserting that even freed *hommes de couleur* must never be allowed to exercise "the slightest authority over a white man" (71). Eugène's wife, Zoé, a *métisse,* has rejected the marriage proposal of a French merchant in the interests of racial decorum, thereby protecting the white male from an unspeakable alliance. Her internalization of the taboos of the plantation is encapsulated in *her* designation of his desire as a "shameful project" (67). She thus becomes custodian and guarantor of the very system that denigrates her. The refusal of interracial mixing (of which she and her husband are products), and the consequent protection of whiteness is thrust back on the nonwhite woman, so that women, whatever their color, are shown to be the primary guarantors of white supremacy. Both episodes—concerning the repugnant Artaban and the hyper-assimilated Dérima and Zoé—are contained and marginalized within a single discrete chapter each and have minimal repercussions for the rest of the novel. Colonial anxieties are therefore held in check, notably in the presentation, or rather the sublimation, of slavery. Moreover, as we have seen, the novel distinguishes itself from most successors (and indeed from its primary intertext, *Paul et Virginie*) through the culmination of the central love story not in death but in marriage and the perpetuation of the planter line in a new generation.

However, despite these apparent markers of ideological security, the novel in fact ends up communicating a much more ambivalent and uncertain version of Creole legitimacy and morality than its plot summary suggests. Even its title conveys a fundamental incongruity. The signifier "amours," although immediately juxtaposed with Zémédare's name (in a title that gives priority to the male, even though Carina's and her family's story is dominant), designates a plural (female) romance plot. It is the white Creole heroine, guardian of virtue on the plantation, who recklessly jeopardizes her future happiness with the valiant Zémédare by falling for the French libertine Mélidore.[17] True love, for reasons of female inconstancy and poor judgment, runs neither smooth nor straight. More generally, the shakiness of narrative authority (a fragility conveyed most notably in the novel's treatment of time and space) is intrinsically connected to the uneasiness of white colonial authority. To this extent, and even though white Creole identity appears on the face of it to be less besieged than enshrined, the novel can be considered as heralding and exemplifying what Toumson calls the siege mentality of the *colons*.[18]

Thus, an ironic voice, or what Bhabha calls a "certain uncertain writing," systematically undermines the virtue and solidity of the Creole elite, casting doubt on its legitimacy and endurance. The island's inhabitants, especially its women, are, with the exception of Mme Sainprale, damned with faint praise. In the novel's opening pages, the narrator notes that the mold for the Martinican woman's face "seems to have been endowed by the Graces" (7), suggesting a universal, classical, and quintessentially white beauty. The narrator continues, "There are very few countries where you can see, keeping everything in proportion a greater number of pretty women [. . .]. Their complexion, a little colored, paints sentiment and appeals to tenderness. Almost all have very beautiful skin" (7). Skin, the signifier and vector of racial purity, is "a *little* colored" and "*almost*" always beautiful (my italics). Less subtly, the praise for the supreme morality of Martinican women is undermined by the eponymous heroine herself who, for much of the novel, behaves like a petulant, superficial, and wayward child, entirely lacking in judgment, and by the portrayal of other women such as the one who led her into her unsuitable engagement, her manipulative companion Mme Bélimé. The master, described as "the best of all men" (7), and ostensibly presented as a benign patriarch, is equally subject to ambivalence. For example, in a remarkable assertion, and one that is never explicitly called into question on the narrative register, the narrator declares, "the inhuman master . . . he doesn't exist in Martinique; considered with horror by all, he would soon be forced to leave the island" (42). Sequence of tense and punctuation here combine to convey Bhabha's "certain uncertainty," a perspective that undermines the ostensible thrust of a sentence appearing to establish planter rectitude and inter-planter surveillance. The ellipsis points that follow the subject, the inhuman master, destabilize the categorical qualifier, "he doesn't exist," opening up a space for reflection and doubt, despite the definitive denial of such a creature's existence. This negative clause is in turn undermined by the past participle "considered," suggesting conversely that such monsters *have* indeed existed and have been viewed with horror by Martinicans. The subsequent conditional, "he would soon be forced," propels the past tense into the projective mood, and gestures toward the hypothetical or contingent: *if* such a master existed, this is what would happen to him, "soon" functioning as a somewhat unstable deictic. It is as though the sentence cannot quite sustain its own message, and instead fractures under the weight of its untenable assertion.

As the above example suggests, the source of this narrative ambivalence and tension is fundamentally connected to time, and this tens(e)ion originates in the time lag between the date of publication of the novel (1806) and its historical setting (1740s–70s). The plot unfolds in a period that is presented as a golden moment of impregnable colonial power. External threat (the 1758 invasion by the English in chapter 4 of the novel) is swiftly and easily neutralized, and internal revolt equally quickly quashed (Artaban and his wife are put to death). And yet the novel was written and published at a time of heightened uncertainty for the plantation owners of the Antilles, within a few years of the French Revolution (1789–99), in the immediate aftermath of the Haitian Revolution (1791–1804), and shortly after France's repossession of Martinique in 1802. The French revolutionary wars and the Napoleonic Wars (1802–15) were ongoing. The novel's diegetic time is inflected at key moments by the anxieties of the writer's present, anxieties that are manifest most notably in oblique references to the French and Haitian revolutions. The novel therefore lends itself to a dual reading, right from an incipit—"Martinique [. . .] is today the most flourishing, the most precious colony owned by France" (7)—which at once elevates and diminishes the colony. For although this opening line is an apparently unproblematic statement of Martinique's supremacy, the slippery deictic "today" (clearly anchored in the writer's, rather than the characters', present) implicitly conjures the loss of Saint-Domingue, by far France's most important overseas possession, which had been declared a republic only two years before the publication of *Les amours*. Later, in a contrary moment that is almost entirely unprepared for by the novel's plot, Martinique is described in a letter from its departing governor (who, in a detail that underscores the time-lag between narratorial and authorial present, has been posted by the king to the "much more important" governorship of the soon to be liberated Saint-Domingue) as "significantly fallen from the state of splendor in which you might have seen it: all sorts of tribulations have thrown the colonists into dire straits" (136). The line carries narrative authority because of its source; Traversay's conservative politics mean that church, government, and the military are revered sources in this novel. It jars, however, with the textual evidence available to the reader, which does not explore, explicitly at least, the decline of the planter caste.[19] Thus the narrative asserts and destabilizes its ostensible authority, through a discrepancy between diegesis and discourse.

Temporal slipperiness, and notably the proleptic gesture, is a strong feature of the narrative, and one that does not, appropriately enough, lend itself to stable interpretation. At one point Zémédare, an early Antillean ecologist, imagines a public garden in Saint-Pierre, housing "plants and trees which would be useful to all colonists" (33); an authorial footnote tells us that this has now been created, and is already proving useful to Creoles. The note is doubly reassuring; it bolsters the narrator's authority (everything he tells us must be true because this has come to pass) and points to the survival instinct of the plantation owners (the colony will survive because its masters have shown such foresight). Zémédare later asserts the necessity of a plant nursery in Martinique, where colonists can procure the trees they need at a reasonable price, before claiming that this wish will be realized "in a not-so-distant future[. . . .] A sweet premonition gives me the strength to confirm that these ills will soon no longer be held against us" (106). The reader assumes, given the temporal disjunction already established between the "now" of the story and the "now" of the telling, and the short-term cue of "a not so distant future" as well as the projective "sweet premonition," that this nursery, too, exists.

Such flashes forward beyond the temporal frame of the narrative into the writing present can be seen to convey the resilience and endurance of the planter caste, what Mieke Bal, analyzing narrative inserts, describes as a sense of "deterioration [. . .] avoided by an embedded improvement."[20] The narrator reassuringly connects diegetic time with the time of writing, and suggests continuity, endurance, and forward planning by white Creoles. Bal's "deterioration avoided" also nicely captures planters' anxiety regarding the legitimacy of their project, an anxiety apparently sublimated and yet very visible even in this first novel.

More ambiguous, perhaps, because not confined to a footnote, nor dependent on the reader's supplementary interpretation, are two passages relating to Joséphine de Beauharnais (1763–1814), who was apparently related to the Traversay family.[21] Both references invoke Joséphine without explicitly naming her, proof of her celebrity. During an episode recounting one of Mme Sainprale's many visits to other plantations—a device by which the author is able to fill out the island topography promised in his title, and to name other colonists and plantations in a gesture of reassurance and solidarity—she goes to stay with one of the oldest families in the colony. The family had arrived during the lifetime of M. Duparquet, "the first owner of the island" (45) and their plantation had once been occupied by Mme de Maintenon, Louis XIV's second wife. The narrator continues, "This example, in favor of our pretty and kind Creoles, should not be lost to posterity. On the world's most important throne we see. . . ." The sentence tails off, interrupted by the narrator who exclaims, "But what was I going to say? This work should only recall facts that happened well before the French Revolution!" (45). The narrator acknowledges that he has broken through his own temporal frame, but in so doing establishes the long and venerable history of Creoles, and notably Creole women, on the island. In a proleptic, if veiled, reference to Joséphine, he suggests the continuation of a history stretching from the ancien régime into the diegetic present (the 1750s) but also beyond, into the 1800s. In a later episode, Joséphine is visited by a fortune-teller. This device, which can be seen very directly to facilitate temporal transgression on the narrative level by bringing the future into the present, appears to have been based on fact, and features in other Creole fiction and in biographies of the empress.[22] The soothsayer predicts a highly advantageous first marriage for the young girl (who is never explicitly named as Joséphine), and a second husband (also never named) who will bring her fortune and glory: "he will cherish you as though you were the very talisman of his happiness. I can see thrones under your feet" (75).

On the one hand, such moments of prolepsis can simply be read as symptomatic of the novel's "overbearingly omniscient narrator";[23] it is as though the narrator cannot quite bring himself *not* to invoke this local celebrity, now empress of the dominant political power in Europe and beyond. But the narrative flash-forward is introduced with a convoluted and syntactically unwieldy justification, suggesting that this break in the temporal order is symptomatic of a greater anxiety. The narrator, as in the previous example, quickly pulls back from this embedded story, reminding himself and the reader that his story should deal only with "things that happened before the French Revolution." He hopes, however, that the reader will excuse the reporting of what he describes as an "anachronism," what he goes on to gloss, somewhat tortuously, as "an historical fact, whose date is not so distant from us that its place in this work could help those who do not know to what extent she, about whom I have the honor of speaking, is still young and beautiful" (60). The reference to quadragenarian Joséphine's youth and beauty—the adverb "still" signals that we have moved back into the realm of the writing, rather than the narrated, present, and the empress was born in 1763—is consistent with the double-edged glorification of Creole women more generally, which hints at their decadence and dissipation. The ambivalent reference to Joséphine's youth also conjures, ironically, the fact that she was six years older than Napoléon and had not borne him an heir, which would ultimately precipitate their divorce in 1810. Moreover, by proleptically framing Joséphine alongside the French Revolution (twice presented as being outside the narrative scope of this novel), the narrator juxtaposes the Revolution that first saw slavery abolished, and the Creole empress whose husband reintroduced it only four years before the novel's publication.[24] Both brief references to Joséphine invoke her throne, metonymically reinforcing her power, and by extension suggest that the plantocracy is secure under her reign. But the allusion to revolution, like Joséphine's being "still young and beautiful," carries an undertow of fragility. The narrator, in attempting to coordinate the island's past, present, and future, suggests that time is out of joint, and points, obliquely, to his and his caste's lack of mastery of the island's future.

Time is in this novel fundamentally imbricated with space. If the slippages in the temporal frame of *Les amours* emphasize a tension between transience and endurance, so too the treatment of space vacillates between an attempt to assert ownership and control and an encroaching sense of rootlessness and impermanence. Traversay's novel flags its topographical ambition in its very title, and like many early novels includes a surfeit of geographical, topographical, botanical, and climatic material, suggesting a strong authorial desire to locate, fix, anchor, and to name island space. Corzani suggests that these devices in the early Creole novel reflect not only a "love for the native land," but also the "the need to preserve it and to keep control over it."[25] Lennard Davis has argued that "the seemingly neutral idea that novels must take place in locations was actually part of a structure of defenses that gave eighteenth-century society a way to justify the ownership of certain properties."[26] Such strategies testify—even, or perhaps especially, in this earliest Antillean novel—to an insecurity of ownership, and are indeed consonant with Davis's "structure of defenses." The extensive lists of flora and fauna, and the detailed geographical coordinates and topographical features which run through these texts, testify not to topophilia—a term coined by the geographer Yi-Fu Tuan to describe "the fondness for place because it is familiar, because it is home and incarnates the past, because it provides pride of ownership and creation"[27]—but to a neurosis deriving from the spatial and temporal insecurity of the slave-owning class. Such features reflect an already pronounced nostalgia for a home/land recently acquired, still only partially known, and already obsolete. The sense of (surface) coordination and control conveyed by the exhaustive lists of flora and fauna, or the meticulous surveys of circumscriptions, parishes, and towns, masks a greater insecurity in space, one connected to a lack of temporal and chronological depth. The opening chapter, "Description of the town of Saint-Pierre and its environs, and some general ideas about the topography of the island of Martinique," in a convention already established by travel writers, and that will remain a strong feature of later Creole novels, provides the dimensions of the island and methodically sketches its eight districts, twenty-eight parishes, and three major cities, naming rivers, lakes, and major plantations. This logical, almost Cartesian, approach, suggests a superficial coordination of elements of the island environment, consistent with topography's investment in the surface features of the land.

In an early episode, the Sainprale family go for a walk in their garden, a lush space of plenitude and profusion, where rivers never dry up and where food is abundant. The episode includes an extensive catalog of trees and fruits typical of this novel and of colonial discourse more generally: these include the cashew, sapodilla, cinnamon, cherimoya, soursop, custard apple, apple thistle, mango, orange, sweet lemon, bitter lemon, "and a whole infinity of other fruits that it would take too long to enumerate here" (24). Water is as fertile as land in this paradisiacal space: "mullets, loaches, tadpoles, brown crabs, and other river fish could be seen in great numbers: you could also fish for crayfish of a prodigious size and exquisite flavor" (23). Such Edenic projections of the plantation were commonplace in early colonial writings and, as Jefferson Dillman has convincingly shown, served above all to act as a screen or a "rhetorical bandage" concealing the horror and suffering that lay behind them.[28] The narrator goes on to describe a wooded area within the garden, in which trees,

> for the owners of this residence ["demeure"], had particular names which had been given to them by M. Sainprale's grandfather, by his son, and by M. Sainprale himself. A monstrous baobab, which had a circumference of almost 80 feet, and which covered a surface of 400 square feet, was called the marquis of Duquesne; a superb acoma was designated by the name of grandfather; a huge fromager was named My Father's Marriage; a beautiful lecythis, whose magnificent flowers spoke powerfully to the sexual system of plants, had the name of Melina Ranugi, M. Sainprale's wife. A courbaril, with the most beautiful appearance, had been named Carina, etc. You could see that each one of these retraced the most precious memories. As you breathed in in their shadow, you were carried back to the event that you had wanted to celebrate by planting them, the mind and the heart delivered up to the most joyous ideas and to the most touching sentiments. (23)

On one level the scene, rooted in Traversay's own experience of plantation life,[29] is a classic of colonial discourse. The episode is framed through a run of terms pointing to ownership, endurance ("owners"; "residence") and linear transmission ("which had been given to them"). The wood is explicitly linked to memory; trees are guarantors of the continuity between past and present and of an ancestral lineage inscribed in the land. Naming, which here has a strong mnemonic function, is the Adamic preserve of the male, and is put at the service of patriarchy and the heterosexual order. Women feature only as wives and daughters (a few paragraphs later we learn that M. de Sainprale has planted a "young wood" as Carina's dowry), destined to ensure the continuation of patrilinearity within the Creole family. The trees named for men are, predictably enough, associated with height, girth, and enormity, while those named for women are evoked in terms of their beauty, flowering, and sexuality. Yet these trees, planted by the family, speak above all to temporal shallowness. Planted by M. Sainprale's father, their expansiveness in space—their circumference, surface, and shadow are emphasized—signify not any chronological depth, nor the steady sedimentation of time, but rather compensate for its absence. To this extent, as the passage acknowledges, they are undoubtedly vectors of short-term rather than ancestral memory, for a Creole family whose existence extends only two generations back.

Trees' connection to familial memory is revisited later, in one of the novel's longest chapters, "On the plantation of trees." This chapter takes the form of an article written by Zémédare to honor the deceased Mme Sainprale, who had herself despaired of Creoles' neglect of their homes—the novel suggests that this neglect derives from both aesthetic insouciance and a more existential rootlessness—and notably, their aversion to planting trees. We can assume that the subject was close to the author's heart as, among the texts inserted after the second volume of the novel, Traversay includes a brief essay entitled "On the felling of trees and on plantations." In this essay, he exhorts the government to encourage the planting of trees and to discourage their felling, and laments the lack of wood available for building houses and sugar mills in Martinique, which means that the island is obliged to import wood from the United States. (The felling of trees for the purpose of building plantation infrastructure is unsurprisingly considered to be a legitimate rather than a reckless or damaging activity.) Traversay also argues, in proto-environmentalist mode, that "cutting down trees perceptibly alters the course of rivers and clearly diminishes the number of springs, which are so precious in this fiercely hot climate" (202). In the novel Zémédare, as an authorial *porte-parole,* launches an energetic defense of planting, highlighting trees' aesthetic, environmental, and economic functions: they enhance the appearance of property, produce shade, and can be sold as timber. But what he privileges above all is their very concrete association with putting down roots; connecting time past, present, and future, the planting of trees is an existential intimation of the *longue durée.* He laments the fact that early planters would, ironically, eschew such planting because of a tendency, even among those born on the island, "to consider their establishment on the island as being very limited in time" ("d'une durée très limitée," 104).[30] Today's (second- or third-generation) colonist, he insists, has no reason to experience a sense of ephemerality, which was

> forgivable for the first inhabitants of the Antilles who, each day, and at every moment, regretted their homeland, and could find no joy at home, having had such great difficulties to overcome and such huge dangers to surmount . . . ; but these sad times are no more; let us love the land in which we were born [. . .]. Our fathers fertilized with their sweat the plantation that, in their tenderness,

they bequeathed to us [. . .]. Shall we abandon their bones to foreign hands? Shall we rob our children of their inheritance which we only received on the understanding that we would transmit it to them? On the contrary, let us put all our efforts into increasing for them its value, so that they will be able to enjoy their stay ["séjour"]. (104)

Zémédare exhorts his countrymen to settle in the Antilles, physically but also psychologically, emotionally, and existentially. Through the sedimentation of time, Zémédare argues, the alien island becomes a *patrie;* through habituation, the plantation, called the *habitation,* becomes habitable, hospitable, home. Or, as contemporary geographers might put it, space, invested with a sense of time, becomes place. Connecting time past, present, and future, the bones of the fathers are the foundation of their children's inheritance in the future; (patri)linear transmission and inheritance is again privileged ("Our fathers fertilized with their sweat"; "bequeathed"; "heritage"; "which we only received"; "transmit"). And yet, in a typically double-edged moment, Zémédare's plea for rootedness is undercut by the final word of this highly charged passage, "séjour," whose etymological root "jour," a day, reinscribes transience and evanescence; any sense of permanence and longevity is unsettled through a closing signifier emphasizing the *courte durée.*

Zémédare goes on to imagine a colonist showing his wife and children around the trees that he has planted, in a passage typical of the novel in its gendered division of agency and passivity. Many trees commemorate a happy event, "the return of an old friend, the arrival on the island of a governor or of a kindly administrator, his wedding day, the birth of each of his children." The copse is also a memorial garden, housing "the urn installed in the memory of his mother, or of a virtuous female friend"; the male *colon,* in Romantic mode, can thus visit the woods so as to "nourish this sweet melancholy, which is a real need of the soul" (105–6). Again, however, the memorial function is temporally restricted, connecting back to the previous generation and no further. Here and throughout, trees are domesticated and inherently part of the plantation culture: there is no mention, for example, of the trees that predate the colonial moment,[31] those mythologized forests that early settlers, in a heavily romanticized trope in Creole writing, had to clear in order to begin the plantation project. In closing this meditation on trees, Traversay quotes a fragment of La Fontaine's tale "The Old Man and the Three Young Ones," which, through a story of young men mocking the long-term planting project of an octogenarian, advocates responsibility to subsequent generations and a sense of care for the future: *"My great nephews will owe this shade to me/Well well! Are you denying to the sage/The right to care for the pleasure of others?/Even this is a fruit that I can taste today!"* (106, italics in original). If La Fontaine associates the planting of trees explicitly with altruism ("the pleasure of others"), the practice is mobilized here to convey a familial project. Planting is presented as a way of providing for the future, which depends on an (optimistic?) investment in continuity and self-perpetuation—the "others" are very clearly identified as the old man's kith and kin, if not his immediate progeny. And yet, what is excluded in the fragment deployed by Traversay is the fate of the nephews, for whose putative future the old man toils: as many contemporary readers would have known, all three of the young men die in misadventures (the first, as it happens, on the way to America), and the family line is thereby terminated, undercutting, in familial terms at least, the sense of a provision for the future generation.

This sense of a constricted past, or of a radically foreclosed future, extends to the novel's brief treatment of prehistory. Among the many visitors to Mme Sainprale in her final illness is M. Tamony, a natural historian and botanist, who is particularly interested in the rock and mountain formations of the island. (Tamony, a metropolitan, is accompanied by a local and well-respected botanist, lending local credence to his conclusions—remember the emphasis on the authenticity of local knowledge in this novel's preface.) In a striking correlative to the shallow roots of the plantation's trees Tamony, in a series of geological observations, asserts the belatedness of the island's geological features, rather than their primal connection to a prehistoric past: "Nowhere in Martinique can you see primitive mountains; their formation can be dated [. . .] to the period of violent natural convulsions, *much later than the creation of the world*" (74, my italics). Other absences and idiosyncrasies are noted, which signal the exceptional status of the island in time and space: Tamony finds "none of those blocks of hard stone [. . .] which can be found in almost all other parts of the earth" (74). The geologist regrets the general paucity of important minerals; hard stones such as granite occur in unusually small quantities, and when they do, they appear to have been imported. If such hard stones are notably absent, more abundant is a "white substance, very friable, which easily dissolves in water" (75). Mary Gallagher notes that "in French, the word for duration, 'durée,' has the same etymology as 'dur' (hard or unyielding)."[32] The absence in the island's geological substructure of *dureté*, with its etymological link to *durée* and endurance, and the characterization of subterranean land as "friable"—something that disintegrates easily and slips through the fingers—should be read in terms of the colonizer's sense of ownership of the land. The scarcity of hard materials, sedimented over eons, and the abundance of this powdery soluble substance, underline impermanence and insubstantiality, and gesture to the chronic unease of the planter in space and time.

I have argued elsewhere that stones and bones in postslavery writing function as traces, which constitute a material connection to an otherwise unavailable primeval past. Specifically, these ancient formations and relics provide a numinous link to a prelapsarian time and space that preexist the plantation.[33] Here, in a very different construction, the lack of anteriority of stone, mineral, and ancestral bone is the geological corollary of the arboreal roots described above. The bones of grandfathers, relics of a recent past, the superficial roots of the island's trees, and the absence of any "primitive mountain" or "hard stone" betoken shallowness, illegitimacy, and a lack of mastery of time and space (it goes without saying that the novel makes no reference to any precolonial past—historical time begins with the first planter, M. Duparquet, 45). White Creoles are thin on the ground, demographically (the recurrent extended lists of planter surnames should be read as consolatory litanies, working against this sense of isolation), and thin *in* the ground too. Both the anteriority and the future of the island are shown to be compromised, uncertain, foreclosed. Traversay, confidently announced by Joyau in his introduction to the novel's second edition as a "Créole de vieille souche" (of old stock, but literally of old stump, the arboreal referent having a further layer of [ironic] biographical resonance),[34] works, perhaps despite his best ideological intentions, to undermine any idea of Creole antiquity, and explores rather the extent to which place is inseparable from displacement, possession from anxieties around dispossession.

Les amours, unlike subsequent Antilles novels, does not revolve around the threat of collapsing racial identity, incestuous desire, or thwarted maternity; it eschews the apocalyptic endings of later Antillean novels, which figure the plantation as a literal and metaphorical dead end. The institution of slavery—and with it the sanctity of whiteness—is apparently presented with a confidence no longer available to such writers as Levilloux or Maynard, who were writing in the wake of English, and on the cusp of French, Abolition. And yet as we have seen, the narrative voice undercuts the certainties of (diegetic) plot and (topographical) plotting. My analysis has focused on the temporal and spatial anxieties experienced by the white Creole, anxieties that might be seen to converge with those of the more classic postcolonial subject, for example the Black Caribbean writer. There are many other tropes in Traversay's *Les amours* that connect him to subsequent generations of postcolonial writers, from his pronounced ecological awareness; to an authorial alter ego, Zémédare, who reflects on the business of writing and the vagaries of literary reception; to an investment in and celebration of the local. In all three respects—environmentalism, metafictional self-awareness, and localism—there are strong commonalities with the *créolité* writers, for example. Seeking out, analyzing, and problematizing such commonalities might enable us to move beyond Derek Walcott's pessimistic binary diagnosis of postcolonial Caribbean writing as "a literature of revenge written by the descendants of slaves and a literature of remorse written by the descendants of masters."[35] In the final analysis, such textual work might also enable a nuancing of Said's model of contrapuntal reading, elaborated in *Culture and Imperialism* and deployed most famously in regard of Jane Austen's *Mansfield Park* (and what it—supposedly—didn't say about slavery).[36] As well as scouring the canonical metropolitan nineteenth-century novel for gaps and *non-dits,* so as to identify the submerged presence of empire at the heart of a text ostensibly unconcerned by it (texts written by white Creoles are, after all, axiomatically saturated in the ideologies of colonialism), the contemporary critic can, through the fractures, fissures, and disjunctions operating in narrative, understand how the apparent security and comfort of colonial discourse is destabilized from within. Such a contrapuntal reading reveals the extent to which early writings intersect with, and serve to complicate, our understanding of the Antillean literary tradition. At the same time, though, the contrapuntal challenge for the contemporary reader is to revisit these texts without making them bear too much interpretative strain, so as to avoid revising, incorporating, and co-opting them to fit what we might call an *analeptic* postcolonial agenda. In other words, the nineteenth-century postcolonialist should bear in mind Stephen Greenblatt's wry observation: that what one hears when one tries to speak with the dead is "one's own voice."[37]

2 Unsettling the Pigmentocracy
Levilloux's *Les créoles* and Maynard's *Outre-mer*

I'd sell my soul for white skin.
—Louis de Maynard, *Outre-mer*

LES AMOURS *de Zémédare et Carina* unfolds, as we have seen, in a period presented as a golden moment of impregnable colonial power, between the mid- and late eighteenth century. In this respect the novel is both the first and the last of its kind. Indeed, the apparently untrammeled security of ownership that the narrative explores comes under strain in the novel's discourse, a strain that derives from a tension between diegetic time and the historical period in which the novel was written. This split leads to what I have called, following Homi Bhabha, a "certain uncertain writing,"[1] in other words a writing that is permeated by anxiety, despite the comfortable ownership conveyed at the level of plot. This next chapter examines two novels published thirty years after Traversay's: Joseph Levilloux's *Les créoles; ou, La vie aux Antilles* and Louis de Maynard de Queilhe's *Outre-mer* (both 1835), novels that put mixed-race male protagonists at the heart of narrative, and that are explicitly haunted by the sense that the plantocracy is coming to an end. Both novels therefore overtly explore an anxiety and insecurity consigned to the margins of Traversay's novel. The destabilizing factors that had troubled Traversay, writing two years after the establishment of an independent Haiti, and that are only partially repressed in his sentimental novel of white endurance, are placed front and center of these Gothic novels. In Estève O'Reilly, hero of *Les créoles,* and Marius, antihero of *Outre-mer,* we encounter for the first time the interstitial figure of the *métis* or *mulâtre,* a figure who would become a key focus for later writers, both French and Antillean, from Balzac to Baudelaire to Séjour. The tragic destinies of both young men, and the apocalyptic endings of their respective entourages, point most obviously to the ferocious threat that *métissage* poses to the plantocracy.

Traversay, Levilloux, and Maynard, although in some cases prolific essayists and journalists, are all one-hit novelistic wonders. The thirty years separating their narratives wrought critical and irrevocable changes to the status of white Creoles in the Antilles, heightening the "siege mentality" discussed in my previous chapter. Léon-François Hoffmann describes the period between 1789 and the Restoration as a long succession of atrocities, during which "monarchists opposed republicans, Parisian delegates opposed local assemblies, rich planters opposed 'petits blancs,' whites opposed *hommes de couleur*, blacks opposed mulattos, soldiers opposed civilians, French troops opposed English soldiers."[2] By the 1830s Haiti, only obliquely referenced by Traversay, serves as a conspicuous cautionary example to other colonies. It is foregrounded in Levilloux's preface as an "out of control and half-deserted carcass" (13). Maynard, meanwhile, states that Haiti's independence foreshadows the loss of other colonies (I 147); it is cynically upheld as a shining example by the unscrupulous Marius to encourage resistance (II 134), and is declared a revolutionary role model by the maroon Scipion as he foments support for revolt (II 153). If Saint-Domingue has by 1835 been definitively lost to the French, Martinique and Guadeloupe, still reeling from the aftershocks of the Haitian Revolution,[3] are poised precariously between several further revolutionary moments: the plantocracy was profoundly destabilized by the July Revolution of 1830, itself an outworking of the 1798 French Revolution. The situation at home in the Antilles was no less turbulent: a number of slave insurrections (including the Carbet insurrection of October 1822, the February 1831 revolt in Saint-Pierre, and the uprising in Grand Anse in 1833) had been brutally repressed, but their cumulative effect had left the planter caste shaken.[4] Meanwhile, the Charte des îles of April 1833 formally granted suffrage to the *gens de couleur*, which furthered the owning caste's sense of fragility, while 1834 saw the launch of the *Revue des colonies*, edited by the prominent *homme de couleur* Cyrille Bissette. And these novels are also written only a decade and a half before the 1848 revolution, which would bring with it the definitive abolition of slavery.

The abolition of the slave trade by Great Britain in 1807 added to the malaise of the planters. If, for French reformists, this British initiative appeared to cede the moral high ground to the perfidious Albion, such measures were presented as recklessly liberal initiatives by conservative commentators, who made much of the fact that Britain was now lumbered with the fiscal burden of having to compensate plantation owners.[5] Meanwhile changes in world sugar markets, instigated by the Haitian Revolution and France's loss of its most productive colony, were firmly in place by the 1830s, and meant that France had been relegated to a second-rate power, while the British islands were reaching the apogee of their development. As Dale W. Tomich puts it, "between 1815 and the middle of the nineteenth century, the world sugar market was quantitatively and qualitatively restructured around the dominance of British capital."[6] Britain, an enemy so easily vanquished in Traversay's novel (see chapter 4 of *Les amours*), looms much larger in both of these later novels, and now represents a potentially fatal challenge to the Creole worldview. If France, and Europe more generally, are suspiciously revolutionary places—the progressive ideals of the protagonists have been inculcated outside the colonies and are portrayed as being fundamentally incompatible with life there—it is England, birthplace of Estève's enlightened father and Marius's adopted homeland, that poses the greatest threat to the status quo. Not only is Estève O'Reilly the son of an English planter (the discordant Irish patronymic is passed over without comment), but the first word of Levilloux's preface names the philosopher Francis Bacon, and this preface also reflects on Thomas Gray and Shakespeare. In *Outre-mer*, both Marius and his beloved white Creole, Julie, have been contaminated by time spent in England, and this novel too is suffused by references to the perfidious Albion, not least in the presentation of father figure and mentor to Marius Sir William Blackchester. Marius and Julie, like Estève and his friend Briolan, have been enlightened (in other words polluted) by their experiences abroad. Julie has endured what the narrator describes as the tragedy of a French education, exhibits an "excessive love" for Shakespeare and Byron, and her father worries that reading *Othello* has triggered "her sensibility for blacks" (I 158). In a letter to his mentor Sir William *Black*chester, a name that at the very least evokes the enslaved rather than their masters, Marius complains that England has poisoned him with democratic ideals, inculcating a "disastrous enquiring mind" (I 31) that values the soul over the skin. England is dismissed by the marquis de Longuefort, the benign planter-patriarch of *Outre-mer*, on his very first encounter with Marius, as having "far too many theories" (I 43). (The role of England as a contaminating source of liberal values reverberates throughout Antillean writing, as we will see in such novels as *Qui a tué le béké de Trinité?*).[7]

If white Creoles in the period cultivated a "pugnacious waiting game,"[8] their writing is characterized by a profoundly melancholic mode. Acutely conscious of the decline of the plantocracy, in their journalism, fiction, letters, and memoirs they seek to present slavery as a natural and universal fact of human existence (referencing the ancient world and the Bible to suggest slavery's perennial and immemorial nature) or framing their justifications in familial or in gendered terms. Just as the authority of fathers or husbands over their children or wives was a natural and indisputable fact of life, so too was the authority of the white master over the Black slave. The plantocracy is figured by both Levilloux and Maynard as being on the verge of destitution. The latter, in another self-justifying preface, invokes his own overbearing patriarch, who has "seen flames engulf [his] land and revolts that have piled up corpses in Grosse Roche." Maynard continues, "all colonists know only too well that it is no longer possible to compose pretty volumes, smelling of rosewater or orange flower, about events occurring in their society." Jacqueline Couti interprets this as a jibe at Traversay's *Les amours*,[9] which she reads as the epitome of the "over-sentimental romance," and which is one of the few extant fictions in the Antilles at the time. Whether this is the case or not, Maynard makes it abundantly clear that things have changed profoundly for the plantocracy.

Both *Outre-mer* and *Les créoles* center on the thwarted love of a young mixed-race protagonist for a white female. Their date of publication, 1835, falls in the middle of a period of white Creole literary production (1815–48) during which, as Roger Toumson has shown, there was an obsession with racial distinction and with the opposition between whites and *mulâtres*, the latter being represented as sinister and transgressive. As we saw in my introduction, it is highly significant that the term *béké* gains visibility around this time, and that, in the metropolitan context, this is the precise year in which the words *race* and *whiteness* are for the first time associated in the dictionary of the Académie Française.[10] Both novels are convoluted racial melodramas, shot through with incredible twists and turns of plot and with scenes of Gothic excess. A number of shared literary topoi reflect the hemorrhaging of social, political, and economic power away from the white ethnocaste: in addition to explicit references to the threat posed by rebellious slaves (revolts and poisonings, torture, pillaging), natural disasters such as hurricanes, cyclones, and shipwrecks are prevalent, as though to suggest that even the gods are aligned against the planters. Both texts, much like Traversay's *Les amours*, include a surfeit of geographical coordinates and topographical descriptions, gesturing toward an insecurity of ownership of space, and an attempt to anchor or fix an unsettled position. Both register a high degree of generic anxiety, an anxiety perhaps mirrored, given the novelty and the instability of the form, in the youth and mixed origins of their heroes. Levilloux and Maynard, in their prefaces, reflect explicitly on the validity of the fictional enterprise, and, like many later Caribbean writers, posit a hesitant but self-justifying authorial persona. Both have criticisms to make of all three castes, although the insistent reduction to three is itself an anachronistic strategy of containment, in a context where much more complex racial permutations were commonplace, a fact acknowledged even within the novels themselves.[11]

The few critics who have discussed these texts have often done so from a comparative perspective, and this is indeed the mode in which I approach the two novels. I have argued elsewhere, for example, that whatever their ideological differences, the novelists are in striking harmony in their presentation of the Black mother, figured as a source of phobic disgust. The threat posed by the mulatto/*métis* can be read as an outworking of the primal interracial desire of the white man for the Black woman, the original sin that causes the Manichean certainties on which the system depends to be transgressed.[12] Other critics have privileged the representation of the mulatto, a figure who in these novels is for the first time placed center stage. Critics have generally preferred Levilloux's text to Maynard's "reactionary" or "mulattophobic" novel, and it is hard not to agree with Richard Burton's assessment of *Les créoles* as being "perceptibly more liberal on the subject of miscegenation."[13] My key interest in this chapter is to attend more specifically to the construction of whiteness, a concept put under much more obvious pressure in these novels of *métissage* and (covert) mixing than in Traversay's *Les amours*. The very fact that Estève passes as white (unlike Marius, who is immediately recognizable as mixed race and who never expects to be treated as anything other than a damned representative of his caste) destabilizes the neat categorizations on which the plantocracy depends, and makes him a disruptive and destructive figure. Inevitably, perhaps, Estève's mixed status is unmasked, and his transgression is punished. But what happens to whiteness in these novels when it is put under pressure from within? How is the plantocracy presented at a time when it finds itself under acute historical pressure? And how do white characters shore up an identity so obviously under threat?

Les créoles: Color Trouble

Levilloux's life story and family history remain obscure, although a recent reprint of the novel establishes his birth date as 1805.[14] The uncertainty surrounding his biography has produced a number of disparities: he has been referred to as Jules and as Joseph,[15] has been identified as both Guadeloupean and as Martinican (despite the fact that he declares himself

Martinican on the frontispiece of the novel), and, most strikingly of all, is described by critics as white Creole and as mixed race. Although Corzani and Burton tentatively suggest that he was a mulatto,[16] Chris Bongie makes what I consider to be an irrefutable case for the author's belonging to the white slave-owning caste.[17] Such identitarian ambiguity seems especially appropriate for a novelist who is markedly more ambivalent than Maynard in his presentation of race and skin color on the plantation.

Les créoles; ou, La vie aux Antilles, Levilloux's only novel, is set in France, Guadeloupe, and the fictitious Île des Solitudes. The novel opens in Navarre, where Jamaican-born Estève O'Reilly is introduced into an elite French school, and immediately becomes friends with Edmond Briolan, also the son of a plantation owner. Edmond realizes to his shock that Estève is *métis* but can pass for white because his mother was a *mulâtresse*. Their intense and highly sentimental friendship—by far the most passionate and fully developed relationship in a novel that ostensibly turns on the heterosexual romance plot—is fundamentally enabled by their metropolitan meeting ground. Estève and Briolan are angry young men, whose frustration with the caste system in Martinique has been cultivated in France, and whose sympathy for the principles of the Revolution is unshakeable: they are later described as being exiled from their "philosophical Eden," France (64).

On the sudden death of Briolan's father and the destruction of his plantation by a hurricane, Estève invites him, his mother, and his sister, along with the family's elderly freed slave, Iviane (also Mme Briolan's closest confidante), to take refuge on the O'Reilly plantation in Guadeloupe. Iviane had originally belonged to O'Reilly and had been wet nurse to his son before being sold on to guarantee the secrecy of Estève's mixed-race origins. This separated her from her biological son Bala, now a maroon chief. Against the backdrop of a rebellion fomented by Bala, Estève falls in love with Briolan's sister, Léa, and their marriage is arranged to the delight of both families, neither mother nor daughter doubting Estève's racial purity. However, Iviane, eager for vengeance against the slave-owner who removed her from her son, exposes Estève's mixed blood and slave rebellion intervenes. In an apocalyptic conclusion, the lovers are slaughtered, to be reunited, under Briolan's watchful eye and to the disapproval of his mother, in the grave. Briolan dies in the Battle of Sierra Negra alongside Guadeloupean-born General Dugommier.

Like Traversay, and unlike Maynard, Levilloux sets his story several generations in the past (both displace their stories by approximately fifty years). But while Traversay chooses a time of apparent security (the

1740s–1770s), *Les créoles* is set against the background of the French Revolution, and the preface conveys foreboding and a sense of imminent change: the novel opens on the cusp of transition, at a time when "nothing had changed," and yet also at a point when the Revolution is projecting "a troubling light" (4). The narrator notes that a "malaise which always precedes serious crises" prevails in the colonies, and that "men could feel the old world crumble under their feet and were already throwing themselves into that near future in which a new society would have to be reconstructed" (9). While Traversay, in an attempt to shore up a sense of power that is beginning to ebb away, chooses a peaceful historical context, *Les créoles* addresses head-on the impact of the French Revolution on the colonies, and foregrounds the clash of value systems between a metropolitan elite and a planter caste. But this caste, although small, is not homogeneous: it is itself riven between *grands* and *petits békés,* but also by internal political tensions regarding the *homme de couleur,* tensions epitomized in this novel by Thélesfore and Deshauteurs-Desvallons. As its title suggests, *Les créoles; ou, La vie aux Antilles* is also an anthropology, or even an ethnography, of the Creole caste. The novel is saturated with sometimes contradictory generalizations on the attributes and comportment of white Creoles (the word *béké* does not feature). Hence, as we shall see, Levilloux and Maynard, despite the coincidence of their publication dates and their plot similarities, are in striking disharmony in their politics.

Levilloux describes the literary preface as having a preparatory educative function (it is a "space of necessary fomentation allowing the unguent to be absorbed by the flesh," 3), and his preface to *Les créoles* is therefore especially significant, distilling, in an apparently straightforward, even didactic, way, detached from the intricacies of the fictional plot, his view of racial identity in the Antilles. The author attempts in his opening pages to characterize the three different castes in the islands; here we already see a stark difference with Traversay who, in declaring that "the population of our islands is made up of two species" (*Les amours,* 184), spectacularly excluded the most numerous caste, Black slaves, from his ethnography. Levilloux's exercise in racial profiling obsessively tethers together "character" and "physiognomy" (the latter word, almost never used by Traversay or by Maynard, occurs with remarkable frequency in *Les créoles*) to articulate the key features of the three types. And yet Levilloux's typology is significant less for the "essentialist attributions and value-laden racial stereotypes" that Gésine Müller identifies there,[18] than because of the points at which these color-coded certainties are put under pressure, in other words the moments when physiognomy appears to offer no stable relationship with character, caste, or color.

Levilloux's typology begins with white Creoles, and homes in immediately on their intellectual capacities. They are described as being of "light intelligence, in general uneducated ['incultes'], but lively ['vives'], penetrating, enthusiastic about the magical, disdainful of European philosophical knowledge" (4), lines that encapsulate the ambiguity surrounding his presentation of white Creoles more generally. First, the opening qualification of Creoles' intelligence with the adjective light ("légère") both bolsters and undermines their ability. Müller, for example, translates the expression as "intellectual lightweights,"[19] and read alongside the terms that immediately follow it—the adjective "incultes," the enthusiasm for the "merveilleux," and a disdain for European philosophy—whites can indeed be seen as uncultured, superstitious, and uneducated. However, this reading is in turn undermined when located in the context of the next paragraph, on the *homme de couleur,* who is shown to exemplify both the "intellectual qualities of whites" and the "corporeal vigor of blacks": the relationship between Black and white here is clearly predicated on the age-old contrast between white intellect and Black brawn. And from this perspective, the "light" intelligence of white Creoles points rather to their nimble and deft intellectual capacity, as though they might wear their learning lightly. Such a construction plays on familiar Enlightenment connections between light, knowledge, and whiteness.[20] And yet Levilloux continues, in the following lines, and in a manner with which we are familiar from *Les amours,* to damn Creoles with faint praise. They are hospitable (a key Creole virtue, as we know) but also haughty, easily carried away, foolhardy, reckless, generous, and casual or easygoing ("faciles") in business. The white nobility that they claim as their own ("They pride themselves on the nobility of the color white," 4) is set against more vulgar, flighty, and unsubstantial qualities that return us, here and throughout, to notions of levity, hot-temperedness, and, above all perhaps, pretentiousness.

Levilloux moves onto the *homme de couleur* in the next section of his preface. His description, surprisingly brief given the centrality of this figure in *Les créoles,* rehearses familiar stereotypes regarding the ambition and opportunism of this caste. But it also suggests, as we saw above, that in the merging of (white) intellect and (Black) vigor, the mixed-race individual combines the best of both racial worlds. The third and last type, "black slaves" are, predictably enough, described as ignorant, cruel (notably in their propensity for poisonings), and cunning. But the narrator stresses that their apparent stupidity is often "calculated," and also points to slaves' capacity for "sublime devotion." If devotion is consistent with the stereotype of the contented slave, the highly charged adjective "sublime" connotes grandeur, the spiritual, and the ineffable. Slaves, moreover, exemplify "virtues that one is surprised to encounter in this state of degradation," and most notably of all are "endowed with a poetic imagination" (4). Here, and despite the brutalization with which slavery is explicitly presented, the enslaved are associated with poetry, the imagination, and the sublime, in a manner that recalls Caliban's appetite for beauty and verse in Shakespeare's *The Tempest*. Indeed, their affective responses to the world around them (a capacity stated rather than illustrated, given how marginal slaves are at the diegetic level, but that is nonetheless given a certain priority in the novel's preface) stand in stark contrast to the repeatedly mentioned philistinism and superficiality of white Creoles.

The preface thus sets the tone for a novel that continually destabilizes the very stereotypes on which it appears to depend. If the intelligence of white Creoles is both asserted and subverted in these opening pages, it is repeatedly undermined at other points in the novel. Estève and Briolan are imbued with revolutionary principles acquired in France, principles that are incompatible with colonial life. But their "candid and virtuous ignorance" (9), and their impetuous and idealistic naïveté, are generally seen as morally superior to the stasis and conservatism of white planters, who are satirized and often openly ridiculed. The Creole inhabitants of the small town are described in terms of parochialism, a propensity for gossip, and limited intelligence: "who is unaware of the inquisitive habits and the faultfinding habits of the planters resident in small towns, people whose emotions and ideas are every bit as limited as the circular figure of the horizon?" (64). An elderly Creole, on learning of Estève's *métis* identity, wonders how whites could degrade themselves by mixing (literally and metaphorically) with him; but the old man's credibility is undermined in the next line, which sees him compared to an ignorant feudal baron, and personifying a "naïve indignation" (68). Thélesfore, a young "thoroughbred Creole," is also in love with Léa; his ignorance and self-importance (he is described as being "born to dominate," 63) means that he cannot tolerate her preference for the cultured and accomplished *métis* (in a key scene, Léa faints in admiration of Estève's violin playing). Indeed, the characterization of one white Creole, puffed up by his nobility of the skin ("enflé de sa noblesse d'épiderme," 68), can be said to describe the entire planter caste, the self-importance conferred by whiteness offering a powerful counterweight to inherited ideas around nobility and social standing, and the very concept of white nobility being shown to be only skin deep.

The most heavily mocked individual in the novel's cast of pretentious whites is Monsieur Deshauteurs-Desvallons, a relative of Mme Briolan, who comes to her aid in her moment of destitution. Described as "the perfect example of old school Creoles" (the expression "Créoles de la vieille roche" mobilizes geological rather than arboreal depth in the attempt to suggest longevity), descended from one of the earliest planters to arrive on the island, he is clearly meant to be read as a typical, rather than an unusual, *grand béké*. Like many of his ilk, he is a pretentious and ostentatious show-off, a man who is proud to "porter l'épée," descending from the nobility of the sword, and yet who yearns for further markers of nobility (the narrator derides his "ridiculous mania for nobility," 62). His status anxiety is evidenced in the fact that he has invented a second, semantically opposing, term to his birth name, in a bizarre attempt to further distinguish himself and to "mark his origins out as unique" (62). The lofty-sounding Deshauteurs is tethered to, and semantically cancelled out by, the lowly sounding Desvallons, his original surname, in an invented patronymic that claims both the higher and the lower ground, a peculiarly explicit example of social climbing and the character's "lofty pretentiousness" (67). (The ridiculing of white Creole names by such modern writers as Houël, Confiant, and Cabort-Masson has long historical precedent.) Deshauteurs-Desvallons "affected to have deep knowledge under a smattering of literary expertise" (the French original, "une *teinture* de belles lettres," connects color, in the form of dye, with feigned or affected learning, 62). He is, moreover, a philanderer and an avid lover of mixed-race women (at one point he is complicit in the attempted rape of Placide's daughter), while his wife, like many Creole spouses, "took her revenge through her fidelity and through an excessive hatred for women of color" (62).

During a party thrown by Deshauteurs-Desvallons to welcome the Briolan family and Estève and to distract them from their misfortune (further evidence of the centrality of Creole hospitality), the young men find themselves at the center of planter attention, in a crowd scene that I shall quote at some length in the original as well as in translation:

> Surrounded by colonists, Estève and Briolan were overwhelmed by ingenious or crazy questions about France, and about the events and the men of the Revolution. In general, the speakers were full of light and brilliant observations, their ideas more remarkable for their elegance than their accuracy. Their

reflections were shrewd without ever getting to the heart of the matter, their ease in getting to grips with external relations, marvelous. So, their minds skipped around from subject to subject, gracefully skimming them, with the help of voices that were alert and eager for new emotions. However, a few rare minds did distinguish themselves in their aptitude and knowledge, and by their passion, which burned as brightly and as vigorously as the local sun. But they too showed no sign of being able to generalize in any profound way; you could tell that climate, work, and morals had arrested the development of these male intelligences. To every question, our two friends offered sober and prudent answers in which glimmered, nonetheless, general principles which, much to their surprise, elicited real sympathy in the crowd, but whose slightest consequences would have caused a storm. (65–66)

(Entourés de colons, Estève et Briolan étaient accablés de questions ingénieuses ou insensées sur la France, sur les événements et les hommes de la révolution. En général les causeurs abondaient en traits légers et brillants, en idées plus remarquables par la tournure que par la justesse. Les réflexions étaient pénétrantes sans atteindre le fond de la question, la facilité de saisir vivement les rapports extérieurs, merveilleuse. Ainsi leurs esprits sautillaient de sujet en sujet, les effleurant avec grâce, à l'aide d'organes éveillés et avides d'émotions nouvelles. Cependant quelques rares esprits se distinguaient par la force et le savoir, par des passions énergiques et brulantes comme le soleil de leur zone. Mais chez eux aussi, point de généralités fécondes; on sentait que le climat, les travaux et les mœurs arrêtaient le développement des intelligences mâles. À toutes les questions, nos deux amis faisaient des réponses sobres et circonspectes, où perçaient néanmoins quelques principes généraux qui, à leur grande surprise, excitaient une vive sympathie dans l'assemblée, mais dont la moindre conséquence aurait enfanté l'orage.)

The passage, as well as signaling the distance between colony and metropolis, again underscores the levity and superficiality of white Creoles. While appearing to applaud their conversational skill, adjectives such as "brillants" and "légers" bring us back to the ostentatious and the lightweight (the use of the latter adjective is less ambiguous here than in the earlier example). Indeed, at worst, Creoles' interventions are characterized as "insensé" (extravagant, nonsensical, even insane). Meanwhile verbs such as "sautiller" (to leap) and "effleurer" (to touch lightly) suggest their propensity to jump from one topic to another, or to skim the surface of a subject, rather than engaging with any depth. In structural terms, the fact that two successive sentences begin with "however" and "but" epitomizes the narrator's tendency to give with one hand, to take away with the other, and then to go on to further nuance, refine, or even contradict this second, already nuanced or attenuated, position. The distinguished minds, introduced by the sentence beginning "however," are not only "rare," but are themselves unable to grasp the broader implications of the Revolution. In a further concessive, the subsequent sentence beginning with "but" further undermines their grasp of the general repercussions of what is discussed, as well as suggesting that plantation life is incompatible with (male) intelligence. Their conversation is impressive for the turns of phrase employed rather than for its accuracy or depth of engagement; white Creoles are left bemused by Estève and Briolan's political discourse, and their response to it is ostentatious, unenlightening, and ultimately self-harming. At the end of the passage quoted, the planters enthusiastically welcome the very ideas that will bring about the end of slavery.

If established, and still prevalent, ideas around white intellectual and cultural superiority are thus undermined, Levilloux goes further still in his ambivalent anthropology. Color, and the characteristics associated with it, is repeatedly unsettled and shown to be unsettling, so that "physiognomy" is not only untethered from "character" but also from itself: in other words, and in distinction to *Les amours* and *Outre-mer*, not even the face can be taken at face value. The instability of skin color as a marker of "racial" categorization is flagged from the opening of the novel, when Edmond's father warns him in a letter not to take "external signs" at face value, as they are so frequently deceptive for observing subjects. Briolan senior continues, "Sound out, question all Creoles. They will be few, so it should be easier to discover their origins and to escape any dangerous friendships" (12). His son not only resists this conservative paternal interdiction but, in giving his blessing to and actively facilitating Estève's marriage to Léa, radically destabilizes the founding principle of the plantocracy. Color, moreover, is unreliable, even unseeable. Indeed it is often a quality invested in, and confirmed or secured by, the presence of the other; the entire plot springs from the fact that Estève's mother's death liberates him from "the living proof of his color," inspiring his father to "raise the *métis* to the rank of whites" (9). That he so nearly gets away with it, and that so many others have (Estève argues that the phenomenon of passing is widespread, and aspires to join the ranks of "so many families, proud of the so-called purity of their blood, and whose fingernails have for such a long time carried the coat of arms of my race," 79), clearly asserts the ubiquity not just of racial mixing, but much more transgressively, of passing.

There are other significant instances where color is malleable, radically destabilized, or prized from its habitual associations. This is most notably the case when protagonists are first presented to the reader. While Marius in *Outre-mer* personifies the coming together of the simple categories of "Black" and "white," Estève represents a more complex form of mixing as son of a white (English) father and a mulatta slave. In other words, his "pure" white ancestor on his mother's side is two generations back, and we are told in an early footnote that this is a "nuance which can be confused with European blood" (8). Indeed given the profound racial ambivalence that was associated with the Irish at precisely this point in the nineteenth century, Levilloux might well be seeking to cast a shadow over even Estève's paternal origins, registered in the spectacularly unconvincing English patronymic, O'Reilly.[21] Again Levilloux suggests that color is a much more slippery attribute, or indeed a more easily adopted and shed construction, than Maynard would concede. When introduced into a metropolitan school, it is the mixed-race Estève's *whiteness* that is emphasized. The attention of his schoolmates is drawn to the remarkable "paleness of his skin" and the "insipidness of his complexion"; Estève even succumbs to blushing. Meanwhile his "pure-blooded" white friend Briolan, soon to be his bosom buddy, is described as having a "melancholic color" (8), a fact that is repeatedly invoked throughout the novel (21, 76, 110, 148, 277). The etymology of the word melancholia is doubly freighted with color connotations, linking to blackness ("melas" in Greek), and "colie," bile, traditionally yellow-green. Briolan therefore represents a more visibly off-white position than his *métis* friend. This opening episode sets the scene for multiple scenarios in which color codes are worried, suspended, or subverted entirely.

Several chapters later, the reader is introduced to the novel's two representatives of white Creole femininity, Mme Briolan and her daughter Léa. The latter's virginal whiteness is associated with sickness rather than health, as she sports "the whiteness of a convalescent" (28). Meanwhile Mme Briolan, more incongruously, is repeatedly associated with blackness. Dressed in widow's weeds because of her husband's recent death, she has a "brownish complexion" and "black eyes" (34). More significantly still, for a novel in which dress functions both as a stabilizing marker of social class and as an outrageous disguise donned as a travesty of established codes (as we see below, the novel features a scene where Blacks dress as whites),[22] she wears accoutrements associated with the *femme de couleur*: her head is covered in "a brightly colored madras handkerchief," while on her ears "hung large and heavy gold earrings"

(64–65). The somber garb that covers her body is in sharp contrast to her highly colored headdress and oversized earrings.[23] She is attired in a manner stereotypically associated with exoticizing images of the mulatta, the enemy of the white Creole woman generally, and a figure especially reviled in Levilloux's fictional universe.[24] Joan Dayan describes the "uneasy similarities" that bound together Black and white and that were often manifest in clothing, and notably the madras: "First used as a headdress by slave women, who took a sign of servitude and adroitly turned it to their own advantage,"[25] white women's adaptation of the brightly colored and knotted headpiece registers a kind of secondary appropriation, a relaying of vestimentary codes that worries or undoes the binaries of enslaved and free. And beyond these highly charged color codes, other aspects of her description resonate with the stereotypical portrayal of the mulatta. Her gait is "nonchalant," her gestures "languorous"; indeed, it is telling that Levilloux presents her as a typical *Antillean*, rather than Creole, woman: "The entirety of her physiognomy exuded the carried away and determined, but sensitive and loving character of the Antillean woman" (28).

There are many further examples of this chromatic slipperiness, points where characters are shown, almost inexplicably, to change color, or where color shows a proclivity to distort itself or even to disappear altogether. Perhaps unsurprisingly, such moments occur at points of political upheaval, moments of crisis and transformation, and notably where whiteness is put under political and historical pressure.[26] For example, as the maroon rebellion led by Bala takes hold (the narrator notes in passing that the planters are incapable of appointing a leader, comparing them to medieval barons in their lack of discipline, self-indulgence, and heightened sense of individualism, 182), all involved "had the look of resurrected pale ghosts: whites were lit up by a wan reflection and the ebony color of the blacks had disappeared to make way for a blueish white ['livide'] hue" (183). The whiteness that envelops both Blacks and whites is ghostly, unhealthy, even pathological, again undercutting the association of whiteness with health and cleanliness, and destabilizing this color as the unique preserve of the *colon*. As interwhite tensions grow around the position of the *homme de couleur,* Thélesfore is himself shown to turn yellow: "rage turned him yellow, and bile rather than blood surged to his face" (244). This encroaching yellowness is especially significant in the case of Thélesfore, pillar of the pigmentocracy. He is Estève's rival for Léa's love and the most virulent critic of *métissage* in the novel, a character who is notably distinguished from Deshauteurs-Desvallons, for whom the "prerogatives of the skin" are overtaken by paternal instinct, and by sexual attraction to the mixed-race women with whom he fulfils the biblical edict to "be fruitful and multiply" (62). The only possibility for reproduction, it is suggested, is outside the stilted world of the plantocracy; but Deshauteurs-Desvallons's heavily mocked (liberal, if not libertarian) views and behaviors are not condoned within the moral universe of this novel.

At other points this color trouble is intimately connected to the psychosexual dynamics of the plantation. Iviane's memory of blackening baby Léa as she feeds her—"Often face of mine all black would come down on her face all white and would blacken it" (247)—draws on the repertoire of noir horror that permeates this Gothic novel, and which is especially concentrated in the portrayal of Iviane.[27] But it also, more subversively, reinscribes the realities of intercaste intimacy, underscoring the potential for such figures as the *da*, the nanny, to disrupt fixed color boundaries. Iviane is, indeed, a profoundly troubling presence: her breastfeeding of Black (Bala), white (Léa and Edmond), and mixed-race (Estève) children allows her to cross intimate racial boundaries and otherwise forbidden frontiers. She has also, however, worried the boundary necessary for the healthy heterosexual and homosocial order.

Both Estève and the woman he (almost) marries—crucially, not only is the union unconsummated but the "yes" that would officially tie her to Estève is prevented by Iviane's interruption of the wedding—have suckled at the same breast, and indeed even the relationship between Estève and Briolan, based on homosociality rather than kinship, is itself threatened by this inappropriate infantile intimacy. Thus, through her association with milk, saliva, and the breast, Iviane destabilizes the boundary between the "clean" white mother (personified in Mme Briolan) and the abject Black mother, undermining by extension the apparently secure binary oppositions and suppositions on which the plantation is founded, and which resonate throughout the text. Léa's loss of control when dancing is connected to this. As she moves like a woman possessed by "the demon of dance," the narrative voice announces that "she will die, she dies" (71). As Couti argues, "when associated with acute pleasure," the repeated verb "mourir" conjures sexual arousal, even "*la petite mort* (the little death) orgasm."[28] Léa is possessed by her love of music, which is shown to be an intensely primitive impulse, gesturing toward her contamination by blackness. Later, when Bala's partner, Soubaïna, saves Léa from the clutches of Iviane, "the compassionate Soubaïna supports Léa's pallid head on her ebony breast" (172). Here, the reference to the "ebony breast" recalls the familiar stereotype of the *da*, while serving also to emphasize the contrast between Soubaïna's ebony breast and the whiteness of the young Creole woman. As well as stressing Léa's purity, the proximity of the two women also suggests her potential contamination by blackness, through the implication of the topos of breastfeeding. Just as Léa's convalescent whiteness suggests sickness rather than health when we first are introduced to her, so too her pallid head "echoes her sepulchral pallor and prefigures her death."[29] Once more, whiteness exists in a threatening and inappropriate proximity to blackness, and is repeatedly unmoored from associations with health, continence, and sanctity.

Later, in a characteristically bloody incident, a group of Black prisoners led by Bala revolt and murder their mulatto jailer, provoking anger and a desire for vengeance among the assembled *hommes de couleur*. While a panic-stricken Estève attempts to calm this tension, arguing for intercaste fraternity rather than hostility, the crowd of *hommes de couleur* point to the corporeal evidence of the jailer's mixed origins (exactly what kind of evidence is not specified, but it may be the fingernail that is also named as the index of Estève's identity). They then announce portentously, in a biblical-sounding injunction, that the traces of the two bloods will be washed separately, never to mix again. The line, which closes chapter 16, is repeated, almost verbatim, in the opening of the following chapter: "The traces of the two bloods shall be washed separately and will never again commingle" (114, 115). This unique instance of cross-chapter repetition and relay—of a highly incongruous, indeed bizarre, statement, issuing as it does from the mouths of the *métis* caste themselves—might seem to encapsulate and confirm Bongie's summary of Levilloux's position. Bongie argues that the author of *Les créoles* "embraces in theory the mixing together of Estève and Léa, of métis and Creole, but remains pathetically constrained by the 'clear' categories that the novel would confuse and yet upon which it also depends."[30] Bongie's deconstructivist approach means that he is less concerned than Müller to identify straightforwardly "essentialist attributions and value-laden racial stereotypes,"[31] instead reading against the grain to show how Levilloux's novel reinscribes "the values of a prejudiced world to which it is ostensibly opposed."[32] Both Müller and Bongie, however, end up at the same conclusion, concurring on Levilloux's racism. Similarly, Couti asserts Levilloux's "racial biases." Iviane's revelation of Estève's mixed race springs from "a desire to protect Léa from a fate worse than death"; Couti concludes that "surprisingly, even a murderous *négresse* with an acute hatred for white people cannot let such an ignomy happen."[33] This analysis misreads, in my view, the intervention of the Black slave, who is primarily motivated by a highly personalized revenge toward her ex-master (O'Reilly had separated her from her son Bala), and who will in turn murder Léa through poisoning. In other words Iviane is much less invested in protecting the plantocracy (a system that she understandably despises as it has not only enslaved her, but has also separated her from her son), than she is with wreaking revenge on the O'Reillys. Her gripe against the white family is intensely personal rather than political or ideological. In any case, her intervention in the end also secures the plantation's demise: she poisons Léa, whose death leads to the death of Estève.

Levilloux's novel cops out, on the diegetic level at least, by having the lovers slaughtered by Bala's maroon band rather than united in an intercaste marriage. But in emphasizing Levilloux's "prejudice" and "racial bias," all three critics (Bongie, Müller, and Couti) underplay the profound ambivalence in his presentation of white Creoles, an ambivalence that takes the form of both an anxious ethnography in which whiteness is at once celebrated and undermined, and a more radical unmooring of color from conventional associations. In this context the portentous injunction quoted above—that the two bloods be washed and kept separately—serves only to underscore the impossibility of "unmixing" castes, functioning less as a proverb or mantra than as a subversive affirmation, a recognition of the challenge posed to the binaries on which the old order depends, but which are now definitively and irreparably breached. Couti rightly argues that Levilloux, like Maynard, blames "creolization, miscegenation, and Republican ideals of racial equality for the death of Creole culture."[34] However, it is perhaps in our understanding of Levilloux's view of that culture that our readings differ; as I have argued, Creole culture is itself shown to be inward-looking, unenlightened, degenerate, and unsustainable. If the white Creole clan at the heart of the narrative is fractured and ultimately annihilated, other familial models are also explored and celebrated. The happy family of the well-named Placide, a mulatto overseer, stands in stark contrast to the fate of the senile elderly Creole who employs Placide, and to the dysfunctional and exhausted Briolan clan. Placide is associated with gravity and wisdom, easy authority, and is energetic despite his advancing years; his peaceful and contented life—Briolan exclaims, "Placide, you possess happiness!" (197)—distinguishes him from the lightweight and anxious white Creoles. Placide's serenity is directly connected to his "numerous progeniture," described as a "a security belt of beauty and strength" (192) and repeatedly invoked by the narrator. The attempted rape of Placide's daughters by Desvallons and a band of marauding whites marks a low point in white debasement, but it is also a moment of white defeat: the corrupt and perverted white mob is overpowered by mulatto strength, virtue, and family loyalty. The dissipation and dissolution of the white Creole family is taken a step further by Maynard, in a novel that is an elegy for the "good old days" of the plantation, and a lament for contemporary degradation.

Outre-mer: Whiteness Assailed

Although some uncertainty surrounds Louis de Maynard de Queilhe's biography, we know substantially more about him than we do about Levilloux. Born in 1811 to a planter from Quercy, Maynard's mother was born in Vauclin, Martinique, in 1778. Louis, the eldest of four children, moved to France as a young man and was active in Parisian cultural and literary circles between 1833 and 1835. During this time, he was an energetic and well-connected journalist and art critic, and a close friend of Victor Hugo; he was championed by Henrich Heine, Victor Schœlcher, and Hugo, among others. In a twist worthy of his own fictional universe, he was killed in a duel aged twenty-six, apparently by his brother-in-law.[35]

Outre-mer tells the story of Marius, a talented and ambitious young mulatto who was educated in England under the guidance of his adoptive father, Sir William Blackchester. Although neither of his parents, as it turns out, is dead, Marius, like many a protagonist in the nineteenth-century bildungsroman, is effectively if not literally an orphan in search of his roots. An essential part of his education will be unlearning the truths inculcated in him by his progressive guardian, truths that will be countered by that other father figure and Martinican mentor, the marquis de Longuefort, whose title is an almost perfect anagram of "qui Marius" and who will eventually be revealed as Marius's biological father. Blackchester—whose very name suggests a dangerous affinity with the enslaved—has "abused his credibility" by telling of the harsh treatment of slaves, but Marius will be charmed by the modest wealth and happiness of the slaves he encounters (I 53–54).

On arrival on the island, Marius falls instantly under the spell of, and promises to marry, the beautiful and manipulative mulatta Flora; he ends their relationship, however, when he surprises her in a compromising scene with a young *béké* (the word makes its fictional debut in this novel, as *béquet*),[36] a scene that confirms his prejudices regarding women of his own caste. He then befriends the marquis de Longuefort, who introduces him to plantation life, and debunks many of the myths that his progressive mentor Blackchester had inculcated; reeling from Flora's disloyalty, Marius decides to take a newly arrived slave as his wife, hoping that such a woman will, in her ignorance and racial "purity," help him to recover from Flora's venality and guile (all mulattas, Marius concludes, are prostitutes). The marquis offers him one of his slaves, Jeannette, and Marius duly marries her; but before long—and largely thanks to Flora's interference—Marius discovers his new wife in flagrante with the same young *béké*. He murders the comte de Longuefort in a fit of jealousy and withdraws from Jeannette, causing her mental collapse; he then falls in love with the marquis's daughter, Julie, who has recently returned from France. She has been influenced by that country's more liberal views and, susceptible to the mulatto's charms, falls in love with him. When Jeannette, unable to bear Marius's cruelty, commits suicide, the way appears to be open to the young couple. But Julie, although in love with Marius, bows to her father's desire to marry her off to a worthy (white) suitor. The jealous Marius, with the help of a band of maroon slaves, murders three successive fiancés or husbands and, as the plot spirals toward its melodramatic conclusion, Marius kills Julie too when she appears to reject him one more time (although as she dies she utters the words "My Marius, I did love you," II 178). In the final denouement Marius realizes that the marquis is his father and that an old Black woman (Dorine), who had been in cahoots with Flora, is his mother. This makes him the killer of his brother, his sister, his brothers-in-law, and, eventually, in the novel's closing suicide, himself.

The novel charts the demise of the plantocracy through the destiny of the Longuefort dynasty. Maynard, like Traversay, uses the degradation of the Creole house both literally and figuratively as reflecting the planter caste's lack of long-term (psychological, emotional, and financial) investment in the colonies: "The colonies, alas, through a lack of guarantees and rights, have always resembled and resemble more than ever today, houses attacked by fire, from which all escape as quickly as they can, taking with them whatever treasures they have been able to salvage [. . .]. Colonists see themselves as merely passing through a land of exile; their wings are perpetually open, to allow them to rediscover their former homeland. Hence the little care they take with their plantations and with anything that could embellish their overseas existence" (I 10). And yet the novel's first volume is also a celebration of the values of the plantocracy and an exploration of the lure of whiteness, revealing the hypnotic and mesmerizing power of both on those excluded from their privileges, notably the ambitious social climber Marius.

From his first encounter with the marquis, Marius is fascinated by his as yet unacknowledged father, who clearly embodies the (uncontested) virtues of plantation life. He swoons in the presence of this "white haired gentleman, who knows what his forefathers were and continues their line" (I 46); whiteness is associated with nobility and grandeur, with the head (intellect and intelligence), and most importantly, with a clear paternal line that guarantees genetic certainty and continuity. Ironically, the marquis may know his ancestors, but is until the last scene of the novel entirely unaware of his son. The association developed here between the head, masculinity, continuous transmission, and whiteness—a cluster of connotations deeply imbricated in the paternalistic system of the plantocracy, and that will be spectacularly demolished in the murder narratives explored in chapter 6 of this book—is reinforced in the portraits of the ancestors (all of whom were soldiers or churchmen) brought from the family castle in Picardie to Martinique by the marquis to adorn the walls of his Martinican house (I 50). Marius feels "small and trivial" beside this "grandiose" figure, described as "sage, soldier, seigneur, and patriarch" (I 46). In a bedtime drama that revolves around the father rather than the Proustian mother, Marius realizes that he urgently "wanted to see the marquis before going to bed" (I 46); he remains infatuated by the marquis, right through to the end of the novel when he intervenes to protect the older man from the impending slave revolution that he has largely fomented, and whose explicit aim is to overthrow the white oligarchy.

The narrator claims that Martinique has a more noble history than Guadeloupe, and the reader is left in no doubt that the nobiliary particle in Longuefort's name (so often a spurious marker of noble origins, as modern writers insist) is genuine. He was a loving husband to his deceased wife, a devoted father to his son and daughter, and a just and generous master to his contented slaves. His skin is frequently compared to marble, his fairness (whiteness and even-handedness are synonymous in this novel) is stressed, and he is shown to epitomize the values of classical civilization, being explicitly compared to Pompey, Roman soldier and statesman (I 43) and to an "aristocratic Plato" (II 132). In an early plantation scene, a crowd gathers to watch two slaves, one of whom has stolen the other's wife, engage in a cutlass fight. While others fear to intervene, the marquis, Moses-like, effortlessly parts the crowd, separates the fighting slaves, and in the process sustains a severe injury to his arm; yet he adjudicates in favor of the slave who has wounded him, a slave who has come from another plantation, on the basis that he is the wronged party, and that "our duty is to do justice on the spot" (I 47). The assembled slaves then join the marquis in saying the Our Father together; Christianity, justice, paternalism, and whiteness all conjoin in an episode that sees the benign patriarchal order (temporarily) restored. A later scene stages a set piece of interplanter solidarity: the marquis visits M. Nicole, a *petit blanc* and Flora's father, another foil to the virtue embodied by the marquis. Nicole's plantation is an incestuous regime of internal reproduction. He has fathered many of the workers himself and encourages them to interbreed with each other. This corrupt and self-serving regime contrasts with that of the marquis, which is shown to perpetuate the values of ancient French nobility rather than New World opportunity: "He had brought with him to the colonies intact and unaltered in any way the almost feudal tradition of the noble castle in which he had been raised" (II 109).

This astoundingly constant association of the white (French-born) father with probity, moderation, authority, and virtue is entirely consistent with the starting premise and underpinning tenet of critical whiteness studies. Here it is sustained through the contrast between the marquis and his dissolute (Caribbean-born) son. The count's townhouse (located in Saint-Pierre, seen here as in other nineteenth-century writings as a hedonistic capital, the "Clamart of the islands," I 5), is a locale firmly at odds with the austere regiment of the Des Rosiers plantation, and indeed with the more upstanding characteristics of the city of Fort Royal. It is the setting for frequent orgies of alcohol-fueled sexual debauchery, to which the count invites "the most amusing range of colors" (I 83), but not whites, who do not form part of the "colored" population and of which caste the count is the sole representative. In one episode he becomes jealous of the lover of his preferred *négresse,* Clara. The count threatens to have the slave castrated, insisting that he be made a eunuch and taunting him in front of the assembly with a knife. Whimsically changing his mind, he then commands that the slave and Clara be given a bedroom, guarded by a Black child, so that they can spend a single night together, before being sent to different plantations. This grotesque spectacle of abusive and megalomaniacal white power forms a clear contrast with the probity and moderation of the father's regime and, significantly, the debauchery is interrupted only by the old man's arrival: "It was the marquis de Longue-fort; sad, austere, frowning, resembling the gothic statue of a French knight, standing in the doorway of this bad place [. . .]. A sense of modesty, or rather a sense of respect intermingled with fear, nailed each of them to their place. They covered their faces with their hands or with their handkerchiefs. You would have thought that God had come down into this bedroom and had caught them all, men and women, in the act of sin" (I 86). The divine analogy is explicit; the marquis's appearance (in both senses—his long white hair is repeatedly referenced in the novel) acts as an instant stop on depravity, literally immobilizing the revelers and causing them to cover themselves because of their shame. If the marquis is explicitly compared to God, the "bad place" conjures hell, and the count the devil himself. The all-powerful father, although dried up by age, manages an ejaculation that is, once again, superior to that of his youngers: he issues "a tempest of cold hail, a hundred times more terrible than all the outbursts of a furious young man" (I 87). The *non du père,* an intervention carrying the full weight of paternal authority, interdiction, and shame, is directly connected, moreover, to the degradation of the *nom du père;* the "pure and honored name" bestowed on the marquis by his forefathers was bequeathed by the old man, in turn, to his son, only on the death of his mother. Once again transmission is a purely white masculine enterprise, and white (male) virtue is conceptualized according to a visual archive of Christian imagery. As Richard Dyer has shown, whiteness is associated with "purity, spirituality, transcendence, cleanliness, virtue, simplicity, chastity,"[37] and in this instance with godliness itself.

The orgiastic excesses of the young count are shown to be exaggerated priapic performances, symptomatic of a fragile or threatened masculinity. On the intervention of his father, he "affects a confidence that he didn't have," falling into an armchair where he "plays nonchalantly with his knife" (I 87). The phallic associations are manifold; pathetically fondling his (unused) weapon, he is reduced to a sullen child amusing himself with a toy. Elsewhere, for all his sexual adventures with mulatto and Black women, the planter's son is presented as inherently feminized and weak. He dresses, for example, in diamonds, earrings, and golden silk. It could be argued that this foppish dress is merely an expression of a dandyism shown to be widespread in the colonies; a later suitor of Julie's, M. de Chalençon, also bedecked in diamonds and lace, is described as a "doll on springs" (II 8). Even Scipion the African, the leader of the band of maroon slaves and Marius's rival, is gently derided for his cerise satin, his white gilet "à la Robespierre" (II 136), and an excessive interest in his appearance. But while these men are mocked for their ostentatious dress, their sartorial choices are clearly made with a view to heterosexual conquest, whatever their disappointing effect on women (Scipion is surprised that women aren't "jumping to embrace him," and takes several hours to ready himself for a visit from an unimpressed Flora, II 146–47). In other words, if masculinity in the colony in general is associated with foppishness and an excessive love for jewels and ornament, it is only the count whose masculinity seems explicitly threatened by this. He exhibits "the coquetries and the puerile vanity of a young girl" and is said to resemble "a weak woman in childbirth" (I 80).[38] More significantly still, the narrator momentarily invokes "the secret tortures of a life lacking desire, or of guilty desire" (I 80), a line that points not to a (transgressive, but normalized) desire for Black and mixed-race women, but to a still more unnamable, taboo desire: homosexuality. Implicit throughout the count's portrayal is the idea that the glorious and virile nobility of the past is degraded (feminized and indeed entirely corrupted) by life in the colonies. If white femininity is entirely incompatible with colonial life (all white women are written out of the narrative through death), something would also appear to be rotten in the state of white masculinity: only the elderly marquis survives the apocalyptic ending, and all four young male Creoles (the count and Julie's three husbands) meet violent deaths.

While *Les créoles* features characters whose nobility is only skin deep (the narrator satirizes, as we saw, their "nobility of the epidermis"), *Outre-mer* insists on the Longueforts' honorable but ultimately tragic lineage, a line (linearity is crucial) that is "always golden, but always bloody" (II 125). The planter's name, whose connotations of strength and longevity appeared entirely appropriate in the first volume, assumes an ironic undertow in the second. The marquis comes from excellent stock; he is related, through the Condé line, to the Bourbon dynasty (four of his ancestors have died defending them), while the marquis himself has fought the English in their 1794 invasion. He ruefully notes in the second volume that none of his ancestors had the luxury of dying in their beds: their destiny rather is to be killed by poisoning, on the battlefield, or on the scaffold, "whether belonging to the king or the people" (II 125). Indeed, as the second volume unfolds, a sustained parallel is developed between the egregious fate of the monarchy in France and that of the white Creole plantocracy. The marquis comments to Marius, "you've just seen a throne fall, a throne that should never have collapsed" (II 125). Moreover, classical references now betoken not longevity but rather anxiety and fragility; the *béké* caste "in their disdainful majesty, mostly resembled those sublime Roman senators who waited, reclining in their seats until their Gallic conquerors designed to slit their throats" (II 80). As the July Revolution brings to an end the Bourbon dynasty, and with it the title that distinguishes the marquis (the latter commends the obsequious Marius who persists in using this title), the old man shows his daughter the portrait of another ancestor, soldier, lawyer, and chevalier of the two orders (II 89). The ancestral portrait is now associated with lost glory, and the head linked to humiliation and defeat rather than to intellect and gravity; the marquis has witnessed this forefather guillotined during the French Revolution, his head shaved and his neck bare. And by the novel's end, rebellious slaves tear the portraits from the wall and dance around them (II 179) in a final carnivalesque interruption of the old order, a scene that dramatically stages the decapitation of the Longuefort line and the dawning of a new (dis)order.

Outre-mer, at the level of plot and characterization, presents a less ambivalent view of the plantation system, and of racial identity, than *Les créoles,* and the chromatic economy of the novel is much less malleable. The social crime mentioned at the start is not slavery but mixing, and this crime has endured, we are told, despite early efforts to penalize masters who had fathered mixed-race children. Maynard's novel, moreover, does not trouble the pigmentocracy in the way that *Les créoles* does. The only point at which the phenomenon of passing as white is invoked in *Outre-mer* is in the character of Balisier le blanc, a pretentious and smooth-tongued character (I 65) named for a red flower and whose exaggerated claims to whiteness (like his nickname) only underscore his shaky white credentials. He is an object of ridicule, instantly recognizable as a mimic man, and thus no threat to the established order, a fact that lends credence, ironically, to his statement that "you are either white or you are not" (I 65). Moreover, and crucially, unlike Estève, Marius is instantly recognizable as a mulatto. Although talented, he is a manipulative character, a deeply racist social climber turned serial killer; his untrammeled evil ensures his own destruction.

I have argued elsewhere that familial configurations in *Outre-mer* systematically eliminate white femininity, and that the novel stages a family drama that moves "outre-mère," beyond the mother.[39] And in this coercive whiter-than-white regime, women are absent, either idealized but departed mothers, or virginal angels, both archetypes being designed to keep racial transgression at bay. White femininity is, it seems, incompatible with life on the islands. The marquis's wife, Julie's mother, is already dead at the start of the text, and Julie is murdered at the end. Even the perverted mirror of Longuefort's plantation, the incestuous Nicole *habitation,* is endowed with an excessive male progenitor and is strikingly without a mother figure. Meanwhile all three white protagonists prove fatally vulnerable to the seductive power of the nonwhite. The primal transgression between the marquis and Dorine leads to Marius's conception. The comte de Longuefort is murdered by Marius as he attempts to seduce the enslaved Jeannette, and his (their) sister Julie is also killed by Marius in a crime of passion. This is, then, a novel about white masculinity, in which the original sin of the father causes the destruction of the plantation. The general, and seemingly inescapable, sexual dysfunctionality of the novel, a dysfunctionality that takes on a claustrophobic character because of the way it plays out within a single clan, is not to be found in *Les créoles*, with its relatively conventional narrative of thwarted heterosexual desire between one couple, and of passionate homosocial friendship between another. (The attempted rape of Placide's daughter stands as an aberration that further underscores white Creole brutality and the caste's sense of being "born to dominate," 63, a version of white supremacy that the novel systematically unpicks.) Marius's dual obsession, with Julie and her (his) father, testifies to the fetishization of whiteness in the novel, a fetishization that leads to the repression of his visible and undeniable Black heritage. The second generation Longuefort family is torn between the twin transgressions of miscegenation (which opens the family line to the "too different," as Valérie Loichot has shown), and incest (subverting filiation by the choice of the "too much the same").[40] Threatened by the risk of racial transgression in the form of Marius (the incest plot emerges only in the final denouement) the white family is shown to turn in upon itself, defensively poised to ensure its own annihilation. In this way Maynard deflects questions of racial equality leading to legitimate interracial marriages onto the question of incest, which cannot lead to anything other than an illegitimate family romance.

If *Les créoles* stages an encroaching and inescapable color trouble, *Outre-mer* locates the trouble in the machine firmly in the psychosexual dynamics of the plantation. Whether it be in the portrayal of the effeminate and possibly homosexual younger son, the incestuous relationship between Julie and her brother, or the perverted plantation of M. Nicole, the absence of the white mother, and the threat to femininity in general, have corrupted the plantocracy. The collapse of the Briolan and the Longuefort families, whose patronymics are ironic (the noun *brio*, from the Italian, connotes mettle, fire, and life in the first; the second naming strength and endurance), resolutely signals the end of the planter line and the stark impossibility of regeneration.

3 Sympathy for the *Béké*?
Glissant and Chamoiseau

DECLAN KIBERD, writing of Ireland in the late nineteenth century as the landed gentry's grasp on ownership loosened, notes that the novel became in this period "almost impossible." He suggests that one could have written "a novel of manners focused on the Anglo-Irish ascendancy, for manners would soon be all that its members had left—but what of the insurgent masses and landless laborers beyond the castle walls?"[1] The French Caribbean novel, like its Irish counterpart, seems in the same period to be a similarly inhospitable literary space for those "beyond the walls" of privilege, reflected in Antillean writers' proclivity for the novel of manners, known in French as the *roman de mœurs*. Novelists such as Rosemond de Beauvallon (*Hier! Aujourd'hui! Demain!*, 1885) and Clémence Cassius de Linval (*Cœurs martiniquais*, 1922) authored unapologetically "big house" novels, which were primarily concerned with the codes and norms of white Creole society and its ebbing world. And while the novel of manners assumes some intersection between the personal and the social in characters' navigation of social codes (often via the device of the intercaste romance) the perspective remained one of privilege. Indeed, the gravitational pull exercised by this subgenre endured well into the early twentieth century. Drasta Houël's *Cruautés et tendresses: Vieilles mœurs coloniales françaises* (Cruelty and tenderness: Old French colonial morals, published in 1925, but also, significantly, set between 1830 and 1848), and Daniel de Grandmaison's *Rendez-vous au Macouba: Roman de mœurs martiniquaises* (Meeting at Macouba: A novel of Martinican morals, 1948) explicitly flag in their titles a concern with morals, behavior, or manners, whether deemed colonial (Houël) or Martinican (Grandmaison). Their action is restricted to the domestic setting (Grandmaison's murder mystery plays knowingly on this "big house" confinement). In distinction to Maynard and Levilloux, these writers marginalize political history to focus on marriage plots, love across social (and racial) strata, and inheritance.

As the twentieth century progressed, and as Negritude catalyzed the release of poetic energy and fired a new political consciousness, fiction, while less visible (or audible) than poetry, also assumes a more political charge. The most striking Antillean novels written during departmentalization and in its wake were by women. The remarkable cluster of female-authored novels mentioned in my introduction, by such writers as Mayotte Capécia, Jacqueline Manicom, and Michèle Lacrosil, tell the story of primarily mixed-race women, and detail their protagonists' damaging obsession with whiteness and their internalization of racial inferiority. These often-harrowing stories of alienation are intimately linked to the imbrication of sexuality and skin color, and protagonists are shown negotiating the false promises of departmentalization. But the encounter with white privilege staged in these works is a predominantly metropolitan experience. While these protagonists have undoubtedly been shaped by the conventions of the plantocracy and by the hierarchal color codes in operation in Guadeloupe and Martinique, their painful encounters with racism are designed primarily to show up the deceptions of departmentalization for subjects newly arrived in France, rather than to foreground the peculiarities of the local Antillean situation.

This outpouring of female expression foreshadowed and contributed to what we might call the golden age of Antillean fiction, one ushered in by the publication of Glissant's first novel, *La lézarde* (*The Ripening*, 1958),[2] and an era that arguably endures today. It is for this reason that I have devoted the remaining chapters of this book to this extraordinarily vibrant period. This chapter will focus on Glissant and Chamoiseau and chapter 4 on Vincent Placoly, while major writers such as Maryse Condé and Raphaël Confiant will be discussed in later chapters. However, and in keeping with my wish to include lesser-known authors, and to move beyond the hallowed ground of elite, middle- to high-brow fiction, I also include populist writers such as Marie-Reine de Jaham and Henri Micaux, and genres such as crime fiction and the family saga. The transition staged here, from chapter 2 to chapter 3, marks a temporal leap of over a hundred years, from 1835 to 1964, a leap explained by the fact that, as Jack Corzani bluntly but with some reason puts it, much literary production in the first half of the twentieth century is "undistinguished, bland, and monotonous, reflecting a widespread conformity."[3] But although this represents a significant jump forward in publication history, the settings of the novels remain similar: both Glissant and Chamoiseau are drawn back to the early to mid-nineteenth century, a diegetic choice undoubtedly motivated by the heightened anxiety that characterized white culture in the years before the abolition of slavery.

The preceding chapters, in their analysis of early Creole fiction (Traversay's *Les amours,* Levilloux's *Les créoles,* and Maynard's *Outre-mer*), have helped us better understand the ways in which *béké* writers considered and constructed themselves in fiction at various critical junctures or even moments of crisis in the nineteenth century: in the immediate wake of the loss of Saint-Domingue, as momentum built around the Abolitionist crisis, and as the position of the planter became increasingly precarious when the *homme de couleur* acceded to full and equal citizenship. This chapter might seem, then, an unconventional juxtaposition, even anachronistically out of place, in the transition to modern novels by two of the most important writers not just in the French Caribbean, but in world literature more generally, Édouard Glissant and Patrick Chamoiseau. In other words, the texts analyzed here offer a modern, even postmodern, and what we might call a postcolonial perspective, on the same turbulent time period explored by the white Creole authors of the nineteenth century. The chapter focuses on Glissant's *The Fourth Century* (1964) and on two novels by Chamoiseau, which, although published a decade apart, are companion pieces that unfold in the same space-time of the plantation: *Slave Old Man* (1997) and *Un dimanche au cachot* (2007).

As we have seen, the vast bulk of Caribbean fiction, although haunted by slavery, takes place after its abolition. While these three novels are unusual in the prominence given to slavery they also, in Glissant's case, explore what came after (as far as 1946), or, in Chamoiseau's case, insist on a before and an after. Both *Slave Old Man* and *Un dimanche* are haunted by the stones and bones that bear mute testimony to the precolonial period; and both open and close with a frame narrative set in the present day (in the latter case, with an author constantly distracted by calls to his mobile phone), a distancing mechanism that reasserts the fictionality of the story. So, slavery and the degradations it incurred is not the full story in any of these novels. But the *béké*—and crucially, in all cases it is the slave master or mistress rather than a post-Abolition or contemporary avatar of the planter—nonetheless occupies significant diegetic and affective space. In all cases, it is a nuanced and complex character who emerges, and one who is frequently treated with authorial empathy. These three novels are exceptional within the fictional output of their authors, and highly unusual in the Caribbean tradition generally, in that they give unusual access to the inner lives of *béké* protagonists, allowing them to speak in their own voice or through the mode of free indirect discourse, facilitating the interplay of proximity and ironic distance so strongly associated with the form.

Édouard Glissant's *The Fourth Century*

Glissant's second novel, a historical epic that unfolds between 1788 and 1946, is the only text in his substantial body of work to give significant space to the *béké*. His first novel, *The Ripening* (1958), isolates the *béké* "in an enclave";[4] subsequent novels afford him a relatively minor role.[5] But this early fiction foregrounds the three emblematic figures of the slave, the maroon, and the master (incarnated, in fact, by two contrasting *colons*), putting this idiosyncratic quartet at the heart of a complicated and intertwined transgenerational family saga that spans centuries of the Martinican past.

The novel tells the story of rival slaves, Longoué and Béluse, brought on the same boat from Africa to Martinique, and sold, respectively, to enemy planters, La Roche and Senglis. These characters and their descendants will interact with each other over the course of the novel, and indeed provide some of the core dramatis personae for Glissant's subsequent fiction. Longoué, bought by La Roche, immediately escapes, becoming a maroon, a healer, and a storyteller in the hills of Martinique. Béluse, Senglis's slave, remains on the plantation. Their roles as refuser and acceptor are thus determined, although the interactions and interbreeding of their descendants means that subsequent generations will deviate from their apparently pre-scripted familial roles. While the enmity of the Africans remains unexplained until the end of this novel (Béluse sold Longoué into slavery in Africa), the source of the colons' mutual hatred is quickly exposed: both were lovers of the same woman, Cydalise Marie Eleonor Nathalie (shortened to Marie-Nathalie), who out of spite chooses the pathetic and physically incapacitated Senglis, a man who repulses her, over the proud and dominant La Roche whom she loves obsessively until her death.

The novel has been said to "completely renew the genre," specifically in its foregrounding of a very unusual relationship between maroon and master.[6] This is a relationship held to be devoid of Manicheanism,[7] in which Glissant "refuses to project the world in black and white."[8] Rather, the dialectic of white versus Black, slave versus master, is complicated, undermined, and renewed: the white community is split between the universes of Senglis and La Roche, while the Black community coalesces around the hills, a space of resistance, and the plain, at once a space of submission and assimilation but also, as Richard Burton insists, of opposition.[9] Moreover, the doublings and echoes on which the novel is constructed (most obvious in the parallel rivalries between slave and slave, master and master, which resurface for example in the murderous rivalry of Liberté Longoué and Anne Béluse for the same woman) cut across ethnocastes, working to attenuate any sense of discrete or hermetically sealed worlds. And, most significantly of all, perhaps, in featuring not one but two planters, Glissant refuses any singular, monolithic, or stable version of white Creole identity. Most Antillean novels, if they feature a *béké* at all, include a single, totemic master—this is the case, not just for the other novels discussed in this chapter, but in this book as a whole—who is held to encapsulate the values associated with the *béké* caste, or, more rarely, to provide a foil to them (as we will see in Placoly's *Frères volcans* and Cabort-Masson's *Qui a tué,* discussed in later chapters). In *The Fourth Century,* however, Glissant's creative bifurcation of planter identity allows him to explore instead the tensions and hatred that exist *between* characters supposedly "on the same side," as well as the complicity that can occur between maroon and master.

Names, vectors of either power or dispossession in postslavery literature, carry heightened significance in this novel, whether they are entirely absent, or signal correlation ("Everyone ended up resembling his own name," 170) or extravagant dissonance with their referent. Glissant devotes significant space, and not a little humor, to the official conferring of names on the ex-slave population after Abolition. Indeed, names in this novel are significant even when referring to inanimate objects. *Rose-Marie,* the slave ship that brings Longoué and Béluse to Martinique, for example, is an especially ironic misnomer: Marie, that ubiquitous signifier in white Creole society, directly invokes Christianity, and specifically female virtue, while the rose is associated with delicacy, fragrance, and pristine prettiness. This is, however, an abject vessel harboring extreme human brutality and degradation. Once its cargo of human suffering has been delivered, the ship is washed of excrement and vomit, and becomes "truly like a rose," but one whose sap is sourced in a "living manure pile" (14).

But it is the names of characters that are most heavily freighted with meaning, and the names of the curious quartet mentioned above, are intrinsically connected to the psychodynamics of the plantation. La Roche (rock) conjures solidity, strength, stubbornness, and longevity, qualities reinforced in the name of his plantation, L'Acajou, mahogany, a hardwood prized for its durability and resilience.[10] Everything, from his "dreadful iron hand forcing wills to bend" (128), to his antipathy toward "gray zones or compromises" (189), to his seven (legitimate) children, points to willpower, dominance, and the capacity for endurance, qualities so central to the white Creole imaginary, as we have seen in previous chapters. He stands "direct, erect, and ready for attack" (102), the seminal father, the patriarch of patriarchs. La Roche's plantation prospers in part because of his steadfast commitment to consolidation and expansion (clearing ground, that primordial and romanticized planter activity; the obsessive drive to increase his slave stock), and in part because he has negotiated a sensible marriage, founded on profit rather than passion, with a rich (anonymous) woman who produces many children. But the qualities linked to La Roche's patronymic—notably his stubborn pursuit of hardline slaving tactics, at a point when they have been declared illegal—also precipitate his end. Disorientated by the collapse of the plantocracy, and with it the absolutes that had defined his world, he finds himself unable to accommodate to "the ambiguousness of the marketplace" and to the "dissolution" of modern capitalism (183). Symbolically his death coincides with the official end of the institution that has defined him, "not three days after the slipshod formalities of Abolition" (185). Utterly deranged, but as fanatical as ever about increasing his stock in human flesh, the elderly *colon* dies on the *Rose-Marie*, now a clandestine vessel and "the last ship of the slave trade" (188).

The name of La Roche's wife is not revealed; in contrast to his deceased lover, she has a purely functional status as begetter of his many heirs. But his four daughters, significant as "products" of this marriage, are named or even overnamed: Marie-France-Adelaide, Marie-France-Eloise, Marie-France-Claire, Marie-France-Nathalie. These forenames allow La Roche to perpetuate the memory of his lover, Marie-Nathalie, while at the same time asserting, like so many of his white Creole *confrères*, his political affiliation (France), his religion (Marie), and his social status (each name ending with a classic French appellation).[11] The profusion of hyphenated signifiers suggests abundance and excess; as in every other aspect of daily plantation life, naming allows the planter to choose freely and copiously from plentiful resources. These excessive monikers are also an attempt to attenuate any status anxiety, naming an identity that is, or aspires to be, more French than that of the French. At the same time, however, the names register constriction and lack of choice: the recurrence of the *same* names from daughter to daughter, names that are themselves variations on a theme inherited from a deceased white Creole woman, also suggests paucity, enclosure, and that ubiquitous Creole trope, the return of the same. Meanwhile La Roche himself, whose forenames we never learn, is noticeably unencumbered by the proliferating Creole names with which other characters are (often ridiculously) weighed down; the definite article and monosyllabic substantive connote certitude, and suggest a one-to-one equivalence between surname and character that only underscores the sense of rocklike indestructibility.

In contrast to the sturdy simplicity of La Roche, the name of the other planter, Gustave-Anatole Bourbon de Senglis, complete with nobiliary particle, is endowed, because of its excessive pomposity, with irony. His first and second forenames, respectively, are a Swedish royal name (meaning staff of the gods), and a name deriving from the Greek for sunrise. His third, from a French royal house synonymous with colonial expansion (Réunion island used to be called the Île Bourbon), appears to further the associations of regal might encoded in the first. But the Bourbons, like Senglis (and indeed La Roche), are by now a threatened line. Louis Philippe, a Bourbon and the last king of France (his reign coincides with the turbulent backdrop to the story of Senglis and La Roche, 1830–48) will rule over the last days of the monarchy in France, and the dissipation of royalty brings about the end of slavery. These names, used by Senglis's wife to taunt him (112), register fragility rather than power.

If the patronymic La Roche conjures verticality, Senglis, an inversion of Glissant—this Creole *verlan* of the author's name is another perverse doubling—suggests something more slippery, inchoate, friable, and unformed. He is from the start associated with abjection: we first encounter him nauseous from the "stench of Negroes," clutching a "squeamish handkerchief" (17). He sways with seasickness in the choppy sea (21), "spews" his words (72), and drools (77). He is said to be "every day [. . .] bent more crooked beneath his hump" (93), a hump that itself appears to be in flux, at one point "almost all the way down his collar" (77). In a scene that appears on the face of it to represent the nadir of sadistic abuse, Gustave-Anatole punishes his slaves by forcing them to eat his underarm hair and to smear themselves with his baby's stools. But such "little perversions" elicit only laughter and scorn in his slaves, who understand his gestures as the "depraved hatred of a puny man," the games of a "feeble idiot" (111). These obscene games are dismissed by the utterly disenfranchised enslaved population as pathetic power plays. Senglis occasionally attempts to elevate himself, metaphorically but also physically, from the abjection in which he is mired. Goaded by his wife's discussions with overseers on the plantation, "some sudden nobility increase[ed] his stature, like an old tunic you notice one day and instinctively put on" (76). But such moments are rare and short-lived: he is "instantly rid of the tunic and back with the reality of his hump" (76). Indeed, Senglis's plantation is slipping away, cast adrift because of the madness and malaise of its inhabitants. Its topography is imagined as a suppurating lesion, a space of decline directly contrasted with La Roche's estate: "the long, smoky, constantly progressing wound, like lines of algae and mud drifting with the currents on the sea, was not there the way it was around Acajou, for example, where it meant the arable land was advancing into the primeval mess" (96–97).

The names taken by, or given to, Africans are significant too. Longoué's self-conferred name, *long oué,* long cry, registers both the maroon's heroic resistance to the plantation machine, and a sense of duration. It therefore resonates with similar qualities to La Roche; once again, maroon and master are shown to inhabit cognate rather than contrasting metaphorical space. In stark opposition to his fellow African, whose self-naming is a primal gesture of self-possession, Béluse, named by the mistress, is saddled with a degrading label. Designated for (the aspiration of) reproduction, deriving from "bel usage," the correct use, in other words copulation, Béluse is exploited as a stud by a mistress who cynically engineers the coupling of her slaves and "took some extra perverse pleasure in disrupting the clandestine amorous arrangements of her managers and overseers" (61). Béluse's utilitarian and debased name thus reflects the dispossession of the slave body; transformed into a surname in later generations the name, connected very explicitly to service, continues to bristle with the degradations of slavery. When the "son of slavery" is finally born he is given the name Anne by Marie-Nathalie (called after the "Constable of France," the Duc de Montmorency, 1493–1567); the flagrant inappropriateness of the name in terms of the gender, social status, and lineage of its bearer means that even Senglis queries its aptness (111). As in so many other novels of slavery, naming, often connected to shaming, is on the plantation a resource exclusively at the disposal of the master, another function that, as the narrator puts it in another context, is entirely "at the pleasure of their possessors" (23).

As well as the power to name, one of the key symbolic manifestations of white power is, as we saw in the introduction and in previous chapters, the master's gaze, which in this novel is constructed not just as a vector, but indeed as the source, of his supremacy. La Roche, "an absolute and maniacal Patriarch," stands as the archetypal master, and is unsurprisingly endowed with a "gaze that made them all, sons, employees, slaves, and freedmen, shiver" (128). His privileged ocular vantage point is emphasized; from the height of his steed, he is endowed with untrammeled vision, and this oversight allows him to instill terror in those on whom he gazes: "High on his horse [. . .] he would stare thoughtfully at those who had incurred his anger," so that even his sons become "more fearful than ever of his fixed stare" (128–29). In his interactions with fellow planters, in moments of crisis, La Roche's gaze is again synonymous with authority: in one instance he "looked [the planter] up and down without a word and the foolish man fell silent" (165). In all these respects he conforms to the type of the all-powerful, because all-seeing, planter, the embodiment of absolute colonial power.

Longoué, however, emphasizes the limits of the look—"The master did not really exist except when he was looking at you"; "as if he could only rule by establishing a flow that dried up as soon as he turned away" (62–63)—and he is the only character in the novel who dares return the gaze. The fact that Longoué, while still aboard the slave ship, holds the *colon*'s gaze, immediately signals the soon-to-be maroon's unique status (even his fellow planters are subjugated by La Roche's stare), and his exceptional capacity for resistance. This exchange of looks establishes their relationship as a power *dynamic*, founded on exchange and reciprocity, and inaugurates a series of unconventional encounters that seal the pact between master, maroon, and maroon's descendants. Longoué, having escaped to the hills, takes the risk of returning to the Acajou plantation to liberate Louise, the slave who had cut him free, and whom he will deliver from brutal punishment to become his partner. The maroon, now armed with a knife stolen from the master's property, is confronted with a somnolent La Roche, sleeping "almost provocatively" (82); his inability to see the intruder renders him especially vulnerable. Rather than killing him, Longoué passes over; the master's foolhardiness in leaving his door open is, for the maroon, symptomatic of a certain innocence and bravery, qualities he "should not take advantage of" (82). It is as if an unspoken code of honor already governs relations between the two warriors. And, in subsequent years, Longoué continues to guard La Roche's plantation, ensuring that his property (and that of Senglis) are not attacked by his comrades. La Roche in turn protects "his" maroon and the maroon's descendants. This complicity continues to the end of their lives, and even beyond the lifetime of the maroon. On his deathbed, Longoué declares "La Roche, that's a man. Ah! Yes, that is a man" (134). Later, when La Roche rescues Longoué's son, Melchior, from certain death at the hands of a group of planters, his fascination with the primordial maroon resurfaces: "He could not bring himself to leave Melchior. Old times coming back like this had him full of life again. He was almost begging for an insult, some gesture, some sign that would have reminded him of his man marooned in the first hour" (164). Melchior, like his father, returns the master's gaze and interacts with him as an equal, offering counsel and notably encouraging the marriage between La Roche's daughter and Senglis's son: "Perform the marriage. The boy is more able than his father and you love your daughter. She will be happy" (164). Such moments of complicity between planter and maroon radically rewrite the conventions of the novel of slavery, which stage the relationship between master and rebel slave as one of inevitable antagonism.

Of particular interest to critics is the scene that unfolds between La Roche and Longoué, who meet by chance after ten years. They stare silently at each other, "unstirred by any fear that might disrupt their scrutiny" (101) and then take turns to speak in languages which the other cannot understand. La Roche speaks French, while Longoué responds in his own African language. In this "dialogue that was not a dialogue," "each one closed in upon his own injury" (102), the men relate the defining experiences of their past: for La Roche, the loss of Marie-Nathalie, for Longoué his experience of captivity and the shock of arrival in the New World. As Keijiro Suga argues, the scene "touches upon the secret of communication" in Glissant's work: "Instead of seeking a compromised, very limited exchange in rudimentary Creole, La Roche and Longoué opt for their own languages that sustain eloquent speeches." In this scene, "their respective monolingualism found a means of inner transcendence."[12] La Roche hands to Longoué a little casket and a piece of ebony bark, in which he has had the portrait of "his" maroon sculpted. These "objects of damnation" seal a "quasi-notarial pact according to which he cedes to [Longoué] the space of the hills."[13] As Bernadette Cailler observes, "For a few moments the dialectic of master and slave fades away, giving way to the singular reality of two human beings equal in suffering and anxiety. Together, in the end, they smile."[14]

Richard D. E. Burton notes that the Senglis plantation is a "matriarchy or rather, a gynocracy," set in clear opposition to the masculine realm of the hills,[15] suggesting that power resides with its mistress, Marie-Nathalie. Certainly, her husband bends to her "cold grip," and therefore to "the feminine law ruling the plantation" (64); she has the power to name slaves and to engineer their coupling (if not to control the outcome of pairings). She frequently carries her riding crop (57, 58, 62, 66, 67, 77), an image that haunts La Roche long after her death (129) and which is a conventional symbol of white planter power. Marie-Nathalie wears a riding habit but yet eschews the horse from which the *colon*'s whip is usually deployed, choosing instead to travel on and between plantations by foot; her whip is used on vegetation, or to lash out at the air in paroxysms of mania. It is an instrument of sexual titillation when she consents to marry Senglis (she caresses the "oh so fragile flower" of a hibiscus trees with the whip, 58), and later is deployed in a delirious sadomasochistic sex scene with her husband, the only time it is used on human flesh ("the flash of the crop descending to graze his crippled back," 77). The crop, it could be argued, is therefore merely a prop, symbolic of an attenuated or even reluctant power, never deployed from the panopticon heights afforded by horseback, and indeed limited to erotic (sadomasochistic), rather than colonial, power.[16] Not prepared to pit herself against La Roche, she chooses a more easily vanquished mate, a reaction of insecurity rather than of authority. She towers over her handicapped husband, whom she has married not only to punish La Roche, but also so that she can enjoy "the certainty, the stability, the chance to dominate a weak person who would consent" (103). Male subjection does not necessarily equate to white female power.

As the novel continues, the mistress, as in many other plantation novels, disintegrates, physically and psychologically.[17] Marie-Nathalie, whose name doubly connects to ideas of Christian birth and maternity (God's mother and Christ's birthday), displays a fanatical and neurotic obsession with having Béluse, rather than herself, produce children. Although she invokes pragmatic reasons for this "multiplication project"—she and her husband will no longer be obliged to rent male sires from neighbors—we are also told that the couple is "mysteriously immune" (112) to the lure of profit, a fact that renders them spectacularly unsuitable for the positions they hold. And indeed, the extravagant care bestowed upon Béluse and his wife, both of whom are allowed to live in the *grand'case*, is disproportionate, eerily indulgent, and economically nonsensical. As the longed-for baby fails to materialize, Marie-Nathalie's descent into madness accelerates; she ignores even her own newborn, conceived in an "inexplicably inattentive" moment with her husband (94), and is instead consumed by the mystery of Béluse's apparent infertility.

Glissant repeatedly underscores the degeneration of the Senglis plantation, hermetically sealed from the outside world, and more conspicuously associated with signifiers of death and disease than with life. In contrast to the La Roche plantation, "a beehive" (97) of production and reproduction, where the *colon*'s decision to mate the slaves who were fit to reproduce generated "fifteen of them, with no other cost" (44), here reproduction, like production, is inherently compromised, and male slaves in particular no longer fulfil their reproductive function (64). Béluse himself is metaphorically "stillborn" on the estate (30), just like the premature baby who arrives at six months gestation to the planter couple, and who is mentioned only in passing (57). The plantation is a "den of decay," "a sluggish canker," in which everything is "rotting away in debasement and shamefulness" (96–97). The extreme physical and psychic contamination of the place suggests that the pathologies of sexuality and slavery are intimately interconnected.[18] The mistress, and by extension the plantation over which she presides, is associated with a plethora of signifiers registering stasis and rigidity. She is described, for example, as "*impervious* to time, *dead* in her *inflexible* and *steadfast* dream, she mourned daily for this birth that had become her obsession. Béluse [. . .] was no longer afraid of her *dead* gaze or the mournful *mask* where you could see her *stiff* wrinkles underneath the cream" (109, my italics). The eventual arrival, after six years, of Béluse's child, in fact only compounds Marie-Nathalie's condition; she is momentarily overwhelmed by a "surfeit of pleasure" (112) before disengaging from the boy, just as she had her own son. This birth heralds the "final downfall" of the plantation (109) and quickens her retreat into insanity.

Marie-Nathalie thus epitomizes white Creole degeneracy; she is the site of collapse of the rational order, and as the novel proceeds she is increasingly associated with figures of the uncanny: a funeral doll (93), a mummy (104), a ghost (109), and finally a zombie (137). She can also be seen to have much in common with other deranged, insane, or psychologically vulnerable mistresses, the prototype of whom is Charlotte Brontë's Creole heiress, Bertha Mason, also her historical contemporary. A series of diegetic and discursive coincidences links the two women, not least the semantic echo that connects the names of their objects of desire, Rochester and La Roche, a consonance that is borne out in the men's shared (masculine) characteristics such as authority, cruelty, and overpowering sexual charisma. Rochester's French-speaking daughter is called Adèle, La Roche's Adélise. Like Bertha, Marie-Nathalie degenerates from beauty to beast in a shockingly sudden manner. Bertha as a young woman had been "the boast of Spanish Town for her beauty" (*Jane Eyre*, 352), just as Marie-Nathalie's "radiant, unexpected beauty" charms all around her, but disappears "from one word to the next" (56). Senglis considers his wife to be a "loose woman" (71), while Rochester compares Bertha to a "professed harlot" (*Jane Eyre*, 355). Bertha is confined, famously, to a third-floor attic room,[19] while Marie-Nathalie is cloistered within the big house. The unhinged laugh that characterizes both women, a "magnificent burst of hysteria" for Marie-Nathalie (77), an unhinged and preternatural "cachinnation" (*Jane Eyre,* 130) for Bertha, are manifestations of mania; they also are forms of physical release connected to sexual desire.[20]

Critics have long disagreed, because of the notorious slipperiness of the designation Creole, about whether Bertha Mason is white or Black. Brontë's novel is ambiguous on the issue, so that some (most famously, Gayatri Spivak) read her as white,[21] others as being tainted by the stain of racial mixing: Rochester, who has dealt, in both senses, with Bertha's father, ominously insists that he has never seen her mother (*Jane Eyre,* 352). Within the racial economy of the text, this ambivalence is the source of her monstrous and uncontrollable behavior. In other words, as H. Adlai Murdoch argues, Brontë's portrayal of Bertha ensures that she remains "insistently, inscrutably interstitial."[22] Or, as Marcus Wood argues, "she is a tabula rasa on which readers and characters project their fear or guilt."[23] Whatever about her racial identity, Bertha's "figurative position," as Valerie Beattie shows, "sustains her literal one: her primary symbolic color is black, connoting the unconscious, the unknown, the repressed."[24] This figurative positionality is similarly central in Glissant's drawing of Marie-Nathalie, in a novel that is suffused on almost every page with highly symbolic references to color. The mistress is occasionally associated with whiteness: she is "white as manioc" (67) and appears after death as a "white zombie" to Béluse (137). But these examples contain her "whiteness" to either the figurative or the supernatural. She is, however, more fundamentally associated with blackness, in a manner that opens up at least the possibility that she is of mixed race. She is connected, in her first diegetic appearance, with a yellowing headdress (62). La Roche, as he bares his soul to Longoué, castigates Marie-Nathalie's use of makeup to cover up "filth." He goes further; as he recalls their passionate courtship, he unequivocally casts himself and his lover at opposite ends of this color spectrum: "Because all the sand we rolled around in, she and I—I saw it as endlessly white and she saw it black. It was black inside her and I did not know it" (103). Such a scene recalls the markers of (Black) Creole identity deployed so ambivalently by Brontë. Crucially, though, while the markers of Bertha's blackness are absurdly visible (the "blackened inflation" of her "savage face," *Jane Eyre,* 327), Marie-Nathalie "sees" Black, and at the same time *is* Black—on the inside—attributions that might suggest either on the one hand a nonracialized use of the word, or on the other hand an essential quality that is not merely skin deep. For example, it both echoes, and diverges from, the description of La Roche as being "half nigger *in his head* despite his blue eyes" (58, my italics). In the latter example, "blackness" is unequivocally linked to race, but it is also an imagined, or even self-appointed, condition (the precise valency of "nigger" is unspecified, but is contextualized, strangely perhaps given the enslaved narrators of this section, alongside his status as a "hothead," a "madman," and his proclivity for "insane" stories). For Marie-Nathalie, though, blackness suggests a temperamental disposition to depression, but also, as I will argue below, a fundamental incompatibility with La Roche, and with the world of exploitation and domination (of Blacks) with which he is synonymous.

Marie-Nathalie, although an orphan (orphan status in Creole fiction, as we have seen, is often connected to the uncertainty of specifically racial origins), enjoys a happy and sociable childhood, during which her proximity to slaves is emphasized, in terms of both narrative voice and plot. The bulk of *The Fourth Century*'s narrative, even when appearing to form part of "the subjectless omniscient narrative of the past," emanates as Celia Britton shows from the maroon Papa Longoué.[25] But Marie-Nathalie's story is narrated, in the first instance, by the old slave who initiates the newly arrived Béluse to the history of the plantation. Longoué defers to the old man—"at the start of *his tale,* therefore, she bloomed like a blue pool brimming with morning sunshine" (56, my italics)—who remembers her vividly, and with an almost paternal affection ("she made your heart glad; everybody, masters and slaves, made a fuss over her," 56). In other words, her story, uniquely, is doubly relayed by enslaved and maroon, the old man's narrative sitting within Longoué's. Meanwhile the "nous" perspective of the enslaved community (including the "old folk" who so often convey her story) acts as a kind of chorus. These voices comment empathically on her choices ("they could not understand why she had not married the lord of the low house," 57), amplifying, and enigmatically and poetically summarizing her story ("riffle on the surface of the water, chalk mask, sea fire, cloistered dead woman," 56), and acting more generally as privileged witnesses, guarantors, and even makers of her story: "all of this was what the slaves knew [. . .]. They pieced the story together bit by bit, almost without meaning to, like it was their job. Because not one of them would miss a chance to go against her, she was *so changed, so distant,* and so amazingly married to the humpback" (58, my italics).

The origins of Marie-Nathalie's decline are therefore specifically connected to her separation from slaves: their disdain for a young woman "so changed, so distant" suggests a prior relationship of contact and easy intimacy. The text is not clear on what exactly precipitates her removal or withdrawal from their world. The house slaves (as ever, the privileged source of information relating to her) confide that she is learning to read and write; her withdrawal is also clearly linked to adolescence, as she reemerges among them a woman. But the transition, described in English as a "split" (the French "écart" means gap), whether linked to literacy or to puberty, is undoubtedly to be understood as an initiation into the symbolic order of the plantation, both linguistic and sexual, an order founded on a binary division between Black and white. She emerges not just as a woman, but as a *white* woman, having nothing more "in common with her surroundings," no longer to be seen "at the head of the little band of wide-eyed black children she used to watch over" (56). Ironically, perhaps, the band of black children recalls the plantation environment of Joseph Zobel's bildungsroman *La rue cases-nègres,* and indeed the transition experienced by Marie-Nathalie in many ways mirrors the trajectory of that novel's Black protagonist, José Hassam, for whom literacy, growing maturity, and immersion in the world of white culture (albeit through the colonial school), creates an unbridgeable chasm between him and his peers. This process of internalization instils a heightened sense of self-consciousness and a feeling of guilt in the young boy, who also, suddenly and damagingly, realizes he has nothing more in common with his erstwhile Black companions.[26]

Immediately after the description of this "split," in a significantly positioned scene, Marie-Nathalie walks with her crop, whipping trees and mauling hedges, when she suddenly comes across a slave convoy. Her reaction is a highly ambivalent one of self-restraint, emotion, and isolation, all of which find their source in this splitting of the self. She realizes "that her lot was to love all her life the very thing she ought to flee forevermore [. . .] clenching her fists, biting her lips, alone and fallible and erect, without a sound, in all the delirium of trees and birds" (57). The reference to the love object ostensibly points to her passion for La Roche; but her physical reaction, generated by the spectacle of human suffering with which she is unexpectedly confronted, but which is not described in any detail, would seem also to be rooted in repression (biting her lip, clenching fists, silence). Marie-Nathalie escapes into the "delirium" of nature, perhaps, to avoid seeing what is for her unseeable; in this respect her reaction resembles that of other deranged mistresses for whom blindness is a necessary strategy to cope with the horrors of plantation life. But the strange juxtaposition of the words "alone and fallible and erect" suggests a mistress for whom the realities of her position are at the very least a source of ambivalence, possibly even shame. Separated from, then suddenly faced with, slaves, the "thing she ought to flee forevermore" might also be understood, not just as La Roche, but also the institution with which he is indissociable, slavery.

The encounter with the convoy, bracketed off typographically, as though to suggest that the scene remains unassimilated in narrative and psychological terms, has a sudden and profound effect on Marie-Nathalie, "as if a force connected to the trees and sky suddenly loosed its fury on her." She is rendered "motionless for a long time, a statue rent by the pounding of an indifferent sun. But her hatred as well as her love turned in only one direction: toward the same blue-eyed lord" (57). The unidentified force unleashed on her in this scene, and notably the further reference to a "split," powerfully inscribed in this image of a rent statue, suggests extreme, indeed overpowering, psychic conflict: she is immobilized, frozen to the spot, and the fact that the scene acts as a narrative lacuna points to a profoundly traumatic event. Read in the context of the association, both discursive and diegetic, of Marie-Nathalie with blackness, it suggests (Black) disavowal, an impulse described by Celia Britton, in an essay that brings Freud's concept of disavowal into dialogue with Fanon's "white masks" syndrome, as an identification with whiteness that causes "an ambivalent ego defense in which the subject both recognizes and refuses to recognize an unwelcome perception."[27] Moreover, as Britton argues, "it is the sight of the black stereotype that triggers an urgent need to identify oneself as white."[28] A more "stereotypical" image of blackness than the slave convoy is, in the time in which the novel is set, barely imaginable: images of shackled people, tied together with forks around their necks, was a visual cliché ubiquitous in paintings and engravings of the eighteenth and nineteenth centuries. The spectacle of suffering triggers in the mistress a very literal impulse to "turn in only one direction," and La Roche's blue eyes, key signifiers of whiteness, are invoked at precisely this moment. But Britton is careful to distinguish Fanon's (highly race-specific) version of disavowal from Bhabha's; as she argues, Bhabha's conflation of the responses of the white and the Black child "fails to see how, *because* both black and white participate in the maintenance of the black stereotype, the mechanism of identification works very differently for each."[29] And this difference inheres precisely in the notion of *splitting*, relevant only to the nonwhite subject, and that is here associated in several key instances with Marie-Nathalie's experience. Thus Bhabha's gloss on the second of Fanon's two primal scenes (the more famous first scene, "Look, mother, a Negro!", involves a white child) is more useful, for our purposes, than the first: "the black child turns away from himself, his race, in his total identification with the positivity of whiteness which is at once color and no color."[30] So too the convoy episode—we could read it as a primal scene—causes Marie-Nathalie not to see the realities of slave suffering, but to turn only in "one direction": to the imago of the white master. This turn to blue-eyed whiteness, however, is via the "delirium" of trees and birds. Disavowal is connected to psychosis, and to a loss of touch with reality; from this point onward, the mistress is, to put it colloquially, "away with the birds," and the origins of her descent into madness can be located in this encounter.

The layers of makeup used by Marie-Nathalie as her madness progresses, often designated in the novel as a mask, and even specifically as a white mask (the slaves call it a chalk mask), are described in Glissant's original French by the somewhat antiquated term *fard*. As a substantive in contemporary French, *fard* is generally translated into English as "blusher." But the word originates in the practice of cosmetic whitening first deployed in the Renaissance, and was most commonly used, between the Renaissance and the Enlightenment, to describe whitening rather than reddening skin (although blushing is also a key, and culturally charged, marker of whiteness).[31] Indeed whitening becomes in this period a "real tyranny," as Catherine Lanoë notes, with "alabaster skin coming to be seen as the very foundation of beauty."[32] Used idiomatically, for example in the expression "sans fard" (without dissemblance or embellishment), the term is connected to the mask, and to ideas of artifice and deception, and is therefore, Lanoë notes, loaded with pejorative connotations: "When it is identified, 'fard' is always condemned in modern French, as it lies and deceives in a context where transparency is de rigueur."[33] The makeup with which Marie-Nathalie plasters her face is therefore linguistically, culturally, and historically loaded: it can be read either as a compensatory performance of whiteness, for a woman to whom this identity does not come naturally, or more radically as an attempt to conceal her true (nonwhite) identity. Her appearance recalls Bhabha's description of the stereotype as the scene of desire "for an originality which is again threatened by the differences of race, color, and culture." Bhabha argues, via Fanon, that the disavowal of difference "turns the colonial subject into a misfit—a grotesque mimicry or 'doubling,' that threatens to split the soul and whole, undifferentiated skin of the ego."[34] In this grotesque mimicry of whiteness, what is, perhaps, at stake is the disavowal of "the knowledge of one's *own* blackness, for which the equivalent 'fetish' is the white imago."[35] In this case the imago is the made up, in both senses, porcelain face, a construction of the *self* that is an even more fundamental and intimate imago than the blue eyes of the other, La Roche. This casts in a different, racialized, light La Roche's two enigmatic references to Marie-Nathalie's darkness, quoted above, both of which point to the unknown (remember that Marie-Nathalie is an orphan) and indeed the concealed, and play on notions of the cosmetic and the substantial. As we saw above, he focuses on her "covering herself with makeup to hide *who knows what filth* on her body, layer after layer, mummifying herself," and states that "it was black inside her and *I did not know it*" (103–4, my italics). Like Rochester, kept in the dark about Bertha's family origins, these statements point to Marie-Nathalie as an unknown quantity, both "dark continent" in the Freudian sense, but also, suggestively, dark Creole.

And it is perhaps in this context that we should understand Marie-Nathalie's attachment to Béluse, which at once mirrors, and yet significantly departs from, La Roche's man-to-man relationship with Longoué. The reader has no reason to doubt La Roche when he states that his ex-lover "probably never will be bold enough to fornicate" with the enslaved sire she houses and spoils (104). Rather, the desire for blackness, and specifically for a Black child (rather than a white one) is a phantasm, an ultimately spurious way of reconnecting to childhood, to the "band of wide-eyed black children" and to an identity repressed through the binary structures of the plantation. It might also provide an answer to the questions posed by Cailler in her appraisal of the novel: Marie-Nathalie's erratic behavior, for Cailler, "evokes a profoundly neurotic milieu, in which sexual fantasy presumably has a significant role." The critic states that desire is central in these scenes, "but experienced by whom? And for what?" She rightly argues that Glissant's "delicate handling" of these elements in *The Fourth Century* means that they are deliberately left vague and uncertain;[36] hence, I would argue, they open up the possibility of more complex racial identities than those acknowledged explicitly at the level of the diegesis, and in working on the level of suggestion rather than explicit statement, have an even more powerful impact on the reader's imagination.

Martin Munro describes Glissant's intention, in *The Fourth Century,* as being "to incorporate all of the contradictory elements of Martinican history into a dialectical movement that synthesizes, while reaffirming their relational complexity, all of the 'basic human components' that created Caribbean Creole societies." Emphasizing "interdependence and contact" rather than "discrete racial, social, and familial categories," Munro argues that the Martinican writer thus seeks to diminish "any residual dichotomy between the 'suffering slave' and the 'haggard maroon,' between the hill and the plain, resistance and compliance."[37] While this dynamic has been understood primarily in terms of the Longoué–La Roche relationship, I have argued that the portrayal of the "insistently, inscrutably interstitial"[38] Marie-Nathalie operates, on the level of suggestion and ambiguity, as an even more potent and radical example of this incorporation of contradictions. By insisting on "other sides" and third spaces, the novel complicates the fixity and dualism—Black/white, mistress/enslaved, mad/sane—on which the plantation depends. Glissant thus troubles, and indeed undermines, the largely binary representations of subjectivity, based on the elaboration of fixed markers of racial and cultural difference.

The Fourth Century mobilizes and reworks a cluster of images that will be reprised by later novels, and perhaps most notably in the work of Patrick Chamoiseau, the subject of the second half of this chapter, and whose entire literary output is profoundly and explicitly imprinted with the work of his mentor and friend Glissant. I begin with an overview of the presentation of the *béké* in Chamoiseau's novels, before looking at two novels that give him particular diegetic and affective space: *Slave Old Man* (1997) and *Un dimanche au cachot* (2007).

Patrick Chamoiseau and the Planter's Gaze

Patrick Chamoiseau's early fiction affords the *béké* little space. His first and second novels, *Chronicle of the Seven Sorrows* (1986) and *Solibo the Magnificent* (1988), foreground the urban Black population of Fort-de-France during and after the period of departmentalization, and make limited explicit reference to slavery. Indeed, in *Solibo,* the *béké* is a discursive, rather than diegetic, presence; the sporadic references to him are rooted in the psycholinguistic structures of the postplantation Antilles. These references emphasize, for example, the protection offered by a (highly cultivated) whiteness—night is "whiter than a sunless *béké* under his take-a-stroll umbrella in the middle of a cane field" (*Solibo,* 13)—or underline the continuing economic stranglehold of the caste (a detective asks a bewildered suspect what he does for the *béké,* 96). Such moments show how "language and economic realities reflect and naturalize each other,"[39] and also speak to what one critic of Toni Morrison has called "the potency of white absence," a form of insidious but invisible domination in postslavery societies.[40] In *Chronicle,* the *béké* appears in a single episode, a dream sequence, suggesting the extent to which the trauma of slavery remains unprocessed, located in the Antillean subconscious rather than assimilated into historical memory. "Afoukal's eighteen Dream-Words" issue from a loyal slave who saves his master's life when he is poisoned by maroons. As Abolition looms Afoukal helps his master bury his riches; he is then murdered by the master, who fears Afoukal's return to uncover the treasure. This set piece of slave memory haunts the Antillean imaginary and is immortalized in other novels. *Chronicle* insists, then, both on the predatory cruelty of the master and on the utter subordination of a slave who had "learned to love the master" (118) and who "understood him when he split my skull open on this jar" (119).

The rather summary and one-dimensional representation of evil embodied in the *béké* of *Chronicle* will, however, be nuanced and expanded in successive novels, in which the *béké* becomes an increasingly pathetic, empathetic, or abject character, *both* vindictive and vulnerable. *Texaco* (1992) can from this perspective be considered a transitional text, in its more sustained exploration of the slave past, and in the way in which the omnipotence of the master is tempered by his paranoia and exhaustion. We first encounter plantation life through Esternome, who is born on the plantation and becomes "the houseboy of the Big Hutch" (43). Treating the field slaves with disdain, the young boy is enchanted by the opulence of the big house and obsessed by its rhythms. His attachment to *béké* culture is so unquestioning (on his liberation he is reluctant to leave) that his more militant daughter, Marie-Sophie, appears embarrassed by his lack of resistance. But the master's cruelty in *Texaco* is clearly shown to be founded on weakness. His home, a "diffuse magic" of beams and planks, inspires awe in the slave population, precisely because it possesses a power that the master doesn't have. Esternome wonders "what kind of strength could have erected this" (43) and slaves gaze upon the building as they would later observe cities or cathedrals. If the house "dominated the whole, seemed to inhale all," its owner "didn't get so much respect" (44). By projecting an impression of permanence and invincibility, the house's structure compensates for the fragility of its owner, "frail and feeble" (the French term "débile" also connotes idiocy; *Texaco,* 61), "soft-bellied" (45) master. Whiteness, then, betokens in *Texaco* not strength, but rather fear, anxiety, and disease: on the death of an animal the anxious *béké,* fearing poison, "would pounce, whiter than his own linen" (35), as the overseer's blade opened the beast's belly. The "translucent" breasts of the mistress (43), that fascinate the young Esternome in their conjoining of exoticism and eroticism, are in fact the manifestation of a mysterious malady, euphemistically described as an "unreal innocence" contracted during her journey to the islands when her schooner was shipwrecked (39).

The mistress is an "ex-strumpet" of the Salpêtrière (39),[41] one of hundreds of *filles du roi* sent off to the Americas in the late seventeenth century, with the aim of providing wives for the colonists in order to increase the white population, the most famous fictional incarnation of whom is Manon Lescaut.[42] An ethereal and unstable presence (her mysterious illness is likely to be syphilis), she is miserable in a "horrible plantation" from which she repeatedly tries to escape, or more accurately, to rise above. She has a "childish laugh" (39), and her "candid gaze" seems to "lift her out of this filthy plantation"; she floats off "like the clouds and filled the world with perfume and flowers" (39), or disappears "into the shadows" (46). Childlike, and apparently childless, her innocence and innate generosity (she gives scissors, thread, and cloth to Marie-Sophie's grandmother, encouraging her to become a seamstress) is unusual; we can infer that her compassion derives from her status as a "fallen woman" who does not conform to the restrictive sexual codes on which the plantation was founded. Many of these motifs are reprised, and explored in more depth, in two later novels, *Slave Old Man* and *Un dimanche au cachot,* novels that further explore, through the prism of the plantation, the younger novelist's relationship with his mentor and friend Édouard Glissant.

Slave Old Man

Chamoiseau's early fiction, like his coauthored essays, is dedicated to Glissant, and many of his novels open with an epigraph from him; a later novel, *Biblique des derniers gestes,* features Glissant as a (ghostly) character. But Chamoiseau's *Slave Old Man,* uniquely, enters a fictional terrain strongly associated with Glissant (the uplands of the maroon) and, moreover, embeds the words of the mentor and friend in the text itself, giving the elder writer a privileged space at the start of each chapter. These epigraphs—short passages from the theoretical essay *L'intention poétique* (1969), and the then unpublished work "La folie Célat," later revised and included in Glissant's *Le monde incréé* (2000)—continue and amplify the intertextual relationship that Chamoiseau began with his mentor in his very earliest writings. The "entredire," in its references to the cask (38), or to La Roche and Marie-Celat, suggests an especially privileged relationship with the novels *The Fourth Century* and *The Overseer's Hut.* In providing a thematic frame, image, or anecdote to introduce each of the seven short chapters, the "entredire" invokes the call-and-response structure of the oral *conte;* indeed despite the fact that the text is identified as a novel on its front cover, it has more in common with the fable or tale. A dialogic relationship, based on similarity and difference, amplification and divergence, is thus established between Glissant's and Chamoiseau's novels of slavery and marooning. The novel, a compact and intense psychological investigation of slave escape (the title in English excludes the hound that had been named in the French title, *L'esclave vieil homme et le molosse*), turns on the intensely intersubjective relationship between a trinity of characters (maroon-master-mastiff).

Extended passages of free indirect discourse afford access, through a stream-of-consciousness narrative that typifies the irony and intimacy associated with that discourse, to the inner life, and increasing anxiety, of the master. And yet the reader's first encounter with the *colon* might suggest permanence and stability. Just as the name of Glissant's Acajou plantation is italicized throughout *Le quatrième siècle,* if not in its English translation, here apparent dominance is inscribed even in typography: the substantive, master, is consistently capitalized, and is, in its first usage, tethered to its colloquial synonym, *béké*. But the title functions as a pleonastic and hyperbolic assertion of strength, a compensatory gesture propping up through punctuation an otherwise inadequate power. Although he boasts the ubiquitous nobiliary particle (in the French original he is said to "vibrate" with the particle, suggesting a humorously disproportionate pride), we know this to be a likely spurious marker of ancestry, and also symptomatic of nostalgia for a disappearing world. The *béké*'s wife and children "scrape by amid the mahogany redolence of the Great House" (5); once more the architecture of the house suggests power and a permanence that the *béké* lacks. If everybody suffocates in this anachronistic, we might even say pathological, space (the sons for example are "pale and peevish"), women suffer most. His daughter "flutters her lashes over staring eyes" (5), suggesting vacancy more than coquettishness. If the gaze is source and vector of knowledge of the other, therefore of sexual desire, this empty gaze conveys an ontological deficit, the absence of desire, and a perversion of the sexual order. Meanwhile the mistress's "ugly theatrical laugh that accents her mute melancholy" (5), a troubling image of aphasia and excess, registers profound communicative difficulty. This is a darker, more sinister image than the mistress's "childish laugh" of *Texaco,* one that directly recalls the deranged mistresses of *The Fourth Century* and, of course, Bertha's unhinged and preternatural "cachinnation" in *Jane Eyre* (130), and prefigures her yet more unhealthy laugh in *Un dimanche au cachot.*

The sense of a disappearing world is foregrounded in a novel whose opening pages categorically describe the plantation as being "disenchanted, without dreams, without any future one might imagine" (7).

This casts in an ironic light any apparent show of *béké* strength: at the start of their pursuit, the planter is (apparently) part of a familiar and terrifying triad: "the Master, the horse, the mastiff: an accord as old as eternity seemed to unite them" (25). The apposition of these three substantives, so highly charged in the slave imaginary, appears to indicate a united and impenetrable colonial front. But the description of this plantation alliance as being "as old as eternity" is profoundly ironic, in a novel in which trees, stones, and bones point to an ancient prehistory (and therefore, presumably, a future) uncontaminated by the shadow of this ignominious, but temporally contained, past. Moreover, the reader knows, from the novel's opening pages, that this apparently "eternal alliance" is dissipating. And as the text progresses, the surprising proximity of those historic enemies, dog and slave, a proximity generated by the horrific conditions that both have endured in transit from Old World to New, becomes increasingly apparent, allowing Chamoiseau to situate the hound, as Doris Garraway argues, "firmly within the circuit of abuse and denaturation that is slavery. Like the African captives, the hound is commodified, purchased, and transported across the ocean, subjected in the process to extreme abuse and physical depletion." He too has endured the horrors of the slave ship, becoming "the unlikely double of the old man, who alone understands him."[43]

The power that the planter "puts on"—one thinks of Senglis's tunic in *The Fourth Century*—is therefore merely a uniform to be donned and doffed, rather than an innate characteristic. Astride an Arabian horse, accompanied by his hound and sporting a pith helmet, he embodies all the visual clichés of mastery, and is notably associated with the color white; he "clothes his absolute power in white linen" (5), and on Sunday plays his mother-of-pearl mandolin. But these possessions, symbols, and peripheral attributes, as Valérie Loichot argues in another context, function merely as "stamps of authenticity" that in fact register "a lack in being and authority." Meanwhile the insistence on whiteness also conforms to the "confusion of having and being," which, she argues via Fanon's *Black Skin, White Masks,* is so prevalent in the construction of the Martinican subject. Fanon's infamous case study in this regard was Mayotte Capécia; but Loichot, in a fascinating reading, applies Fanon's insights into the lactification complex not to a Black or mixed-race author, but to the writings of *béké* author Saint-John Perse. Just as Mayotte, Capécia's protagonist, imagines herself white via her possessions (nice clothes and jewelry), the source of Fanon's excoriating reading, so too, Loichot argues, Perse's "father-master constructs his own whiteness and social position by his tools."[44]

Perse, as well as being the iconic *béké* poet and memorialist of the Antillean plantation, is a particularly resonant figure for my analysis of both *Slave Old Man* and *Un dimanche*. He is obsessively referenced by Chamoiseau, in both theory and fiction, and like Glissant, appears as a ghost at the end of *Biblique des derniers gestes*. Both novels include intertextual allusions to Perse, *Un dimanche* being especially saturated in references to the Guadeloupean poet. In *Slave Old Man*, the *béké* remembers an unidentified "very pale woman, with a very white arm, beneath a wide-brimmed hat with bobbing lace" (80)—she may or may not be the planter's wife—a line that directly conjures Perse's "Written on the Door," with its references to his daughter's "very-white arm among her black hens."[45] Whiteness, for both writers, is associated with a de-individualized woman who secures or guarantees the patriarch's position. The woman's disembodied body parts are used by both Chamoiseau and Perse to authenticate whiteness in a context of suspected contamination: the father's mule-colored skin is emphasized by the poet, while in Chamoiseau's novel the white arm is invoked just after his memory of "plan[ning] ports on the tresses of mulatto women" (80). Sexual adventures with mixed-race women are therefore connected to the colonizing mission itself: the conquest of space, and the establishment of infrastructure to perpetuate colonial expansion, are part of the same drive to dominance that motivates the carnal conquest of nonwhite bodies. Indeed, the reference to *mulâtresses* is itself embedded in references to his erection of white buildings (the "dispensaries of marble" he had raised; the "white cities" he had founded). This fleeting memory of interracial intimacy, profoundly troubling to the certainties on which the plantocracy depends, requires a compensatory, even neutralizing, (re)assertion of white mastery, whether vested in the stabilizing figure of the white woman or in the upright white constructions that function as monuments to the colonial drive, and to a highly racialized sense of mastery and masculinity. For, as Loichot puts it, "in the Caribbean colonial context, whiteness has to be constructed from both sides and consists only in constructed attributes lacking being: one *has* whiteness rather than *is* white."[46]

The plantation, as we have seen, is a debased and doomed space, in which masters "seem more like fermenting matter than like living people" (7). In a description strongly reminiscent of Glissant's abject Senglis plantation, and which recalls, in its English translation at least, the inverted authorial patronymic used in that novel, we are told that "everything is slipping sideways: a kind of chemical decomposition, impalpable but major" (12). With the escape of his most docile slave, the master realizes that his world "défolmante" (the Creole word, meaning to destroy or demolish, is used in the English translation, and is typographically emphasized: it resonates with the French *déformer,* but also includes "fol," crazy). It is in this process of decomposition, deformation, liquidation, and psychological disintegration, that the *béké,* like the old man and, indeed, the dog, emerges transformed, remade, one could even say creolized.

Initially, the episode is framed through a conventional list of colonial triumphs ("he had fought so hard to clear this land, beat back the savages, attend to those *nègres* [. . .] he had popped off bombards against Carib rages [. . .] He had buried [. . .] He had blasted [. . .] He had planted [. . .] He had modified [. . .] He had sold [. . .] He had bought . . . ," 79–80), which stages the colonial endeavor as a heroic, individualistic, and self-sacrificing project of possession, exploitation, and domination (what the narrator describes as "the heroism of the personal chronicle," 79). Like the page and a half of Perse's *Éloges* analyzed by Loichot for the density of reference to ownership (conveyed in the repetition of "my" and "I have"), this short and dense section of Chamoiseau's novel is suffused with active verbs of conquest.[47] But as this breathless litany continues (the *béké,* like the hound, is on the move, in pursuit of the old man) the self-justifying, indeed delusional, pieties of the colonial mission are pierced, both by an increasing sense of physical and psychological disorientation, and by an incipient sense of shame. The run of negative clauses which sit around the narrative of domination expresses the master's sudden lack of understanding of the world around him ("The Master had no idea what to do any more"; "He did not know whether . . ."; "The Master no longer knew"; "The Master did not understand," 78–83) and registers a profound ontological crisis and a loss of control. The master is disorientated in both space and in time. Described in the novel's opening pages as a kind of anachronism, "a conquistador fallen from a fold in time" (5), he is also incapable of finding his way through the woods, a space most obviously associated with the flight of maroons, but also invested, unlike the shallow tree roots of Traversay's *Les amours,* with temporal depth and precolonial innocence: in both senses, this is a space that is highly threatening to any facile narrative of white mastery.

As his journey toward self-consciousness continues, the planter reflects explicitly on the "tumultuous shames" that he has experienced, and which he had ascribed, in the first instance, to original sin: "but the Masses had brought no peace. Nor had the confessions. The feeling of shame remained coiled on the inexpressible, the unpronounceable, on the invisible and the unavowable—of which he knew nothing" (79). He is unable to recognize his sense of "unavowable" shame as being connected to the original and *collective* sin of slavery, which is why the Catholic rites of confession and mass-going provide no relief. But, in a highly significant passage, as the *béké*'s examination of conscience continues, he is transformed by an intimation of his role in the past:

> He did not feel he was returning empty-handed, having lost a *nègre* or been made mock of by an ingrate of a Maroon. He was returning bearing something he could not name. His fatigue had disappeared; the shame and fear had melted away. The tears had dried on his face but above all, within him. In him, now, other spaces were bestirring themselves, spaces where he would never go, perhaps, but where one day no doubt, in a future generation, hopefully in the full radiance of their purity and legitimate strength, his children would venture, as one confronts a first misgiving. (109)

He leaves the forest absolved or cleansed of his shame, and experiences a sort of catharsis, which allows him to envisage a future founded not on the hierarchical rules of the plantation, nor on racial and sexual stratification, but rather on a value most prized and privileged by Chamoiseau, (self) doubt and misgiving.

Slave Old Man therefore closes on a note of optimism; the narrator suggests that, for the descendants of the *béké*, there is a possibility of transformation and opening to the outside world. Lorna Milne analyzes the old man's "identitarian metamorphosis,"[48] a term that could be extended to include the master, who ends the novel crying alone in the woods. As Milne observes, this passage, which closes the story of the slave's escape, suggests "the possibility—even if it is provisional—of possible future rapprochements between *békés* and Créoles, anchored in the formative experiences shared by their ancestors in Martinique."[49] In an autobiographical essay, *Écrire en pays dominé* (Writing in a dominated land), published on the same day as the novel, the author connects not only with his "moi-Amérindien" and "moi-Africain" but also his "moi-colon," and lays claim to "the planter's gaze" (49). Such gestures further testify to the impulse to see identity in this postslavery society in nonbinary, transcultural terms. The urge to transcend the self, and to identify with the experience of the other, is an especially radical and transgressive ethical aim when that other belongs to the master caste, and will be revisited and nuanced in *Un dimanche au cachot*.

Un dimanche au cachot

Published a decade after *Slave Old Man*, and sharing a focus on the experience and inner world of the *béké*, *Un dimanche au cachot* is both an amplification of, and a significant departure from, the story and themes examined in the earlier novel. Also in seven sections or movements, this is a longer and more complex novel, which reprises the protagonists of *Slave Old Man* (the master, his pallid wife and whining sons, and his mastiff), extends both the dramatis personae of this text and their life stories, and includes a much more developed frame narrative set in the present day. This frame includes postmodern features that foreground the self-awareness of the author/narrator and the fictionality of the text in hand; such signature Chamoiseau devices include conversations between the "reader," the "author," and the "educator," all three avatars of Chamoiseau himself, as well as a metafictional commentary on the progression and quality of the narrative in hand. This is, moreover, an intensely metafictional reflection on slavery, which includes extended meditations on Faulkner, Perse, Césaire, and Glissant, four writers repeatedly identified in the novel as being from different "sides" of the plantation color line, and whose influence on Chamoiseau is well established in previous texts.[50] And if these four writers haunt the present-day narrative, the nineteenth-century story (the largest part of the novel) includes another writer, Victor Schœlcher, a major, and perhaps surprisingly sympathetic, character. The French abolitionist visits the Big House as the unnamed son of a porcelain manufacturer, and, through his writings in his little black notebook (although the Alsatian was a prolific author, these are unmistakably the work of Chamoiseau), becomes in many ways the "ethnographic double" of Chamoiseau himself.[51]

The novel's explicit interest in matters of skin color and race is signaled in an early section of the frame narrative, playfully entitled "The Anguish of Sir Moreau de Saint-Méry." Moreau's "proliferation of bizarre phenotypes" (25), discussed in my introduction, was a notorious attempt, through what Chamoiseau calls "clean lines and hermetic compartments" (25), to account for, and ascribe personality traits to, all possible racial permutations in the Antilles, a project that continues to haunt the Antillean imaginary. Chamoiseau compares this obsessive investment in the gradations of skin color with the (equally absurd) racial history of the United States, where the color line categorically separated "two imaginary absolutes," and where you were either Black or white. He continues, "In the Antilles there was no line. Just a racist contraction of white Creoles in a flood of unpredictable métissages" (27). This "contraction" (the French original, "une crispation raciste," has much stronger connotations of an involuntary reaction to an external stimulus of, for example, fear, and also connotes psychic tension), and its absurd outworkings, are thus foregrounded at the metafictional level, will become central to the diegesis of *Un dimanche*.

The novel includes several intertwining timeframes and melding characters. The present-day frame narrative concerns a disaffected young girl, Caroline, the daughter of drug addicts, who has taken refuge in the dungeon of the Gaschette plantation. The narrator's friend Sylvain has called him out of the indolence of a Martinican Sunday to talk to the troubled adolescent, and the result of this intervention is the hallucinatory and oneiric narrative of a young woman called L'Oubliée (Forgotten One), who was condemned to this same dungeon in the eighteenth century. Her story mirrors and merges with that of Caroline herself (both are neglected; both take refuge in a space associated with horrific abuse), gesturing toward the cycles of transgenerational trauma that have affected the Antillean psyche, and that find their origins in slavery.

The text deepens and darkens the perspective on slavery offered by the earlier novel. For Chamoiseau's readers, the plantation depicted is a by now familiar world of stagnation and slow disintegration, where machines date back to the time of Père Labat, and where "not a stitch has moved in the direction of new techniques" (141).[52] In this novel, significantly, decline is most often, and most eloquently, voiced by Schœlcher himself. Usually described as the "visitor," an outsider endowed with a clarity of vision that the inhabitants of the plantation, master and slaves, are denied, he "watches questions searches" (66). He perceives that the "pathetic" planter is "in osmosis with the Plantation" which is "breaking down." Moreover, he explicitly describes the "abjection" (66, 68) of the plantation, also using such terms as "obsolete" (140) to describe its profound dysfunction. The novel deals with some of the most horrific events of the slave past, including the repeated rape of the young heroine, L'Oubliée, by an elderly *colon* who is also her father. And yet while it plumbs the horrors of planter atrocity and slave suffering, it does so in such an abstract and ambivalent register (for example, the words rape and incest are not used) that the traumatic aftereffects are often displaced into metaphor or euphemism, and yet are all the more powerfully suggested.

The Master (again unnamed, but consistently capitalized) is reduced to an empty cliché: he is for example "an undiluted power," "the sun" of the plantation (61), "the omnipotent" (64), statements that jar absurdly with the already established degeneration of his plantation. As in the previous novel, the beloved dog no longer obeys his master's commands, while the master himself observes that his gestures have been blunted. Moreover, his gaze is also empty (137); and, when he attempts to explain the brutal hierarchies of plantation life to Schœlcher, even he lacks conviction ("he no longer believes what he says," 66). Power is repeatedly shown to be ebbing away from him, so that "nothing stands up anymore" ("rien ne se dresse," 138).

The *béké*'s anxiety regarding race, established early in the story, is encapsulated in a single sentence that features four, racially charged, references to color: "he caresses his children's blondness, their yellowing mops of hair ['tignasses flavescentes'] whose emergence he had worked out in advance, the pale skin of a wife chosen purely for her whiteness: a circle of purity in this mangrove which infects the human" (65). The circle has highly sinister connotations. This is a community living in a situation of apartheid, and a family cynically created, even genetically manipulated, by the "omnipotent" phallic father (64). The family is incapable of liberating its members and refuses to admit others. Closed in on itself, paranoia and fear of hybridity transform the family, and by extension the plantocracy, into a sterile dead end, in contrast with the external mangrove, which is buzzing with life (those familiar with Chamoiseau's work know the cherished status of the mangrove, its value as a repository of diversity and energy, and will recognize the irony in its association with infection). And, as in *The Fourth Century* and indeed in so many other novels of the plantation, decline is primarily vested in the destiny of the "pallid" (*blême*) white woman. Her laugh, or rather its absence, is again a key indicator of her physical and emotional decline: "The mistress no longer laughs under her melancholy. She no longer has the debris of those dramatic laughs that signal that she is still there: she remains diaphanous, airy, silent, walks around like a zombie throughout the house, followed by her train of blond children who haven't cried for a long time" (166). His wife's whiteness is emphasized, as in earlier novels, but the emphasis seems, once again, to betoken illness and racial anxiety rather than security. The narrator describes a "master and his so-white" (106); the racial adjective, here transformed into a substantive and conjoined with a (compensatory?) intensifier, reduces the woman to a simple racial type.

The *béké* family is therefore pulled between two equally inadmissible urges, incest (which results in a lack of genetic renewal, leading to degeneration and even disappearance) and *métissage,* obliquely suggested by the word "flavescentes," which names a color between yellow and gold, the present participle registering a process (of darkening?) rather than a fixed state. For all the father's calculations, the threat of mixing hangs inexorably over the circle, which is hermetically closed to the outside. Rebecca Hartkopf Schloss reminds us that Creoles, however much they insisted on their own whiteness, were considered by metropolitan French to bear the stain of mixed blood (the "tâche de sang mêlé").[53] The density of reference to the color white, rather than suggesting ancestral certitude, points to a profound anxiety regarding racial origins. Meanwhile the truly "white" man in *Un dimanche au cachot* in fact comes from outside the plantation. Schœlcher is directly and unproblematically associated with the whiteness and delicateness of the porcelain he sells. If his abolitionist discourse is a direct ideological threat, his education and the sophistication of his artistic and musical tastes, which establish his superior cultural capital, equally destabilize the uncultured *colon*.

The specter of mixing that haunts the family circle in this early episode is embedded, it emerges, in the *béké*'s family history, and inevitably resurfaces later in the novel. The exhausted master imagines that he sees his dead father, figured here as a sort of colonial archetype, even a caricature, and the source of a profound inferiority complex in his son. His hypermasculinity is suggested by the accumulation of substantives—he is "conqueror discoverer conquistador"—as well as by a network of adjectives that describe him as solid, fixed, and hard (138). He is strongly associated, like Glissant's La Roche, with the all-seeing gaze: he "sees in [his son] who knows what, and is ashamed of what he sees," and he is also described as "the old decipherer" (138–39). Indeed, in marked contrast to his son, living from hand to mouth, and "from one desire to the next" (140), the father had been endowed with foresight (the term *prévoir* is repeated three times on page 138). In this ghostly paternal apparition, several highly charged references suggest the old man's proximity to the slave: his odor is "close to that of blacks" and, like Perse's patriarch, he has "tobacco-colored cheeks" (138).[54] This episode prefigures a later confrontation with the dead father, which takes place in a more degraded context (and which recalls the paternal disappointment inscribed in the faces of family portraits of Maynard's *Outre-mer*). In a parallel scenario to that of Chamoiseau and Caroline in the frame narrative, the *béké* tries to coax L'Oubliée out of the dungeon, and here again the Guadeloupean poet is explicitly named. The master, who has "fallen from on high, like Perse," "sees what Perse no doubt saw in his old age: this general flux which distances him from everything, and which transforms the imaginary of the predatory colon" (239). This "flux" is connected to racial identity, and the scene coincides with the novel's definitive revelation of a story hinted at earlier in the novel: L'Oubliée, the girl in the dungeon, is in fact the *béké*'s half-sister. His father had impregnated her mother, Congo, and then embarked on a sexual relationship with his own daughter.

The *béké* remembers how his father would return to the Big House smelling of Black women; despite his efforts to wash away their "inescapable musk," in particular that of Congo, in the end their smell became *his* odor (248). The words rape and incest are absent, and as already mentioned an affective ambiguity surrounds this relationship, so that Congo has to "fight against her own feelings for the old man" (251). This is in part because of the hazy context of drug taking: the old master gives her datura to smoke, with its "aftertastes of pleasure" (251). The abusive nature of the relationship is nonetheless clear, as is its traumatizing effect on L'Oubliée. In the revelation of this foundational crime, which conjoins *métissage* and incest, the *béké* recognizes his own face in the countenance of his half-sister. This section (247–55) is shot through with references to the yellowness, and to the smallness and vulnerability, of the "chabine": she is a "yellow face," a "yellow child," a "little yellow thing," "a little yellow thing without a shell," a "little yellow comma," even a "yellow consternation," or is described in Creole terms ("cribiche jaune," "moune jaune"—little yellow thing; yellow person). Crucially, this yellow face reminds the planter, not just of his (and her) father, but also of his lineage more generally, the purity of the family line besieged by the "round" of Black faces that now suddenly come into focus: "his father's face. His mother's face. The faces of his ancestral line. And then this round of dark faces, black living faces . . . the quivering and living world, all these presences which glistened with an infinite nuance, and which relayed each other" (261). And, as he is visited by this ghostly circle of interconnected and blended countenances, the master is for the first time endowed with the power to see: "his childish gaze distinguished them without distinguishing himself from them [. . .]. He *saw*. He wasn't afraid of being in what he saw, of following along the line of what he saw, of existing in that way . . . *faces, faces, great trouble in their gazes* . . . he saw them, saw them there, re-saw them with a precision that had disappeared since this eternity had been planted, lofty, in a depth of himself. He stuttered . . ." (261, italics in original). These dark faces, with their infinite nuance, and from which the *béké* is incapable of distinguishing himself, at once recall, and contrast starkly with, the yellowing family circle with which the novel opens, defensively (and we now know, futilely) poised to repel the outsider, hermetically closed in on itself in a stark manifestation of the "crispation raciste" identified by the frame narrator.

Garraway identifies the "pervasiveness and lure" of a psychosexual fantasy at the heart of the plantation imaginary: an "illegitimate family romance that installs the white father as perpetually in pursuit of his own mixed race daughter."[55] While the master observed, and indeed was "bound by," the rules of kinship in his legitimate family, miscegenation under slavery allowed "two parallel yet entirely conflicting sets of norms relating to desire and kinship [. . .] in the shadow family, the slave master was theoretically 'free' from all constraints and social norms governing sexual relationships with his legitimate kin and could explore his incestuous desires at will."[56] Discussing the incestuous logic dominating Moreau's infamous taxonomy, she quotes Werner Sollors, for whom "one of the ironies of tabular or mathematical representations of race is that they model racial amalgamation as an allegory of repeated incest,"[57] a model that represses the possibility of white women starting interracial families of their own. Although Moreau, like Chamoiseau, does not mention incest explicitly, Garraway argues that Moreau's allegory "is more than an accident of diagrammatic convenience."[58]

The revelation of this concealed past causes the *béké* to fall into the "infernal vault" of the dungeon, also described as a "fetid uterus," and, like the woods, a space of initiation, transformation, and eventual rebirth. This new vantage point—for the first time the master sees the plantation from below, rather than from the heights of his steed—reveals to him, in an expression that recalls Freud's *unheimlich,* "that which he thought he would never in his life see" (262). This radically destabilized new perspective offers a vision of decline (deformed buildings, advancing forest, wilted fields); in a hallucinatory apparition he is visited by a crowd of elderly and injured slaves, who have come to look silently at him. One of the slaves offers his hand "as one would help a shipwrecked man," in a gesture of generosity and reconciliation (264). Meanwhile L'Oubliée, to the surprise of all (including the "reader"), returns to the plantation after surviving the horror of the dungeon. The scene is illogical, maintains the "reader," but the "writer" insists on her return, "so that the scene remains engraved in the Master's memory. He makes it into a key scene in the transformation of this *planter* who saw the end of slavery" (268). In other words, the scene is crucial precisely because her return disrupts expectation, confounds the codes of the plantation order, and radically rewrites the myth of *marronnage:* "It confronts him [the reader in the first instance, but also possibly the writer and indeed the master] with the impossible" (268).

This novel, then, offers no neat diegetic resolution. Any triumphant narrative of slave escape from torture is undermined by the fact that L'Oubliée gracefully and silently resumes her position in the slave hospital (although in the last pages of the novel it becomes clear that she has marooned again). Moreover, any teleological trajectory of the *béké* toward self-awareness or even shame, such as that experienced, despite the oneiric and profoundly nonlinear nature of the novel, by the *béké* protagonist of *Slave Old Man,* is also destabilized by master's pleasure in sending La Belle back to the same horrific dungeon, commanding L'Oubliée to tend to her grandmother's wounds there. The reader interprets as intensely ironic the *béké*'s reference to "*justice,*" a word that "rings in his ears" as L'Oubliée emerges from the dungeon (306, italics in original). Work on the plantation resumes, and although the *béké* walks with a slower step, hesitates, stops to think (309), his "transformation" is apparently minimal. Indeed, any voyage of (self) discovery would seem to be the preserve of Schœlcher, who is struck by nausea and horror on realizing his own familial implication in slavery and tries to liberate L'Oubliée from her self-imposed imprisonment. It is clear that it is only the "great winds of change" (again, Perse's "Vents" is invoked), in other words Abolition, that "might" bring the destruction of the machinery of the plantation, along with the architecture and contents of the Big House (309–10). The message stands in stark contrast to that of *Slave Old Man:* it is systemic political change, rather than personal conversion, that will bring about the end of slavery in the Antilles.

In the closing pages of *Un dimanche,* when the present-day narrator sits down to eat with Caroline and Sylvain, he imagines he sees Perse and Faulkner, who emerge from the ruins of the Big House, passing but daring not to look at the *cachot,* while from inside the "shitty dungeon" emerge Césaire, Fanon (mentioned for the first time), and Glissant, "improbable ghosts" who, "like L'Oubliée, *look* around them" (312, italics in original). The novel closes, then, on a categorical assertion of difference, both of experience and reaction to that experience; the white writers have been housed in the ruins of the Big House, while their Black colleagues have been confined to the horrific space of the dungeon, here associated with excrement. Chamoiseau would seem to insist here on the fact that what Bhabha calls the "houses of racial memory" are differently invested, and that the burden of slavery, like its inscription in literature, is always unequally shared.[59]

All three novels discussed in this chapter, in positioning *béké* characters if not in the emotional center ground, at least in a significant affective annex, grapple with the ethical challenge, for contemporary Black authors, of writing the *béké*. All attempt to give a nuanced, reflective, and psychologically complex voice to the experience of the "other," and to escape simplistic moralizing strictures. Glissant, for example, sees madness as indissociable from mastery: from the grotesque hysteria of the Senglis couple to the feral excess of La Roche, all three planter protagonists are mad, while vulnerability and exhaustion would seem to be the inevitable characteristics of Chamoiseau's *colon*. And both writers powerfully suggest that white women suffer the burden of plantation life more intimately than men. Such attempts to humanize the *béké* have not escaped critical commentary, and in some cases have caused discomfort. Writing of the scene of exchange between La Roche and Longoué, discussed above, Jack Corzani suggests that Glissant prefers a "sympathetic" approach to the *béké*.[60] Marie-Christine Rochmann considers the same scene to be somewhat implausible, arguing that it is only because we are in the realm of the symbolic (what, she asks, is the meaning of the return of the barrel, the integrity of the hill, these two sovereignties?) that the kind of exchange depicted is possible. The novel, she argues, "far from showing the hunting of maroons [. . .] signals instead their relative tranquility," while the feudal contract imagined in the novel, which would assign to each side its own territory (the maroon on the hill and the white on the plain), denies the fact of slavery and suggests rather a consensual "cohabitation."[61] Meanwhile in her appraisal of *Slave Old Man*, Milne identifies a "glimmer of hope—albeit tentative," reflected in the "hesitating and jerky rhythms" of the closing movement, where the provisional possibility of dialogue between *békés* and the Black population is intimated.[62]

Slave Old Man emerged not just at a high point of *créolité*, with its message of inclusivity, hybridity, and its celebration of the multiple strands that constitute Antillean identity, but also as the 150th anniversary of Abolition loomed. Raphaël Confiant has suggested that *In Praise of Creoleness*, which appeared several years earlier, was at its inception an attempt to "reach out" to, and to "come to an understanding" with, the *béké*. He claims that in drafting this essay in the late 1980s he, Chamoiseau, and others had organized a series of meetings with prominent *békés* in an attempt to initiate dialogue with this caste.[63] The appearance of the novel, along with its companion essay, undoubtedly tapped into and contributed to discussions around the memorialization of the past. The sesquicentenary of the following year, 1998, was marked by a short letter, instigated by Roger de Jaham and signed by over four hundred *békés*, which recognized slavery as a crime against humanity several years before the Taubira Law in 2001 gave this legal status.[64] The sudden self-awareness of Chamoiseau's "melancholy" *béké* (109), transformed by a journey of self-discovery that is every bit as destabilizing and transformative as the maroon's, might therefore be read as resonating with a collective taking stock, a tentative first step by the *béké* caste toward racial reconciliation, and toward a rejection of plantocratic power structures by those who had established and profited from them.

And yet the (tentative) optimism discerned by Milne in *Slave Old Man*, like the "cohabitation" that Rochmann criticizes in *The Fourth Century*, would seem to be dissipated in both authors' later fiction. The "relatively optimistic and consensual"[65] vision promoted by Glissant in this novel will be ended by the author's return to Martinique in 1965, when the pessimistic tenor of novels such as *Malemort* and *The Overseer's Hut* becomes much more marked. Meanwhile, Chamoiseau's 2007 plantation novel, *Un dimanche au cachot*, radically rewrites *Slave Old Man*, showing the *béké* to be infinitely less open to transformation than in the earlier novel, and affording Schœlcher a surprisingly crucial diegetic, if not political, role.[66] One of the defining features of the commemorations of the 150th anniversary of Abolition in 1998 was the conscious attempt to rewrite the Schœlcherist script on which the centenary celebrations of 1948—largely driven by Aimé Césaire, in the immediate wake of departmentalization—had depended.[67] Much subsequent debate has involved a highly critical revisiting of the Schœlcher myth—the ongoing attacks on statues of the French abolitionist being an especially conspicuous aspect of this memory work—and an almost universal rejection of the elevation of the great white liberator to the detriment, or even exclusion, of slave agency. *Un dimanche* might therefore be considered a revisionist revisionist novel, which complicates the portrayal of both the *béké* and the maroon of the earlier text, and questions any too-easy narrative of local racial reconciliation, all the while restoring a place to the now rather unfashionable metropolitan abolitionist.

Meanwhile all three novels, while showing undoubted sympathy for the *béké*, also enshrine distance at the narrative level; all, as I argued in my introduction, make powerful use of the intimacy and irony afforded by free indirect discourse. In the novel we examine in our next chapter, *Frères volcans* (1983), which also, incidentally, includes a very positive appraisal of Schœlcher, we are entirely immersed in the psyche of the *béké*; his perspective is predominant, he speaks entirely in the first person, and we gain access to this sympathetic old man through the unimpeded intimacy of his fictional diary.

4 Empathy and Estrangement
Vincent Placoly's *Frères volcans*

> I don't feel that I'm a prisoner of any race.
> —Vincent Placoly, *Frères volcans*

VINCENT PLACOLY (1946–1992), "perhaps the most undeservedly neglected" Antillean author according to Celia Britton,[1] was a writer, teacher, and left-wing activist. Born and educated in Martinique, he spent most of the 1960s in Paris and took part in the events of May 1968, an experience that undoubtedly whetted his interest in revolution and political change. Returning to Martinique in 1969, Placoly helped establish, and then became leader of, the Groupe révolutionnaire socialiste (1971), which was committed to independence for the islands.[2] In his short but prolific career he authored three novels, a significant number of essays, and over fifteen plays. Two of these dramas place *béké* characters front and center: *La Fin douloureuse et tragique d'André Aliker* (The sad and tragic end of André Aliker, 1969) revolves around the real-life murder of the eponymous communist journalist, a killing suspected to have been at the behest of the *békés* whose corruption Aliker was in the process of exposing, while the unpublished *Scènes de la vie de Joséphine-Rose Tascher de la Pagerie* (Scenes from the life of Joséphine-Rose Tascher de la Pagerie, 1988) was commissioned by the Conseil Général de la Martinique to mark its acquisition of the Pagerie domain, and appears to have left little trace.

If these works register a longstanding interest in social justice generally, and in the position of the *béké* in Antillean society in particular, it was undoubtedly Placoly's 1983 work, *Frères volcans*,[3] a diary-novel written, controversially, from the perspective of a sympathetic (i.e., abolitionist) *béké*, that gave fullest expression to this preoccupation. The novel conforms, on a very basic level, to a subgenre of North American fiction, what Robert Fikes Jr. calls "white-life writing," a term that describes novels written by Black authors that center on white characters,[4] and which has attracted significant recent attention from US-based critical race scholars of literature. Like critical whiteness studies generally, the "white-life" narrative both maps onto, and emanates from a radically different context to, the Antilles. It bears repetition that whites are in the United States the unmarked category against which difference is constructed, the "unexamined norm" (although, as mentioned in my introduction, a less secure norm today than at the time when many of these US novels were written). The minority status of white Creoles in the Antilles, on the other hand, ensures that they are a highly marked category. George Lipsitz's observation that whiteness "never has to acknowledge its role as an organizing principle in social and cultural relations"[5] is only partially and problematically relevant in a society where nonwhites outnumber whites in such significant proportions. On the most fundamental level, then, white characters tend to occupy a peripheral rather than a central diegetic space for twentieth- and twenty-first-century Antillean authors, even if their fiction remains haunted by the memory of slavery. The novels explored in my previous chapter, by Glissant and Chamoiseau, are unusual in the substantial space they afford to the master and mistress and, as I argue in chapter 3, in the ways in which the reader's empathy is mobilized for white characters. But even in these cases, the *béké* remains a secondary figure within the overall textual and affective economy. The novels that revolve around the killing of white Creoles, discussed in my closing chapter, are more influenced by the modes of crime fiction than by white-life and crucially, like the works by Chamoiseau and Glissant, are primarily concerned with the stories and interior life of Black protagonists rather than white. And if demography plays a role, so too does cultural politics. In the postwar USA, many Black writers (such as Zora Neale Hurston and James Baldwin) could be seen as making inroads into white readership, seeking out greater publishing opportunities by taking up subjects outside preconceived notions of the "negro problem."[6] In the Antilles, however, in a period galvanized by the political and poetic energy of Negritude, and further enriched by writers and thinkers for whom the outworkings of slavery have been fundamental, it is precisely because of their positionality as *Black* that authors have been primarily read and valued.[7] While Fikes can describe the mode of white-life writing as "persistent," having attracted novelists of the stature of Hurston and Baldwin,[8] and while John C. Charles notes that nearly every significant Black novelist of the twentieth century "abandoned (albeit momentarily) the white hero in favor of white protagonists,"[9] *Frères volcans* is unique in Black Antillean literature in the priority it affords to, and the intimacy with which it scrutinizes, the *béké* hero. For reasons to do with its singularity, then, the novel warrants detailed discussion in any consideration of whiteness in Antillean fiction.

Working out of Fikes's initial and fairly descriptive typology, and in a manner that resonates directly with Placoly's project in *Frères volcans,* Veronica T. Watson has theorized "the literature of white estrangement," a genre that critically engages with whiteness as a social construction and that makes visible "the unseen, unspoken, and unevaluated nature of whiteness."[10] Such narratives deconstruct the mythology of whiteness, ostensibly from within. While in some cases these novels of white estrangement were produced to satisfy white readers, they also can be seen as "trickster" texts that embed "critiques of whiteness within texts that seemed to celebrate white racial ascendancy."[11] Moreover, as Watson comments, this writing "gives voice to that which has been repressed within Whiteness. In these black-authored texts, there is often an unarticulated longing in white characters for what they have lost or turned away from: their fuller humanity, which is most often symbolized by their relationship with African American people."[12] This sense of estrangement, as well as a pervasive longing for what whiteness has lost, or perhaps never securely possessed, is a strain that runs throughout *Frères volcans,* and is particularly vested in the narrator's relationship with Black characters. The narrator-diarist, like so many literary *békés,* is the last in his line, and throughout the novel, in a familiar trope, his declining health is metaphorically linked to the decay of his caste, a decline that he explicitly and repeatedly connects to the cursed heritage of slavery. The narrator believes that the institution has ruined the planters themselves, sucked human relationships (both within and between castes) dry, debased art (58–59), and stunted the evolution of the Caribbean basin more generally (109). The *béké*'s vital organs are in a state of disintegration (15), while society more generally suffers from a "gnawing plague" (46), and is "eaten up by secret maladies" (62). Even children's bodies are defective ("porte des tares," 62). Sick from its own history, white society is, moreover, conspicuously unable to cure itself. The narrator's doctor, Raff, cautions defensively against "Negro drinks," noting that "these people [. . .] were not made to understand the science of the Enlightenment" (18). And yet Raff's practice owes as much to serendipity, one might even say quackery (the narrator likens his practice to exorcism), as to rational science: his outlandish "trouvailles" include a purgative from Holland and a cream from Brazil to prevent sweating (15–18). Such extravagantly sourced and much vaunted remedies are consistently bested by the local plant-based cures of his servant Némorine, who is indeed more trusted by the narrator.

As the novel's prominent references to *Hamlet* would suggest, then, something is rotten in the plantocracy, in the body of the protagonist and in the body politic, and the novel is saturated with references to illness, plague, and physical suffering. The novel features no young Creoles, no children, and no sexual relationships of any kind, whether based on love (an admittedly rare phenomenon in narratives about white Creoles) or abuse (so common in fiction exploring master-slave interactions and their modern avatars). The protagonist is surrounded by other, apparently equally sexually inactive, old men: his doctor, Raff, who is his confidant, counsellor, physician, and intellectual sparring partner;[13] the visiting Creoles who attempt to dissuade him from his abolitionist views, and in whose features he reads "the ravages of time, gray hair, dulled eyes" (53); or his wrinkled Black servant Abder. Only Vive, the well-named former lover, offers a vibrant and feminine contrast to this male gerontocracy, but she is invariably associated with frivolity and gossip, and is killed in the uprising of 1848. The novel thus exemplifies, in its almost parodically masculine viewpoint and its claustrophobic sense of interiority, a strand of white-life fiction identified and analyzed by Charles, which centers on "white heteropatriarchy," and notably on "private, domestic spaces, and especially intimate relations—in other words, on signs and scenes of white privacy."[14] Charles's focus on masculinity, and his concern with "the psychological deficits and moral failings" of white men, provides an especially resonant way into my discussion of *Frères volcans*.[15] These novels, according to Charles, stage "a powerful discursive inversion," in that it is white characters, rather than Black, who are depicted as "bound, even enslaved and imprisoned, by mainstream ideals and traditions."[16] For Charles, the focus on white privacy "might seem an evasion of political and social critique."[17] In Placoly's novel, however, in which sexual intimacy, as mentioned above, is strikingly absent, privacy acts rather as the enabling condition for extended political reflection, and indeed political and social critique is placed front and center of *Frères volcans*. But as we will see in the second section of this chapter, the narrator's reflections on sexual politics are markedly less enlightened than his reflections on race.

Whatever the divergences between white-life writing in the United States and the Antilles, in terms of scale of production, tenor, diegetic detail and authorial motivation, the broader implications of a Black writer representing white subjectivity in an intimate, sympathetic, and reflective mode are central to my analysis here; this positive affective relationship deviates from the "critical dictum" that writing by Blacks "always registers a fundamentally dissident position" with regard to whiteness.[18] Like other novels of the white-life genre, *Frères volcans* stages "self-conscious representations of whiteness that disrupt conventional notions of racialized power and privilege."[19] It cultivates sympathy for its protagonist because he is drawn to Black culture in all of its various manifestations: medicine, music, spirituality, and religious rituals, political discourse (significantly, given his servant Abder's political fluency, not the exclusive preserve of white Creoles in this novel), and, above all, language. This affinity with blackness in turn creates a reciprocal empathy between Black frame narrator (the diary purports to be a document found in a library by an unidentified contemporary historian, who has transcribed it and supplemented it with a preface and a postface) and white diarist-protagonist. In a radical opening salvo, the historian declares that he has discovered "between the lines of the other, a face not so different from my own" (12). This cross-racial identification is further enabled by the fact that the *béké* remains unnamed throughout. On the one hand he is unburdened by any alienating, or even ridiculous, Creole name, like those that feature so prominently in the other novels discussed here. On the other hand his anonymity enhances readerly empathy: as one critic comments, "the narrator is so close to us that he doesn't receive a proper name."[20] A Black novelist, via his fictional alter-ego historian, writes in the voice of a white master, an abolitionist *colon,* and, as one critic puts it, "a narrator with white skin but a blackened mask,"[21] who in turn enjoys an easy intimacy with his Black servants and wishes to get under *their* skin, attempting to "see things through their eyes, to think with their intelligence" (95). The novel is shot through with references to "them" ("la population noire," "les nègres"), and, conversely, to "nous." But this is a (real life) writer whose ostensible "them" is, of course, his own people.

This complex affective structure, along with the language employed by Placoly, in its antiquated lexicon and its often imperious and moralizing tone, has a peculiarly vertiginous effect on the reader, who can easily forget that the text was written in the late twentieth century by a Black author. The portrayal of the "barely fictional"[22] narrator is a feature that was commended, for example, by the commissioning editor for Seuil who, in rejecting Placoly's manuscript for its lack of vigor and its dryness of tone (the novel purports to have been originally conceived as a scholarly monograph), applauded the author's "ability to get under the skin of the character."[23] Structure and style combine to facilitate a kind of double consciousness, which consistently invokes, and attempts to trouble, the them/us racial boundary that is so frequently referenced in the novel, and on which the plantocracy depends.

In all of this, the sense of introspection conveyed by the diary form draws the reader into the world of this nineteenth-century character, creating an effect of empathy but also estrangement. The first section of this chapter looks at the implications of Placoly's use of this intimate form, as well as examining the diary's ambiguous relationship with the frame narrative that surrounds it. In a second section I consider the novel's explicit reflections on language, a focus of many white-life novels, described by Stephanie Li as the reconfiguration of "how we understand the relationship with whiteness as well as the importance of language to racial constructions."[24] Language, in its imperfect relationship with the reality it shapes, masks, conceals, and distorts, is of course a perennial literary topos. But it is specifically in its inability to convey the new political realities promised by Abolition that language is found to be especially wanting in the novel: this inadequacy is an obsessive point of reference for the narrator. In the final section of the chapter, I consider the portrayal of gender in this narrative of "heteropatriarchy,"[25] examining what Marie-Agnès Sourieau, the only critic to comment on gender (and then, only in passing), calls the novel's "resolutely masculine" system.[26] From the novel's first page, which announces that we "cannot expect beautiful women to have taste" (14), and indeed from its gendered title, which draws on the rhetoric of Negritude to posit the volcano as brother, this is an unapologetically masculine take on the colonial world. Paternalism, patriarchy, and the plantocracy are inextricably interconnected: culture and politics are the exclusive preserve of men, and male power and impotence are core concerns that are anxiously intertwined and interrogated in the novel. If *Frères volcans*, through a process of white estrangement, has new and often quite radical ways of representing white subjectivity, it remains embedded in a very questionable approach to gender politics, one that is a disappointingly familiar feature of male-authored French Caribbean fiction.

Interiority, Self-Consciousness, and the Diary

Frères volcans unfolds in Saint-Pierre, the oldest town in Martinique and, in the 1840s, the island's cultural capital. The city has a somewhat mythical status, considered, until the devastating volcano of 1902, to be the bastion of white Creole society in contrast to the "blacker" city of Fort-de-France (in reality both were predominantly inhabited by the enslaved and their descendants). The novel reports, from the perspective of a politically enlightened *béké,* on the cataclysmic months leading up to and succeeding the abolition of slavery. The diary is presented in two sections. The first is comprised of eight entries, composed between 2 January and 3 February 1848, and the second of six entries from 25 April until 11 June of the same year. The entries are of strikingly uneven temporal and spatial dimensions: some take up a page or two, and cover a single day, while others are significantly lengthier (for example a single entry, on 3 February, runs to fifty-four pages and covers the entirety of Lent). Separating the two sections is the slave revolt of 22 May 1848, an unnamed temporal division constructing the diary around a "before" and an "after" the slave revolt. The month-long silence between 25 April and 25 May (the entry marked with the former date is revealed a page later to have been written on the latter, as the diarist turns away from writing during this turbulent month) means that the diary reflects, even in its dating method, the chaos and instability of the period and, crucially, occludes any direct account of 22 May. The horror of that day is suggested in the anachronistic, indeed analeptic, date attributed to the entry (25 April), and in the disorientated and staccato style with which the second section opens, notably the stuttering "I saw," a phrase used repeatedly, at times frenetically, in the first page of section two, opening almost every sentence. The phrase introduces a succession of violent acts witnessed by the narrator: the burning of buildings and boats, the destruction of the Sannois home in which thirty people, including Vive, are killed,[27] the sight of friends' throats being slit and their brains blown out, and an all-encompassing sense of death and destruction (79). These events, invoked as a barbarous litany but not processed (nor even dated) into a coherent story, register the narrator's profound trauma, and point to the limitations of his language to describe them.

The sense of introspection generated by the diary form is intensified by the fact that the novel takes place almost entirely indoors. This interior space is not the sprawling villa known as the *grand'case,* the almost obligatory setting for novels by and about white Creoles, but rather a symbolically downsized townhouse. The familiar optical clichés of mastery (panoramic oversight of workers and factories; the enjoyment of an unencumbered sea vista or garden; the vantage point of the veranda) give way to a heightened sense of self-reflexivity, which generates a conspicuously claustrophobic tone. The narrator's home, the former Hôtel Desgrottes, a name that gestures toward enclosure and retreat, is located between the respectable Rue d'Orléans and the Rue de la Confession, a dirt track reserved for servants, and this latter street name further reflects the intensely confessional and intimate nature of the novel. The cramped liminal location in which the novel plays out (cramped relative to other *béké*-centered, rather than Black-centered novels) demonstrates the distance the master has traveled from the spatial and racial hierarchies of the plantation. The narrative arc of many "white-life" novels means that resolution, as Charles explains, "depends on the white protagonist, and implicitly the white reader, undergoing a kind of moral reform that frequently includes a symbolic repudiation of his or her possessive investment in whiteness."[28] Here, however, the dramatic "repudiation" of these values is symbolic *and* material, and indeed precedes the opening of the novel: the *béké* has already liberated his slaves and rejected the values of the plantocracy by the time he begins his journal. Hence, this highly self-aware protagonist occupies from the outset of the story a position of moral enlightenment that many characters in white-life novels only attain as the novel progresses. He regrets that his caste has not developed an adequate "method of self-investigation" (33), a phrase that resonates with the confessional mode registered in the name of his street. And, for example, unlike many fictional *békés* who turn a blind eye to the inequalities of slavery, he provides a vivid account of slave punishment and suffering (29). The novel, then, is less a journey toward enlightenment and humanist values than a sustained philosophical reflection on how, or rather whether, such values can be understood, adopted, and applied in a postslavery context.

The narrator at one point observes that "episodes are less important than the situation that gave rise to them [. . .]. No episode exists in and of itself" (96). The journal, despite a subtitle that promises a chronicle, omits the most salient episodes of May 1848, to make way for the reflections of local writers, politicians, churchmen, planters, or former slaves, and for metacommentary on these reflections by the narrator himself. The diary thus emphasizes the failure of any individual to fully understand what was happening. Both master and slave are caught off guard by the events of that month: "dictator or victim, soloist or choirboy, we are actors released on stage without a director, a producer, an audience, or any rehearsal" (98). And like a real-life diary, the novel reads very much like a work in progress, a text that is being written alongside, and often overtaken by, the events it describes. It is replete with hesitations, uncertainties, doubts, self-interrogations, and cites a range of conflicting perspectives on the events recounted (and indeed it is very often in conflict with itself). It thus frequently denies stable interpretative ground to the reader. Indeed, it is only in the frame narrative that a clear and unambiguous commentary emerges on the false promises of Abolition.[29] The preface refers to a liberty that was "so subtly stolen" from slaves (9), while the postface closes with the observation that "the slave of yesterday, to whom France opened the gates of universal suffrage, remains today the very essence of an outsider" (126). Such a devastating political assessment, bookending a novel whose twists and turns make, at times, for a politically disorientating read, gives the lie to the mythology of Abolition and clearly connects the historical circumstances of 1848 to the continuing societal problems in the Antilles and France at the time of the novel's writing.

Like so many other Caribbean novels, this is an intensely self-aware text, saturated with references to other writers. Placoly references classical sources (31, 34), metropolitan writers (Montaigne, Lamartine, Hugo, Baudelaire, and Chateaubriand, to name only a small number), well-known (in the nineteenth century) Creole poets such as Parny and Léonard, and invented *béké* authors such as Villiers and Leyritz.[30] The narrator intersplices these literary allusions with references to real works of botany or history, for example, and quotes historical documents such as letters and political tracts. Above all the *béké* is influenced by the writings of abolitionist Victor Schœlcher, described as a "man of action [. . .] a man of patience [. . .] a man of faith [. . .] and a visionary" (73).[31] The intense intertextuality of the novel is doubled and enhanced at a structural level by the observations of the frame narrator, also an admirer of Schœlcher, and who likewise reflects, like the *béké* diarist, not only on the text we are reading, but also on literature more generally. This unidentified author-historian is yet another restless authorial double, whose relationship with the real-life Vincent Placoly is so ambiguous that most critics have conflated the two; their positions mirror each other and their voices at times would seem to converge with the viewpoint of Placoly himself.[32] The frame narrator-historian had been working on a historical essay about the events leading up to Abolition, but finds himself jaded by the repetitive and clichéd accounts found in the archives. His writer's block is dramatically interrupted when he happens upon a manuscript, contained in a single thick notebook, and written in clear and faultless handwriting, which "burned my eyes," and which offers a striking counterpoint to the "outdated moralizing of ebbing empires" (11) that had so fatigued and frustrated him. Shedding "the tight-fitting uniform of university research" (10), he diligently copies out the journal's pages one by one to produce the novel that the reader holds. Frame narrative and diary will continue to mirror each other, as we shall see, in their mistrust of vacuous or overblown language, their frustration with existing literature, their antipathy to cliché, their respect for Victor Schœlcher, and, it has to be said, their dismissal of women, a point to which we return in the closing section of this chapter.

Language, Self, and Other

Language in the novel is presented in largely binary terms. "Black" language, whether Creole or, in a single instance, French, is consistently shown to be a source of expressivity and plenitude. On hearing his servants talk, for example, the narrator comments that "Negro allegories, especially when presented in our language, dig deep into the history of humanity" (16). He later reflects on Creole etymology, pondering the Creole word *houcler,* the last link in a "very long and interwoven chain" (the metaphorical chain connecting the two terms conjuring its much more literal usage in slavery), which began with the French verb *roucouler* (to warble or to coo). The observation gives way to a celebration of the Creole language, which in this novel is clearly, with the exception of Léonce, discussed below, the preserve of Black rather than white characters, and associated with untrammeled expressiveness, energy, and movement: "How rich their language is, and how it transfigures the world of sentiment! The rivers of language are indeed eternal!" the narrator observes, going on to compare "Negro language" to alluvial deposits of gold and diamonds (24). At other times this language brings reassurance and relief: looking onto the rue de la Confession the Black voices he hears "sing in my ear, just like their laughs, freed from all shackles, making my readings (the only true source of joy) calmer" (46). The spoken words of Black servants stimulate in the narrator the desire to listen "deeply" (95), while Abder, conversing with his master, finds "in the depths of his language the ability to talk to me equal to equal" (85). The language used by Blacks is thus associated with gravity, richness, plenitude, adaptability, liberty, joy, and the capacity to transfigure rather than to debase or distort.

Such overwhelmingly positive attributes stand in conspicuous contrast to the language of whites, both written and spoken (in other words, this is not a novel that, in the manner of some novels of *créolité*, elevates orality over the written word, although Black language falls exclusively into the former category). Vive and other Creole women are repeatedly associated with stultifying gossip, which makes the narrator "dizzy" (42). If female chatter is denigrated, so too is Creole literary production, which is repeatedly judged to be empty, vapid, and derivative, and passively consumed by uncritical and easily sated Creoles. Local theaters show "plays for simpletons, insipid trifles, worthless sketches for the pleasure of primped up men and women bedecked in lace and silk" (48). The two invented Creole poets, Villiers (scathingly referred to as the national poet of Martinique, and associated with *soties* and *bons mots*, 20) and Leyritz, are subject to particularly virulent criticism. In an incident reported by Vive, the former slaps the latter in the face for having accused him of plagiarism (42), but both are repeatedly associated with a lack of originality and authenticity, and are presented as passive absorbers and redrafters of existing work. The narrator derides local Martinicans' efforts to rote learn Villiers's poetry, not only because his verses "sound wrong," but also because they are politically useless. Given current political circumstances, poetry should, according to the narrator, incite action (21). But even when the narrator finds literary satisfaction in Villiers's writing, he undercuts any sense of his poetic skill. Quoting the poet's description of "the eternal gaiety of the colonies," he notes that the phrase is suggestive and rich. But this felicitous expression is instantly dismissed as the product not of talent but of serendipity; the author has somehow got lucky, produced an interesting expression without any sense of the full meaning of the phrase: "I know his narrow mind, and the great pretention with which he cultivates his futile garden." The narrator concludes that the poet was referring, literally, to the insouciance of Creole youth (17), rather than making a more abstract point, presumably about the political immaturity of the islands.

In his insistence on the poor quality and mimicry of Creole writing, Placoly reprises a familiar trope. Chris Bongie, invoking Baudelaire's 1861 dismissal of Leconte de Lisle's work as lacking originality and "any power of conception or expression," reminds us that it is "a cliché of literary history that the single most defining characteristic of literature written by Creoles in the nineteenth century is its unoriginality."[33] As we have seen, Chamoiseau and Confiant are also scathing in *Lettres créoles* about the literary sensibility of the white ethnocaste. They dismiss colonial writings as exercises in the scribal ("la scription") rather than the literary ("l'écriture"): planters, usually illiterate themselves, only used the pen to fill in birth and death registers, accounts books, or legal or criminal texts.[34] And Chamoiseau features the philistinism of the *béké*, a figure more interested in the bottom line than in lines of verse, in *Texaco* (48). But Placoly goes further, to suggest something more disturbing: if Creole literature lacks originality and vigor, this is most crucially an inherent symptom of language itself, both literary and spoken, and derives from the fact that language has been fundamentally deformed by slavery. Slavery and poetry are, he argues, incompatible. The narrator reflects repeatedly and at length on the inadequacy of the words available to express the situation of Creoles, and even to accommodate a new postslavery world order. For example, he laments that "the emptiness of our literary soirées, the hubbub of our theaters, cannot hide the misery of our humanity. I feel that each and every one of us suffers from an extraordinary ill, which is even more terrible because the words don't exist to express it, and indeed in doing so one would lose one's life" (58). This is not the linguistic frustration of the modernist hero, grappling with the desire to purify or to clarify language, and attempting to navigate that unbridgeable gap between what we mean and what we utter. Nor does the extract register any surrealist project of linguistic emancipation. Rather it underscores the extent to which language is incapable of expressing the "misery" of slavery, the "extraordinary ill" invoked but not named. The realities of inequality, degradation, gratuitous corporal punishment, and cruelty have so indelibly marked the psycholinguistic superstructure of Creole society that language can neither express the current reality, nor would it be able to reshape itself to accommodate any postslavery regime: "the knife turned back into the wound, whipping, *quatre-piquets*,[35] and sequestration: *the master knows no other language*" (29, my italics).

Words are distorting and inadequate, then, *because* they are embedded in and constituted by a history of abuse and violence. Moreover, the language through which slavery and the plantation have been conceived and described is the preserve of the ruling class; it has therefore been cannily manipulated by the master to construct, sustain, and even at times to deny entirely the status quo. The term "slavery" itself, for example, is woefully inadequate to describe the horrific realities of its referent for the enslaved. But crucially, it can also be avoided by slave owners themselves in the interests of whitewashing the brutality it (fails to) name. Pécoul, a *béké* deputy, in a (historically authentic) letter sent to all planters, emphasizes the weight of words, and urges a euphemistic approach. "We must beware," he declares, "in constructing sentences with the word *slavery*, that we aren't guilty of deforming the reality of colonial life" (57). Such "atrocious colors" distort "the natural authority of the farmer ['agriculteur] over his worker!" (57). (Pécoul cites the hackneyed examples of the boroughs of London, where famine and begging are rife, as examples of a more brutal social order.)[36] Placoly here echoes US poet Audre Lorde, whose observation, made in the same year as this novel appeared, that "the master's tools will never dismantle the master's house," similarly exposed the futility of the linguistic tools "of a racist patriarchy" being used "to examine the fruits of that same patriarchy."[37] If Placoly, as I argue below, is less attuned than Lorde to the gendered nature of the language available to us, he is certainly sensitive to the extent to which these same tools can be cynically repurposed, by the master himself, to buttress his own egregious dominance through the canny control of language, and notably, here, in the substitution of the word "farming" for "slavery."

Several pages later, in a further reflection on language prompted, typically, by his sense of alienation from the codes of Creole social life (here, a society dinner characterized by "sophistry"), the narrator asks,

> Is there a language in which words cover entirely the reality of the facts they designate? In which synonym, metaphor, and redundancy are inconceivable? And which excludes all rhetoric? Are there peoples who pillory poets? Peoples who consider grammarians to be crazy, or who view the observers of language as pleasant imbeciles whose hamstrings need to be cut so that they don't err from household tasks? As I listened to the artificial chat circulating around the wealthy table, without participating in it, I was struck by regret. (64)

This is an apparently wistful lament for a language freed from the falsifications or distortions of the literary enterprise, in which there is a simple equation between signifier and signified (although, in a moment of not uncharacteristic inconsistency, this easy equation of word and thing is one of the reasons he dismisses Villiers in the quotation given above). Poets, grammarians, and linguists are presented as the agents of a suspicious craft, one that seeks to theorize language itself. Such theorizing is connected not to any enhanced awareness of or sensitivity to the power of words, but rather is associated with the "artificial chat" and sophistry that envelops the white Creole world. And yet the narrator himself exhibits a marked penchant for the figures of speech and the rhetorical flourishes from which he appears to wish to liberate himself and his caste (for example, in his analogy of Creole as a precious stone or metal, or in the metaphor of language being freed from its shackles).

The passage's opening interrogative ("Is there a language . . . ?") appears to summon as a response Creole, a language that offers a rich, because untheorized and unselfconscious, contrast to the empty rhetoric of French. Elsewhere, as we have seen, Creole is presented as a natural resource, in the analogy with gold and diamonds, for example. But the *langue des nègres* (it is almost exclusively associated with the enslaved) is not named, and the contrast is in any case not an entirely unproblematic or secure binary opposition, not just because Creole derives in part from French, but even within the novel's own terms. The first reference to Creole explicitly associates it with allegory (16), while later, Creole's capacity to "transfigure" (a term that conjures metaphor or analogy) the world of sentiment is valorized. But what we can say is that the *langue des nègres* offers an authentic contrast to the artificiality of French, just as the slave world more generally is associated with energy and vigor rather than affectation and decline. The extract's sudden and rather brutal reference to "cutting the hamstrings" of the observers of language relocates, into a sentence ostensibly about the distortions of the literary, the motif of slave torture, grounding the observation in the violence of the local context. And the narrator's reflections, sparked by dinner-table discussions on the need to maintain slave subjection through hunger and fear, are themselves brutally interrupted by an example of Creole violence, when Mme de Brenne, the host of the party, punishes her slave Gaîté in front of the guests, making him the scapegoat for an accidental injury sustained by her grandson. The hypocrisy and cruelty of whiteness, fundamentally connected to a penchant for sophistry, is again underscored.

The French language, in which the slave regime has been conceived, shaped, and realized, is therefore inescapably and axiomatically the preserve of master rather than slave. But it is also, paradoxically, the language in which Abolition has been conceived. In the wake of 22 May 1848, this language cannot bend itself to accommodate new realities, and is unavailable to the ex-slave population, who "drag around with them words that sound like gongs" (91) and for whom the word "work" is a term endowed with such abstraction that it "rings in their heads like the bells of Pentecost" (120).[38] The percussive clanging of the French language in the mouths of the ex-slave population (the association with bells and gongs suggests noise, harshness, dissonance, and a lack of subtlety and malleability) registers the chasm that continues to exist between master and ex- (in name only) slave. The Black population knows "that there is no possible dialogue between present liberty and the former master who they might well run into on the street; so, they fall back on the law" (91). But this recourse to French legalism leaves the Black population vulnerable to law's linguistic seduction and its false promises: "Anybody coming from the faraway republic that invented for them the word Abolition would be welcomed" (91).

The narrator speculates that what is needed is an entirely new language, what he describes at several points as a "universal language" (33) or a "common language" (111), which has liberated itself from the shackles of a system that normalizes such monstrosities as slavery. He imagines a future in which the lexicon of slavery (whip, dungeon, chain, "so many shady words") will vanish from use, so that French, described as the language of "progress," will brighten, become enlightened ("s'éclaircit," 61). While slaves have not changed (how could they possibly, the narrator asks, suggesting that their subaltern linguistic status precludes the self-awareness necessary for change), white Creoles have been obliged to change "fundamentally and irreversibly." In another example of Creole's capacity for metaphor, the old man observes that "history had thrown us to the wind, as they say in their black language, and we felt that words were losing their power" (89). If mastery is first and foremost the mastery of language, then the ebbing of white power is of necessity experienced by the master caste as linguistic disempowerment, however unequal the power relations between Black and white remain.

These linguistic reflections, predicated on the existence of "us" and "them" (Creole is in no sense a lingua franca in this novel), are tied to a broader concern with understanding the other. As we have seen, this is a narrator keen to shed his skin, to get beyond, or even to be delivered from, the self (he wishes to be "cured" of himself, 12, for his caste to be "finally delivered from ourselves," 87, and later for his people to "escape ourselves," 113). He wonders, in one of those rhetorical questions that suffuse the text and that create a dialogue between self and soul, intensifying the sense of isolation (no answer is ever forthcoming), "How will history judge us?" This may be a vain question, he concedes, before concluding, in a remarkable statement, that "we are other people and the universe is whole" (47). In asserting the interconnectedness of all Antilleans, and of humanity more generally, the narrator insists on the fact that identity is founded on a dynamic and respectful openness to the other, rather than on defending the unitary, the same. In this the diegetic narrator mirrors the observations of his historian-avatar, who, as we saw above, discovers, "between the lines of the other, a face not so different from my own" (12). In the diary's closing pages, the narrator engages directly with Abder on the subject of Abolition, asking him, "What will liberty bring your race?" The servant answers, "We shall need time to appreciate its value. The blood of our race has been drained [. . .]. You who have been unable to teach us anything, and who haven't prevented our desire for liberty becoming a reality, you have more to learn than us" (114). The exchange is predicated on what looks like an absolute cleavage between subject and object, "us" and "you"; and yet it resolves itself into a gesture of inclusion and solidarity. "When he said *you*, he didn't point his finger in my direction [. . . ,] he opened his arms to me [. . .]. We watched the sun rise together" (114). In this poignant closing moment of resolution, optimism and fraternity, which recalls the complicity of Longoué and La Roche in *The Fourth Century*, the sun rises on a new day in post-Abolition society. These "frères volcans," one Black, one white, meet the day together as apparent equals.

But Placoly's novel is more pessimistic than Glissant's about the likelihood of intercaste communication and, ultimately, the possibility of equality. The novel also insists that the challenge for the Antilles is not merely to enshrine such equality in law, but also in everyday practice; for, as one character prophetically comments, "You can regulate the economy, reform work practices, and moderate the law. The spirit of the caste escapes the power of governments" (106). The destruction of plantation slavery has not undermined a political economy still founded on an exploitative plantation model, and the "spirit of the caste" endures in a contemporary context that remains marked by staggering inequality. The brutally depressing diagnoses contained in the preface and postface, which have the advantage of the frame narrator's historical hindsight, give the lie to any evolutionary narrative of progress, enlightenment, and equality.

Patriarchy, Decline, and the Mal de Viv(r)e

In one of his many about turns, hesitations, or self-contradictions, the narrator of *Frères volcans* wonders whether he has judged the poet Villiers too harshly, before in the next breath, in a comment that segues from literary criticism to personal invective, dismissing the poet as a "doddery little man" who has earned, because of his lifestyle, the rumors of his having contracted a sexually transmitted disease from women in the port (33–34). The narrator prays to God that a place will be reserved for Villiers in the poetic Pléiade of posterity. The episode is evidence of the narrative's internally unstable viewpoint. But more tellingly, its unadulterated misogyny (men are artists, albeit failing ones and, like the narrator, literary critics, while women are prostitutes, sexual commodities for writers and artists, and carriers of disease) is symptomatic of a novel that, right from its gendered title, seeks to occlude, and at times even to vilify, white Creole women. This dubious, and at times vicious, presentation of femininity is, I would argue, the crucial impediment to full readerly identification with the narrator, and perhaps also explains critical reticence toward the novel. It also, in conjoining the emptiness and mimicry of white (literary) language and the debased nature of Creole women, points to a more profound anxiety to which I return in the conclusion of this chapter.

The plantocracy in this novel is a highly gendered supersystem, in which women are conspicuously marginalized; when they do appear, they fulfil unidimensional roles. The narrator's mother is mentioned only once, when he remembers "the worry in my poor mother's eyes, she who was so good" (63). She is a benign force, but not one endowed with speech or agency. Another white Creole, Mme de Brenne, as we saw above, viciously and unfairly punishes her slave Gaîté, and voices the novel's most reactionary views regarding the treatment of slaves. The novel's only other mother, Mme Laguerre, is described in a single episode, when she visits the narrator with Vive and her other daughters. The narrator offers her a hand-bound devotional book, *The Imitation of Jesus Christ*.[39] In return, she and her daughters listen to him talk about his health, and then present him with "the gossip of the entire colony" (37); male culture, piety, and serious-mindedness are met with female indulgence and frivolity. More generally, mothers are shown to happily delegate their sole responsibility, the education of their daughters. In a hypocritical and opportunistic manner they outsource this role to entirely incompatible agencies: on the one hand young girls' spiritual instruction is entrusted to the Sisters of Charity; on the other, "omniscient *das*" induct girls in the ways of seduction during "nocturnal lessons" (37). White piety and chastity, and Black sexual savoir-faire, are uncomfortable bedfellows, a fact that is surely meant to explain the malaise and moral ambivalence of white Creole women in the novel. Above all, mothers are motivated to secure financial and social advantage for their daughters. They understand that "money talks, in town and in bed"; hence they "enthusiastically release their fillies ['pouliches'] at the colony's purses," while their daughters quickly learn to chase status ("courir l'établissement," 37).

If mothers are presented as weak, frivolous, morally hypocritical, or excessively attached to society and its gossip, the novel insists on the gravity of the narrator's father, to whom several entries are largely devoted. The diarist observes that "A child's first education consists in watching the father and listening to the mother who, in a warm and low voice, sketches the father's portrait" (71). Mother and child in this image are entirely subjugated to the *pater familias,* whose association with the portrait immediately elevates him to the world of art and culture and conjures those ancestral paintings of male forebears common in Creole literature. Throughout the novel the deceased patriarch is an overbearing presence for the narrator—the son dates his withdrawal from local aristocratic society to his death (62)—and their relationship is framed as one of both continuity and rupture. Like his father, the diarist is a cultured bibliophile; he has inherited the paternal library, as well as his father's (relatively) liberal views—the older planter is no abolitionist—and his progressive relationship with slaves and workers. The narrator now devotes himself to rebinding his father's books, in an attempt to protect this paternal literary heritage from the ravages of the hot climate.[40] He observes that he began by restoring the local books published in 1835 (19).

In this choice of 1835 as the start date for his conservation project, we can assume that the protagonist must also have been occupied with the texts discussed in chapter 2, *Les créoles* and *Outre-mer*, the two most notable Antillean novels of that year, which are in many respects haunted in advance by the events of 1848 presented in *Frères volcans*. These works also foreground, as we saw in chapter 2, specific anxieties around paternity and patriarchy. And from this perspective the intertextual references to *Hamlet*, as well as registering societal dysfunction and identifying with (British) liberalism, resonate with and add depth to the father-son relationship explored in this novel, tainted by a sense of filial belatedness, inferiority, and even guilt. The clean lines of patrilinear inheritance have been sundered by a narrator who has sold off his father's land, spectacularly rejected his value system, and opted for cultural conservation rather than agricultural production; in a further echo of the destiny of the hesitant and ineffectual Shakespearean son, the *béké* has, for reasons that even he fails to understand, refused marriage with an eminently suitable and devoted younger woman. Both father and son have confided in and taken advice from slave-turned-employee, Abder, while the elder planter had allowed his young slave, Zembi, to cease working in the fields to indulge his talent in making drums (a particularly benevolent decision, perhaps, given the association of the drum with both slave leisure and resistance). Instead of opening schools of religious instruction for slaves, the father comments that planters should instead found an institute of arts and crafts, open to all castes, to develop manual and engineering skills (71). But although the father is presented as a relatively enlightened master, and a model of probity and foresight, he is no dissident to the system. Rather he is a vigorous and enthusiastic planter, who is associated with clichés of hypermasculinity and with the gendered paraphernalia of mastery. Like his son, he is attuned to questions of language, and to the values encoded in it; but in contrast to his son's admiration for "black" language, he values "the equilibrium of the French language" and the "riches of Western thought" (20). He regales his young son with stories of murder, torture, and sea battles (20). When the voice of paternal interdiction and command intervenes, it is entirely embedded within the more brutal realities of slave punishment: "when you don't hear the rattling of slave drums, get the dogs and the pistols on the scene" (40). He is also presented as a godlike figure: the Gospels and the word of the father are interlinked (19), and the father himself suggests that the plantation conforms to a divine rather than a man-made order: "The word of man is in vain," he comments (20). When the narrator dreams that the Domaine has burned down, his father, accompanied by his Bible, acts like an Old Testament prophet as he "reassures his people of the imminence of divine justice" (26). And again, he is an authoritarian upholder of the values of slavery: the divine justice invoked in this scene is clearly to be visited upon the slave rather than the master.

It is because of this paternal connection that the narrator, despite his progressive values, retains a wistful vision of colonial nostalgia connected to the security and innocence of childhood, a very literal form of homesickness. In a scene that can be considered a set piece of colonial literature, the father invites his son to observe a vista of white mastery: "the mill and the boiler houses, the slave huts and the distillery" (no slaves are mentioned). The father exhorts his son to admire "the durability ['pérennité'] of things" (19). But the reader, like the narrator, knows that this durability is fatally compromised, both by the future actions (and inaction) of the son, and by the course of history. In a second imagined revisiting of the plantation the son comments, "I remember those years when my father still possessed le Domaine" (25), a statement that can be read at once as an expression of filial nostalgia, even guilt, and, given the curiously generic plantation name and the anonymity of its owner, the regret of a Creole everyman, confronted with the imminent end of the plantocracy and its domains. The narrator recalls how "the high, green, and vigorous canes resemble the arms that cut them. Fruit trees give as much as they can, plums, apricots, plump *icaques*" (25). In this colonial metonymy, a *locus classicus* of white Creole discourse, the institution of slavery is reduced to an arm, and worker and sugar cane blend into a seamless, unified, and highly idealized unit. The passage, in its opening injunction ("I remember"), its nostalgia for childhood, its celebration of Edenic profusion (indeed one of the plantations visited by the narrator is called Eden), and its loving list of local fruits, recalls Saint-John Perse's poetry of a plantation childhood, *Éloges*. In a further resonance with Perse's poetry, the narrator remembers "the patriarch's gnarled hand" extending over "the horizon of his lands" (63); this hand, metonymically invoking age, experience, and labor, but also possession and power, stands in marked contrast to the youthful ("green"), vigorous, but entirely depersonalized slave hand. If writers such as Joseph Zobel famously focused on the time- and work-worn hands of laborers (notably Man Tine in *La rue cases-nègres*), these extremities are conspicuously associated with dispossession rather than possession.[41] Here, as in the depiction of Perse's father in *Éloges,* the image of the father's hand "condenses the portrait of all men of his rank, class, and socio-historical position."[42] The hands also stand as a reminder of the degeneration of the contemporary plantocracy, a state of decline that is specifically connected to a lack of connection to labor and the land.

If the patrilinear ties that bind son to father (slaves and servants in common; the inherited library and love of literature; an interest in language) are emphasized, this only serves to accentuate the radical way in which they are shattered by the narrator's sale of the plantation, but also by his mysterious (even to himself) refusal to marry, which prevents the perpetuation of the name and the family line. The novel repeatedly suggests that the rot that has taken hold in white Creole society, founded in slavery, is primarily expressed in male sexual and reproductive inhibitions. The narrator concedes that he would have lived a life of "passionate happiness" (40) with Vive, the adjective signaling a union fueled by sex as well as love, and indeed he continues to see her in erotic terms. She is a frequent late-night visitor, her arrival accompanied by bursts of heat ("bouffées de chaleur," 39), his gaze drawn to the sexually charged parts of her body: the play of the sun on her hair, her light dress, her breasts which have "matured like wild pomegranates" (39) or "her naked shoulders [...] her back the color of a ripe orange" (42). Yet his detachment from the body, even his impotence, is also suggested in a concentrated network of references to inactive organs and underused muscles in the novel's opening pages. The narrator observes that his organs are abandoning him (15), and admits that in his youth he had been insufficiently active, due to his preference for card games and salon chat over horseracing and the "exercise of the muscles," both activities highly coded in terms of conventional masculinity and physical vigor (16). His body has been "closed to passion" (16), a state he equates with death. Later he admits that "when you're alone the circulation of your blood slows" (36), and states that

Creole men more generally "have deserted our wives' wombs" (62). The (unsuccessful) project of reproduction in the New World is figured in the familiar gendered terms of the colonial enterprise, based on allegories of imperial male activity, or rather in this case the absence thereof, and by extension of female passivity and submission: "If we haven't managed to fertilize ['féconder'] American society, it's because we have been corrupted by slavery" (62). The gendered division of labor is entirely familiar here, but the geographical referent is ambivalent—the reference to American society names neither Black nor white, and indeed conjures peoples native to the Americas as much as it does those transplanted there. But given the exclusively white-on-white relationships explored in the novel, and the importance placed on white procreation, the line points, at the very least, to the failed project of reproduction within the white ethnocaste, a failure that is clearly and repeatedly presented as one of male withdrawal and desertion, and which is epitomized in the narrator's relationship with Vive.

When Vive is given space to speak in her own voice she is, despite the narrator's disdain for her intellect, an educated and astute observer. She expresses herself in a highly metaphorical language that is suffused with paradox, but that emphasizes female silence, confinement, and sexual frustration. She claims that Creole women are "condemned to dream of the closed doors ['huis clos'] of freedom [. . .] languishing after the voracious chimera of their blood and their vitality" (43). The reference to menstrual blood reinscribes (failed) reproduction, reminding us of the abandoned wombs of the colony. Women are "weighed down by silence, as our illusions are voiceless. Nothing that we do, or dream, is of any consequence anymore" (43). But more commonly the narrator, by his own admission, "speaks for" women (40) and for Vive, appearing almost pathologically fixated on both the corruption of white female flesh and the inadequacy of the white female mind. His discourse, which vacillates between apparent sympathy and outright phobia, continually conjoins references to women with notions of sex, desire, and erotic pleasure, or, more commonly, with their absence. He notes that women are "confined very young in a pleasureless harem," that they "die more than they live," and that society constrains them in a steel girdle: "This slow death can be seen in their face, and on their gaze which they pass over everything without seeing it" (40). In a startling denial of both his own sexual desire for Vive, and the fact that he jilted her, the narrator claims never to have been attracted by "these [Creole] women," claiming that it was his ex-lovers who "convinced me that it was better for me to end my life alone" (37).

Tellingly, this revisionist version of his past immediately follows a passage that reprises the casual slippage between femininity, prostitution, and the female quest for pleasure. Courtesans are legion in Saint-Pierre, he observes, and young women long for marriage. But "the idleness of their situation makes them put too much importance on bodily pleasure" (38). Vive, meanwhile, already associated with frivolity and gossip, is in a remarkable series of textual put-downs depicted as an intellectually limited and even dishonest character. She "cannot see the deeper meaning of things," is occupied with "the most pointless futilities," and fails to grasp "the flavor of reality" (42). As she "swirls around" the books in his library—yet again male intellect is met with female levity, frivolity, even dizziness—he wonders when she will resolve "to extricate herself from the games of society" (42). Moreover, she is later revealed to be intellectually duplicitous. Her entry in a prayer-writing competition, organized by the town's women as part of the Easter celebrations, has, the narrator suspects, been "plagiarized from somewhere," a charge that recalls and indeed surpasses the earlier association of white Creole writing with a lack of originality and mimicry. Although Vive's dishonesty is not confirmed within the novel, the narrator is of course correct (75).[43] Vive's death, somewhat curiously in such an introspective text, is distanced in narrative terms (it is relayed by Abder) and granted minimal narrative and emotional space. When the servant reports the historically accurate death of thirty people in the Sannois home, the narrator states merely that he later "learned that Vive was among them" (102), while in the last reference to her, Raff informs the narrator that her family has decided to leave the colony as a result of her death (109). Vive therefore leaves little trace, diegetically, emotionally, or genetically.

If Vive, like white women more generally, is extensively discredited and eventually written out, the text has strikingly little to say about Black or mixed-race women, an absence all the more telling given the repeatedly stated frustration of white women and the extent to which white men have rejected their bodies. White male sexual withdrawal from white women is not unusual in French Caribbean writing; in *The Libertine Colony*, for example, Doris Garraway discusses early Haitian narratives in which white men are depicted as having "shun[ned] women of their own race," and we see similar sexual preferences operating in a wide range of Antillean novels, such as Drasta Houël's *Cruautés et tendresses*, Daniel de Grandmaison's *Le bal des créoles*, Guy Cabort-Masson's *Qui a tué le béké de Trinité?* and Patrick Chamoiseau's *Un dimanche au cachot*. But in these cases, as in Garraway's examples, this withdrawal is in favor of Black and mixed-race women (in Garraway's study, for example, it operates specifically in favor of freed mulattas, around whom she claims a "veritable cult was developing").[44] What is remarkable in *Frères volcans* is the extent to which the unbridled interracial libertinage analyzed by Garraway, and indeed the extramarital relationships sustained by masters with slaves and freed women in so many Antillean novels, is entirely displaced, disavowed, and repressed. The novel's only Black female character is the faithful servant Nemorine, a much less fully drawn (and less intellectually gifted) character than her coworker Abder, and interracial relationships are otherwise notable for their absence. Effaced from the diegesis, they are similarly absent from the narrator's otherwise extensive reflections on the new political reality faced by the Antilles. This repression points to a libidinal dynamic that can only originate in the psychosexual dynamics of the plantation. We saw in our second chapter the extent to which *Black* femininity had to be rendered abject by the anxious male narrators and (white) authors of *Les créoles* and *Outre-mer*, in order to neutralize the threat posed to the white male values at the heart of the plantocracy.[45] The portrayal of white femininity in *Frères volcans*, while overwhelmingly negative, is less strikingly abject than the depictions of Black women in the earlier novels. Vive, like the few other white women depicted, is not associated with savagery or primitiveness, for example, nor is she depicted in anatomically hideous terms. And yet the attempt in all these novels, by Black and white male writers, on the one hand to contain and marginalize women, and on the other to stress the barren, profoundly unregenerative nature of Creole society, suggests that *Frères volcans*, set only thirteen years after the novels of Maynard and Levilloux (and all but referencing them explicitly in the allusion to 1835), resonates with many of the concerns discussed in these earlier texts, and yet significantly departs from them. Specifically, although the novel shares earlier novels' concern with white male power, control, virility, legitimacy, and sustainability, it spectacularly occludes the transgressive intercaste sexual relationships that they foreground.

The narrator's homosocial relationships are prominent in the novel: the only "intimacy" that he experiences is with his servant Abder (112), who, in his subtle grasp of revolutionary politics and in his (somewhat anachronistic) references to Black nationhood, is presented as a political visionary, a "Niger Phlegmaticus" (50) greatly admired by the narrator. His friendship with his physician, Raff, occupies similarly generous narrative space. Nonetheless, the narrator is unambiguously presented as heterosexual. And in this respect the longing for Black language that so preoccupies the narrator throughout the novel expresses a fantasy of desire that acts as a screen for a much more profound desire, for blackness itself. The narrator's fixation on the (oral) language of blackness is a metonymy for a desire that cannot speak its name. The energy and plenitude of blackspeak is specifically rewarded with life, energy, and vitality, while Creoles live a "slow death" (45) and suffer from a "mal de vivre" (47), a generalized condition that bespeaks the sexual deficit at the heart of the novel (it is also, surely, a *mal de Vive* and her ilk). Self-disgust is further channeled through the repeated emphasis on the debasement and sterility of white Creole literature, which is dismissed as mimetic, uncreative, endlessly reproducing the same, rather than being open to and energized by the new.

It is surely ironic, then, that for all the insistence on the relationship between "nous" and "les nègres," and for all the rhetoric around the need to embrace the other, there are so few characters, at the diegetic level, crossing the color line, even in their imagination. When they do, moreover, their behavior is presented as highly transgressive, and is rewarded with punishment, even catastrophe. In the opening pages of the novel a drunk male, Léonce, interrupts a dinner party in honor of the Epiphany, insulting the white Creole host. The latter says that he would challenge the intruder to a duel but "will not dip his sword in mulatto blood." Léonce responds in Creole, invokes the French Revolution as heralding the end of the plantocracy, and is ejected from the party declaring "Nou caye pété yo" (our houses are not for them, 19), a retort that rather eerily prefigures the mantra mobilized by the Liaynnaj kont pwofitasyon (Anti-exploitation League) during the 2009 strikes, "La Guadeloupe cé pa ta yo" (see my conclusion for further discussion of these events). And yet what appears to be a confrontation between the white and the mixed-race castes is revealed by the narrator to be an internal standoff between two white Creoles—Léonce is in fact a *béké*. The narrator wonders why the colony rejects as a mulatto the son of a rich planter family fallen on hard times (18–19), Léonce's real name being Alexis-Louis de Préville. In order to maintain their stranglehold, the novel makes clear that white elites banish those who threaten their survival on *both* economic and racial grounds. And toward the end of the novel the much-derided poet Villiers is killed in a duel with another white Creole for having injected his poetry with "negro color" (103)—a canny literary move, perhaps, given the inadequacy of his verse, but one that leads to his annihilation.

If it is the prerogative of the caste to exclude white sons fallen on hard times—their poverty threatening to dilute the capital concentrated in white hands—the plantocracy will equally not tolerate proximity with, or boundary-crossing into, blackness, even (or perhaps especially) in the imaginary space of literature. In other words, the boundaries policed by the white Creole plantocracy are not exclusively, or even primarily, racial, but encompass the economic and even the cultural.

Watson concludes her study of the US white-life novel by drawing on a theoretical concept elaborated in the Caribbean, creolization. She states that "creolized" aptly describes a "radical white subjectivity that is willing to embrace the darkness within itself as a metaphor for the internalization of [the] oppositional black gaze." This vantage point would mean that "traditional performances of Whiteness" could be estranged, and a "critical white double consciousness" developed. Embracing this gaze, she suggests, "could lead to an interracial healing that has long eluded us."[46] This is a view with which *Frères volcans,* in its prolonged theorizations of race and explicit criticisms of whiteness, and in its closing scene of complicity between master and ex-slave, would appear to be in sympathy. But theories of race are, in Robert Young's oft-quoted statement, "covert theories of desire."[47] Placoly's novel, in playing off Black language against white, and in repeatedly asserting the inadequacy and moral bankruptcy of white women, displaces a more profound anxiety. The narrator only once describes the degeneration of Creole society as specifically "racial," noting the need for a future generation that would inject "new blood" in the circulation of property and observing that "progress and *métissage* can loosen the yoke of class superiority" (47–49). He thus projects racial mixing and intercaste sexual relationships into an unidentified future, directly connecting them to the outworkings of Abolition. The use of the conditional mood ("une génération qui assumerait [et qui] injecterait un sang neuf [et qui] abolirait l'esclavage," 49) is a markedly more open-ended and hesitant temporal marker than the concrete certainty of the future tense, itself a spectacularly inappropriate tense to describe a pervasive reality that is already, in the present-day of the novel, of long historical standing. The reader knows racial mixing to be a phenomenon as old as the plantocracy itself, one that occupies the diegetic core of the 1835 novels that the narrator is, presumably, in the process of rebinding, and that it is itself a key trigger for the events at the core of the present novel. This single reference to *métissage* is therefore an act of profound and quite startling discursive disavowal and self-delusion, which mirrors the diegetic absence of any such threat to the clean white lines of the plantocracy. Indeed, the inert old men and frustrated white women of the plantocracy embody a crisis of desire according to which we might reinterpret the novel's title. The volcano, rich with local significance for a novel set in the shadow of Mount Pelée, is often a symbol of male phallic power and the capacity for sexual eruption. Here, however, its eruption can be seen to symbolize what one critic, writing in another context, describes as "the erosion of the political and economic power of the island's white elite."[48] Moreover, its force is sublimated into a fraternal rather than heterosexual mode, an entirely appropriate recasting for such a sexually dormant and inhibited novel.

Placoly's narrator at one point observes that "we become fearful when once familiar things become strange, when our perception is confronted with the other side of the objects of our world" (26). *Frères volcans* is undoubtedly a "disconcerting" text for the reader, generically and diegetically,[49] a work in which familiar things are indeed made strange, and in which the story of the "other side" is so remarkably absorbed into the narrative of the (Black) writer/historian. If it has, according to Britton, a "calmer tone and a clearer structure" than Placoly's other novels, characterized as they were by "obscure references" and "surreal and chaotic" speech,[50] *Frères volcans* remains, as Seguin-Cadiche claims, "an experimental and difficult novel," which "has generated populist critiques that fundamentally misunderstand the author's intention."[51] The instability and claustrophobia of narrative voice, the antiquated linguistic register, the extended philosophical passages, as well as the "dryness of tone" and "lack of warmth and vigor" of *Frères volcans* (reasons for its rejection by Seuil, as we saw above)[52] make for a challenging read;[53] because of its heightened introspection, and its explicit disregard for historical or biographical "episodes," it might be better termed a "white mind" rather than a "white-life" novel. But the profound self-absorption of this white mind shows the protagonist to be frequently detached not just from blackness, but also from whiteness. Declaring, as we saw in our opening epigraph, that he is a "not a prisoner of any race," a fact that he thinks redeems him, he can be seen to be imprisoned instead in an entirely solipsistic worldview. Conversely, the impulse toward the other, and the ability to see "a face not so different to my own," suggest the desire for transcendence—of his caste, of language, and even of the self.

The protagonist is, then, a contradictory and in many respects a sympathetic narrator, an "honest man" who, as one critic puts it, gains the reader's esteem through his "desire for objectivity, his sensitive and fair judgment."[54] But the impulse toward the other that characterizes the narrator's relationship with blackness is entirely absent in the portrayal of the white male's "other" other, femininity. The anxiety around white femininity means that the diarist cannot be read in purely progressive or liberal terms, and that the reader's esteem is often in flux, so that empathy goes hand in hand with estrangement. In the excess with which femininity is treated, one might, for example, be able to read the imprint of authorial irony, given the fact that Vive is a knowledgeable, energetic, and sympathetic foil to most of the male characters. Similarly, the little space devoted to her death could be seen to register the emotional as well as sexual repression of the narrator. But the slippery and highly ambivalent relationship between author, frame narrator, and diarist undoubtedly complicates our reading of the novel. Critics, who have generally remained silent on the presentation of sex and desire in the text, have tended, too readily perhaps, to conflate the voices of frame narrator-historian and author. And yet the frame narrative, short as it is relative to the diary, reinforces rather than troubles the treatment of women in the diary. It is perhaps understandable, given the diary's historical setting in 1848, that women authors are entirely excluded from the heavy freight of intertextual reference; but the late twentieth-century frame narrative, which finds space for Hugo, Césaire, Hearn, Schœlcher, Voltaire, Zola, Gauguin, Sartre, Fanon, and Robert Peel (to whom is given the penultimate, and highly ironic, line, "the white race is incontestably the sole barrier against the invasion of barbary in the colonies," 126), names not a single female author or political figure. In his only reference to female writers, the frame historian describes their output as "hot air from women overheated by the humidity of the tropics" (11), perfectly replicating the dismissive view of the diarist regarding woman's potential for cultural activity. In this sense the novel appears to share ideological space with the *créolité* writers, who would emerge on the Antillean literary scene in the years following the publication of *Frères volcans*. Lorna Milne has argued that "the Creolist writer, in order to assert a masculinity threatened by colonialism, is still bound to a masculinist aesthetics which necessarily casts his literary 'forefather'—the *conteur*—and all his descendants as male."[55] The privileged and mutually validating relationship between author, historian, and diarist, as well as the density of intertextual reference to exclusively male writers, and the diegetic treatment of women characters (both Black and white females are shunned), places male creativity at the core of narrative, and entirely dismisses not only the possibility of biological reproduction, but also of female cultural production. The priapic excesses of the (Black) male heroes of *créolité* are dramatically absent from this novel; but its protagonist embodies, despite (or perhaps because of) his extensive theorizations of race and gender, an equally questionable version of masculinity.

5 "Here, It's Black or White"

Marie-Reine de Jaham's *La grande béké* and the Unbearable Whiteness of Being

> Anything that reminds us of slavery is taboo. And everything reminds us of slavery.
>
> —Marie-Reine de Jaham, *La grande béké*

As I argued in the introduction to this study, the white Creole population has remained, with some notable exceptions, culturally reticent, and at times entirely inaudible, in the wake of the abolition of slavery. The collapse of the economic and ideological system on which the colonists depended ensured that the concerns of white Creoles quickly came to appear highly anachronistic and reactionary, not to say politically incorrect. The short-lived cultural efflorescence of the early nineteenth century discussed in the first two chapters of this book, which saw, in addition to the publication of the white Creole-authored novels discussed earlier, the founding of important periodicals and journals, was curtailed by history, and had little momentum and a very limited cultural afterlife. Small wonder that by the 1840s we witness such a striking reduction in the number of texts published by a group faced with much more pressing challenges. But the shrinking of cultural production is most noticeable in the second half of the twentieth century, a period in which *békés* found themselves conspicuously on the wrong side of history, notably with regard to the Vichy regime. David Macey describes *béké* enthusiasm for Vichy, which is discussed in more detail in relation to Guy Cabort-Masson's *Qui a tué le béké de Trinité?* in my next chapter, as a "final planter revolt intended to seize back the political power that had gradually been acquired by the black-mulatto middle class,"[1] while decolonization, the dominant political movement of the 1960s, further destabilized the plantocracy. Reluctant to raise their heads above the parapet for fear of drawing further attention to the egregious iniquities of their privilege in the post- and even neocolonial world they now inhabited, *békés* retreated into their gated residences, preferring coastal locations (the Békéland of Raphaël Confiant's title, also discussed in the next chapter) to the more central urban settings of Saint-Pierre and, later, the Route Didier in Fort-de-France. This second half of the twentieth century coincides also with the extraordinary efflorescence in Black writing, a literature that played a significant role in heightening Antillean political consciousness, notably regarding slavery and the continuing privilege of the *béké* caste.

It is surely no exaggeration, then, to claim that *béké* writing in the late twentieth century has been almost exclusively associated with, and channeled through, a single literary voice, that of Martinique-born novelist Marie-Reine de Jaham (1940–).[2] Jaham, who grew up in Saint-Pierre before moving to the United States and then France, authored ten novels between 1989 and 2007, all set in the Antilles, as well as a number of Creole recipe books. She also founded the cultural association Patrimoine créole (Creole heritage) in Paris in 1993, and the Cercle Méditerranée Caraïbe, which aimed to explore links between the Mediterranean and the Caribbean, in Nice in 2002. In a context of almost blanket cultural invisibility, she, like her relative by marriage Roger de Jaham, quickly acquired an iconic, if double-edged, status: both have a background in advertising and seamlessly transitioned into cultural activism, becoming spokespeople for, and insider-critics of, their community. This dual position is reflected in the local reception of her work. *Antilla,* for example, devoted its front cover to the release of her first novel, *La grande béké,* with the headline "Scandalous Book. When a *Béké* Judges Her Fellow *Békés,*"[3] and Raphaël Confiant recounts elsewhere that she was "boycotted" by other members of her caste during her "brief stay" in Martinique in the wake of the novel's appearance.[4] Yet she has been conspicuously packaged and received in terms of (colonial) authenticity and representativity, in other words as a writer who speaks for, and whose work offers privileged firsthand access to, her caste more generally. In this sense Jaham's authorial image, channeled through her public interventions and mediated via the marketing of her novels as well as in her journalistic and critical reception, mirrors that of the postcolonial (subaltern) author who, as Nicholas Harrison has shown, is routinely seen to be both a "representative" type and as attempting to "represent" his/her people.[5]

This representativity is a function of both textual and paratextual features. The titles of early novels (*La grande béké; Le maître-savane*) name an entire caste as well as an individual protagonist. Meanwhile the publisher's blurb stresses biographical continuity between author and protagonist ("like her heroine, Marie-Reine de Jaham is a *béké*: a descendent of those French colonizers who settled in Martinique from the fifteenth century onward"), while the author herself also plays up the commonalities between the life of fictional heroines and her own biography.[6] Her debut novel, a first-person narrative told by an elderly Creole woman, is dedicated to "all the Grand Békés who have existed or who will exist in the future" (7). Such editorial and authorial gestures have been replicated in the journalistic domain. An article published in *Antilla* in May 1989 to mark the release of *La grande béké* reinforces Jaham's representative status: the novel's cover, featuring a blue-eyed, slender-nosed white female face superimposed on a recognizably Caribbean backdrop, is juxtaposed with photographs of Suzanne Dracius and French author Catherine Lépront, while the article in question, by Confiant, characterizes the work of these three authors as, respectively, colonial, diasporic, and exoticist. The French newspaper *Le Monde,* a year later, mobilizes the Martinican author's image to similar, equally representative, effect: her photograph is carefully positioned between that of Aimé Césaire and Suzanne Dracius, in a triptych unmistakably representing white, Black, and *métisse* Martinicans.[7] Meanwhile in a second (not unsympathetic) account of the novel Confiant, who in 2013 would himself explore this "most secret of worlds," devoting a crime novel to the shady world of *béké* corruption (discussed in chapter 6), urges the Antillean public to read the novel on the basis that it "reveals what *békés* think of us and brings us right into the closed world of our former masters, unveiling their collective unconscious."[8] Even Benjamin Ngong, who is otherwise highly critical of her approach, reads Jaham's emergence as a moment of "breaking the silence,"[9] again suggesting that she speaks for her otherwise voiceless caste, and inverting, presumably unintentionally, the "coming to voice" trajectories of subaltern or marginalized subjects, and notably writers from colonial contexts, as they began to express themselves in literature.

Jaham's popular and populist novels—Confiant notes that *La grande béké* "flew off the shelves" of Fort-de-France's bookshops,[10] and her novels have routinely gone through multiple print runs—occupy a markedly different space in the cultural sphere to any of the fiction that we have thus far examined. Her work has been compared to television soap operas such as *Dallas* and *Dynasty* (Jaham was resident in the United States when these series were at the height of their popularity), with sugar rather than oil providing the economic impetus for the plot. Chris Bongie has described Jaham as "the Jackie Collins of Franco-Caribbean historical fiction,"[11] arguing that she, along with a writer such as Tony Delsham, is received and packaged as part of the postcolonial "low brow," as the author of "page turners" rather than aesthetically resistant (Glissant) or postcolonial middle-brow (Condé) novels (although the locally published

Delsham is presumably more dependent on a local Antillean readership than Jaham, published by mainstream French publishers). Like the US soap operas mentioned above, the novel's overarching thematic preoccupations are with blood, genes, legitimacy, inheritance, and inter- and intra-clan warfare. But Jaham's writing is arguably misrepresented in some of these appraisals; her fiction, and notably her historical trilogy, is well-researched, often supplemented by maps, references, and glossaries, and firmly located in, and informative about, its various historical contexts. And while plot devices such as the cliff-hanger and intergenerational clan warfare are indeed, as in soap opera, structuring motifs in her fiction, her novels are not especially concerned with sex; in this respect her fiction is far removed from the "bonkbuster" genre so closely associated with Collins, Danielle Steel, and others, and similarly diverges from the American soap genre in this respect.

Whatever nuances exist in plotting and characterization, however, it is hard to disagree with A. James Arnold's criticism that Jaham's writing recycles "the most hackneyed clichés of empire,"[12] nor with Bongie's view that her novels rehearse "many of the ideological assumptions of nineteenth-century 'creolist discourse,' redeploying any number of long-established clichés (both positive and negative) about Martinique," and emphasize "the central role of her people, the *békés*, in shaping the island's history."[13] And it is certainly true that Jaham, although often critical of the excesses of *béké* behavior, is generally an apologist for her caste. As Ngong observes, a novel such as *Le sang du volcan* is "outrageously negligent of the subject of slavery, even if this operates as a backdrop to the story." This novel, as he argues, includes over 150 characters (including a dizzying array of historical figures), of whom only eleven are Black.[14] For Pierre Pinalie-Dracius, meanwhile, the author remains unforgivably "closed to historical reason" in seeming to absolve her caste for the ills of slavery.[15] Her fiction is shot through with nostalgia for slavery, and foregrounds progressive and tenacious, if not always sympathetic, white Creoles. This explains, for example, why the eruption of Mount Pelée in 1902, which destroyed the town of Saint-Pierre, citadel of *béké* culture, looms so large in her fiction.[16] Jaham's plucky Creole protagonists often find themselves in opposition to the "dinosaurs" of the past, engaging in a struggle for the modernization and liberalization of the Antillean economy.

The combination of questionable literary style and dubious ideological credentials has ensured that Jaham has been, with the exception of the small number of analyses mentioned, almost systematically excluded by scholars of Caribbean writing. Her absence, as argued in my introduction, is most conspicuous in studies that focus on Antillean women writers, many of which take as a starting point the male-centeredness of the Antillean literary tradition. In a context in which, despite its stylistic and ideological shortcomings, early Creole fiction (which is generally much less readable than Jaham's "page turners") is receiving serious critical attention, the extent of her neglect is perhaps surprising. Jaham's role and unique status as modern-day *porte parole* for her caste make her a necessary and significant inclusion in this book. But she is, moreover, also crucial because of the gendered perspective that she brings to bear on modern Creole society. Whatever the ideological thrust of her fiction in terms of racial politics, and however nostalgic her fiction might be for the plantation, all of Jaham's novels foreground female experience: from the eponymous (anti)heroine of *La grande béké* (1989); to the legendary ancestor of the Solis clan, Anna Akwaba in *L'or des îles* (1996); or the privileged protagonists of *Le sang du volcan,* Charlotte and Phoebe, who manage the plantations; and even a youthful Joséphine de Beauharnais, famously an ancestor of the author, presented in the novel's opening chapter as a questioning proto-feminist. *Bwa Bandé,* a crime novel set in Saint-Martin, features a female anthropologist-investigator as well as a female murderer, Mama Love, a voodoo priestess. In contrast to the paternalistic patriarchs who people so many of the novels that we have thus far examined, and in marked distinction to the white mistresses imagined by other Antillean writers, fading half-presences who haunt rather than inhabit much male-authored Antillean fiction, this is a fictional world in which white women hold significant diegetic weight and wield considerable power.

This chapter concentrates on Jaham's first novel, *La grande béké* (1989), a *succès de scandale* that quickly generated five editions, and garnered significant journalistic, if not strictly critical, attention in the Antilles and in metropolitan France.[17] The novel is of particular interest because of the way it perpetuates, but also nuances and at times radically revises, many of the tropes associated with white Creole writers with regard to gender and race. For example, in its unsympathetic and often callous heroine, Fleur, it radically rewrites the script of white femininity. Moreover, Jaham appears at several points to debunk the foundational and self-sustaining myth that *békés* are descended from nobility, a common reference point in the fiction we have examined thus far. Fleur insists rather on the fact that "the blood of cavaliers and buccaneers" runs through her veins (17, 232). And yet elsewhere, and precisely at the moments when landowners come into contact with the white commercial class ("cod merchants, *petits blancs* from the bottom of the pile," "en bas feuille," 172), this hybridity (an exclusively white-on-white hybridity) is denied. When the *internal* caste hierarchies of the plantocracy appear to be put under pressure, the "aristocratic origins" of the caste are reasserted (172). Rather than celebrating the coming together of cavalier and buccaneer, the novel romanticizes lines of ancient noble planters through its loving litanies of *béké* names (de Poincy; Ducasse; Bélain d'Esnambuc), recalling the consolatory gestures of early fiction, in order to lament the erosion of a system in which such *grands békés* held a clearly demarcated position *within* their own caste: "Somewhere along the line, the thread broke. We became bastardized and true decadence ensued" (83). Within the novel's set of caste-based hierarchies, then, the titular adjective "grand" in the worldview of the author and her characters is almost as significant as the noun it qualifies—one of the reasons for her hatred of Lorigny, her archrival, is his inferior merchant status—and functions as a legitimizing byword for ancient planter stock. The "bastardization" that Fleur laments is the mixing of *grands békés* with lower-class whites; the lip service paid to difference, alterity, and hybridity is merely an alibi, not only for (white European) sameness, but indeed for a highly rarefied kind of whiteness, in which difference cannot be accommodated, but represents rather disintegration and degeneration. Therefore the inestimably greater threat of racial difference has to be kept in check, in remarkably atavistic ways, in *La grande béké*.

Jaham's first novel is set squarely in the period of decolonization (May 1965) and reflects the especially acute sense of political insecurity experienced by the Antillean plantocracy as global colonial empires disintegrated. Algeria, in particular, looms large in the novel as an ominous postcolonial reference point, occupying an analogous structural position to Haiti in white Creole fiction of the early nineteenth century. Mickey, the novel's hero, served as a paratrooper there, while Fleur's son goads his mother with the example of Algeria, cautioning that France will let its overseas departments go, and predicting that the first political reform will be the redistribution of land, the most sensitive, and deeply resisted, of all political reforms in the Antilles. The fate of the *pieds noirs* serves as a warning to whites more generally. Such reflections lend a particularly anxious tenor to the familiar rhetorical signatures of colonial nostalgia and despair, so prevalent even in early Creole fiction, and add an especially pressing sense of historical legitimacy to the (perennial) view that the plantation system is coming to an end. Fleur's plantation is described as "disintegrating," like time itself (15), and the elderly protagonist reminds herself, in a typical self-address that foregrounds her caste status, that "Béké, you are dust and unto dust you shall return" (15).

Fleur declares early in the novel that "I am the plantation" (14), and is shown to embody *béké* society generally: the heart attacks she suffers in the course of the novel are clearly to be read, like the organ failure of Placoly's narrator in *Frères volcans*, as a synecdoche of the state of her caste more generally. The only daughter of the island's richest planter, Fleur is Martinique's most important landowner; she owns one-fifth of the island, acquired by mostly foul means between the 1902 volcano that wiped out her family and the diegetic present of the novel. In her old age she contrives, through a series of elaborate and manipulative moves, to disinherit her children, in part because of her barely concealed revulsion for them, and in part because she wishes to secure the future of the island's economy by founding a cooperative trust, in which all sectors of society will (appear to) have a stake. Her grasping, untrustworthy children (all are inept or dishonest businesspeople) wish to wrest control of the plantation from her, and to inherit her vast holdings. Fleur thwarts their avarice by bequeathing her land to her metropolitan grandson, Mickey, the son of Fleur's son Raoul, conceived with her long-deceased American lover Duke. Mickey, whom she has never met, is a cocky seventeen-year-old who was brought up in the Parisian suburbs. He predictably takes time to adapt to his new environment, eventually proving his mettle with laborers, managers, and union representatives. He also overcomes his grandmother's opposition to his romance with Camilla, also newly arrived and identified, initially and erroneously, as the granddaughter of Fleur's archrival, and in her view, inferior, Lorigny, only to be revealed as an almost equally unsuitable (in Fleur's eyes) jobbing actress and dancer. By the novel's end Mickey has assumed control of the plantation and is poised to marry Camilla, while the eponymous heroine, in an anachronistic and unbelievable denouement, enters the convent in which her saintly cousin and erstwhile love rival, Marie-Hélène, has lived as a nun since her rejection by Fleur's husband Robert.

The novel opens and closes in two symbolically charged spaces, the bedroom and the convent respectively. Fleur's bedroom is the novel's dominant location. Analogous to the boardroom so privileged in 1980s soap opera, this is the room in which most of Fleur's shady deals are conducted. Although it is a highly feminized theater, it is not a site of sexual, or even emotional, intimacy.[18] It is a space entirely saturated in whiteness: indeed, the room is presented as a *mise en abyme* of the white face, its two windows compared to lidless eyes that perpetually survey the now dormant volcano that had wrought such devastation on the previous generation (16). Elsewhere, "the walls are white [. . .] the bedspread made from a heavy white lace [. . .]. White too is the raw silk that covers the divan, as well as the cushion that sits on the English chair at my dressing table," a table covered in ivory-handled hairbrushes (16). But this conspicuous whiteness is a contrived one, the result of careful interior design and, for all that Fleur insists on the simplicity of her bedroom, it is the result of the acquisition of luxury commodities and accoutrements. The insistence on whiteness within the overall economy of the novel clearly does not, cannot, connote virtue, innocence, or purity. Fleur is a ruthless and Machiavellian character, her "rich bitch" machinations recalling the unscrupulous, and often criminal, activities of a villainous antiheroine such as Alexis Colby of *Dynasty*. She has, for example, taken advantage of the wholesale obliteration of documents in the wake of the 1902 volcano to redraw (in other words, expand) the boundaries of her holdings, and bribes officials to ensure her preferential treatment in land deals. She goes so far as to have the founder of the Crédit Antillais, Maurice Hazart, assassinated when her credit dries up. Her sexual relationships, with one notable exception (she still mourns Duke, Mickey's grandfather and her only true love) are motivated by greed rather than love: she has an affair with a geologist in order to learn about the risks posed by the mountain, and she seduces, marries, and is repeatedly unfaithful to, her cousin's fiancé, Robert Mase de la Joucquerie, out of financial self-interest. Even Fleur's emotional responses, which are often coded as white—she "blanches" in fury (387), her voice is described as being "white" with anger (117, 173, 188), and at other times she succumbs to a "white rage" (387)—conspicuously reject the conventional association of whiteness with piety, innocence, and benevolence.

If the commodities with which Fleur surrounds herself (silk, ivory, lace) are self-conscious markers of caste rather than virtue, whiteness and its associated iconography is also mobilized to conceal and deceive rather than to reveal. In her bedroom, for example, a heavy white curtain hides a secret door, which facilitates her Machiavellian plotting: it allows her to receive her informants in secrecy, and provides an escape route for the bankers, politicians, and, presumably in the past, lovers, who visit her clandestinely. The two portraits that hang above Fleur's bed (one of her parents, painted from the only photograph of them to survive the volcano, a second of the protagonist herself) are inauthentic, even phony, projections. The paintings form part of the visual apparatus of white power around which the novel is structured, and play on the interrelated clichés of whiteness and mastery. Frequently, as we saw in the fiction of Maynard and Chamoiseau, these ancestral images are used in fiction to suggest the dominance and superiority of the painted subject, in order to accentuate the debasement of the colonial present and the inadequacy of the planter's descendants. But in this novel, the images are highly contrived fictions. The first is a heavily doctored and unsatisfactory likeness. At Fleur's instruction, the painter has removed the baby in baptismal robes (Fleur) who had been at the center of the original sepia-toned photograph, an excision that registers not only the protagonist's lack of sentiment and nostalgia, but also her rejection of the pristine innocence symbolized by white baptismal robes. Although repainted ten times, the final version does not do justice to the "violence," "appetite," and "mocking attitude" (17) of the white patriarch's smile, all presented as quintessential planter qualities by the narrator. The second is a posed portrait expressly conceived by its commissioner to play on the visual clichés of white mastery, and to communicate a sense of power and femininity. Fleur's highly stylized portrait is an exercise in self construction, a clichéd white Creole pose that accentuates the potential for brutality (she holds the totemic "riding crop with an ebony knob," 17), but also the conventional markers of white femininity (her "nose is small, and the skin is smooth as polished ivory," 17).

In both her emotional reactions and in her physical environment, then, Fleur's conspicuous whiteness is spectacularly detached from any sense of piety, Christianity, goodness, nature, or virtue. Instead the convent, and in particular the figure of Marie-Hélène, are associated with a simpler, less manufactured whiteness, one more directly imbued with selflessness and virtue. The convent is peopled by "white troops of nuns" (218) and "white silhouettes" (220), images in which whiteness is not associated with lavish accoutrements, and where any sense of individualism is subdued to the collective. The saintly Marie-Hélène acts as a loving and forgiving foil to Fleur, becoming, despite the latter's treachery, her closest confidante. Marie-Hélène's whiteness is associated with natural features (the white hibiscus, 221; unrefined white cotton, 384) whose simplicity stands in stark contrast to the linen, ivory, and lace of the *grand béké*'s room. Moreover, the nun's ethereal and spiritual qualities are emphasized: she is "diaphanous" and "radiant" (384). Named for two culturally loaded versions of whiteness, the Christian and the classical (the mother of Jesus, synonymous with virtue, and the heroine of Greek myth, synonymous with beauty), Marie-Hélène thus occupies, according to a familiar virgin/whore, saint/sinner dichotomy, the position of the conventionally "white" female.

If Fleur's whiteness is a contrived and materialistic image that serves to undermine rather than bolster any claims to innocence or purity, it functions in another, much more problematic way too, that is, as a foil to a repertoire of crudely drawn versions of blackness. Throughout this novel, there is an obsessive, even grotesque or abject, quality in the depiction of Black bodies, depictions that very often overlook the Black face (thereby deindividualizing the nonwhite population) in order to focus on limbs, hands, and feet, and that run the gamut of racist stereotypes. Typical of this is the portrayal of the anonymous market seller, whose "huge quivering mass" and arms "the size of hams" (174–75) embrace the *béké* in gratitude for her commitment to renewing the island economy; the Black woman is unindividualized but outsized, animalistic but pathetically grateful. Meanwhile the island's taxis are "overflowing with blacks" (234). But it is specifically in the portrayal of Fleur's workers that this problematic, and indeed highly anachronistic, reproduction of racist tropes is mobilized. Blacks are repeatedly deindividualized in a series of crowd scenes that pit Fleur and Mickey against them ("Les Noirs" move as a group in such moments, at one point opposing Fleur with "a stone face," 143) and in which white intelligence systematically wins out. Moreover, the physical brutality of the plantation is only sporadically acknowledged, and is inscribed, as in other plantation novels such as *La rue cases-nègres* and *De nègres et de békés,* on laborers' feet. Da Eudèse suffers from the elephantiasis so ubiquitous in the Caribbean novel, Arsène has lost toes in an industrial accident and has had half his foot cut off by coworkers to save his life (150, 213), while Roger's misshapen toes are "spread like a fan" (212) as a result of decades of toil. But these injuries and deformities, despite their grotesque nature, never prevent the workers from resuming work, a double gesture of containment: the injury is confined to the corporeal extremities, and the compliant victims return happily to the Big House and the factory.

Two characters are described in particular physical detail, Marcel (Fleur's godson, the treacherous son of her loyal servant Roger) and Eudèse, both of whom routinely interact with Fleur in the gleaming space of her bedroom. This space, as well as being, as we saw above, a contrived repository of caste identity, also acts as an enabling location for the prolific production of racially loaded images, continually reinforcing the Black/white binary around which the novel turns. In the novel's opening,[19] Eudèse is presented in a profoundly stereotyped way that recalls the mammy of US fiction and film, the "jolly, fat, black woman who works as a nanny, cook, or housekeeper [. . .] for a white family to whom she is devoted." This "fantasied" figure "accepts her condition of servitude absolutely."[20] The sixty-year-old complicity that exists between *da* and mistress is devoid of any racial or intercaste tension, suggesting rather an unchanging and benign plantocracy. Much as Marie-Hélène acts as a *moral* foil for Fleur, Eudèse acts as the necessary *racial* counterpart who guarantees her mistress's whiteness. Blackness is, therefore, entirely at the service of whiteness, both diegetically and discursively.

The novel's opening, like the famous first scene of *Gone with the Wind* (1939),[21] establishes some of the clichés associated with Black female servitude: Eudèse's girth, her swollen legs, and enormous bosom are emphasized. As Maria St.-John has argued in relation to the 1939 film, "wherever she appears, Mammy is big,"[22] and associated with darkness, earthiness, and fleshiness. Indeed, in the film's first scene "Mammy fills up, indeed extends beyond, the window frame," suggesting that "the filmic frame will prove too narrow to contain her."[23] So too Eudèse's "enormous frame blocks out the light" (12) in the novel's opening, a scene that already associates the blackness of even the devoted Eudèse with a dangerous capacity to engulf whiteness. Black plumpness stands in stark contrast to the shrunken physique of the white woman, an "old mummy" (19) rather than a "mammy," whose withered sexual organs (she tells us repeatedly that her breasts and thighs have been "emptied out") register old age, exhaustion, and asexuality. Both are octogenarians: there is therefore no suggestion that Eudèse has suckled her white mistress. But she is primarily associated with orality (food and gossip) and corporeality (the breast and the bodily realm generally), and with attempts to feed, or more commonly, to make Fleur drink. Eudèse's coffee is renowned in the island for its excellence and is the first product she brings to Fleur. The steaming dark liquid, itself a product of slave labor, in an analogy that conjoins stereotypes of race, corpulence, and consumption, is described by the narrator as being "as black as a negress's ass" and is drunk by the gaunt white woman from a porcelain cup described as "tiny" and "fine" (13).

This opening episode, in its multiple contrasts (Black obesity and white emaciation; ivory and ebony; coffee and porcelain) sets the scene for a story that, to a remarkable extent given its date of publication and its historical setting, and despite the fact that many of the characters are deemed to be of mixed race, revolves around an entirely polarized, and highly simplifying, version of "blackness" and "whiteness," a point to which we return below. Indeed as St.-John argues with regard to Mammy, "she is big across time as well as space" because hers "is the face of timelessness."[24] Like Mammy, Eudèse is one of the most persistent stereotypes of Black femininity in the white imagination, and her transfer to the small screen only reinforced the clichés (cheerful servitude, unwavering loyalty, enormous girth) associated with this role.

The portrayal of Marcel, an untrustworthy mulatto who is in cahoots with Lorigny, while also emphasizing physical enormity, has a markedly different tenor. On his first appearance the *béké* notes that he has put on an inordinate amount of weight ("il a démesurément grossi," 58) and elsewhere his corpulence, barely contained by his clothing, is described in grotesque terms. His "obscenely enormous thighs" (93, 261) and knees (359) strain against his too tight trousers. He is frequently seen sweating. In a rare, and highly loaded, description of the Black face, his "little" eyes are "drowned in fat" (58), and later he has the "big fat face of a baby, trembling like jelly" (359). In such descriptions, Marcel is reduced to what Marcus Wood calls the "lumpen stereotype" of slave depictions,[25] compared to a sumo wrestler (261) and a "big heap" (367). These excessive portrayals convey a revulsion that is absent from depictions of the caste of happy servants, among whom the only tension is a jockeying for the favor of the white mistress. Marcel, as a disloyal employee working against Fleur to undermine her business, must be violently neutralized at the textual level by descriptions that emphasize both the threat and the disgust represented by Black corporeality.

The emphasis on the outsize dimensions of the Black body, as in US plantation fiction and film, naturalizes the division of domestic labor and the economic, physical, and sexual exploitation of the slave regime. Such a division is reinscribed in the various racist mantras and proverbs that weave through the novel ("a well-to-do black is just a little mango thief sat under the *béké*'s trees," 140; "Black sweat is white wealth," 207), which originated in slavery but continue to speak powerfully to the novel's political status quo. The depiction of Eudèse conforms perfectly to this logic. But in the specific spatial and historical context of Martinique, the extravagant dimensions of the Black body, and in particular its spreading, uncontainable quality (splayed toes, thighs breaking through trousers, Blacks "overflowing" the taxis that transport them) should also be understood as a metaphor for the demography of the island. Repeatedly framing the population as a simple Black/white, *nèg/béké* binary, the protagonist obsessively bemoans the fact that she and her people are swamped by Blacks ("Here there are blacks and *békés*, three hundred thousand blacks and three thousand *békés*," 199) and the novel is punctuated by crowd scenes in which "les noirs" confront Fleur and Mickey. This demographic insignificance, which posed much less of a problem for whites under the secure color lines of the slave regime, has required the *béké* population to move with the times and to make adjustments in the wake of departmentalization. And this explains the particularly venomous depiction of Marcel, who represents a much bigger threat to the plantocracy than the happy servants. In a typical narrative move, whites are constructed as the victims of Black success, and societal change is presented as entirely degrading for the white Creole. Fleur speculates resentfully that Marcel will own a chain of supermarkets in twenty years ("and where will the plantation be?") and marvels at the ease with which ex-slave owners can greet the great-grandsons of the slaves they whipped and tortured as Monsieur the Deputy Mayor or as Monsieur President (82). Meanwhile Fleur claims that in the wake of departmentalization, "the *béké* hushed his voice, lowered his eyes, shrugged his shoulders, dropped his trousers, ready to do whatever necessary to maintain his privileges: money, home, lifestyle. What else can a white minority do, faced with such a crushing majority of blacks?" (83). Such vitriolic, even hysterical, diagnoses, spectacularly incognizant of the foundational degradations of slavery, and willfully ignorant of the ongoing extent of white privilege and Black exploitation, foreground the "siege mentality" and persecution complex of the caste, discussed in early chapters of this monograph, and which remain an enduring strain in contemporary *béké* discourse.[26] The novel treats with particular disdain economically ascendant, or well-to-do Blacks (Marcel and his ilk) and, moreover, projects blame for the disappearance of Creole culture onto a Black population no longer willing to do the *béké*'s bidding. The protagonist wistfully wonders how much longer Creole meals such as the "chou-coco" (a local delicacy, palm heart salad) will be prepared, for example, and laments that it is now impossible to find Blacks who will scale a coconut tree (33). But the threat to Creole culture is, according to the narrator, entirely the fault of the Black population, whose growing sense of injustice and determination to resist the master's command impoverishes society more generally.

The novel's plot is primarily concerned with Fleur's attempts to answer the question posed above: what indeed can the white minority do to protect itself from invasion or contamination by blackness? Her response takes two forms, one political, the other familial, both invested in self-protection and containment. On the one hand her business foundation, conceived as a way to expand the power base of the plantocracy

"*Here, It's Black or White*" 151

and to ensure buy-in from well-to-do non-*békés*, has the appearance of a progressive and forward-thinking initiative. Fleur recognizes the unsustainability of the current business model, in which rum and banana production is propped up by France. Her project is presented to the reader as a pragmatic solution to the multiple economic challenges facing the local economy, and, significantly, women are the first to welcome this solution. But Fleur has ensured that her own self-interest is protected. Her foundation is a cynical solution that will ensure that money stays within the island, bolstering *béké* privilege, benefitting the already privileged Black middle class and neutralizing the threat of an increasingly politicized Black underclass. It is an initiative that seeks to concentrate and contain wealth rather than opening economic opportunity up more widely.

The second, and diegetically, more significant solution that Fleur engineers is a familial one. In striking contrast to so many other fictional *békés* who are haunted by being the last in their line, and for whom the possibilities for regeneration have been stifled, Fleur has five children (including Raoul, Mickey's father, named for Fleur's beloved father, and who was killed in World War II) and counts 112 descendants. Rather than providing comfort or security, however, this numerous progeny inspires anxiety and, more often, disgust. Within the affective economy of the novel, it is Fleur's revulsion toward her own (legitimate) children, rather than her overt racism or even her wicked deeds, that most radically rewrites the script of white Creole femininity, vested in notions of virtue and maternity. Fleur is strikingly devoid of maternal instinct, variously referring to her children as worms (16, 82), sharks (46), hyenas (47), vultures (83), snakes (154), and parasites (203), and ridiculing them savagely. She is, for example, disgusted by the "fat woman sweat" of her daughter Elsa (45), whom she describes as "a bag of lard dripping with bonhomie" (46). While Fleur is bedecked in Chanel, she compares her children to provincials in their Sunday best (247). And throughout the novel, the metaphor of the "cuvée pervertie," the infected or perverted vat or barrel (32, 47, 48, 75, 150, 178, 334, 357) is repeatedly mobilized. The metaphor, rooted in the plantation infrastructure, describes the vat of rum ruined by a single drop of inferior alcohol. Fleur's project is to destroy this perverted barrel and, in so doing, to regenerate the family line.

Fleur's solution to the "infected vat" is the introduction of (an at first reluctant) Mickey, whom she hopes will learn about, and then take over, the running of her business. Mickey, whose "foreignness" is registered in his incongruous forename (like that of his grandfather Duke), is transplanted into the organism of the plantation. Fleur repeatedly insists on the fact that he is "new," has a "new eye," and that a "different blood" runs through his veins (35, 245, 246, 239). At one point she uses the analogy of the speck of dust in the oyster shell, a foreign body which is eventually transformed into a pearl (79). In another *mise en abyme* of the familial project, also based on the idea of incorporation of the "other," she uses the horticultural analogy of grafting to describe her attempt to engineer the survival of her plantation and her caste (the two are repeatedly connected by the protagonist). A keen gardener, she eventually and after much effort manages to breed a rare, and extremely beautiful, black orchid, and connects her botanical enterprise explicitly to her attempts to save her caste:

> I sharpen the end of the graft meticulously, taking care to cut cleanly into the stem, then I scrape the bark to expose the plant's flesh. From a clean incision, I make a deep, almost horizontal nick in the creeper chosen to be the host. I watch the white blood of the orchid form with satisfaction. Finally, using a pair of pliers, I seize the graft and stick it into the wound I've just made. [. . .] Look, I've taken this degenerate plant, which couldn't flower, and I've just performed a transplant. An orchid will grow from it. A black orchid, the most beautiful and the rarest of all. [. . .] *Békés* have become like this plant. And for them too, I'm in the process of carrying out a graft. (212–13)

The graft or transplant works on the principle of insertion, incorporation, or contact from an outside organism or body, and compensates for a defect or lack in the host. The passage emphasizes the contrived and manipulated nature of this transplant, the dominance of the first-person pronoun underscoring Fleur's control, as she describes her meticulousness, the clean lines of the horizontal incision, and the carefully chosen "mother" plant. The reader might at first see in the black orchid an (albeit crude) reference to a nonwhite element in, or product of, the graft or transplant, given the extent to which color positions in this deeply shadist society, and especially in *béké* writings, are expressed and reinforced through analogy, metaphor, and association. However, the familial graft is here realized through the imposition of Fleur's illegitimate, but resolutely "white," Parisian grandson. He is only "new" or "other" in one very limited sense—he has had no contact with the plantation or the plantocracy. Thus, the "sang blanc" of the flower could be seen to be the more resonant metaphor for the engineering at work in the text. Strikingly, Mickey's position is not primarily envisaged as husband or familial sire. Rather, his new blood and energy are to be harnessed in labor, administration, and management of the plantation, and eventually, but only secondarily, with a *béké* spouse chosen by Fleur. The novel's follow-up volume, *Le maître-savane,* sees Mickey miserably married to his cousin Irina.

Fleur describes the *béké* family as a "huis clos" (operating behind closed doors—the same expression is used by Placoly to describe the life of Creole women, as we saw in chapter 4) and observes that "you always find a common ancestor somewhere in *béké* families" (79), while another character asks, "aren't we all to a greater or lesser extent cousins?" (294). And yet, surprisingly, this consanguinity is presented in a rather matter-of-fact manner, and the novel is less haunted than many others by the threat of endogamy. Rather, as we saw above, Fleur stresses, although also denies, the inherent "hybridity" of the *béké* caste—hybridity being understood as a fusion of nobleman and buccaneer, in other words as a white-on-white combination. Meanwhile Fleur's repeated references to the perverted, infected, or corrupted vat apparently have nothing to do with inbreeding or endogamy, and refer specifically to her own, individual, "inestimable mistake," that is, marrying into the "cursed" Mase de la Joucquerie clan, over whom a "very heavy heredity" hangs (35). This *béké* family's genetic predisposition to alcoholism and madness aligns them with those "hellish" families "worthy of the Atrides and the Antilles" (35). Generations of the Joucquerie clan have been hidden away in Martinique's principal psychiatric hospital, Colson, while Fleur's first husband was a drunk, and genetically prone to madness and infidelity. In these respects, and in his final immolation (he burns to death in bed, from a lit cigarette, and Fleur, pregnant with Duke's child, is helpless to save him), his fate recalls that of Charlotte Brontë's mad mistress, Bertha Mason, rather than that of the classic planter patriarch, and his depiction notably contrasts with that of Fleur's beloved father. This is why she looks to her own grandson rather than her husband's (Mickey's special status as "love grandchild" is repeatedly mentioned).

By the novel's end, the Mase de la Joucquerie dynasty has survived; what has not been contemplated on the narrative register, however, is any form of intercaste union with local "Black" Martinicans. This Black population, at the novel's end as at its beginning, occupies universally subaltern positions (servants, laborers, and tradesmen), and remains diegetically and discursively, as well as economically, at the service of whiteness. The new blood injected by Mickey (North American from his father, French from his mother, but also *béké* from his grandmother) facilitates a steadfastly white-on-white combination, and one destined to be reinforced rather than diluted by marriage to Camilla. If the novel pays lip service to the embrace of otherness (transplant, the formation of pearl from grit, and the graft) as necessary preconditions for the caste's survival, the rejuvenation and cross-fertilization envisaged are of a controlled, highly engineered, and monoracial kind. As Fleur declares at one stage, "Here it's black or white, all or nothing" (307). The project to preserve the family line and the plantation has also been a mission implicitly, but quintessentially, designed to reinforce racial binaries, and in so doing to "préserver la race." And in this respect the comparisons drawn between this novel and the US soap genre are peculiarly relevant. For Patricia Zimmerman, *Dallas, Falcon Crest,* and *Dynasty* "operate as arbitrators between two interconnecting ideological constructs: capitalism and familialism." She argues that these series "constitute economic relations as *family* problems of patrilinity, reproduction (both of babies and wealth), incest (between relatives or companies), sexuality (whether as the eroticization of power and money, or as the primary explanation for corporate decisions), and mothering."[27] *La grande béké* is strangely but perfectly encapsulated in this description of a US genre that, although set in some of the "blackest" states of North America (Texas; Georgia), was spectacularly and exclusively concerned with white characters (Diahann Carroll's Dominique, in *Dynasty,* the single exception that proved the otherwise exclusively white rule). The realities of plantation life mean that Jaham's protagonists live in proximity with Black characters. But like the 1980s TV series that Zimmerman describes, the novel's protagonists are entirely insulated from sexual or romantic contact with Blacks. The "otherness" that Fleur so desperately craves as a source of regeneration and vitalization is in fact shown to be a quest for spectacular sameness.

In March 1998, as Martinique and Guadeloupe prepared to celebrate the one hundred and fiftieth anniversary of the abolition of slavery, a TV film based on *La grande béké* was screened over two Saturday nights, in France and the Antilles, in a primetime slot on a mainstream French channel.[28] Named for Jaham's debut novel, the plot in fact comprises the story of this novel and its follow-up, *Le maître-savane* (1991), although it takes enormous liberties with both. Alain Maline's film relocates the story from the 1960s to a contemporary setting in the 1990s, a transposition that in turn necessitated further diegetic changes: for example, Fleur's son Raoul dies by suicide rather than in World War II. Moreover, the casting of some key protagonists modifies their novelistic portrayal. Joby Bernabé plays Marcel, no longer associated with the grotesque corpulence of his novelistic avatar, but a svelte, smooth, suit-wearing, and utterly corrupt bourgeois. The novel's hero Mickey has been renamed a more Gallic-sounding, much less "other," Marc.

The film is markedly more melodramatic in tenor than the novel, in part an effect of the rather lurid 1990s soundtrack, and maximizes the resources of the audiovisual medium to indulge in a range of stereotypical features not present in the original novel in order to accentuate a sense of local color for a metropolitan audience. The servile class is even more strongly caricatured in the film than in the novel: perpetually drunk, childlike (at times barely comprehensible), and inanely smiling and dancing. In a series of exoticist scenes, barely clothed (exclusively Black) bodies engage in the pleasures offered by the island: sun, sea, alcohol, zouk, and, in particular, sex.[29] There are also scenes of laborers cutting cane with machetes that would not be out of place in Euzhan Palcy's 1983 adaptation of *La rue cases-nègres*. And, while the novel's narrator states that by 1965 the traditional checked dress of the *da* is now reserved for marriages and funerals, and that Eudèse wears only European dress, in the film, set in the 1990s, she is consistently bedecked in traditional Martinican costume, and is also associated with the voodoo doll, given to Irina to help her conceive. In short, for all that Camilla cautions Marc, in one of their first filmic encounters, to forget all that he has learned about the Antilles—postcards, beaches, *doudous*—the TV movie is in many respects an unreconstructed indulgence in precisely such clichés.

Space does not allow a full discussion of the multiple changes made in the transition from page to screen, although as the above examples suggest, the adaptation tends to accentuate rather than minimize some of the exoticist tropes and racist excesses of the novel. Undoubtedly, however, the most significant change is the foregrounding of, and central diegetic space afforded to, intercaste sexual relationships and the reactions they provoke. These relationships were ubiquitously denied in a novel whose "black and white" binaries projected a fantasized, unbearably white, version of Antillean life. This major rewriting has much to tell us, perhaps, not only about the creolist discourse of Jaham's first novel, but also about the evolution in attitudes toward race, skin color, and white privilege in the decade separating the publication of the novel and the broadcasting of the film. The film significantly expands and rewrites, for example, the role of a minor character in the novel, Fifi Zécoté, a down-at-heel *béké* ("*béké* en bas feuille*,*" a *béké* at the lowest leaf), who had once been a prosperous landowner, and who had been ostracized by his caste. Fifi is excluded from *béké* society, not for having fathered a child with a Black woman (a ubiquitous, but often denied, transgression), but for having recognized the child officially as his.[30] (The fact that this social outcast is employed by Fleur as part of her inner circle clearly asserts her independence from the dictates and dogmas of her peers; and yet this independence of mind does not apply to her own bloodline.) But by far the most significant change made in the film is the radical recast(e)ing of the novel's central love story. Camilla, in addition to having shed her white skin in the transition to the small screen (she is reinvented in the film as a beautiful Black woman), has also, somewhat mischievously, been renamed Camilla Fanon. The iconic surname of the author of *Black Skin, White Masks* clearly aligns the character with radical anticolonial and antiracist politics. A high-profile journalist who works for the main Antillean broadcaster, RFO, Camilla is the daughter of a murdered trade union leader, a politicized, fiery, and independent young woman who initially resists the attentions of the handsome Marc. Fleur's grandson, played by Anthony Delon, is presented, initially at least, as a carefree playboy whose decadence is partially redeemed by his humanitarian work in Bosnia and Rwanda. Marc pursues Camilla, from whom he receives regular, if rather labored, lessons on the ills of slavery, the inequalities that continue to blight the island, and even a definition of the term *béké* itself. Unlike Mickey, whose contact with Africa had been as a paratrooper in the brutal war of Algerian independence, which saw the forced repatriation of white colonizers, Marc's primary experience of the continent is in his beloved South Africa. Feted by the late 1990s as the "rainbow nation," and serving (however problematically and imperfectly) as a template for reconciliation and interracial healing, South Africa (never mentioned in the novel) is clearly mobilized to assert the desirability of transcending apartheid-based regimes.[31]

As in the novel, Fleur contrives to separate the couple, bribing Camilla with a one-way ticket to Paris, and arranging Marc's marriage with Irina. But here her impetus is explicitly framed as an attempt to prevent racial mixing ("*békés* don't marry Blacks" is a repeated mantra), rather than the desire to prevent marriage to an unsuitable white woman. Indeed, Fleur's reaction is shared by Camilla's mother, who is disgusted by the fact that Marc is not just white, but a *béké*. Even though Camilla accuses her mother of being "every bit as racist as them," Mme Fanon continues to view the romance as a betrayal of her husband's political beliefs, and of the Black people more generally. The film therefore gives space to contemporary Black disdain, or even revulsion, for the planter caste; and Fifi's daughter, for example, refuses to see him because he is a *béké*. Such contempt for the plantocracy is entirely absent in Jaham's novel, in which Black characters' interactions with whites are framed in terms of either subservience, gratitude, and awe, or, much less commonly, treachery and deceit. Here, in other words, the foundational interdiction of inter-caste marriage is shown to be as much the credo of the Black population as the white.

The fate of Irina, Marc's first wife and half-cousin, is markedly more typical of white Creole female destiny than that of Fleur. Unlike Camilla, whose naked body features in several sex scenes that unfold against the backdrop of an erotic soundtrack, Irina is never seen having sex with Marc. She is isolated and frustrated in the plantation: treated with disdain by her husband, who rejects her sexually, she endures several miscarriages, and is eventually, through a convoluted series of plot turns, murdered. Marc in the end marries Camilla with the blessing of his grandmother, who has understood that "the world is changing." That he is free to marry Camilla due to Irina's death is significant: within the value system of the novel, divorce is avoided not primarily, perhaps, for moral reasons, but in terms of financial dissipation (Fleur too, despite her miserable marriage, does not divorce). The film's idyllic final scene shows grandmother, happy couple, and mixed-race toddler cavorting on the veranda, the (newly enlightened) matriarch no longer immured in the convent, but integrated into, and looking out onto, this happily creolized brave new world. The family is observed by loving servants, chuckling with joy and basking in the reflected happiness of creolized family life.

The changes made in the adaptation of *La grande béké* suggest the unacceptability of Marie-Reine de Jaham's whitewashed novel for both a mainstream French and for an Antillean audience in 1998. This year of the 150th anniversary of the Abolition of slavery was, after all, a high point in the memorialization of slavery, and the film was extensively featured in France's many television magazines, which also included feature-length interviews with its three stars, Delon, Line Renaud (Fleur), and the less well known Keen de Kermadec, who played Camilla. That the film, in rewriting the novel's plot, itself falls foul of many other racist stereotypes (most notably, perhaps, in the way it plays up rather than down the giddy devotion of Fleur's servants, but also in the exoticized and eroticized presentation of Camilla) is captured in many of the press reviews. One critic mentions the film's "unhappy love stories, Machiavellian plots, murder, and redemption," going on to note that "we are immersed in romantic and crime fiction ['roman rose et roman noir'], and can only beg for more."[32] Several articles flagged Kermadec's mixed background in a manner that further commodified the actress as a product and source of pleasure to be consumed by the Western spectator: "Breton, Antillean, Carib, and Indian blood creating this charming cocktail."[33] Only Sophie Berthier gives a more critical account: as she argues, the film, "while claiming to denounce Antillean 'Apartheid,' in fact keeps all the key characters in their place; the bad guys are greedy Antilleans in cahoots with powerful Whites; the good characters are the Black domestics, devoted in body and soul to their blond mistress."[34]

Unsurprisingly, perhaps, for the novel's author, the adaptation was a disappointment; making no reference to the recast(e)ing of Camilla, Jaham regrets that the film was a "vector of neither the valorization nor understanding of Creole culture."[35] Jaham's understanding of "Creole culture" is here strikingly limited, and will itself evolve in the course of her novelistic career. For example, the Solis family, one of two clans at the heart of her historical trilogy, is structurally positioned as the "pure white" family. They descend, however, from a non-*béké* ancestor, the formidable and legendary Carib, Anna Akwaba, whose Indigenous origins are immortalized rather than concealed in the names of subsequent female characters. But here and elsewhere in her fiction, it could be argued that slavery remains marginalized, denied, repressed; the nonwhite ancestor, significantly, is not contaminated by slavery, but rather preexists it. Similarly, it is telling that in *Le sang du volcan,* the often-cited curse that hangs over Mount Pelée is not connected to slavery, but rather to the extermination of the Carib population. We are told early in the novel that the mountain was the site of the death of thousands of Caribs, who flung themselves from the mountain to escape the European invader. The inequities of postplantation society are continually sublimated in such references, which seek to register an awareness of the suffering wrought by colonialism all the while averting the gaze from the horrors of slavery.

Marie-Reine de Jaham radically rewrites the script of female Creole identity in *La grande béké.* By troubling the association of whiteness with virtue, and by putting at the novel's center a monstrous mother, she fundamentally revises a discourse that we can trace back as far as Moreau de Saint-Méry, who noted that "maternal tenderness" is a particularly exalted virtue in Martinique.[36] But in other respects the novel is consistent with, indeed an extreme example of, creolist discourse, willfully blind to the traumas of slavery and to the continuing struggles of the ex-slave population. This is a novel in which creolization, moreover, is not so much repudiated, but seems rather not to exist at all as a viable option. In this respect, in terms of Creole-authored fiction, the novel might be said to have more in common with the earliest Antillean novel, Traversay's *Les amours de Zémédare et Carina,*[37] than it does with later nineteenth-century texts explicitly haunted by the threat of miscegenation. In other words the novel, like Traversay's inaugural Creole fiction, does not so much reject such postcolonial tropes as hybridity, in-betweenness, and the contact zone, as propose a world in which such positions are unthinkable. Indeed, at the discursive rather than the diegetic level, the ambivalence and complexity that I identify, in the first chapter of this study, in the 1806 novel, are markedly absent in the 1989 work, an absence all the more remarkable, indeed strikingly anachronistic, given the novel's relatively recent publication date.

Finally, there remains something troubling in the novel's primary metaphor, the infected or perverted barrel, corruptible by a single drop of inferior rum, and which at all costs needs to be destroyed by the protagonist to guarantee the quality of the superior commodity produced on her plantation. Although Fleur describes the "heavy heredity" that hangs over her husband's family, there is a curious silence regarding the specific source of this infection. This metaphor of the infected barrel does, however, implicitly recall the "one-drop rule" of racial categorization. Indeed, this rule is explicitly invoked with regard to Fleur's son, André, the only member of the family to embark, albeit briefly, on a relationship with a "dark palmed" woman (50), before bending to his family's demands to end the relationship; he is now unhappily married to a *béké*. Distant in history, the story is glossed over quickly by the narrator, who notes in passing that all *békés* are familiar with the signs of the "drop" of Black blood resurfacing ("c'est 'la goutte' qui ressort"): darkened gums and palms and, in particular, a sclerotic yellow color (50). The phrasing that here describes André's lover perfectly replicates the description, just a few pages earlier, of Fleur's despised mother-in-law, whom she describes in a markedly similar way. As we have seen in previous chapters, yellow is a highly loaded color, often mobilized by Antillean writers (*békés* and non-*békés* alike) to suggest, often without naming, racial mixing and miscegenation. It is notable for its almost entire absence in a novel that revolves around blackness and whiteness, and is therefore highly significant in the description of Fleur's mother-in-law. Her eyes are a washed out blue and, crucially, she is also a "sclerotic yellow" color (34). This single description of the matriarch of the Mase de la Joucquerie line, with its emphasis on an unconvincing whiteness (pale eyes; sclerosis) points to, without naming, the possibility of a miscegenation that dare not speak its name. These loaded references to color do just enough to infer, without stating, that the corruption of the line might in the end be connected to blackness, the ultimate alibi for this grand Creole whose investment in the integrity of her own white genealogical line leads her to pass over her (legitimate) children in favor of her "bastard" grandson.

6 Killing the *Béké*

Crime, Fiction, and White Death

> Here in paradise, nothing ever happened.
> —Agatha Christie, *A Caribbean Mystery*

THE ASSOCIATION of the Caribbean with laid-back indolence, torpor, and inertia, on the one hand, and on the other with unbridled passion, loss of control, and excess, has provided the impetus for many murder mysteries, crime novels, and police procedurals set in the islands. Examples include Agatha Christie's *A Caribbean Mystery* (1964), Susan Bowden's *House of Shadows* (2003), Mike Myers's *Deadly Eyes* (2012), Timothy Williams's *The Honest Folk of Guadeloupe* (2015), Don Brun's series of murder mysteries set in English-speaking islands, and most recently *Death in Paradise,* the spectacularly successful British TV series set on the fictional island of Sainte-Marie, a thinly disguised Guadeloupe.[1] French writers, too, have exploited the locale in novels such as Brigitte Aubert's *Requiem caraïbe* (1997) and Stéphane Pair's *Élastique nègre* (2017). Many of these works play on the closed and bounded contours of the island space, which provide "the perfect geography for the clue-puzzle mysteries that dominated the golden age of crime fiction"; the island acts as an "ideal place for a group of strangers to become a temporary community of potential murderers," much like the country-house murder mystery familiar in the work of Christie and others.[2] But these novels also play on a broad range of stereotypical tropes, constructing the Caribbean as a place of heady and transient touristic encounters, a hotbed of illegal drugs trafficking, or of particularly lax, if not corrupt, policing (only Bowden's novel, set in a deserted plantation villa, foregrounds in any explicit way the slave past). To such well-worn exoticist clichés as sun, sand, sea, sex, spice, and rum, we might therefore add another: murder.

If the Caribbean backdrop provides a propitious setting for European and American writers, crime fiction holds a powerful appeal for local Antilleans too, often allowing novelists to rewrite the exoticizing tropes deployed in Western versions of the genre. Novels such as Daniel de Grandmaison's *Rendez-vous au Macouba* (1948) and *Le bal des créoles* (1976) adopt and adapt the style and codes of the Agatha Christie whodunit. More recently, and testifying to a strong local appetite for the genre, Caraïbéditions has launched a "*polar*" series, in which such authors as Ernest Pépin and Raphaël Confiant have published novels, including the latter's *Bal masqué à Békéland,* discussed below.[3] Loïc Léry's *Le gang des Antillais* (2016) explores violent gang culture in France in the 1970s. And crime is of significant and increasing interest for Patrick Chamoiseau to judge by his recent novels: *Hypérion victimaire* (2013) centers on a serial killer and *J'ai toujours aimé la nuit* (2019) is a self-styled thriller. In a more noticeably subversive mode, a striking number of Antillean novels place an (apparent) murder at the heart of the story, only to undermine this narrative starting point. Perhaps the most famous example of this tendency is Chamoiseau's *Solibo magnifique,* a novel that presents as a police procedural but that in fact describes the death, by natural causes, of the eponymous storyteller. Condé's *Traversée de la mangrove* (1989), like *Solibo,* opens with the discovery of a dead body, but the novel is an extended meditation on the identity of the deceased (Sancher too has apparently died of natural causes) rather than an attempt to identify his (nonexistent) killer. More recently Gisèle Pineau's *Le parfum des sirènes* (2018) similarly opens with the discovery of a corpse; the protagonist (who eventually solves the mystery of the death) is repeatedly compared to Miss Marple, and the novel self-consciously references the television series *Cold Case.* But here again, and even though narrative closure is brought about in a way that Chamoiseau and Condé refuse, there is no crime, rather a death by misadventure. All these novels conform to "a line of French-Caribbean literary works that, in questioning (neo)colonial patterns and practices, propose investigations largely void of crime stories."[4] So while classic detective fiction "traces a story from effect to cause," requiring "that everything be explained rationally,"[5] the French Caribbean crime novel frequently eschews logic and Cartesian rationality, leaving as many questions open as answered, or rather posing questions that are in the end irrelevant or unanswerable. As Jason Herbeck argues, "In diverging from the formulaic reproductions of the mass-distributed genre in French and elsewhere, the French-Caribbean detective novel calls into question the very traditions it so often transgresses."[6] It could be argued that the rules and codes of crime fiction tend to be honored more, by Antillean writers, in the breach than in the observance.

This chapter is concerned with a distinctive strand within this vibrant and rapidly expanding body of Antillean crime fiction or, as in some of the examples above, fiction that plays with the codes of the *polar* only to transgress them. This strand puts the violent killing of *béké* characters at its investigative center. In historical terms, the murder of *békés* is at once an omnipresent threat (one thinks of the poisonings that haunted the collective imaginary in nineteenth-century texts), and something of a historical anomaly. In her discussion of the real-life murder of Guy de Fabrique, a *béké* who was hacked to death by plantation workers in 1948 during an industrial dispute, Catherine Childers argues that the case "was one of very few in which a *béké* was the ultimate victim."[7] As noted in the introduction to this book, *békés* are usually a relatively minor presence in contemporary fiction and *béké* murder is accordingly rare. That the four novels considered here—Guy Cabort-Masson's *Qui a tué le béké de Trinité?* (1991), Maryse Condé's *La belle créole* (2001), Henri Micaux's *De nègres et de békés: Une journée de chien* (2011), and Raphaël Confiant's *Bal masqué à Békéland* (2013)[8]—all put violent white death at their diegetic center makes them, for this reason alone, worthy of attention. These novels were written over a period of twenty years, by established authors (Condé and Confiant), and by less familiar ones (Cabort-Masson and Micaux); by Guadeloupeans (Condé and Micaux) and Martinicans (Confiant and Cabort-Masson); by both male and female writers. In each novel, the violent deaths, whether of a *béké* patriarch (Cabort-Masson, Micaux, Confiant), lover (Condé), or daughter (Confiant), are mysterious, misrepresented, misconstrued, or simply are not what they seem. Confiant's *Bal masqué* is the most straightforward in terms of generic classification: like other novels in his "Teddyson" series, it is a classic noir novel, "urban in location, masculine in point of view, fast-paced and frequently violent in word and action."[9] In Micaux's *De nègres et de békés* the reader has been a privileged witness to the crime scene and is in no doubt as to the identity of the killer; but the novel includes many elements of the police procedural. Cabort-Masson's novel morphs into a police procedural in its closing section, although it is generically hybrid, and although narrative closure is ultimately denied (the reader cannot be sure at the end of the text who has murdered the eponymous *béké*). Condé's *La belle créole,* meanwhile, opens as the court case that has exonerated the Black man accused of murdering his white mistress draws to a close.

Whatever their generic and structural differences, their varying literary styles (and, it must be said, their divergent literary quality), as well as the range of historical settings and plots, all four novels nail their narrative colors to the mast in one significant respect: they all invoke the white ethnocaste in their very titles. Given the paucity of literary titles that make any such explicit reference,[10] this suggests that crime fiction has a distinctive and provocative generic capacity: it provides a unique platform on which Antillean writers can name the *béké* and put him/her at the heart of the story. (If, as it turns out, *La belle créole* designates a boat rather than a character, its title playfully manipulates readers' expectations by more obviously conjuring the white woman at the heart of narrative.) The genre offers other possibilities too, given the extent to which popular fiction simultaneously responds to readers' fantasies and helps shape those fantasies. On a very basic level, it allows Black writers (and their readers) to trespass imaginatively into this most secretive and exclusive world, much like their awe-stricken characters do within the diegetic space of the novels.[11] Amédée, protagonist of *De nègres et de békés,* is "breathless," "immobilized," and "stupefied" by the beauty of the *béké*'s villa (128), and "dazzled by discovery" as he slips into Blanière's beloved seat (130); and Confiant's authorial alter-ego, Teddyson, masquerading as a caterer in *Bal masqué,* is utterly "paralyzed" ("médusé") in "this *béké* theater" (126). Dieudonné in *La belle créole* is "dumbfounded" (39, 127) when he attempts to talk to Loraine, and enters her bedroom "with the feeling a believer has exploring a cathedral" (40), a room described as a "sanctuary that he only entered tremblingly" (55). Crime fiction, arguably even more than fiction in general, revolves around desire and repulsion; here these dynamics reveal the white Creole world to be captivating and intoxicating, but also highly threatening to outsiders, and at the same time to be a dysfunctional, self-destructive, even toxic and murderous space for those whites who operate within its confines.

What might have motivated four such different writers to put a *béké* killing at the heart of their novels? For Marxist Cabort-Masson, the interconnection between race and class in the Antilles was already a longstanding concern. His polemical essay, *Les puissances d'argent en Martinique* (1984), remains one of the very few full-frontal exposés of white privilege in the islands. A later study, *Martinique: Comportements et mentalité* (1998) also included a scathing critique of the caste. *Qui a tué?* thus emerged during a period of intense reflection on the subject. The other novels discussed here, while undoubtedly reflecting the authors' longstanding interest in race and privilege, can also be considered works of circumstance, which respond more directly to contemporary sociopolitical events. Condé's *La belle créole* (2001) appeared after a series of strikes among civil servants and workers, and in the wake of an independence movement led by the presidents of the Regional Councils of Guadeloupe, Martinique, and French Guiana; contemporary debates around slavery and reparations also form a background to the novel.[12] Meanwhile Micaux's *De nègres et de békés* (2011) and Confiant's *Bal masqué* (2013) were directly inspired by the strikes of 2009, even if these events are not explicitly mentioned in either story: unsurprisingly, given the turbulence of the period in which these novels were produced, they are especially attentive to intercaste tensions and to the challenge to white power in the islands. In Micaux's novel, characters in the 1940s prophetically deploy the infamous slogan that characterized Élie Domota's 2009 campaign ("Guadeloupe is ours!"—"La Guadeloupe est à nous!" 100), while in Confiant's, a key suspect in the murder plot belongs to the militant group called Békés dewo (Out with *békés*, also a mantra of the 2009 strikes), who are described with typical Confiantian irony as a "Stalinist-PolPotist-AlQuaïdesque" groupuscule (21). But even Condé's 2001 novel features slogans such as "out with whites" ("blan dèro") and "fuck off, French people" ("Fwansé foukan"). All four novels, then, explore the racial hostility that remains an abiding obsession in the Antilles, and could be said to spring from a marked heightening of these tensions over the last thirty years.

In structuring this chapter, I begin with the two novels published in the aftermath of the 2009 strikes (Micaux and Confiant), and then move back to earlier novels by Cabort-Masson and Condé. The works written after 2009 deal extensively, if obliquely, with the heightened racial tensions that would come to the fore in that year and its aftermath, and they offer straightforward resolution along conventional crime narrative lines. In moving to two very different novels that precede, and in many ways uncannily predict, the events of 2009, we also transition to novels that deny narrative closure and trouble easy conclusions, and that therefore belong to the strain of "subversive" crime fiction described by Herbeck above. Cabort-Masson's idiosyncratic novel playfully blurs the boundary between fact and fiction to destabilize the reader, while also refusing the conventional codes of the genre (notably in leaving open the question of the killer's identity). Condé, meanwhile, offers "an altogether different variation on the detective narrative typology," in that "the detective narrative (i.e. the novel itself) does not begin until *after* the initial and supposedly definitive investigation represented by his acquittal at the trial's conclusion."[13] Structuring the chapter in this way also allows me to move from male writers to female, and from a discussion of an ebbing white masculinity embodied in fallen fathers to a concern with white female killing (even if Condé's primary focus is Dieudonné rather than his "victim" Loraine). The first two novels, in their explicit treatment of the decline and fall of the planter caste, are doomed family romances: the violent deaths of the white father reflect the disintegration of a caste system founded on paternal authority and patriarchy. Cabort-Masson's novel also places the family at the heart of the social crisis, suggesting that the caste, in order to protect its interests, is capable of the ultimate taboo, the murder of one of its own. Condé's novel conspicuously departs from such narratives: her protagonist is divorced, childless, and lives (threateningly) outside any family structure. My reading of this novel focuses more closely on narrative strategies than on the allegories of decline that structure the other novels (although as we shall see such allegories are present in *La belle créole* too). The peculiar narrative instability of Condé's novel means that it insistently lends itself to a reading that goes "against the grain" of characters' speech. While most characters in the novel espouse a vision of a postracial Antillean society, I argue that Condé's treatment of whiteness and blackness legitimizes, and even mandates, a contrapuntal reading reasserting the centrality of race, and the heritage of slavery, to the understanding of contemporary society.

Whiteness Laid Low

Micaux's *De nègres et de békés* (2011) is set in 1949 and is a displaced meditation on the racial tensions that affect contemporary Guadeloupe after the events of 2009.[14] Plantation owner Michel de Blanière, a once handsome sportsman disabled in a horse-riding accident, lives with his wife, Denise, and daughter Emmanuelle. His marriage is miserable and at times abusive. Conditions on his plantation are oppressive, and against a background of unrest and talk of strikes, Amédée, a laborer, is nominated to intercede with the *béké* with a view to improving the terms and conditions of his fellow workers. (If Blanière's name suggests whiteness, Amédée's racist nickname, Boudin Bleu, blue sausage, names a "blacker than black" hue, and the novel stages repeated confrontations between black and white.) Having rung the doorbell in vain, Amédée lets himself into the *grand'case;* a horrified Blanière finds the intruder in his salon, attempts to strike him with his cane but trips over the carpet, knocks his head on an oak table, and falls to the ground, bleeding but alive. Amédée flees, fearing that he will be found guilty not just of trespassing, but also of having assaulted the *béké*. When Denise comes upon the scene, she seizes the opportunity to murder her incapacitated husband (who had just announced his intention to divorce her) by beating him over the head with a bottle of rum, before denouncing Amédée, whose forgotten hat she uses to incriminate him to the police. The materiality of the plantation is thus mobilized in symbolic and poignant ways. If the *béké* is felled by the ornate objects of his lavish home (the thick rug that trips him up, the pointed corners of the heavy oak table that injure him), the weapon that brutally finishes him off is a bottle of rum, source and product of this economic super-system. Meanwhile Amédée's worn hat, an abject object incongruously out of place in the *béké*'s house, acts not just as a talisman of the former's subjection to the colonial order but as the damning clue that leads ultimately to his death.

Amédée is therefore the only suspect in a crime erroneously, if predictably, deemed "a racially motivated drama" by police—the investigators in *La belle créole* quickly reach a similar conclusion—which must be approached with "the greatest prudence" (144). The novel wryly reflects on a justice system that closes in on a convenient (in other words, Black) suspect, making evidence fit the crime, all the while starting from an unshakeable assumption of white innocence. Although no gun was used in Blanière's killing, it is assumed that Amédée was armed, and even his grandmother's suicide becomes a matter of retrospective suspicion. Amédée eventually takes refuge in the valley of the Galion River where a policeman, thinking he sees a cat or a mongoose, shoots him; Amédée falls into the river dead, shot not because of the danger he poses to police and to society more generally, but in a simple case of mistaken identity.

De nègres et de békés is a crime story in which the perpetrator is known to the reader from the beginning; the point of the novel is not to identify Blanière's killer but rather to encourage the reader to reflect on continuing injustice and inequality against the background of workers' resistance. Although the novel is set in the immediate wake of departmentalization, the conditions of slavery remain. Descriptions of grinding material poverty, dietary monotony, the self-sacrifice of grandmothers, and the summary justice meted out in the case of insubordination, as well as the pitiful state of workers' feet (in an extended passage workers wonder if "they can really still be called feet," 33–34) recalls Joseph Zobel's *La rue cases-nègres,* set a decade earlier in the 1930s, a novel also committed to showing how the degradations of slavery continue to determine workers' conditions. Collective action has proven to be not only futile, but also in fact fatal, and justice, while in the end meted out to neither Black nor white man, is fundamentally invested in white people.

And yet, while not underplaying the tenacity and brutality of the plantation regime, the novel is also a reflection on white masculinity, physical impotence, and the threat posed by white women. The disabled Blanière inhabits an exclusively female space and is profoundly threatened by his wife and daughter. Confined to the home, he has no choice but to ignore Denise's multiple affairs, even when they involve Black men, interracial liaisons which bring to the fore the sexual double standard that characterizes the *béké* caste. These affairs are experienced as an affront to his pride and to the honor of his caste, and he fears above all that "a little bastard might come along and complicate the situation" (60). This fear is intensified by the fact that Blanière has no son, and therefore the patronymic will disappear with him; indeed, his daughter, as in so many other novels, embodies a challenge to the strict racial hierarchy on which the plantation depends. But unlike her mother, whose sexual frustration leads her to Black lovers, Emmanuelle's resistance is intellectual and artistic: she reads René Maran and Aimé Césaire and is a fan of Black music. She taunts her parents that she should have been named Mélanie, a name deriving from the Greek for blackness, and also the name of a fifth-century Roman saint famous for freeing slaves in North Africa. She goads them too on the unsustainability of the plantation system and flaunts her intimacy with Black and mixed-race friends. She has, moreover, a much more nuanced take on racial politics than her parents; she is aware, for example, that her whiteness is an "unforgiveable defect" (63) for some Antilleans.

Michel's physical decline—he is "diminished and vulnerable" (65)—can be read as a more general comment on white masculinity in the context of the patriarchal codes of the plantation. He imagines himself "a debonair and frightening sovereign," and fantasizes about workers prostrating themselves at his feet (48), but such grotesque imaginings only underscore the extent of his frailty. Filled with self-loathing and regret, his physical repulsiveness and emasculation are repeatedly emphasized: he is bloated and obese, drools (50), resembles "an obscene growth" and jelly (50), and is "fat and so deformed" (136). He can only pour himself into his chair, which he fills like a "viscous liquid," and is compared to a cephalopod, which leaves behind a sticky trace (49). This network of images (one thinks of Glissant's pathetic planter Senglis, discussed in chapter 3) repeatedly and systematically deflates any sense of phallic uprightness and mastery, even over the body itself. Michel's is rather an abject, impotent, and defective body unable to function normally, and indeed incapable even of containing itself. The only outlet for his sexuality is a casually abusive groping of his underage servant Virginie. Holding a *tartine* in one hand, he strokes the girl's thighs and crotch with the other. This gesture, although degrading to the servant, is strikingly devoid of the threat of sexual violence. Rather, these are the "mechanical and familiar caresses of a master on his mare's rump, or his dog's muzzle"; they are neither "sensual prelude nor erotic prologue," and indeed are banal enough to leave the servant "indifferent" (55). Michel is pathetically incapable of the conventional transgressions of the desiring white male. Indeed, unusually in this fictional world, the threat of miscegenation is vested solely in his promiscuous wife.

As we have seen in a novel like *Frères volcans,* the physical decrepitude (and more specifically, the sexual inadequacy) of the white man is linked to profound anxieties regarding legitimacy, longevity, and femininity. Michel's murder is triggered not just by spousal opportunity but also by his decision to divorce his wife as punishment for her extramarital activities: if endogamy is the foundational structure that sutures money to power in white families, divorce, as much as intercaste libidinal transgression, threatens that order. His wife's murderous revenge might seem to secure, at least temporarily, the values of the ethnocaste. But as we know, her sexual dalliances with Black men are a threat to this order. And that the couple's only daughter stands as a challenge to the system as well underscores the fragility of its tenure: both women are incapable of living by the patriarchal codes that would secure it.

Whiteness Unmasked

Bal masqué à Békéland is a first-person narrative told from the perspective of Jack Teddyson, second-rate detective and authorial alter ego.[15] Teddyson has been hired by *béké* businessman Michel Dupin de Flessac de Laverdière to investigate the disappearance of his daughter, Marie-Aimée, last seen while partying with other young *békés* during Carnival.[16] Unlike the linear plot of *De nègres,* this is a heady, sprawling, and complicated narrative, in which a superabundance of subplots, red herrings, and dead ends, and a plethora of potential suspects, leave the reader as discombobulated as the hapless Teddyson. But the story eventually reveals itself in its closing pages to be about that most central of all tropes in fiction about white Creoles, inheritance. A Colombian drug cartel has kidnapped, and presumably killed, Marie-Aimée as a way of extracting a debt owed by Dupin. Meanwhile a wealthy uncle has signed his fortune over to Marie-Aimée, a fortune that her father needs to pay off the

Colombians. Dupin attempts to pass off his handicapped daughter, Marie-Aimée's twin, whom he had hidden away at birth, as Marie-Aimée, faking the latter's signature on legal documents that would allow him to access her inheritance. But in the denouement Teddyson, alerted to the twin's existence, asks her to sign her name, which she is incapable of doing. The novel culminates in the suicide of the *béké* patriarch, who shoots himself in front of detective, policemen, his wife, and surviving daughter.

The novel presents a highly polarized world of white privilege and Black subservience. While Teddyson, like his creator a *chabin* (a phenotype of African origin with pale skin and red hair),[17] occupies an interstitial position and circulates, albeit awkwardly, between both worlds, the black and white certainties that originate in plantation hierarchies are continually reinforced. Dupin de Flessac carries accoutrements that suggest the association between privilege, color, and caste (he dresses in white, surrounds himself in porcelain and white linen, and carries a Mont Blanc pen) and references conventional models of macho, indeed violent, white masculinity: he resembles Charles Bronson (26; 192), and is explicitly referred to as a slaver (153). Marie-Aimée is described as a white Creole duchess (the positioning of adjectives in the original French, "la blanche duchesse créole," 43, prioritizing and drawing attention to her whiteness), and is apparently the distant descendant of Joséphine Bonaparte (43). She is said to resemble Catherine Deneuve, an actress associated with an icy clean whiteness. Meanwhile blackness is connected to the experience of exploitation, whether economic or sexual. Dupin's plantation, overseen by "an alabaster-colored overseer," is worked by "an army of ebony-colored workers" (49). Teddyson's long-suffering girlfriend Francelise is said to descend from the Hottentot Venus (36), the stage name of Sarah Bartmann, who was exhibited in "freak shows" in Paris in the nineteenth century, the epitome of degraded and objectified Black femininity.

Unlike the plantation-based intrigue of both Micaux's and, as we see below, Cabort-Masson's novels, this is a deeply urban novel, in which the Fort-de-France setting allows Confiant to embrace and subvert the codes and conventions of the hard-boiled genre. If the classic hard-boiled novel "glorifies white, heterosexual masculinity and projects onto people of color all sexual fears,"[18] this novel revels, to an uncomfortable extent but in a manner familiar to Confiant's readers, in the hyperbolic heterosexuality of the central detective and his conquests (the priapic P.I.; his provocatively dressed and hysterical girlfriend; the sexually adventurous air hostess with whom he meets for casual sex, referred to in highly objectifying terms as La Mauricette) and, inverting one of the key tropes of conventional crime fiction, projects sexual fear and dysfunction onto white people. Of course, the excessive heterosexual conquests of Teddyson and his ilk could be read as a reaction to the degradations of slavery, which, having caused the enslaved male to be displaced by the master, has generated in Black men a compensatory hypermasculinity based on "aggressive heterosexual desire."[19] What interests me here, however, is the portrayal of white masculinity, which is yet again associated with impotence, degeneration, incapacity, congenital defects, and, ultimately, suicide. Early in the novel, for example, Teddyson fears that his scantily clad girlfriend will provoke an erection in the *béké,* "probably his first since the start of the twenty-first century" (17). Dupin's elderly uncle can no longer have an erection, even when his nurse visits (132). But more troublingly, Confiant explores the devastating genetic outworkings of consanguinity among peoples who are "more or less cousins" and who have been "intermarrying for the last three centuries" (162). This description of the extreme endogamy practiced by Antillean *békés* exactly echoes Jaham's in *La grande béké;* but while the system of intermarriage between families is described in entirely benign terms by Jaham's narrator, and indeed is masterminded and facilitated by her as a way to save her plantation, it is connected by Confiant to a much more disturbing narrative of degradation and dissipation.

The sensational unmasking, in the novel's closing pages, of the *béké* patriarch reveals him to be a corrupt businessman whose shady drug deals have led directly to his daughter's kidnapping and murder (the narrator uses the term infanticide) and have had a devastating effect on the island's youth (including whites) more generally. He is also revealed as a spectacularly immoral and inadequate *pater familias:* the incarcerator of his handicapped daughter, and a husband who has caused misery to his wife (also his cousin) throughout their eighteen-year marriage. The infirm twin hidden in the attic recalls, but adds a macabre genetic twist to, the story of *Jane Eyre,* and Dupin's suicide marks the ultimate blow to the paternalistic system on which the plantocracy was founded. As he turns his gun on himself, his "huge body collapsed like a mass on the veranda floor while his brain spread everywhere" (261). He is reduced in the novel's closing pages to an "acephalous body" (261), a headless corpse, recalling the beheaded statue of Joséphine discussed in the introduction to this book, a figure frequently referenced by Confiant in this novel and others. The term "acephalous," used by Confiant here, denotes in anthropology a non-stratified society that lacks political leadership and hierarchy, a structure diametrically opposed to that of the plantocracy. The Dupin family, like Békéland and white Creole society more generally, is an unapologetically patriarchal and paternalistic society, in contrast to the matrifocality of Black Antillean society, but also in contrast to the associations encoded in Josephine's statue. Wives and daughters are (congenitally or habitually) mute, or written out through murder, and are entirely ignorant of and detached from the world of business. The apocalyptic ending of this white Creole family romance recalls the Gothic excess of *Outre-mer,* which, as its title suggests, in many respects bypassed femininity altogether. The white Creole family is here reduced to a reclusive wife and an intellectually handicapped daughter, the suicide and infanticide of the narrative pointing to a profoundly self-destructive tendency in the culture, the acephalous corpse an abject symbol of a superstructure felled.

The Good *Béké*

Qui a tué le béké de Trinité? (1991) is one of three novels written by Guy Cabort-Masson (1937–2002), a neglected figure in Antillean cultural history.[20] The author is deemed by Chris Bongie to be a "little-known scribe,"[21] a judgment that perhaps explains why the critic limits his analysis to Cabort-Masson's essays, articles, and interviews and why, like almost all other critics of Caribbean literature, he ignores his fiction entirely. Cabort-Masson's self-published works are out of print and hard to access even in Martinique; the most obvious memorial to him is a street named after him in his native Saint-Joseph in 2013, although even this memorial somewhat sanitizes his politics.[22] What, then, can Cabort-Masson's poorly executed text, a messy patchwork of styles, unbelievable plotlines, and unconvincing characters, that lurches from an innocent opening reminiscent of classic girls' literature (a little girl, Prudence, plays hopscotch on a Sunday morning before going to church), to a lurid sex romp, and then to classic detective story, tell us about *béké* identity?

The novel is set in Martinique in May 1943, under the rule of Admiral Robert, an especially febrile period in Antillean history that "reinstated the predominance of white *békés* to a degree unseen since the Second Empire."[23] The eponymous hero, Michel de Sainte Lucie, is murdered at home while he sleeps. Sainte Lucie lives, like so many of his fictional *confrères,* in a loveless marriage with his wife (also, not unusually, his cousin) Marie-Josèphe. In addition to his legitimate children, he has fathered a daughter, Prudence, with his servant Judith, whom he continues to visit for sex most Saturday nights. Meanwhile Judith plans to marry Amédée, whose mother had been the *béké*'s wet nurse: the *frères de lait* were brought up in the neighboring island of Saint Lucia, before moving, together, to Martinique. Living under the same roof as Michel and his wife are another couple, Bernadette and Fernand Lannoux, *petits blancs* who have moved in, ostensibly to help the owners run home and business (Bernadette is related to Marie-Josèphe on the latter's maternal *and* paternal lines). But this domestic arrangement has, unbeknownst to the Sainte Lucie family, been masterminded by the most powerful *béké* on the island, Hayot (the family remain today the richest on the island), acting on the instructions of Admiral Robert, who wants to keep an eye on this dissident *béké*.

Michel is, then, the object of considerable surveillance and suspicion in the novel, as he constitutes a threat to both the Vichy regime and to the codes of *béké* society (the fate of both are insistently intertwined here). Most characters, including his wife, Amédée, Bernadette, Judith, and Lannoux have a motive to kill him, as he is an obstacle to their personal and sexual fulfilment. But he is also a thorn in the side of the plantocracy and a threat to the Vichy regime. Indeed, Detective Levesque notes wryly that the entire colony wanted this man assassinated (204). By the end of the novel Levesque, an honest and intuitive investigator, is categorical at least as regards which caste is responsible for the murder. Michel had on the night of his death promised land to Judith and Amédée to allow them to marry; Levesque therefore concludes that the representatives of "the proletarian class" can be eliminated from enquiries, given that they now have no motive, and that the murderer is a *béké*, most likely Bernadette Lannoux.

The novel revolves around a series of absurdly complex triangular relationships—a familiar structuring principle in literature by and about white Creoles—that overlay and complicate the triadic structure of the nuclear family.[24] Moreover the tangles and triangles of the text are not simply erotic. These triangular formations (the novel is set in a commune called Trinité) trouble, in more political ways, the Black-white binary, and the nuclear family, on which the plantocracy depends. Amédée and Michel have suckled at the breast of the Black nurse or *da*, an intimacy that threatens, as in earlier fiction, the pristine separateness of white identity. There is, moreover, at least a hint here that the boys may be more than milk brothers, but also half (blood) brothers. Similarly, Prudence, the mulatta daughter born to a white father and Black mother, troubles the polarities of "black" and "white," just as she threatens the sanctity of the *béké* family.

Cabort-Masson's longstanding interest in denouncing the privileges of the white oligarchy ensures that his *béké* characters run the gauntlet of unpleasant types, from devious spouse (Marie-Josèphe) to Molièresque religious hypocrite (Bernadette) to pantomime villain (Fernand Lannoux, married to Bernadette, sleeping with Marie-Josèphe, but also rapist of the underage Prudence). But white women, as we have seen in other fiction written by Black male writers, inspire the most violent and vitriolic depictions. Marie-Josèphe and Bernadette are parodic phonies, whose showy Catholic faith is expressed in a series of increasingly outlandish and exaggerated performances. They are also sexually promiscuous, even insatiable, women—casually unfaithful to their husbands and happy to embark on a lesbian affair with each other. Besides that, these women are the most likely to have murdered Michel. In this cast of largely incredible grotesques, the most surprising feature of the novel is the sympathetic, if not heroic, portrayal of the central patriarch. Michel de Sainte Lucie is beloved by his workers, offering them financial support to renovate their homes so they will withstand cyclones. He is a socialist, a philanthropist, and an ardent Gaullist, eschewing *La Paix* (the Catholic newspaper revered by his hypocritical wife and by Bernadette) in favor of *Tropiques* (Césaire's journal, banned by the Vichy authorities in April 1943).[25] As in so many other novels, from *Outre-mer* and *Les créoles* (1835) onward, Michel's association with Anglophone culture, what one character calls, in an exact echo of Traversay's 1806 essay, his Anglomania (73),[26] has determined his more liberal philosophy. Named for the English-speaking island on which he was born, and which along with Dominica was the key destination for dissidents escaping the Vichy regime, he is the proud owner of "numerous Anglo-Saxon books" (169), is considered to have been "contaminated" (73) by American democracy, and is active in dissident activities aimed at liberating the island (although doubt is cast on how effective his activities are).[27] This reverence for English liberalism is presented as a positive quality. He is a "a very particular type of Grand Creole," a "rock of profound conviction" (122), and a benign if paternalistic boss. This makes him one of the most sympathetic *békés* in the fiction discussed in this book so far, and this is the primary reason for his elimination.

The denouement in this novel is not the revelation of the culprit; rather, while the murderer remains unidentified to the end, we learn in the closing pages that the novel is based on a real-life murder. Levesque happens upon a copy of *La Paix* in his hotel in May 1945, where he finds a report of the murder of Robert Despointes, an uncanny echo, or *mise en abyme,* of the credibility-defying story we have just read.[28] Both victims are fathers of large families, both murders take place in Trinité and involve details such as the cutting of the electric current to guarantee darkness. Local readers (presumably the self-published Cabort-Masson's primary audience) will know that Despointes was the real-life inhabitant of the "chateau" in Trinité, had a daughter called Marie José, and was indeed shot dead as he slept by a mysterious intruder.[29] Moreover, like Michel de Sainte Lucie, he was the philanthropical owner of a hardware business, known particularly for having helped his workers to build and secure their homes.[30] In unearthing this repressed story, the crime novel morphs into a roman à clef, blurring the boundaries between the fictive (this is, as we have seen, an extravagant and credibility-defying story) and the real. And the reader is (doubly) denied narrative closure—we neither find out, for sure, who killed the *béké* of Trinité, nor do we uncover the precise relationship between this most ludicrous novel and the true-life crime.

But here the murder of the *béké* patriarch, both historical and fictional, carries a different metaphorical charge than in the other two novels. In political terms, Michel's allegiances and indeed his treatment of both daughters, legitimate and illegitimate, position him as the sole "good father" in a cast of reprehensible *békés,* while Hayot (a character wonders whether he is "pater familias or godfather," 167), the corrupt bishop, and even Aimé Césaire, often referred to as Papa,[31] fulfil the role of bad fathers. Martinique itself is torn between de Gaulle and Pétain and his local representative, Robert. White male authority figures dominate all institutions (church, medical profession, politics, and business) and are hypocritical, predatory, and corrupt. Dr. Doumenge has burned the evidence at the scene of the crime, while Inspector Levesque is literally and metaphorically driven away from the investigation by the bishop and put on a plane back to the metropole. All are pathetically in hock to a Vichy regime that has been opportunistically welcomed by many (Admiral Robert attends church flanked by *békés* Lejeune and Hayot), and all are shown to connive with each other to secure their positions. From this perspective, the dissident Michel de Sainte Lucie needs to be neutralized in order to guarantee the survival of the species.

All three novels discussed thus far revolve around, or culminate in, the death of the white father (coincidentally, in each case, called Michel). These dead white men have fathered almost exclusively female children (Sainte Lucie's son Philippe in *Qui a tué?* barely features in the story, while his daughters have key roles).[32] The family dramas are therefore strikingly non-Oedipal: there are no sons to overthrow the omnipotent, castrating father to ensure their own survival, because survival itself is in jeopardy. All are representatives of an already ebbing paternal line and a patronymic brought, in these novels, to a violent end. In this sense all stage a very literal downfall: as white male bodies crash to the floor, any notion that hegemonic power, the law of the father, can be inviolable, impenetrable, and closed off is radically rewritten in the lacerated, bruised, and bloody bodies of the patriarchy. Each novel, moreover, zeroes in on gruesome descriptions of brain injury, cerebral hemorrhage, and cranial trauma. Dupin blows his own brains out, Sainte Lucie is shot in the head by his own weapon, and Blanière's "skull is smashed open" (138) by the heavy bottle of rum. If men are shown to be the "brains" behind business, canny negotiators, cruel overlords, and often corrupt operators, their wives are willfully ignorant, even disdainful, of their activities. These fatal head wounds, all delivered at home, and by their own weapons (the heavy bottle of rum is one of Blanière's prized possessions), suggest both economic unsustainability and a conspicuous capacity for self-destruction.

That is not to say that the three novels share a single ideological message. Just as the decapitated statue of Joséphine, with which we opened this study, lends itself to a metaphorical reading, it would be tempting to read these fictional assaults on male power, and specifically on the head, as pointing to a decapitated and therefore fatally weakened plantocracy. Cabort-Masson does not fit this reading: rather, he suggests that the good father, who embodies the best reflexes of paternalism—benevolence to his workers, attentiveness to his children—is incompatible with the plantocracy and must be removed from within. For Confiant and Micaux, however, the death of the old paternalistic and patriarchal order can be seen as part of a particular crisis linked to the events of 2009: the male power embodied in Dupin and Blanière is in the course of these novels disabled, decapitated, and definitively neutralized. Both Confiant and Micaux, significantly, also feature progressive *béké* characters who are vocal critics of their caste and who refuse the self-segregating, isolationist, and racist tendencies of white Creoles. In *Bal masqué,* Pierre-Marie de Reynaud invests, symbolically, in renewable energy, is in a monogamous relationship with a mulatta, and surrounds himself with local (Black) art and a picture of Nelson Mandela (192), rather than the ubiquitous ancestral portraits that grace other *béké* homes in the novel. The narrator notes that the "ancient haughtiness" of these "descendants of conquistadors" (191) has already faded. And Emmanuelle de Blanière, as we saw above, is intellectually attuned to Black artists and socially intimate with non-*békés*.

Both writers, while highly critical of *béké* society, tentatively suggest the emergence of what Confiant describes as "a new race of *békés*" (191) whose survival will depend on rejection of the established codes of Creole society and authentic engagement with the Black population. Meanwhile the fate of Michel in *Qui a tué?* reinscribes the self-protective instincts of the caste even as it explores an intraclan murder. Just as Julie in Maynard's *Outre-mer* must be removed (by suicide in the earlier novel), so too the dissident Michel, in a novel set a century later, has to be violently neutralized.

La belle créole: Can the Subaltern Speak?

Cabort-Masson's novel reveals itself, in its closing pages, to be a heavily fictionalized version of the real-life murder of Robert Huyghues Despointes. *La belle créole* (the English translation carries the same title), published ten years later, opens, in a nice illustration of the close interconnectedness and temporal endurance of (the same) *béké* families, with a dedication to another member of the clan; the unidentified Amédée is in fact Condé's close friend and collaborator, Amédée Huyghues Despointes, a prominent *béké* and patron of the arts in Guadeloupe.[33] Her novel is set in 2001 (also the year of its release), on an unnamed Caribbean island, a thinly fictionalized and dystopian Guadeloupe.

While *Qui a tué* features, as we have seen, a series of proliferating, overlapping, and incestuous love triangles, *La belle créole* has at its core a classic "treacherous double love triangle"[34] between three protagonists: white Creole Loraine Féréol de Brémont, her Black lover/gardener Dieudonné Sabrina, and the lighter-skinned artist Luc. Loraine, an aging alcoholic (her forename, to any Antillean, conjures the Martinican "blond" beer, Lorraine), is the only surviving member of a very rich family. She is childless; indeed, a teenage abortion necessitated by sex with her father's middle-aged friend (abuse is implied in Loraine's account) has left her infertile. Yet again, sexual dysfunction and sterility are shown to be linked. But infertility, disease, and degeneration would seem to have a congenital grounding as well, affecting white women most profoundly. Loraine's paternal aunt Yolande is also "sterile" (44), while her twin sister died at fifteen from leukemia, an illness that carries a particular metaphorical charge for a caste so invested in the quality of their blood. At Yolande's funeral, *békés* are shown to be sickly and degenerate: Dieudonné, who accompanies his mistress, is struck by their old age, their crumpled parchment-like skin, their washed-out hair and discolored eyes, and the lack of "new blood." They are said to resemble "the last survivors, the increasingly hoary, fragile, and threatened guardians of a time that would never return, but which remained firmly anchored in their nostalgic hearts" (45). Yolande has had to sell off the family treasures, and her house is curiously empty; meanwhile the names inscribed on her gravestone, all of which carry the obligatory nobiliary particle, recall "former splendors and glories" (46). Loraine, like so many of the *béké* protagonists discussed in this book, is the last in her line and will herself die prematurely.

In middle age Loraine embarks on a relationship with a young Black drifter, Dieudonné, whom she initially employed as her gardener.[35] She is a failed writer, art collector, and patron of local painters, who has been thrice married to white men; her alcoholism, coupled with her sexual history (she has had relationships with men from across the color spectrum), means that she is ostracized from her caste, not fitting the stereotypes of virginal purity and sexual reserve that continue to characterize the "ideal" of white femininity. The return of Luc, an opportunistic artist with whom Loraine is infatuated, displaces Dieudonné and upsets the relatively peaceful status quo. Luc attempts to seduce Dieudonné, which triggers repressed memories of Dieudonné's childhood abuse at the hands of a gay man and, despite his own desire for Luc, he reacts with fury. Loraine happens upon the men fighting and banishes Dieudonné. When he returns to her home, she tries to kill him and, in self-defense, he shoots her with her own gun. In the highly mediatized trial that ensues, and to the surprise of most observers, Serbulon, Dieudonné's lawyer, has him acquitted, appealing in his defense to a familiar narrative of slave exploitation and humiliation to explain Dieudonné's actions, "the old stock roles" and "hackneyed motifs" deployed by the cynical lawyer, who does not believe his own narrative (30). The novel opens with this acquittal, then scrolls back to events preceding the death, and forward, to Dieudonné's hopeless freedom and eventual suicide.

This is a(nother) bleak novel, then, in which the self-destructive tendencies of the two main characters mirror, as in the other novels discussed here, a more general societal dysfunction. Despite the trappings and accoutrements of advanced capitalism (outsized plasma televisions, automobiles, designer sports gear, champagne, now preferred by locals to rum), islanders struggle with the most basic exigencies of daily life. Strikes and social disorder are pervasive, affecting citizens' lives from cradle to grave: rotting rubbish casts a pervasive stench, doctors are on hunger strike, electricity blackouts mean that infants' milk quickly sours, and overflowing morgues are unable to refrigerate the corpses they house. Poverty, robberies, rape, and murder characterize daily life; vigilantes patrol the streets (and are themselves frequently murdered); and Port-Mahault, the fictional town in which the novel is set, has, quite literally, gone to the dogs.[36] Left-wing politics offers no hope, but rather is exposed as hypocritical and self-serving: union leaders, whose decisions to cut off vital services cause such extreme hardship for the community, have electricity generators at home, while Mathias Serbulan's appropriation of revolutionary thinkers such as Césaire and Fanon in constructing his defense is a cynical rhetorical posture. The graffiti scrawled on a derelict supermarket ("Whites out"; "Fuck Off, French People," 10), slogans that uncannily prefigure the mantras of the 2009 strikes, are shown to be equally empty, offering only an ironic commentary on a story that explores a Black man's pathetic and self-destructive infatuation with a white woman.

The proliferation of narrative perspectives, and in particular the pervasive use of free indirect discourse, ensures that, until the belated revelation of the facts of Loraine's death (on page 163—the story proper ends on page 176), the truth of what happened is deferred, unstable, and fluid. Dieudonné, following his acquittal, becomes an overnight celebrity; he is variously seen as a "hero of the people," even a film star (11), is admired by his (unknowing) half-sisters as a Lenny Kravitz lookalike (135), and is also a source of fear and dread to characters such as Carla and Ana's grandmother. Throughout the novel, characters describe themselves as being unable to make up their minds about what happened, or change their mind along the way, generating complex maps of misreading of what is, in fact, a simple case of killing in self-defense. Serbulon presents the incident in straightforwardly racist terms, as evidence of atavistic Black male savagery, the humiliated slave rising up in vengeance against his cruel mistress. Serbulon's father, left-wing activist Pierre, sees in his son's legal victory the triumph of good (Black resistance) over evil (colonialism), while others read the incident as evidence of a generalized and endemic abuse of women; as one female character comments, "even though she was a *bekée*, this put her in the interminable list of victims of almighty male power" (87). Milo, Dieudonné's absent father, speculates that the motive was theft, given that his son's best friend, Rodrigues, is a well-known thief. Arielle, Milo's wife, and the only practicing Christian in the novel (it is she who encourages Milo to assume his fatherly responsibilities in Dieudonné's hour of need) uncharitably declares, in the middle of her nightly prayers, that Loraine deserved her fate not because of her caste "but because she was a bad person" (138).

But the key reason for the peculiar indeterminacy of the novel has less to do with the proliferation of narrative perspectives than with the protagonist's remarkable reticence and detachment, and in this respect Dieudonné can be considered a subaltern character. He says nothing in his own defense to the police who arrest him, and is entirely silent in court, allowing Serbulan to "construct his absurd theories" (163). Occasionally he is drawn into reluctant dialogue with others; but his monosyllabic and petulant responses to Dorisca and Ana, women who offer him love and much-needed shelter, testify to his self-destructive and incommunicative nature. His two most significant relationships (with Marine, his mother, and with Loraine) are characterized precisely by the absence of speech. The former is rendered mute by the accident that leaves her paralyzed as a young woman, and the pair lives together in silence for many years, making Dieudonné suspicious of the spoken word and more comfortable with its absence. Loraine is generally so drunk at night that communication is impossible, while Dieudonné in turn is too intimidated to speak to her ("dumbfounded," 39), or able only to stutter a reply. The intimate moments of their relationship are conveyed not only in free indirect discourse, but also in a series of interrogatives, suggesting that Dieudonné himself has only a vague grasp of the details of the relationship ("When did Dieudonné first offer her his arm for her afternoon walks? [. . .] When did he first start running to the Texaco convenience store in the middle of the night to buy her alcohol? [. . .] When did he first start showering her with care and attention?" 41). And Dieudonné's relationship with Luc is even more strikingly a one-way communicative street; although he is flattered that Luc solicits his opinion, he is utterly incapable of answering his direct and provocative questions. When asked about art, he "didn't know what to say" (51), and at other points flatly refuses to answer questions (158); when Luc asks how much Loraine pays him, an especially loaded question in the context of their unequal power relationship, Dieudonné's answer is literally an ellipsis (155).

Dieudonné is especially reluctant to assume or sustain the first person: he speaks in his own voice for the first time only on page 35, and then, merely to tell his grandmother that he is going out. Subsequently he intervenes only very rarely, and briefly, in the first person, and when he does it is mainly for functional iterations (to ask Ana for a place to stay for a night; to give his name to street criminals). In general, then, Dieudonné is the object of other people's discourse (spoken to, at, about, for, and over), and therefore has a curiously weakened subjectivity, or what Nicole Simek describes as a "keenly disturbing evacuation of identity."[37] Readers familiar with Condé's work, and especially her 1989 novel, *Traversée de la mangrove,* know the significance of narrative voice and of first-person access for this writer. This earlier novel, also about the mysterious death of a (*béké*-descended) character,[38] likewise manipulates the conventions of the detective plot to underscore "the importance of the act of reading within and outside the parameters of the text."[39] *Traversée* features a striking oscillation between the first- and third-person narrative (the former generally, but not exclusively, reserved for women characters), a technique that "is indicative of the implicit author's intention to differentiate and problematize the narrative voices of her characters."[40] For an author so profoundly attentive to issues of voice and perspective, writing a novel that turns on a trial, a scenario in which telling one's own story is of paramount importance, the paucity of direct and unmediated access to the central character's inner world is a significant narrative choice. And while, as Jacques Coursil has argued, the use of free indirect discourse means that the reader, more than any other character, has access to Dieudonné's thoughts,[41] this access usually conveys bafflement, lack of understanding, or gives way to other viewpoints.

Because of this scarcity of both direct dialogue and first-person narration, the two instances in which Dieudonné is given extended access to the unmediated expressivity of the "je" are worth dwelling on at some length. The first occurs over halfway through the novel, when he finally feels compelled to unburden himself to the garrulous Dorsica. In the shift from free indirect discourse to the first person, over two pages, Dieudonné has the belated opportunity to tell his story in his own voice. Yet this narrative is primarily a rather pathetic, indeed delusional, defense of Loraine, in which her voice entirely subsumes his. He retains the first-person for only a paragraph and then concedes the "je" to her, creating an extended first-person narrative (hers) within a much briefer one (his). This is less an act of narrative takeover than of surrender. Dieudonné begins by insisting that he was "happy" with Loraine and that she was "always nice"—both observations cast in a strangely childish emotional register—except on those occasions when she'd had "too much to drink" (98). He acknowledges that, when drunk, she would address him in the following terms: "You're so stupid! Dumb as a donkey! Why am I wasting my time with a stupid guy like you?" (98; "Tu es bête! Bête à manger du foin. Qu'est-ce que je perds mon temps avec un type bête comme toi?" 165). But the narrative insists that Loraine lives in a permanent state of inebriation, and the reader can therefore infer that such humiliation was the dominant mode of their relationship. Moreover, in her address to him the slippage in the original French, from the adjectival *bête,* meaning stupid, to its nominative case, *bête* meaning beast, reactivates racist associations of Blacks, and specifically slaves, with both intellectual incapacity and animality.

As Dieudonné's story segues into Loraine's, she emerges as a self-obsessed and delusional grotesque; his assertion that she could laugh at herself, for example, is immediately undermined. She claims to be more talented than Marguerite Duras (another alcoholic writer from a colonial background), but that her "cursed" *béké* status has prevented her success as a writer. Planters, she laments, were simply carrying out the dirty work of the French, who in turn despise them for sleeping with their slaves. Meanwhile they are also hated by Blacks who only remember the bad masters. Indeed, good masters, she claims, get even harsher treatment, being viewed as hypocrites and paternalists, so that *békés* "lose across the board" (98). If she rehearses here some of the key tropes of the *béké* persecution complex—and, unwittingly, as I will argue below, describes the power dynamics of her own sexual liaisons in terms of a spurious and entirely self-serving distinction between "good" and "bad" mastery—Loraine also falls into self-pitying cliché in her presentation of her own history. Her deceased sister was more intelligent, more beautiful, and more loved by her parents than she was; her parents wanted her to be a doctor; her failure at school, along with her three unsuccessful marriages, have disappointed them (99).

The second, and last, passage that affords the "je" position to Dieudonné is an interior monologue (114–16), prompted by his grandmother, Arbella's, revelation that Milo is his father, and that the wealthy businessman wishes to put things right with his son. This shock announcement sparks an extremely violent, but also rather childlike, murder fantasy. Blaming Milo for the deaths of his mother and Loraine, Dieudonné imagines himself stabbing Milo ("I'll bleed him like a pig," 115), then cutting the body up and roasting it on a spit. His fury gives way to memories of the relationship with Loraine, a relationship here constructed as having been poisoned by Luc's arrival; again, Dieudonné is incapable of seeing the abusiveness of the relationship. He remembers her calling him "black trash full of bitterness and spite [. . .] a common nobody" (115). While he knew that she was out of his league, he felt that he had a small space in her life, "like a dog has a doghouse" (115). Once again, his blackness is mobilized in conjunction with worthlessness and with animality.

As well as reiterating Dieudonné's destitution, the passage is significant in its introduction of, and concentration of reference to, the idea of reparation: the verb "réparer" is used four times over as many pages in the original French. Dieudonné's narrative is triggered by Arbella's apparently pleonastic description of Milo's motivation, "it's repairing that he wants to repair" ("C'est réparer qu'il veut réparer," 192—the English translation "making amends is what he wants," 114, losing the repetition and linguistic force of the original French). The term means nothing to Dieudonné, who begins and ends his narrative with a characteristically confused interrogative: "What does that mean, make amends?" (115); "Qu'est-ce que ça veut dire réparer?" (195). Ostensibly relating, here, to the absent father's desire to make good, to repair, the paternal relationship, the word in French inevitably conjures the debate around reparations for slavery, a debate that was especially live at the time the novel appeared: in the wake of the 150th anniversary of Abolition (1998) and the year in which the Taubira Law declared slavery to be a crime against humanity.[42] Later, in more typically political terms, Luc justifies Loraine's support for him by claiming that "she was only paying a small part of the considerable debt accumulated on the part of the Race" (158). More generally, Dawn Fulton argues that the defense narrative mobilized by Serbulon "resonates powerfully with legal arguments that inform the demand for reparations, whereby contemporary society is held responsible for the debts incurred by past generations."[43] But this first, repeated, use of the word is curiously detached from any political context, and therefore both conjures and evades the subject of slavery. Dieudonné typically chooses not to engage with any concept of reparation in personal, but also political, terms. The resigned closing line of his narrative—"What does that mean, make amends? You can't undo what's been done. Change what has already taken shape" (116)—speaks to the paternal relationship but can also be read as a restatement of the irrelevance of slavery for contemporary Guadeloupe.

While characters such as Loraine, Luc, and the Serbulons remain obsessed with the slave past, Dieudonné steadfastly refuses to see contemporary Guadeloupe as conditioned by this ("Oppressed by whom? By what? He was born in the wrong cradle, bad luck!" 53). But his lack of self-awareness and general political naïveté, to say nothing of his constant wish to exculpate Loraine, discredit this perspective, and the diegesis works also to destabilize this postracial discourse. Dieudonné is constructed both in his own free indirect discourse, and in the narrative generally, as a child, or even a baby (as in his reference above to being born in the wrong the cradle) or a fetus (18). He focuses on the anatomical markers of maternity on the childless Loraine's body ("her dejected breasts sagging with the weight of their nipples. Her stomach with its curves like a gourd," 41–42) rather than eroticism, and generally eschews sex with other women. His emotional and intellectual responses are infantile in the extreme. His jealousy of Loraine's dog, Lili, which culminates in his poisoning the animal, is the jealousy of a displaced child ("He couldn't stand seeing her constantly curled up at Loraine's breast or on her knees anymore. He couldn't stand seeing Loraine covering her slobbering little mouth with passionate kisses," 48). Hence his (highly Freudian) desire to murder his father, and yet his simultaneous childish pride, even "jubilation," that his father is "not just some nobody" (131). His inability to take responsibility for, or even to engage with, his son (a boy conceived by Ana on the one occasion that they have sex) is further evidence of immaturity: "Babies made him uneasy" (129).

Celia Britton, in a careful psychoanalytical reading of the novel, links the scenario explored in the novel to slavery but not necessarily to race. Britton identifies a "chain of causality in which plantation slavery creates the matrifocal family, which leads to the son's incestuous desire for his mother, which in turn results in his homosexuality, which in Dieudonné's case arouses Loraine's furious jealousy with regard to Luc."[44] It is this jealousy that causes her to shoot at him, and that in turn prompts his shooting her in self-defense. Britton notes that "ironically, Dieudonné is the only one of this love triangle for whom race is irrelevant."[45] But in taking Britton's argument a step further, I would emphasize that race is irrelevant for Dieudonné not because of any conscious rejection of racial discourses, nor any thought-out ideological position in terms of their meaning in the contemporary Caribbean. Rather it is because of ignorance, or even a childlike innocence. Dieudonné doesn't "understand or share [Luc's] rancor" (158): ignorance inoculates him from anger but leads directly to his own exploitation. In justifying his ignorance of slavery—neither Marine nor Arbella talked to him about the past, he claims—he reinscribes his childlike dependency on (grand) mothers for historical information. He is vaguely aware of a shared heritage with the African Americans he sees in films and on TV, who were "fruits of the same womb," but only momentarily dwells on "how exactly" this had happened, before concluding, somewhat petulantly, that he "didn't know and hardly cared" (158). While Simek suggests that he actively refuses "to grant any privileged hermeneutic status to the historic past,"⁴⁶ I would argue that Dieudonné remains enslaved by his ignorance, an ignorance that is a necessary precondition to his exploitation by Loraine, and one which allows Loraine to treat him as a beast, a child, a subaltern, a *nègre*.

In a sense, then, Loraine's death is the ultimate red herring; in and of itself, it indeed has nothing to do with color, race, or slavery, but is instead a momentary reflex of self-defense toward an out-of-control female by a socially vulnerable younger man. But almost everything else in this racially saturated novel works, if not to insist on the relevance of slavery, at least to suggest that slavery, and the racism that is bound up in its heritage, is not *not* relevant. Loraine is ostracized from her caste precisely because of her relationships with nonwhites. Her claim (itself the product of white privilege) that it is perfectly possible for a white woman and a Black man (i.e., Luc) to be in love—"They're imbeciles who think slavery's still alive today, who can't conceive that a *nègre* in this country can really truly love a *bekée*" (128)—is intensely ironic. She is unaware that Luc's view of her is entirely determined by his desire for vengeance, a vengeance directly, if somewhat simplistically, connected to the slave past (he considers Loraine's patronage, as we saw above, to be part payment of the debt accumulated "on the part of the Race, over the centuries of slave trading, slavery, exploitation of every type and humiliation of every sort," 158). Dieudonné's belief in the equality of suffering across all sections of Antillean society ("loneliness and mourning dwell in both the *kaz nèg* and the master's house," 131) is not only intensely naïve, but is expressed immediately after his childhood memory of being ostracized by rich white children.

Taken together, such moments categorically give the lie to Loraine's supposed colorblindness. It is after all, as Shannon Sullivan has shown, the prerogative of whites to choose Blacks as friends: "to be with non-white people, to go to non-white places, to participate in non-white bodily expressions are further demonstrations of white privilege. Non-whites, on the other hand, do not always have the choice to venture into white spaces."⁴⁷ Loraine is infatuated with the light-skinned Luc, while we know that Dieudonné is very dark skinned. Dieudonné is categorically cast as slave to her mistress; his role is one of abject subservience, gratitude, and loyalty. This relationship is therefore determined by them both "staying in their places" (42), which is why the "enormity of his presence" at Yolande's wake takes him starkly out of his comfort zone: he feels ashamed and doesn't know, quite literally, where to put himself (45). Conversely Luc's relationship with the *békée* springs from the conviction that "she has to be put in her place" (159); by this, Luc aspires to degrade and humiliate her rather than to grant her a position of privilege. At another point he describes sex with Loraine in terms of a murder fantasy: "Sometimes, I imagine that I'm finishing her off. I imagine that her cries of pleasure are death rattles" (80). Both men's responses to the white woman, whether they seek validation or revenge, are fundamentally conditioned by their knowledge, or lack of knowledge, of the slave past.

In *La belle créole,* as in Condé's fiction more generally, readers are forced into an active interpretative role, rather like the novel's police and the judiciary: her slippery fictions, founded on double and triple bluff, ensure that meanings are not secured or legitimized within the texts themselves, and that facts, even when established, can lead to a variety of possible conclusions. But Holly Collins's reading of this novel significantly underplays the overwhelmingly bleak message contained within it. She acknowledges that racial tensions do exist in the novel, but that Condé "shows nonetheless that the Guadeloupean society in which *La belle créole* takes place, and hopefully the 'brave new world' about which she spoke in 1998, are creeping closer to a more open and hopeful conception of identity—one that no longer allows itself to be partially or wholly defined by race and imposed by a racialized color."[48] I have argued here, on the contrary, that race, founded in the experience of slavery, continues to determine the destinies of the novel's characters. The association of Dieudonné with babyhood and animality, his general silence and lack of access to unmediated subjectivity (the slave narrative, in which the enslaved told their own stories, was historically absent in the French Caribbean tradition), the meaninglessness of his eventual liberation ("a freedom he didn't know what to do with," 98), the prominence of a discourse of reparations, his fear of dogs, as well as the comparisons of Dieudonné to a dog (82, 90, 115), his lack of control over his own destiny, and his humiliation in the relationship with Loraine, all point to his subaltern status, a status intrinsically connected to the slave past. Serbulon in the end rejects his own version of the facts, based on his having played the "race card," and decides rather that "an entirely modern drama" is unfurling; but Condé leaves open the possibility that these "old stock roles" (30) are still very much in play in the contemporary Caribbean. This story of a defenseless slave's revenge may well be a cliché, what Dawn Fulton calls "a file that already exists in the jury's memory and needs only to be accessed, prompted by a few key images."[49] But, as the old cliché goes, just because it's a cliché that doesn't mean that it's not true.

Richard Dyer's *White* concludes, much like the present book, with a chapter entitled "White Death." Here Dyer identifies an emergent discourse in the 1990s in which "whiteness, especially masculinity, is under threat, decentered, angry," and is linked in films such as *Falling Down* and *Blade Runner* with reproductive impotence and even homosexuality. The four novels analyzed here, all released in roughly the same period, undoubtedly key into some of these general ideas around masculine anxiety and what Dyer calls the "emptiness of whiteness and its terminal reproductive line."[50] But these novels function in a very specific way as a powerful and flexible mode for interrogating the racial history of the islands of Martinique and Guadeloupe. While, in conventional grammars of representation, everything black or dark is metaphorically linked to danger, fear, or violence, these *noir* novels establish white as the color of peril, deceit, and brutality. Moreover, in their often freewheeling and ludicrous plots, or in the chaotic lifestyles of their drunken, corrupt, sexually capricious, and promiscuous protagonists, they constitute a concerted rejoinder to one of the defining constructions of whiteness, which sees it as conventionally linked to order, rationality, self-control, and endurance. And the novels offer another remarkably consistent diagnosis of the racial tensions in the islands: whatever the apparent premise of narrative, all four are less about the fatal confrontation *between* castes in the Antilles than about a pronounced tendency toward self-destruction (alcoholism, suicide, infanticide, mariticide) *within* white Creole culture itself, via the family, the couple, even the individual. All, in other words, bear out Abder's observation in Placoly's *Frères volcans* that "the master has more to fear from himself than from us" (16).

In none of the novels considered here is the killing that drives the story categorically or unproblematically the fault of Black characters. In this way, these texts invoke and play with a key premise of classic detective fiction, which aligns "mystery conventions with anxieties over contamination, irrationality, and the threat posed to imperial modernity by unassimilated racial and cultural difference," only to offer a powerful rejoinder to it.[51] If some white characters are deeply anxious about contamination by outsiders (Micaux, Confiant), their anxiety is either in the final analysis fatally misplaced, or is cannily mobilized as a convenient smokescreen that enables their crimes (Confiant, Cabort-Masson). Meanwhile, endogamy and suspicion, paranoia and conspiracy are powerfully shown in every novel (even in *Qui a tué* and *La belle créole,* where the dead white protagonist chafes against such conventions) to be at the core of *béké* societal malaise.

Peter Messent has argued that one of the most productive ways of thinking about crime fiction "is its relationship to the dominant social system: to the hierarchies, norms, and assumptions of the particular area, country, and historical period it represents."[52] The genre in this case allows writers to name (the use of the word *béké* in three of the four titles is itself a political act), shame, and kill off white characters. But the inherent racism of the justice system means that, for Micaux and Cabort-Masson at least, the white perpetrator gets away with it, while the patriarch's suicide, in Confiant's *Bal masqué,* is at once an admission of guilt and the ultimate evasion of responsibility. Meanwhile Condé's Dieudonné exemplifies the catch-22 situation for Black males who have been charged with violent crime: even when found "innocent" (albeit it on the basis of an invented defense, and one even more judicially damaging than the facts of the incident itself), they cannot unproblematically reintegrate into a society in which they are already viewed with suspicion and fear. As Condé notes sardonically in *La belle créole* (33), community service, the best outcome for young Blacks convicted of a crime through the justice system, serves only to further enrich the *béké* caste in the closed economic circuit in which everybody, ultimately, is, as the saying goes, "working for the *béké*." Justice cannot be done in any of these novels, because of a color-coded justice system that continues to defer to white privilege and an assumption of white innocence. Finally, only Condé has a Black character kill a white, in a novel that breaks another taboo in foregrounding a white woman who sleeps with Black men. And even then, this killing is in self-defense. The ultimate taboo, of Black murdering white, remains curiously intact.

Conclusion

> Time, at its own pace, carries out its work: *Négritude* and *Blanchitude,* Martinican dramas, are coming to an end.
> —Tony Delsham, *Dérives,* 1999

THIS STUDY of the fictional representation of the *béké* caste in the islands of Martinique and Guadeloupe began with the first Antillean novel, *Les amours de Zémédare et Carina* (1806). Traversay's novel closes with the emergence of a new generation of white Creoles, seamlessly enabled through the marriage of the title characters, who are shown to prosper, and produce children themselves, in a benign Martinique that celebrates their joy with them. In many respects Traversay's novel is, then, both the first and the last of its kind: the easy regeneration of the *béké* line signaled in the novel's ending stands as a rare, if not unique, diegetic resolution, as is the sense of collective joy engendered by the family's expansion. My study draws to a close in chapter 6, with an investigation of *béké* murder and violent death in contemporary Antillean crime fiction. The most recent novel discussed here, Raphaël Confiant's *Bal masqué à Békéland* (2013), culminates in the suicide of the *béké* father, the murder of his daughter, and the revelation of the existence of a second, profoundly handicapped, daughter, whose congenital impairment results from the extreme inbreeding that characterizes the caste. The novels analyzed in the intervening four chapters, which can be read as fictions of whiteness in various guises and disguises, span a period of two centuries and have been authored by both *béké* and non-*béké* writers. All have tended to privilege self-destruction over romance, death over love, deterioration over rebirth, Thanatos over Eros. The congenital impairment of the mute and unnamed Dupin daughter is, perhaps, an extreme example of degeneration; but her fate is decidedly more typical of the fictional *béké* than the radiant, secure, and expanding family line of the beautiful and fertile Carina.

As this book has progressed, I have investigated the emergence of typologies of race and skin color, analyzing the sanctification of whiteness, its canonization in the collective imaginary, and its shifting representations in fiction, and often within a single text. Whiteness is crucially important to the sense of *béké* identity—Pierre Guillaume describes it as the only criterion of belonging accepted by all[1]—and is therefore a fantasized and a fetishized state, and a source of profound anxiety. A key aim of this book has been to pay close attention to a number of early white Creole novelists; these writers have been neglected by critics who often begin their analysis in the mid-twentieth century, and frequently consign earlier texts to the category of preliterature. These early texts are crucial in helping us to better understand the longer genealogy of Antillean writing, and give access to particular anxieties around racial identity and mixing as the phenomena began to assert themselves in the literary imagination. In my closing chapter I investigate another genre, consigned by many to the category of subliterature: crime fiction. And the intervening chapters, discussing Glissant, Chamoiseau, Placoly, and Jaham, offer a spectrum of perspectives on the white Creole. Chapter 3 looks at fiction by the two major French Caribbean novelists of the twentieth century, continuing and deepening this portrayal of dysfunction and degeneration. The Senglis plantation in *The Fourth Century* in particular is shown to be a decaying space of perversion. Meanwhile Chamoiseau's work registers an increasing, and increasingly dark, treatment of whiteness: if his early novels assign to the *béké* a walk-on part, and focus almost entirely on poor Blacks, his later fiction affords greater diegetic space to the white Creole, and specifically to the sexual violence and incest that characterized the perverted sexual economy of slavery. Placoly's *Frères volcans*, discussed in chapter 4, gives the reader a uniquely extended access to the inner world of the white Creole protagonist, through the intimacy of the diary form. But even this more sympathetic *béké*, immured as he is in his own study, is fatally disconnected not only from the Black world outside his window, but even from women of his own caste. The sense of claustrophobia and imminent ending that this novel conveys suggests a profound psychosexual dysfunction. This dysfunction is also foregrounded in Marie-Reine de Jaham's *La grande béké*, the subject of chapter 5, a novel also shot through with anxiety regarding the future of the plantocracy. Jaham's novel mobilizes the language of creolization and mixing in describing Fleur's project of regeneration in *La grande béké*; but the introduction of her grandson Mickey is in fact a perpetuation of the same in genetic terms. And the crime novels discussed in my final chapter similarly foreground anxieties around reproduction, inheritance, and the closed and self-segregating world of *béké* society (almost a contradiction in terms in some of these texts), a world that resists outsiders and, in its attempts to distance itself from the "other" outside, is often peculiarly vulnerable to the threat from within.

These narrative tropes, based on self-legitimizing and linear thought systems, sit at something of a jagged angle to contemporary Antillean cultural discourse. Over the last thirty years, French Caribbean literary theory has been characterized by postmodern discourses and movements that valorize cross-cultural, relational, and mobile models of identity, whether we think of Glissant's creolization, his poetics of Relation and the rhizome, or the *créolité* movement, with its privileged metaphors of the mangrove, the mosaic, and the kaleidoscope. Derek Walcott's injunction to "break a vase" similarly puts an aesthetic of rupture, fragmentation, and radical reassembly at the core of Antillean identity.[2] All stand in contrast to what Chris Bongie describes as a modernist, but "now historically surpassed," version of identity "grounded in a roots-oriented logic of filiation and legitimacy."[3] This roots-oriented approach resonates obsessively instead in the discourse of fictional *békés*, which is marked by a fixation on clean lines of inheritance and with (patri)linear transmission. *Béké* characters in fiction repeatedly appeal to these clean lines of genetic security, thereby asserting their difference from the ex-slave population, for whom history and genealogy have been experienced as an irretrievable series of discontinuities. The *béké*'s wife in *The Overseer's Hut* notes with pride that her "line had resisted so many governors and general intendants with dynastic might" (113). Marie-Reine de Jaham's *grande béké* is the only survivor of "a great line of *békés* rooted in Martinique for three centuries" (17). And in *Eau de café* Confiant's Honoré de Cassagnac taunts the maroon, Julien Thémistocle, that he cannot identify a line stretching from father to grandfather to great-grandfather, because "you blacks are nobody's sons" (227–28). And yet in response, the maroon easily and spontaneously traces his lineage back through generations, while Cassagnac's decade-long attempt to research his ancestry has served only to expose uncertainty, gaps, and silences. The first ancestor comes to Martinique from Anjou "for obscure reasons" and is mysteriously sacked from his job as king's brewer; Cassagnac is unable to find the name of this man's wife. The *béké* is unable, moreover, to answer the maroon's question: "Do you know if your great grandmother allowed a negro to open her thighs?" (The question is especially provocative, given the general tolerance of white men having sexual relations with slave women, versus the taboo that surrounded white women sleeping with Black men.) Moreover, the family line is characterized by marriages between cousins and second cousins, and stunted by infertility, miscarriage, and disability.

Like the whiteness of which they are so proud, then, the linearity at the core of *béké* identity is itself a fiction or a fantasy, a spurious celebration of an illusory purity and certainty, which often sits in tension with, or is indeed overwritten by, another, quite different, geometric formation: the circle. Glissant characterizes the plantation superstructure in terms of circularity, describing it as an "enclosed space" in which "everything was taken care of within a closed circle."[4] The circle is a powerful metaphor in many of the novels considered here, deployed in connection with geography, genealogy, architecture, psychology; this geometric form has a structural role, too, in that novels can often be said to come full circle. Traversay, for example, features a new Creole town built as an amphitheater, surrounded by mountains in the shape of curtains (*Les amours*, 23). The circular horizon is used, as we saw in chapter 2, by Levilloux to describe the closed minds of the *béké* ethnocaste in *Les créoles* (68). Moreover, the romance plot that drives this novel brings its protagonists full circle, returning them to the primal sins of a father who in a single gesture at once recognized, and denied, his mixed-race son. More spectacularly *Outre-mer* in its final denouement unmasks as half siblings its putative lovers: Marius is revealed as the product of an affair between *béké* patriarch and female slave, now catastrophically returned to his origins. And generally, the *béké* family is often imagined, by white and nonwhite writers alike, as a circle. Chamoiseau, as we saw in chapter 3, stages a *béké* father orchestrating a "circle of purity" to keep the forces of contagion at bay (*Un dimanche au cachot,* 65). This is in fact a defensive and hermetically closed community, closed in upon itself, incapable of freeing its members and determined not to admit others. The scene graphically demonstrates how the dread of hybridity has made a dead end of the plantation. Incest is obliquely suggested, as the father caresses children turned in upon themselves, defensively poised to repel the other, and therefore to neutralize the threat of that other taboo, miscegenation. And Marie-Reine de Jaham, too, in her insistence on the "perverted" or "infected" vat again invokes a circular formation to suggest the concentration of (malignant) forces in a small geographic and genealogical universe.

Beyond the fiction considered in this book, the figure of the circle appears most graphically and most shockingly in the incendiary documentary *Les derniers maîtres de la Martinique,* in the family "tree" brandished by octogenarian Alain Huyghues Despointes. The documentary aired in January 2009, during the strikes in protest at the excessive cost of living and high unemployment (according to some estimates, three times higher than in France). In a quirk of timing, the film, prepared months earlier, was broadcast eight days into the strike, reflecting and catalyzing anti-*béké* sentiment in the islands. Romain Bolzinger interviews a number of middle-aged or elderly white men (the representatives of the caste featured in the film are exclusively male), hidden away in gated residences, steeped in economic privilege, currying political favor in Paris, and looking to that capital rather than to Fort-de-France as their political home. In the film's most controversial scene, Huyghues Despointes observes that in mixed-race families, "there is no harmony, and I don't think that's good," and concludes by invoking the *béké* mantra: "We wanted to preserve the race" ("on a voulu préserver la race"). The family "tree" that he produces in support of this remarkable defense of endogamy powerfully asserts that all *békés* are descended from the same ancestor, Jean Assier, and that all are therefore today related.[5]

Huyghues Despointes's dizzyingly circular family tree, which I have discussed in more detail elsewhere,[6] stands as a figure of identitarian concentration and self-containment. Realized as a series of concentric circles rather than as an arborescent structure, the tree in fact resembles a genealogical dartboard, with Assier, the primal ancestor, located at the bullseye, and appears to reduce rather than to extend genetic material. Huyghues Despointes rejoices in the stifling incestuousness of *béké* identity within a radically constricted gene-pool. The overt obsession with purity, and the more covert undertones of the reference to the single ancestor, are typical of a strain of *béké* discourse that fetishizes an uncontaminated and pure whiteness, repelling—and repressing the desire for—a necessary otherness. Jason Herbeck, working out of Glissant's circular plantation model, argues that the plantation's weakness was its very boundary: its "proximity to and *transactional* dependence on the outside world (commercially, technologically, etc.) essentially wreak havoc in the form of mobility, fragmentation, and cultural *métissage,* all of which are considered anathema to the structure's founding principles."[7] As a result, as Glissant argues, the system was unable to evolve, and collapsed everywhere, brutally or progressively, without regenerating its own ways of superseding itself. The white fictional family (the family often stands as a metonymy for society more generally) frequently succumbs to the same pressure, and the above image, although produced in the film as a source of spectacular pride, can also be read as a worryingly incestuous and inward-looking genetic and social graph, exemplifying the "clean lines and hermetic compartments" that are a source of horror for Chamoiseau (*Un dimanche*, 25).

Of course, we are talking here and throughout about fiction rather than real life. The most extraordinary story of all, from a sociological perspective at least, is that this closed and self-segregating community has survived at all, in a postcolonial world in which the dominant narrative has been one of supplanting the colonial overlords. One key difference between the Antilles and other postcolonial societies is precisely the length of *békés'* settlement in the islands—their arrival parallels, and in some cases marginally precedes, that of the enslaved peoples they forcibly brought to the islands and therefore, in Derek Walcott's resonant phrase, master and slave were equally "strange" in these alien islands. Or, to reprise David Macey's comment quoted in my introduction, "a *béké* is as much a native of Martinique as any mulatto or Black."[8] As Yarimar Bonilla has argued, the caste today can be seen to be in rude economic health, although exact figures regarding their ownership of land and business are contested. But as Guillaume argues, the "tacit hatred" with which they are viewed can explode at any point "in the context of social degradation."[9] The 2009 strikes offer a particularly riveting example of this degradation. The predominant motto deployed during this prolonged social unrest, "La Gwadloup cétan nou, cé pa ta yo" (Guadeloupe is ours, not yours), proposed an absolute distinction between "nous" (us) and "eux" (them), the haves and the have-nots, which was in practice a distinction between white and Black. While Bonilla suggests that the motto, as a "complex semiotic vehicle," depends for its power on the shifting indexical function of "'us' and 'them,'"[10] it is almost impossible not to see *békés* as the major constituent of the "eux" identified. Élie Domota's rhetoric, and notably his statement on 9 March 2009 that "either they [*békés*] put the agreement into practice, or they get out of Guadeloupe [. . .]. We won't stand by while a band of whites reestablish slavery,"[11] was deemed so provocative that the attorney general in Guadeloupe instigated a judicial enquiry into his alleged incitement to racial hatred. Huyghues Despointes, too, was tried for incitement to racial hatred and ordered to pay a substantial fine for his inflammatory words. Such examples testify to the extent to which the last decade, in the wake of the strikes, has been marked by a particularly heightened sensitivity to race and skin color, a situation that most certainly gives the lie to my epigraph, the ironic opening disclaimer to Tony Delsham's *Dérives* claiming that the psychodramas attaching to skin color in the Antilles are no longer relevant in the islands. The toppling of the statue of Schœlcher in May 2020 is part of this general move, and the removal of Joséphine's statue in July of the same year finally felled an especially imperious icon of white power.

Societal and political tensions have been further reactivated by the chlordecone scandal. From 1973 to 1993, the insecticide (also known as Kepone) was used in Martinique and Guadeloupe to combat the banana weevil. Ninety-five percent of Guadeloupeans and 92 percent of Martinicans are said to be contaminated by the product, which also causes premature birth, congenital defects, and has been linked to Parkinson's, Alzheimer's, and male infertility.[12] The chemical is associated with a range of cancers, notably breast and, in particular, prostate (Martinique had the highest rate of prostate cancer in the world in 2008 and continues to have one of the highest incidences of the disease). The product was outlawed in France in 1990 but special provision was made for its use to continue in the Antilles until 1993. (It had been banned in the United States since 1976.) While the French state was found to be primarily responsible in the parliamentary report commissioned by Emmanuel Macron and published in November 2019, Garcin Malsa speaks for many Antilleans in observing that the collusive and mutually sustaining relationship between French state and *béké* caste is the source of the scandal: "The State made the choice to satisfy the greed and financial appetite of the descendants of slave owners who unfortunately found accomplices in the political class of Martinique."[13] The tensions around skin color, class, and inequality play out in a particularly emotional way in this ongoing scandal. *Békés*, in denying responsibility for the situation, decry instead the racist anti-*béké* excesses of many of those who demand compensation and acknowledgment, in yet another example of the profound fault line that continues to run through this society.

In all this highly polarized debate and discussion, the emergence of the Tous Créoles! (All Creoles!) movement in 2007 is noteworthy for two reasons: first, in a context of cultural reticence, this *béké*-dominated movement represents an unusually visible intervention into the cultural politics of the islands.[14] Second, the emphasis on intercaste solidarity, and on a shared history and common contemporary preoccupations, represents an unusual opening toward the population of the islands more generally. The movement was founded by the most visible, accessible, and politically engaged *béké* on the islands in recent years, Roger de Jaham (1949–2017). Jaham had been the driving force behind a 1998 letter, signed by 400 of his fellow *békés*, in which slavery was acknowledged to be a crime against humanity ("We remember," "Nous nous souvenons"). The letter paved the way for Jaham's speaking at the 22 May commemorations of the Abolition of slavery in 2006 alongside Serge Letchimy, successor to Césaire as mayor of Fort-de-France, and his establishment of Tous Creoles! was in many ways the culmination of this attempt at political outreach. The movement positioned itself explicitly and unapologetically in the lineage of the *créolité* movement.[15] Its motto ("to create out of our differences a collective work"), language (the terms "creole" and "créolité" are sprinkled liberally as markers of positive cross-cultural interaction throughout the various documents and postings on the association's website), and overarching political agenda (defending human rights and combatting racism, xenophobia, racism, and all forms of discrimination) reprise tropes frequently invoked by the *créolité* writers and by Glissant.

From the start the movement was viewed with suspicion by many, because of the disproportionately heavy involvement of *békés* in the establishment and running of the organization, and because of the undoubtedly *béké*-centered worldview it propounded. Confiant is the movement's fiercest critic. As we saw in chapter 3, he claims that in drafting the *Éloge* he, Chamoiseau, and others had organized, over the course of a year in the mid-1980s, a series of meetings with Jaham and other *békés,* but that the supremacist ideology of the caste had caused the initiative to flounder. The discursive proximity between the two movements leads Confiant to talk of conceptual theft. He likens Jaham's maneuver to "an adversary who helps himself to your ideological tools" and concludes that the movement is a "perversion of *créolité.*"[16] Tous Créoles!, he argues, pays lip service to *créolité,* while remaining "a kind of social ecumenism that would suggest that there is no more class war."[17] He accuses Jaham of appropriating the language of *créolité* to gloss over the very profound inequalities of Antillean society, inequalities that derive directly from slavery. When such celebratory discourse is associated with, or appropriated and instrumentalized by, the *béké,* it clearly takes on a much more incendiary and offensive charge.[18] It remains to be seen whether the election of non-*béké* Gérard Dorwling-Carter as president of Tous Créoles! in July 2020, following the sudden death of Jaham in 2017, will lead to any significant change in political direction for the organization.

Whatever one may think of Roger de Jaham's political and cultural interventions, it is at the very least fair to say that he, in his attempts to reach out to the nonwhite populations of the Antilles, was atypical of his caste. Few other *békés* have put their heads above the proverbial parapet in recent years, and when they have it has often been, as we saw above, with disastrous results. Jaham's sudden death in 2017 has not signaled the end of Tous Créoles! but it has undoubtedly deprived the movement, and the caste more generally, of a charismatic, energetic, and media-savvy figure (as mentioned in chapter 5, Jaham's background was in advertising rather than in the more typical *béké* businesses of rum, supermarkets, agribusiness, or hotels), who acted as an able and persuasive spokesperson for the caste. A recent book launched in his honor by Tous Créoles! in 2019, *Créoles, tout bonnement!,* offers an anonymously authored and entirely self-congratulatory history of the movement (one section is subtitled "The problem with being right too early," 37). The book includes a number of short testimonies, written in "sincerity and humility" (45) by a high proportion of *béké* contributors, including Jaham himself, Emmanuel de Raynal, and Cécile Hayot-Royer, reminiscing about their childhood in the Antilles and, more specifically, on the difficulty of being a *béké* today. These pieces are unreflective about, and often in staggering denial of, the level of *béké* privilege, and are markedly nostalgic for the good old days. Jaham's own memories of anti-*béké* racism, shortage of money ("les fins de mois pas faciles," 48), and of a cramped three-bedroom house, and Hayot-Royer's conclusion that her late passport application was expedited quickly not because she was a *béké* but rather because of her father's friendship with the *préfet,* are misjudged attempts to downplay *béké* wealth and privilege and in many cases exemplify the persecution complex that has come to characterize the caste's interventions.[19] Peggy McIntosh's resonant image of white privilege, invoked in the introduction to this book, as being located in the "invisible weightless knapsack of special provisions, assurances, tools, maps, guides, codebooks, passports, visas, clothes, compass, emergency gear, and blank checks,"[20] is both metaphorically and literally present in this collection of testimonies.

Kate Marsh has shown how nostalgia based on imperial loss can be both de facto and anticipatory, generated in advance of loss as well as in its wake.[21] Pierre Dessalles, as early as 1811, observed that "the colonies are coming to an end,"[22] a sentiment that we find resonating in the work of Saint-John Perse ("We shall not always dwell in these yellow lands, our pleasance . . ."),[23] and later, in 1989, by Marie-Reine de Jaham's *grand béké:* "all the gold in the world won't turn the tide of history" (15). In many respects these gestures can be said to conform to the "stratagem" of the melancholic, defined by Slavoj Žižek as a mode of anticipation of the loss of the love object, which is itself profoundly linked to the insecurity of ownership: the only way to possess an object that we never really had, that was from the outset lost, is, he argues, "to treat an object that we still fully possess as if this object is already lost. The melancholic's refusal to accomplish the work of mourning thus takes the form of its very opposite, a faked spectacle of the excessive, superfluous mourning for an object even before this object is lost."[24] There is indeed something spectacular in Huyghues Despointes's family tree, also encoded in the title of Bolzinger's film, *Les derniers maîtres de la Martinique*. Similarly the images and metaphors through which the caste has imagined itself, or been imagined from the outside, have an often grandiose, and even grotesque, quality: the doomed Roman senators to whom Maynard compares Martinique's planters in *Outre-mer;* the infected barrel, or the perverted vat, of Jaham's last chance saloon Creole family; the extreme figures of the feminine uncanny (doll, mummy, ghost, and zombie) through which Glissant explores white Creole degeneracy in *The Fourth Century;* the sinister circle of familial purity invoked and revisited, in a yet more disturbing manner, by Chamoiseau; the huddle of degenerates who attend Yolande Féréole de Brémont's wake, "the last survivors, the increasingly hoary, fragile, and threatened guardians of a time that would never return, but which remained firmly anchored in their nostalgic hearts" (*La belle créole*, 45), and even the abjectly deformed statue of Joséphine with which we began our study. All partake of the familiar rhetorical signatures threaded throughout the fiction studied in this book: all are focused on the past and preoccupied with regret, and all explore a disappointing (even dangerous) present being continually juxtaposed and contrasted with a comforting but inaccessible past. And yet the security encoded in these texts, images, family trees, and memorials is, in Žižek's terms, a "fake," and in the title of this book, a "fiction." These bathetic and pathetic last gasps make necessarily insatiable demands on a past helpless to fulfill them, inventing, through a kind of parody of mourning (this is literally the case in *La belle créole*) a fantasized past of white purity and security that never in fact existed. In the same gesture, they project a shaky and uncertain future, another fictive maneuver that legitimizes the discourse of victimhood, scapegoating, and persecution that characterizes much contemporary *béké* discourse.

Notes

Preface

1. Chamoiseau, *Texaco,* 47–48. Ninon also refuses to describe slavery to her daughter, while Esternome, in a further occlusion, asks not to have to describe the dungeon "lest we ease the burden of those who built them," 36.

2. Adult reluctance to relay the story of slavery to children is a prevalent trope, not just in Antillean fiction but also in autobiographical writing by such authors as Gisèle Pineau, Maryse Condé, Patrick Chamoiseau, and Daniel Maximin. See McCusker, "'Troubler l'ordre de l'oubli.'"

3. In referring to his preference for numbers over poetry, Chamoiseau evokes the *béké*'s supposed philistinism, a view energetically propounded by the *créolité* writers, and which is often nuanced or undermined in the novels discussed in this book.

4. Dyer, *White,* 68.

5. Butler, *Gender Trouble,* 140.

6. For a polemical critique of this position see "Le décolonialisme, une stratégie hégémonique," an open letter signed by eighty French intellectuals, including Alain Finkielkraut, Pierre Nora, and Elisabeth Badinter. They object to the emergence of concepts such as "race," "racisation" (racialization), and "racisé.e.s" (racialized), as constituting an affront to the values of the Republic. These terms, as Bishop and Roth argue, seek to avoid naturalizing racial categories, stressing instead "the cultural, social, and political processes through which these identities emerge." See "Introduction," 1.

7. Fulton, *Signs of Dissent,* 97.

8. This monograph was completed in the aftermath of the murder of George Floyd on 25 May 2020 by a white police officer in Minneapolis. The outpouring of anger caused by this event, only the latest in a long line of murders of Black citizens by police in the United States, led to antiracism demonstrations across the globe and gave further energy to the Black Lives Matter movement.

9. See Ndiaye, "Gommer le mot 'race' de la constitution française est un recul."

10. As Brozgal argues, "The metaphor of color-blindness is a helpful shorthand in discussions of race-neutral politics and ideology in France, yet it is used almost exclusively by Anglophone scholars in English-language venues. While the figure is both efficient and evocative—one needn't understand the mechanics of the eye to understand how color-blind comes to mean 'race neutral'—it has no literal counterpart in French: the term for the same ocular dysfunction, *le daltonisme*, is not linguistically linked to the difficulty of seeing or distinguishing color, and thus cannot be made to function as an analogous trope." "Seeing through Race," 14.

11. Warmington, "Taking Race out of Scare Quotes," 281.

12. The extent of *béké* land ownership is a contested, and politically charged, issue. In *Les derniers maîtres de la Martinique* (The last masters of Martinique), it is estimated that the caste owns 45 percent of Antillean land and controls 40 percent of Antillean business. Roger de Jaham has frequently estimated *béké* ownership at less than half this figure. See, among many interventions from Jaham on this subject, Fouchet, "La colère antillaise."

13. Jugé and Perez, "Modern Colonial Politics," 187.

14. For example, the exoneration of the policemen accused of murdering of Adama Traoré in police custody in 2016; the ongoing fallout from the *Charlie Hebdo* massacre and subsequent attacks in Paris and Nice in 2015; the continuing rise of the Front National; the racist treatment of Guyanese Minister for Justice Christiane Taubira; MEP Valérie Morano's claim that France is a "pays de race blanche" (country of whites) in September 2015; continuing controversies surrounding the comedian Dieudonné, whose various positions have been supported by Martinican novelist Raphaël Confiant; a number of recent prosecutions for incitement to racial hatred taken by, and against, *békés* in the Antilles.

15. López, "Introduction," 13.

Introduction

1. Stuart, *Rose of Martinique*, 10. Joséphine is prominent in tourist materials, and the Pagerie plantation on the south of the island is one of Martinique's most popular tour destinations.

2. Although locals had threatened to remove the statues no provision had been made to secure them, registering no doubt the risk to public order, and perhaps the inevitability of their removal.

3. Barnes suggests that the act could not "have been executed without the help of machinery," *Cultural Conundrums*, 1. A participant stated, however, that the assailants used only a simple awl (a "poinçon"). https://la1ere.francetvinfo.fr/martinique/enlever-tete-josephine-fut-tres-simple-505015.html.

4. Rumors persist that the head remains hidden in the town hall of Fort-de-France. See Loichot, "Fort-de-France."

5. Figures derived from Schloss, *Sweet Liberty*, vii. Kovátz Beaudoux, in *Les blancs créoles*, also estimates their presence in Martinique at 1 percent, a figure corroborated in Bolzinger's *Les derniers maîtres*.

6. In contrast, white Creole identity has been generously analyzed in Anglophone Caribbean literature, where the work of Phyllis Shand Allfrey and, especially, Jean Rhys, has galvanized critics interested in the intersection of feminist and postcolonial readings. Michelle Cliff, too, has been considered a "white" writer by some. See, for two examples among many, Raiskin, *Snow on the Cane Fields* (1996) and Gregg, *Jean Rhys's Historical Imagination* (1995). The French Caribbean has yet to produce a white novelist, male or female, of Rhys's status.

7. Statues of Schœlcher have been repeatedly vandalized, over many years, in Martinique and Guadeloupe. On the night of 22 May 2020, in a curious prefiguration of what was to come, two statues of the abolitionist were felled in Martinique. The incident predated by several days George Floyd's murder, and therefore anticipated rather than partook in the remarkable series of attacks on statues commemorating whites linked to colonialism and/or the slave trade. More recently, in March 2021, a statue of Schœlcher, erected in Diamant, Martinique, to commemorate the 150th anniversary of the abolition of slavery, was decapitated. A bust of the abolitionist was also removed in July 2020 in Basse-Terre, Guadeloupe.

8. See Curtius, "Of Naked Body," 12.

9. See Barnes, *Cultural Conundrums,* 3.

10. In 1974, Aimé Césaire as mayor oversaw the moving of the statue from the center of the Savannah to a less central position, facing the Bibliothèque Schœlcher, a move that reflected a growing resistance to the glorification of the slave past.

11. Kováts Beaudoux, *Les blancs créoles de la Martinique. Une minorité dominante.*

12. Gosson, "What Lies Beneath?" 236. Gosson quotes and translates Burton, "Trois statues."

13. Revered by nineteenth-century Creoles who frequently claimed common ancestry with her, Joséphine has an enduring and totemic status in both the Antillean landscape and the literary imagination. She is, for example, shoehorned into Traversay's *Les amours* (1806), a novel set long before her birth (this time-bending inclusion is discussed in chapter 1); is the subject of Vincent Placoly's *Scènes de la vie de Joséphine-Rose Tascher de la Pagerie* (1988); and appears as character and authorial ancestor in Marie-Reine de Jaham's *Le sang du volcan* (1997).

14. Brown, "Creole Bonapartism," 46.

15. Gueydon to Ducos, quoted in Sago, "Beyond the Headless Empress," 504.

16. Quoted in Sago, "Beyond the Headless Empress," 504.

17. Brown, "Creole Bonapartism," 40.

18. When the statue was reinstated following renovations to the Savannah in 2010, Joséphine's name had been erased from the plinth, which then simply read "To the Empress born in this colony."

19. The term is used by Césaire in a 1991 letter to the director of the Malmaison Museum (the former country home of Napoléon and Joséphine near Paris,

which reputedly held a replica of the Martinican statue), inquiring about an "exact copy" of the head. At Césaire's behest the town council of Fort-de-France voted to cover the cost of the 42,696-franc plaster cast in 1992. As Kylie Sago argues, such a commitment to the statue's restoration sits uneasily with his evocations of the statue's "cruel loftiness" in *Cahier d'un retour au pays natal*. The head was never reinstalled. "Beyond the Headless Empress," 512.

20. Sago, "Beyond the Headless Empress," 510.
21. Barnes, *Cultural Conundrums*, 2.
22. Chamoiseau and Confiant, *Lettres créoles*, 36.
23. Régent, "Fabrication," 68.
24. Régent, "Fabrication," 70–71.
25. Régent quotes documents by Père Labat dated between 1694 and 1705 that deploy the term "white." "Fabrication," 72.
26. Régent, "Fabrication," 74. By way of contrast the earliest instance of "white" referring to "a race of people" was in the *Oxford English Dictionary* in 1604. Dyer, *White*, 66.
27. Moreau looms large in Antillean fiction. His *Description* echoes in the title and topographical ambition of Traversay's novel, while Chamoiseau's narrator reflects on his project in the opening section of *Un dimanche au cachot* (Sunday in the dungeon), and he is himself a character in Marie-Reine de Jaham's *Le sang du volcan* where his "grandiloquent style" is gently mocked (110–18).
28. Dayan, *Haiti*, 230.
29. Garraway, *Libertine Colony*, 248.
30. Dayan, *Haiti*, 233.
31. Dayan, *Haiti*, 25, 232.
32. Garraway, *Libertine Colony*, 262.
33. Burton, "French West Indies," 11.
34. Benthien, *Skin*, 9.
35. See chapter 2 of *White*, entitled "Colored White, Not Colored," 41–81.
36. Tardon, *La caldeira*, 31.
37. Antoine, *Littérature franco-antillaise*, 35.
38. Gallagher, *Soundings*, 153.
39. Quoted in Maignan-Claverie, *Métissage*, 62.
40. Jenson notes that in the early nineteenth century, "the fact that no term designed to easily distinguish white from black was widely used in colonial society is all the more interesting given that the racially clear term *béké* did already exist." The term "Creole" was preferred, "despite its lexical undoing of racial logic in the midst of an indelibly racially hierarchized colonial society." "Mimetic Mastery," 92.
41. Jenson quotes a letter by Marceline Desbordes-Valmore in which she wonders, "Vous va baï letter à pitit Béqué soldat qui rapporté li, vous tende?" "Mimetic Mastery," 104–5nn40 and 41.
42. Maignan-Claverie, *Métissage*, 62. The term is absent from both Traversay's *Les amours* and Levilloux's *Les créoles*.

43. Dessalles, *Vie d'un colon: Correspondance,* 101.
44. *Wikipedia,* s.v. béké, https://en.wikipedia.org/wiki/B%C3%A9k%C3%A9.
45. Stuart, *Rose of Martinique,* 3.
46. See, among other sources, Raphaël Confiant, http://kapeskreyol.potomitan.info/dissertation1d.html#4.
47. Jenson acknowledges this as the suggestion of Srinivas Aravamudan. "Mimetic Mastery," 105n40.
48. Maignan-Claverie, *Métissage,* 62–63.
49. Confiant, "Quelle est l'origine du mot béké?"
50. Giraud, "Dialectics of Descent," 79.
51. Renard, "Social History of Guadeloupe and Martinique," 1.
52. Bonilla, "Guadeloupe on Strike," 7.
53. Daniel, quoted by Bonilla, "Guadeloupe Is Ours," 130.
54. Glissant, *Caribbean Discourse,* 40.
55. Bonilla, "Guadeloupe Is Ours," 131.
56. Bonilla, "Guadeloupe Is Ours," 131.
57. Chambers, "Unexamined," 189.
58. Turcotte, "Vampiric Decolonization," 110.
59. See Twine and Gallagher, "Future of Whiteness."
60. Morrison, *Playing in the Dark,* 9.
61. Representative titles include: Callanan, *Deciphering Race;* Hall, "'These Bastard Signs of Fair.'"
62. Babb, *Whiteness Visible;* Burrows, *Whiteness and Trauma;* Watson, *Faulkner and Whiteness.* O'Callaghan recently flipped the racial norm on its head: see "Black Irish, White Jamaican."
63. One notable exception is Colette Guillaumin's *Idéologie raciste* (1972).
64. Correct to September 2020.
65. "Le Blanc est enfermé dans sa blancheur. Le Noir dans sa noirceur." Fanon, *Peau noire,* 65.
66. https://www.theses.fr/en/?q=blanchite. Of the twelve theses in which *blanchité* figures as a search item, only one (on Sub-Saharan children's literature) is literary. Correct to October 2020.
67. Chalard-Fillaudeau's "From Cultural Studies to *Études culturelles*" provides a useful analysis of the epistemological reasons underpinning this resistance.
68. Laurent and Leclère, "Introduction," 7.
69. Chamoiseau and Confiant, *Lettres créoles,* 13.
70. Sullivan, *Revealing Whiteness,* 1.
71. Quoted in Dyer, *White,* 9.
72. The following year medical doctor Christophe Oberlin set about dismantling white reification of "blacks": "Blacks exist, however. How often have we heard this statement from a 'white', convinced of his anti-racism? And yet he never asked himself, do 'whites' exist? [. . .] We should also ask the basic question: from

what color is one black, and from what color does one become white?" (*Quelle est la blancheur de vos blancs et la noirceur de vos noirs?*, 41–43). Oberlin's polemical stance and more empirical approach is distinct from the theoretically informed studies mentioned above.

73. Cervulle, *Dans le blanc des yeux*, 11.
74. López, "Introduction," 3.
75. López, "Introduction," 5.
76. Toumson, *Transgression*, 171.
77. Corzani, "Poetry before Negritude," 466.
78. Corzani, Hoffmann, and Piccione, *Littératures francophones II*, 100.
79. Toumson, "Littératures caribéennes francophones," 106–07.
80. See Antoine, *Écrivains français*, 219.
81. Levillain, "Introduction," vii.
82. Macey, "'I Am My Own Foundation,'" 45.
83. Bongie, *Friends and Enemies*, 289.
84. Munro, "French Creoles of Trinidad," 187.
85. L'Harmattan's "Autrement Mêmes" series, under the editorship of Roger Little, has been a crucial intervention, making available obscure early texts and providing critical apparatus and contextual information.
86. Glover, *Haiti Unbound*, xviii.
87. Couti, "Introduction," to Traversay, *Les amours*, ix.
88. On the "difficulty" of the Antillean novel, see McCusker, "Caribbean Novel in French."
89. Browne, *Creole Economics*, 15.
90. See among others Théodose, "'Martinique is ours, not theirs!'" and Sheringham, "Markers of Identity."
91. Adamson, "Préface," 1. Jaham, unlike for example Condé, to whom four articles are devoted, has *only* written about the French Antilles.
92. Glissant, *Poetic Intention*, 122.
93. To take just two examples, critics differ as to whether Joseph Levilloux, discussed in chapter 2, is a *béké* or a mulatto. Drasta Houël, conventionally considered to be a *béké* (see Haigh, *Mapping a Tradition*, 3; Corzani, *Littérature des Antilles-Guyane françaises*, 270; and Maignan-Claverie, *Métissage*, 303) has recently been shown to be a mulatta. See Little, "Introduction," x–xi.
94. Bhabha, *Location of Culture*, 91.
95. Couti, *Dangerous Creole Liaisons*, 20.
96. See McCusker, "The 'Unhomely' White Women of Antillean Writing."
97. Macey, "Adieu foulard," 20.
98. Confiant, *Bal masqué*, 106.
99. Jameson, *Political Unconscious*, 20. Jameson's three narrative horizons, founded on a Marxist critique that resonates strongly in this postslavery culture, are also strikingly applicable: many of these novels offer a "chronicle-like sequence of events in time," "a constitutive tension and struggle between social classes," and

a sense of history, "now conceived of as in its vastest sense of a 'constitutive tension and struggle between social classes.'" *Political Unconscious,* 75.

100. Glissant, quoted by Glover, *Haiti Unbound,* xv.
101. Glover, *Haiti Unbound,* xii.
102. See Burton, "French West Indies," 9.
103. Bongie, *Islands and Exiles,* 218 and passim.
104. Bonilla, "Guadeloupe Is Ours," 131.

1. "A Certain Uncertain Writing"

1. Bhabha, *Location of Culture,* 142, 129–30, my italics.
2. Young, *White Mythologies,* 182.
3. The novel was first published in Paris in 1806 then republished in the series Romans antillais du dix-neuvième siècle. It reappeared, with critical introduction, in the Autrement mêmes series (2017) and it is to this edition that parenthetical page numbers refer.
4. Traversay was born in Rochefort in 1762 and died in Poitiers in 1849. He spent substantial periods of time in Martinique. See the genealogical site http://gw.geneanet.org/lrudeau?n=prevost+de+sansac+de+traversay&oc=&p=auguste+jean. See too Madeleine du Chatenet's biography of Auguste-Jean's brother, her ancestor: *Traversay: Un français ministre de la marine des Tsars* provides useful background on the author.
5. Hoffmann, *Nègre romantique,* 134–36.
6. Antoine notes that the novel is accompanied by "a last-minute plea, hurriedly written in favor of the aristocratic class of the island, who wanted the English occupation of 1794." *Littérature franco-antillaise,* 79. In the document to which Antoine refers, an essay entitled "On the love of the homeland and on the supposed Anglomania of Martinique's planters," Traversay acknowledges that it is thanks to the English that men and property were saved during the French Revolution, but insists that Martinique's planters wish to remain under French rule. The novel, like many successors, is haunted by the threat posed by the English. *Les amours,* 205–6.
7. Chancé, *Histoire,* 18.
8. Toumson, "Littératures caribéennes francophones," 107.
9. Joyau, "Introduction," 9.
10. Corzani, "Esclavage et son imaginaire," 150.
11. Gallagher, *Soundings,* 1.
12. Although the novel appears to have been directly influenced by Moreau—it includes for example a taxonomy of African tribes (62), and an extended exposé of how different physiognomic types determine character and personality (101–3)—it lacks the totalizing schematic thrust of Moreau's text.
13. Traversay himself was a naval officer who fought against British forces in the Caribbean and in the Americas before the French Revolution. See Couti, *Dangerous Creole Liaisons,* 33.

14. Couti, *Dangerous Creole Liaisons*, 55. The heroine of *Paul et Virginie* meets her end, (in)famously, because she refuses to disrobe to facilitate survival during a shipwreck. It is debatable whether the heroine could swim or not, the point of the episode being to underscore her virtue.

15. One of these is intended to serve as "instruction" for the marquis de Bouillé, camp marshal and governor of Martinique; and for President Tascher, intendant of Martinique; another for Father Charles-François de Coutance, apostolic prefect and member of the Capuchins.

16. This contrasts with *Outre-mer* and *Les créoles*, which feature slave nurses whose interracial intimacy compromised the family and the plantocracy. Moreau commented on the inherent contradiction without addressing the power dynamics underlying the phenomenon: "in a land in which maternal tenderness is an exalted virtue, children are pressed to a stranger's breast." *Description topographique*, 21.

17. Couti singularizes the noun in her English translation of the title, "The Love between Zémédare and Carina," *Dangerous Creole Liaisons*, 6.

18. Toumson, *Transgression*, 171.

19. The only other intimation of the caste's decline occurs in the aftermath of the 1766 hurricane, which caused Martinique's planters to despair: "There was barely a family that didn't have to mourn the tragic death of one of its members" (57). The event, significantly, marks the beginning of the end of the saintly Mme Sainprale who, although untouched by the death of any of her family, "was singularly altered by the event" (57). In keeping with the novel's episodic structure, the event is contained in a single chapter and its repercussions are not referred to again.

20. Bal, *Narratology*, 198.

21. Chatenet notes the prominence of the Tascher de la Pagerie family in correspondence between members of the Traversay family. *Traversay*, 331n1.

22. The incident, although disputed, was widely reported. While Traversay suggests that the fortune-teller is white, by affording her the title Mademoiselle David, David Wilkie in his 1837 painting *Joséphine and the Fortune Teller* depicts her as a mulatta, and Marie-Reine de Jaham describes her as Malian (*Le sang du volcan*, 46).

23. Couti, *Dangerous Creole Liaisons*, 29.

24. As mentioned in the introduction, there is no historical evidence that slavery was reintroduced at Joséphine's behest.

25. Corzani, "Poetry before Negritude," 468.

26. Davis, *Resisting Novels*, 54.

27. Tuan, *Topophilia*, 247.

28. See Dillman, *Colonizing Paradise*, 3.

29. Chatenet quotes Auguste's unpublished *Mémoires*, where he mentions "a monstrous baobab carrying the name of 'marquis Duquesne'" (Traversay's

maternal great-grandfather) near Saint-Pierre. The tree, she argues, "perfectly incarnates the energetic character of Governor Duquesne." *Traversay,* 28.

30. The lack of attachment to the land described here contradicts Anthony Trollope's assertion of French planter superiority a half century later, in 1859. For Trollope, this superiority is based not just on organizational and administrative prowess but also on the colonist's desire "to make a Paris for himself, whether it be in a sugar island in the Antilles, or in a trading town upon the Levant." French colonists "cast no wistful glances towards France," whereas the English colonies "are considered more as temporary lodging-places, to be deserted as soon as the occupiers have made money enough by molasses and sugar to return *home.*" Trollope, *The West Indies and the Spanish Main,* quoted by Gallagher, *Soundings,* 206. That Trollope's observations are made within a decade of Abolition is further evidence that planter power was largely undiminished by the official end of slavery.

31. These are the trees that will be valorized by later Black writers such as Césaire and Glissant as talismans of a precolonial past, and as the habitat of the runaway slave.

32. Gallagher, *Soundings,* 85.

33. McCusker, *Patrick Chamoiseau,* 119–26.

34. Joyau, "Introduction," 9.

35. Walcott, *What the Twilight Says,* 37.

36. See Said, *Culture and Imperialism,* 95–116. For a reading that claims that slavery is much more visibly present than Said allows, see Fraiman, "Jane Austen and Edward Said"; see also Bohls, *Romantic Literature,* 40–47.

37. Greenblatt, *Shakespearean Negotiations,* 1.

2. Unsettling the Pigmentocracy

1. Bhabha, *Location of Culture,* 185.

2. Hoffmann, *Nègre romantique,* 100.

3. France had already abolished slavery in 1794, a short-lived decree that Napoléon was notoriously to revoke, prompting the loss of the lucrative colony of Saint-Domingue in the ensuing Haitian Revolution.

4. For an account of these rebellions see Nicolas, *Histoire de la Martinique,* 1: 316–20; 343–48; 353–61. Levilloux includes historical characters such as Ogé and Dugommier in his novel.

5. Ironically, France was to seek compensation from the Haitian government after it won its independence, thereby crippling the Haitian economy for the rest of the century.

6. Tomich, *Slavery,* 7–8.

7. Early novelists tend, anachronistically perhaps, to name England, the historic enemy, rather than Britain, as a mirror in which the more conservative, or less recklessly liberal, values of France can be seen.

8. Oudin-Bastide, *Des nègres et des juges*, 23.
9. Couti, *Dangerous Creole Liaisons*, 76.
10. Régent, "Fabrication," 74.
11. Moreau's notorious taxonomy was already in wide circulation, featuring notably in Hugo's *Bug-Jargal* (1826). Estève, for example, in *Les créoles*, is described as the son of a "métisse," a woman "born of a mulatta and a white" (20). In *Outre-mer* Marius lists several subcategories in his letter to Sir William, including *quarteronne, mestive,* and *câpresse* (I 33).
12. See McCusker, "Figuring Abjection."
13. Corzani considers *Outre-mer* to be "reactionary," and Levilloux's novel to be "much more sympathetic." "L'image de l'homme de couleur," 92–93. Jeune states that the *homme de couleur* is "very roughly treated" in *Outre-mer*. "L'année littéraire 1835," 361. Maignan-Claverie concurs with Corzani's view of Maynard's text and applauds the "liberal and progressive perspective" of *Les créoles*. See *Métissage*, 249, 257. Burton describes *Les créoles* as being "perceptibly more liberal on the subject of miscegenation" than other novels of the period. Burton, "West Indies," 852. Bongie reads Maynard's novel as a "displaced autobiography," a "projection onto the rival class of his own fears (and desires) in a gesture of expulsion that must be understood in terms of René Girard's analysis of the scapegoat." *Islands and Exiles*, 301–2.
14. A Levilloux from the Martinican parish of Case Pilote was a signatory to the "Adresse des planteurs réfugiés dans la ville de Saint-Pierre, aux planteurs des Antilles" in 1790 (see https://gallica.bnf.fr/ark:/12148/bpt6k5457827x/f11.image.r=levilloux?rk=21459;2) and Corzani attests the name from the eighteenth century in Martinique (*Dictionnaire encylopédique*, quoted by Rochmann, *Esclave fugitif*, 46n2). The name does not figure for example in the list compiled at the end of Traversay's novel cataloging planter enrollment in the Conseil Supérieur, nor in the list of ancient families detailed in Petitjean Roget and Bruneau-Latouche's *Personnes et familles à la Martinique au XVII siècle*.
15. Rochmann, *Esclave fugitif*, 46n2.
16. Burton, "West Indies," 852.
17. Bongie, *Islands and Exiles*, 470–71n43.
18. Müller, *Crossroads*, 65.
19. Müller, *Crossroads*, 65.
20. See Benthien, *Skin*, 156.
21. Noel Ignatiev contends that in eighteenth- and nineteenth-century America, Irish Catholics, an "oppressed race" at home, "commonly found themselves thrown together with free Negroes," and that "racial amalgamation" between these two groups was frequently envisaged. That things turned out otherwise "was not the inevitable consequence of blind historic forces, still less of biology, but the result of choices made, by the Irish and others, from among available alternatives." *How the Irish Became White*, 2–3.

22. This cross-caste cross-dressing is a trope of early fiction dealing with slavery: see Hugo's *Bug-Jargal* and Mérimée's *Tamango*. But it is a one-way transvestism, with slaves dressing as masters but not vice versa.

23. Examples of such crossover are rare but not unique; Poirié Saint-Aurèle's "Les Antilles" features a white Creole woman who wears the madras and is "full of coquetterie." For discussion of this "semantic trembling" see Bongie, *Islands and Exiles*, 295.

24. See for example Mme Desvallons-Deshauteur's untrammeled hatred for mulattas.

25. Dayan, *Haiti*, 175, 180.

26. These episodes are distinct from moments of overt mimicry, which tend to solidify rather than destabilize identity. For example, Bala, after an "orgy" of alcohol with the maroons, apes the language and manners of the white man. This mimicry is legitimized because of Bala's uncompromised position as maroon leader, in other words as the arch resistor to the white regime (141). Bala's "good" mimicry contrasts with a later, more debased, example: "There is nothing more naturally grotesque than the negro who, wishing to elevate himself to the dignity of his audience, makes sure not to be himself, but salutes like whites do, takes on their attitudes and manners and mixes them up with his own" (155).

27. See McCusker, "Figuring Abjection."

28. Couti, *Dangerous Creole Liaisons*, 86.

29. Couti, *Dangerous Creole Liaisons*, 90.

30. Bongie, *Islands and Exiles*, 465n2.

31. Müller, *Crossroads*, 65.

32. Bongie, *Islands and Exiles*, 226.

33. Couti, *Dangerous Creole Liaisons*, 84.

34. Couti, *Dangerous Creole Liaisons*, 64.

35. For full biographical details of Maynard, including errors in critics' presentation of him, see McCusker, "Introduction" to *Outre-mer*, xii–xv.

36. See Maignan-Claverie, *Métissage*, 62.

37. Dyer, *White*, 72.

38. The noun used in French, "une femmelette," is often translated as wimp or sissy. Its juxtaposition with "en couches" (in labor) however, necessitates a term that refers to a biological female.

39. See McCusker, "Figuring Abjection."

40. Loichot, *Orphan Narratives*, 129.

3. Sympathy for the *Béké*?

1. Kiberd, *Irish Classics*, 287.

2. The Points reprint frames the novel in these inaugural terms, claiming that it bears witness to the "*emergence of the Antillean word* and to *the birth of a language*" (my italics).

3. Corzani, "Poetry before Negritude," 472.

4. Rochmann, *Esclave fugitif,* 242.

5. For example, the plantation mistress transcribes Anatole's story in *La case du commandeur* (*The Overseer's Hut,* 1981).

6. Rochmann, *Esclave fugitif,* 240.

7. Rochmann, *Esclave fugitif,* 240.

8. Cailler, *Conquérants,* 115.

9. Burton, *Roman marron, passim.*

10. Crosta observes that the Acajou plantation's name is systematically italicized in *Le quatrième siècle,* while that of the Senglis plantation is italicized only when embedded in a paragraph, meaning that "the plantation which causes most suffering to slaves is at the level of typography flagged rather than concealed" (*Marronnage,* 103). This does not hold true of Betsy Wing's English translation where neither name is italicized.

11. Crosta, *Marronnage,* 122.

12. Suga, "*Échos-Monde* and Abrasions," 23.

13. Madou, *Édouard Glissant,* 32.

14. Cailler, *Conquérants,* 116.

15. Burton, *Roman marron,* 72n4.

16. As Macey argues, the "memory of the *béké* on horseback and with a whip in his hand is a powerful and intimidating figure in the Martinican imagination." *Frantz Fanon,* 43. She can be contrasted, for example, with Mme de Soulaga in Drasta Houël's *Cruautés et tendresses,* a mistress who is similarly armed with her whip, which is used against slaves to much more violent ends.

17. See McCusker, "The 'Unhomely' White Women."

18. Crosta, *Marronnage,* 52.

19. Her story famously provides the title for Gilbert and Gubar's foundational work of feminist criticism, *The Madwoman in the Attic,* published in 1979.

20. At other times the relationship works on the level of association rather than direct convergence. In an infamous scene Bertha is described in nonhuman terms: "it grovelled, seemingly, on all fours; it snatched and growled like some strange animal" (*Jane Eyre,* 290). In *The Fourth Century,* it is Senglis who is pictured "on all fours in the middle of the floor spinning like a crazy top" descending with his wife into a paroxysm of mania (77).

21. Spivak, in "Three Women's Texts," categorically describes her as "the white Jamaican Creole," 247.

22. Murdoch, "Ghosts in the Mirror," 10.

23. Wood, *Slavery,* 333.

24. Beattie, "Mystery at Thornfield," 493.

25. Britton, "*Discours* and *histoire,*" 156.

26. See Zobel, *La rue cases-nègres,* 131–32.

27. Britton, *Race,* 40.

28. Britton, *Race,* 41.

29. Britton, *Race*, 42.
30. Bhabha, *Location of Culture*, 76.
31. See Benthien, *Skin*, 139.
32. Lanoë, *Poudre et le fard*, 28.
33. Lanoë, *Poudre et le fard*, 33–34.
34. Bhabha, *Location of Culture*, 75.
35. Britton, *Race*, 41.
36. Cailler, *Conquérants*, 115.
37. Munro, "Rhythms, History, and Memory," 419. The quotation is from Dash, *Édouard Glissant*, 72.
38. Murdoch's terms to describe Bertha Mason, quoted above.
39. Simek, *Hunger and Irony*, 51n30.
40. Chimalum Nwanko, quoted in Burrows, *Whiteness and Trauma*, 187.
41. Houël's *Cruautés et tendresses* features a character who prefers his "healthy African woman" to the "sickly girls recruited for the islands in certain Parisian hospitals," 69.
42. The eponymous heroine of Prévost's *Histoire du chevalier des Grieux, et de Manon Lescaut* (1731), a "fille de joie" condemned to embark for the New World, finds herself imprisoned in the Salpêtrière. On the hospital's role in punishing "fallen" women, see Carrez, "La Salpêtrière."
43. Garraway, "Toward a Creole Myth of Origin," 155.
44. Loichot, *Orphan Narratives*, 107.
45. St-John Perse, *Collected Poems*, 17.
46. Loichot, *Orphan Narratives*, 107, italics in original.
47. Loichot counts sixteen references to ownership conveyed by "I have" and "my" (*Orphan Narratives*, 107). The passage in *Slave Old Man* has a similar tenor and includes at least as many pluperfect active verbs that testify to his dominance, or rather compensate for its absence.
48. Milne, *Patrick Chamoiseau*, 152.
49. Milne, *Patrick Chamoiseau*, 156.
50. Chamoiseau's 2013 essay *Césaire, Perse, Glissant* discusses the three francophone writers of this quartet, writers who have "unexpectedly emerged" from the "inaugural abyss of a new genesis," 49.
51. Knepper, *Patrick Chamoiseau*, 226.
52. Although the *béké* is never named, the novel is set on the Gaschette plantation, a historic site in Le Robert, Martinique. The word *gâchis*, waste, also resonates in this toponym.
53. Schloss, *Sweet Liberty*, 7.
54. The father of "Written on the Door" has "skin the color of mules or of red tobacco." St. John Perse, *Collected Poems*, 17.
55. Garraway, *Libertine Colony*, 277.
56. Garraway, *Libertine Colony*, 285–86.
57. Garraway, *Libertine Colony*, 277.

58. Garraway, *Libertine Colony*, 277.
59. Bhabha, *Location of Culture*, 13.
60. Corzani, quoted in Glissant, *Caribbean Discourse*, 39. Glissant, clearly irritated by Corzani's observation, argues that the economics of the Antillean plantation mean that the *béké*, who was never for the slave "*the real enemy,*" is also in a position of dispossession with regard to the metropole. *Caribbean Discourse*, 39, italics in original.
61. Rochmann, *Esclave fugitif*, 242.
62. Milne, "The *Marron* and the *marqueur*," 69–70.
63. See Vété-Congolo, "Creolization," 781.
64. Bongie, *Friends and Enemies*, 212. The initiative paved the way for Roger de Jaham's speaking at the 22 May commemorations of the end of slavery in 2006 alongside Serge Letchimy, successor to Césaire as mayor of Fort-de-France, and culminated in his establishment in 2007 of the organization Tous Créoles! (All Creoles!), discussed in my conclusion.
65. Rochmann, *Esclave fugitif*, 245.
66. For a discussion of this positive presentation of Schœlcher see Cailler, "Le personnage historique." Schœlcher's centrality is especially unusual for a writer who has tended to focus on the *petit peuple*, anonymous Martinicans, and treats major figures from politics and history (Césaire; de Gaulle; Pory Papy) with ironic distance.
67. See Rabbitt, "History into Story," 1–2.

4. Empathy and Estrangement

1. Britton, "Vincent Placoly."
2. The Groupe Révolution Socialiste was born from a split in the Communist Party in Martinique.
3. The novel's title comes from the poem "C'est moi-même terreur" ("C'est moi-même terreur c'est moi-même/le frère de ce volcan qui certain sans mot dire/rumine un je ne sais quoi de sûr") in *Ferrements* by Aimé Césaire.
4. Fikes, "Escaping the Literary Ghetto." Novels held to belong to a genre that has spawned huge critical interest include Frank Yerby's *The Foxes of Harrow* (1946), Zora Neale Hurston's *Seraph on the Suwanee* (1948), Richard Wright's *The Outsider* (1953) and *Savage Holiday* (1954), and James Baldwin's *Giovanni's Room* (1956). The phenomenon is heavily concentrated in the post–World War II decade.
5. Lipsitz, "Possessive Investment in Whiteness," 369.
6. See Charles, *Abandoning the Black Hero*, 5.
7. As Munro illustrates, in the French Caribbean "black, colonized, or otherwise 'repressed' authors writing back against empire, colonialism, and neocolonialism have been quite rightly praised and promoted." "French Creoles," 187.
8. Fikes, "Escaping the Literary Ghetto," 105.
9. Charles, *Abandoning the Black Hero*, 202.

10. Watson, *Souls of White Folk*, 5. Claverie's description of a poetics of distancing and making strange ("poétique la distanciation et de l'inaccoutumance") resonates with Watson's term. See "L'Auteur au miroir," 60.

11. Watson, "Lillian B. Horace," 6.

12. Watson, *Souls of White Folk*, 132–33.

13. This intimacy between patient and physician features commonly in fiction about white Creole society: see Grandmaison's crime novels *Le bal des créoles* (1976) and *Rendez-vous au Macouba* (1948), among many other titles. Jaham's *La grande béké* also features a close relationship between the elderly female protagonist and her doctor.

14. Charles, *Abandoning the Black Hero*, 9.

15. Charles, *Abandoning the Black Hero*, 54.

16. Charles, *Abandoning the Black Hero*, 202.

17. Charles, *Abandoning the Black Hero*, 9.

18. Charles, *Abandoning the Black Hero*, 3.

19. Li, *Playing in the White*, 190.

20. Seguin-Cadiche, *Vincent Placoly*, 71.

21. Sourieau, "*Frères volcans*," 510.

22. Aubin, "Approche du roman," 33.

23. Quoted in Seguin-Cadiche, *Vincent Placoly*, 290–91. The letter is undated by Seguin-Cadiche.

24. Li, *Playing in the White*, 27.

25. Charles, *Abandoning the Black Hero*, 9, 82, 88, and passim.

26. Sourieau, "*Frères volcans*," 508.

27. This historical event is reprised for example by Marie-Reine de Jaham in *Le sang du volcan*. Sannois is the family name of Joséphine de Beauharnais's mother.

28. Charles, *Abandoning the Black Hero*, 7.

29. Carvigan-Cassin compares the narrative to other studies in colonial and postcolonial deception, "those famously disappointing tomorrows." "Chronique de l'abolition," 109.

30. The Leyritz plantation, in the northeast area of Martinique, is one of the oldest (established 1713), but there is no evidence of a writer with this name. Villiers, also fictional, is distinct from French poet Auguste Villiers de Ile-Adam (1838–89) who was ten years old when the events described took place. The Dessalles family is named, but the diary kept by Pierre, which covers, and extends far beyond, the timeframe of *Frères volcans*, is not invoked by either narrator.

31. This rehabilitation (Sourieau, "*Frères volcans*," 514) of the abolitionist is validated by the frame narrator, who regrets that his writings have not featured on any Antillean school syllabus (*Frères volcans*, 123), and could be seen to prefigure Chamoiseau's sympathetic portrayal of the abolitionist in *Un dimanche au cachot* (2007).

32. This critical read-across is largely due to the fact that the frame narrator is an "accomplished" (in this case, an academic historian) rather than an

"apprentice" writer, according to Lydie Moudileno's typology, who allows the author, in her terms, to reflect self-consciously on "pre-existing texts, images, and established discourses" in much the same way as the reader imagines Placoly might. See *Écrivain antillais*, 197–98.

33. Bongie, *Islands and Exiles*, 319–20.

34. Chamoiseau and Confiant, *Lettres créoles*, 40.

35. A punishment method by which hands and arms are tied to four posts on the ground. See Dayan, "Codes of Law," 49.

36. Later the contention that slaves are happier than, for example, Irish peasants, prevalent in journalism of the period and used as the narrator says to close debate, is dismissed as a "fashionable argument" (60).

37. Lorde, *Master's Tools*, 17–19.

38. In *Texaco* Chamoiseau stages a similar confrontation between newly liberated slaves and the language available to them, and foregrounds the word "travail," work, fusing the signifier with *esclavage* to give *l'estravaille*.

39. In a curious parallel, Thomas à Kempis's *Imitation* also features in Drasta Houël's *Cruautés et tendresses* where it is described as a "sibylline" book, to be "consulted as one would an oracle" (162). It is also the book that the devout Arielle, married to Dieudonné's father, reads in bed in a key scene of Condé's *La belle créole* (136).

40. This affection for the books of the father, and the desire to preserve them for posterity, rewrites the fate of Saint-John Perse's father's library, which had "sunk in harbor" after having arrived from Guadeloupe. Perse notes in his diary that "The son saw the father's mute sadness and forever kept a strange aversion to books." See Loichot, *Orphan Narratives*, 81.

41. Meanwhile the grotesque physicality of the feet, described in such detail by Zobel, and reprised for example by Micaux in *De nègres et de békés* (see chapter 6), is clearly the attribute of slave rather than master.

42. Loichot, *Orphan Narratives*, 103.

43. The quatrain presented by Vive to the narrator is taken from a hymn, "Désir du ciel" (Heaven's desire). See Lambillotte, *Cantiques pour toutes les fêtes de l'année*, 158.

44. Garraway, *Libertine Colony*, 28.

45. See McCusker, "Figuring Abjection."

46. Watson, *Souls of White Folk*, 141.

47. Young, *Colonial Desire*, 9.

48. Joseph-Gabriel, "'Ce pays est un volcan,'" 13.

49. As noted above, the novel is internally unstable, featuring many contradictory assertions, but critics have tended to limit their discussion to generic instability. Clarisse Zimra stresses the influence of Aimé Césaire in describing the novel as a "notebook-journal." "Second retour," 532. Marie-Agnès Sourieau describes it as a "novel-essay," then as a "book-diary." "Frères volcans," 507, 509. The

latter is a term used by the narrator himself ("livre-journal," 12). Aubin sees it as being "at the crossroads of history and the novel." "Approche du roman," 32.

50. Britton, "Vincent Placoly," n.p.
51. Seguin-Cadiche, *Vincent Placoly*, 54.
52. Quoted in Seguin-Cadiche, *Vincent Placoly*, 290–91.
53. The novel, which has received minimal critical attention, is often read comparatively, as though it can best be understood in a broader prism rather than on its own terms alone. Molly Grogan Lynch, in "*Frères volcans*," compares the novel to Patrick Chamoiseau's *L'esclave vieil homme et le molosse;* Laura Carvigan-Cassin in "Chronique de l'abolition" reads the text alongside Lafcadio Hearn's *Youma;* while Clarisse Zimra, in "Second retour au pays natal," situates the novel with reference to Aimé Césaire's poetry.
54. Aubin, "Approche du roman," 33.
55. Milne, "Sex, Gender," 26.

5. "Here, It's Black or White"

1. Macey, *Frantz Fanon*, 46.
2. Marie-Reine de Jaham (née Dulieu) is the wife of Philippe de Jaham, Roger's second cousin. See Paul Michaux's genealogy of *béké* families: http://gw.geneanet.org/pmchx?lang=fr;pz=paul+marie+joseph;nz=michaux;ocz=0;em=R;ei=3911;et=A;p=philippe;n=de+jaham. The *île en île* website announces that Jaham is descended from planters who arrived in the time of Richelieu (http://ile-en-ile.org/jaham/), while her husband also descends from an ancient line.
3. *Antilla* 329, 17–23 April 1989.
4. Confiant, "Trois regards féminins," 26.
5. Harrison, "Representativity."
6. Notably the fact that Fleur, like Jaham's own grandfather, dedicates her life to rebuilding the family plantation destroyed by the Saint-Pierre volcano of 1902.
7. Péroncel-Hugoz, "La Martinique en mots d'auteurs," 15.
8. Confiant, "Trois regards féminins," 26.
9. Ngong, "*Le sang du volcan*," 183.
10. Confiant, "Trois regards féminins," 26.
11. Bongie, *Friends and Enemies*, 292.
12. Arnold, "Institution littéraire," 129.
13. Bongie, *Friends and Enemies*, 293.
14. Ngong, "*Le sang du volcan*," 183.
15. Pinalie-Dracius, "Une Amérique dépassée," 17.
16. Even though *La grande béké* is set in the 1960s, its heroine is haunted by having witnessed the volcano explode at the age of seventeen. In true soap opera style, *Le sang du volcan* closes on a catastrophic cliff-hanger: the volcano explodes as key protagonists drive toward it.

17. In addition to the reviews mentioned above, the prime-time French literary magazine program *Ex Libris* dispatched a reporter to Martinique to interview Jaham about the novel (broadcast 24 May 1989, TF1). In his review of the novel Confiant criticizes Jaham's literary style and her negrophobia. However, her "plague on all your houses" approach (mulattoes and, especially, *békés*, are treated with equal derision), as well as the insights afforded into the secretive world of the *béké* (for Confiant, Jaham is the first writer to have fully explored the role of the *da* or nanny in Antillean fiction), means that the novel is deemed "worthy of interest despite everything." "*La grande békée* [sic]," 15.

18. The protagonist's only erotic pleasure is vested in her relationship with the plantation. The smell of the sap of the gliricidia trees induce in her a "strange trouble," reminding her of sperm, and she is entranced by the "frenzied fornication" of the island's flora (27). In a death fantasy, she imagines herself thrown from her horse and dying face-down on the land (14). Later the pleasure she takes in touching the map of her land ("my finger continues its voyage [. . .] my finger slides south and my heart beats faster," 88) suggests a very literal form of topophilia.

19. This is mirrored in *Le sang du volcan*'s opening, a scene of intimacy and chatter between Joséphine de Beauharnais and her *da*.

20. St. John, "'It Ain't Fittin','" 131.

21. Tara, Margaret Mitchell's fictional plantation, is the name of one of the clans featured in Jaham's trilogy.

22. St. John, "'It Ain't Fittin','" 133. In both 1939 film and 1989 novel the "heavenliness" of white femininity is embodied by a proxy, Melanie (played by Olivia de Havilland) and Marie-Hélène, who stand in contrast to the flawed heroines, Scarlett and Fleur.

23. St. John, "'It Ain't Fittin','" 133.

24. St. John, "'It Ain't Fittin','" 133.

25. Wood, *Black Milk*, 93.

26. In Jaham's *Le sang du volcan* the enlightened plantation master Patrick Solis asks one of his slaves, "Do you think it's easy being a *Béké*?" 83.

27. Zimmerman, "Good Girls," 67, italics in original.

28. *La grande béké*, dir. Alain Maline, broadcast 14 and 21 March 1998, France 3.

29. The film carries a "ten years old and above" warning and features full frontal nudity of the (Black) female star.

30. In the novel, the downfall of this prestigious *béké* line (he was known as Francis de Récoté) is attributed exclusively to the disastrous volcano, which ruined the fortunes of the family, and meant that the family took up residence in "les cases," the slave huts, with some marrying Black women. Although such intercaste marriage is presented as an unfortunate outworking of this disaster, Fifi is a bachelor in the novel (167).

31. The excision of Algeria is undoubtedly connected to the increasing sensitivity to the role of France, and in particular the paratroopers, in that conflict.

Rebranding Marc as a humanitarian worker sidesteps the polemic building around the "war without a name" in the late 1990s.

32. "La grande béké (Review)."
33. Guillermet, "Keen de Kermadec," 41.
34. Berthier, "La grande béké (Review)."
35. See "Interview Dé mó, Kat pawol."
36. Moreau, *Description topographique,* 21.
37. Traversay features as a sympathetic character who is about to travel to Russia in Jaham's *Le sang du volcan,* 50, 89.

6. Killing the *Béké*

1. It is one of the biggest selling British television exports in the world (at the time of writing its eleventh series has been commissioned), offering "a burst of the exotic in the dark depths of a British January." Henderson, "Death in Paradise."
2. Crane and Fletcher, *Island Genres,* 20–21.
3. Pépin, *La darse rouge* (2011). Confiant, in addition to the novel discussed below, has published three other titles featuring Detective Teddyson: *Du rififi chez les fils de la veuve* (2012), *Citoyens au-dessus de tout soupçon* (2014), and *Deux détonations* (2020). An earlier detective novel, *Le meurtre du samedi-gloria,* was published in 1997.
4. Herbeck, "Detective Narrative Typology," 78.
5. Ferrari, *Vulnerable States,* 45.
6. Herbeck, "Raphaël Confiant's *Le meurtre du Samedi-Gloria,*" 342–43. In a later study Herbeck, in addition to the above titles, lists a striking number of novels that include mysterious deaths or "occurrences that some or all characters attempt to unravel," including Jacques Roumain's *Gouverneurs de la rosée* (1946) and Édouard Glissant's *La lézarde* (1958). See "Detective Narrative Typology."
7. For a fascinating discussion of this case see Childers, *Seeking Imperialism's Embrace,* 109–11.
8. While Delsham's *Dérives* (1999) also features the murder of a *béké* and his Black wife, the event serves as background to the story. Marie-Reine de Jaham's *Bwa Bandé* (1999) takes place in Saint-Martin.
9. Kinsman, "Feminist Crime Fiction," 157.
10. In addition to the various editions of Jaham's *La grande béké,* there are only three further fictional titles in the BNF catalog that include the signifier: *Béké!* (2010), *Quand je serai béké* (2013), and *Le béké de l'île aux fleurs* (2004). Correct to October 2020.
11. Confiant, having set a previous *polar* in the secretive world of Martinican Freemasons, comments bluntly in an interview that *béké* society is "the most closed of all Martinican milieus." "Bal masqué à Békéland."
12. Collins, "Towards a 'Brave New World,'" 78.
13. Herbeck, "Detective Narrative Typology," 71, italics in original.

14. Micaux was born in Guadeloupe in 1935, worked in Africa as a colonial administrator, and then as a teacher in Burgundy. He has written approximately a dozen works of poetry, drama, and prose, but his writing is almost entirely neglected, both in the Antilles and beyond. This was his fifth published work.

15. Békéland is the local nickname for Cap Est in the François commune, where most *békés,* having deserted the urban centers of Fort-de-France and, after the eruption of Mount Pelée in 1902, Saint-Pierre, now live. It is known as the Neuilly of Martinique, and during the 2009 strikes required a special police presence. See Guillaume, "La résistance du pouvoir béké," 297. The novel's front cover features an immediately recognizable sketch of Confiant, and Teddyson's other physical characteristics (his pock-marked skin; dark glasses the "color of goose poo," 63–64; and his "frizzy mop of reddish hair," 97) playfully conjure the author.

16. Confiant has fun, as in other novels, with the unwieldiness of *béké* names—his daughter is later referred to as Marie-Aimée Dupin de Flessac de Machin-Chouette, 26. Dupin is also the name of the first great detective of the genre, Edgar Allan Poe's Parisian polymath.

17. His teeth are yellowed by cigars and resistant to Ultrabright toothpaste (32), the lenses of his glasses are yellow-brown, and at points he is shown to become yellower still ("I went pale, or rather I got yellower," 32).

18. Reddy, *Traces, Codes, and Clues,* 94. While the novel has received no academic criticism, Alain Léauthier makes a salient comment on the novel's presentation of women in a review: "a stupid and venal black companion, an older mistress who is utterly immoral, another, fairly stupid one who is devoted to him and then finally, the ultimate local cliché, the mulatta who inevitably is the mistress of a *Béké.* You would think that comrade Confiant had never met one of those '*famn doubout*' [upright women] who salvage the country from these weak and womanizing men." "Bal masqué à Békéland," n.p.

19. Arnold, "Gendering of *Créolité,*" 25.

20. Born in the commune of Saint-Joseph, and trained as a teacher, Cabort-Masson fought against the French in the Algerian war alongside Sony Rupaire and Daniel Boukman (there is some debate as to whether or not he officially joined the FLN), founded a vocational college in Martinique, is credited with designing the Martinican national flag (a reflection of his nationalist convictions), and was a vociferous critic of white privilege.

21. Bongie, *Friends and Enemies,* 354.

22. See Noël-Ferdinand, "L'homme Guy Cabort-Masson."

23. Under Robert, elected leaders were replaced by white Vichy sympathizers, while he "used the naval officers and sailors in Martinique as a kind of personal 'Praetorion Guard.'" Childers, *Seeking Imperialism's Embrace,* 29.

24. In terms of "love" triangles Michel, married to Marie-Josèphe—a religious hypocrite whose name conjoins two of the three figures in that other iconic triangle, the Holy Family—is in a longstanding sexual arrangement with his domestic servant Judith. Marie-Josèphe, Michel's wife, sleeps first with Amédée

and then with Lannoux; Judith, who is in love with Amédée, is obliged to have regular intercourse with her master; Amédée and Michel, *frères de lait,* are both in a relationship with Judith. Dr. Doumenge is in love with Marie-Josèphe. Lannoux and his wife Bernadette are both sleeping, unbeknownst to each other, with Marie-Josèphe. This incestuous lesbian relationship (the women are doubly related to each other, on both their maternal and their paternal lines), instigated as Marie-Josèphe comforts Bernadette on the fall of Admiral Robert, is the most ludicrous in a series of outrageous plot devices clearly contrived to expose the hypocrisy of *béké* society. It comes hot on the heels of Marie-Josèphe's liaison with Lannoux, during which she masturbates him in church, before making love to him atop the tarpaulins stored in her husband's warehouse. In such moments, the novel descends into a hyperbolic and lurid romp, in which sexual intrigue (and even sexual orientation and appetite) evolves at staggering speed, such that the inspector's description of the story as a "politico-sexual magma" (191) stands as a conspicuous understatement.

25. Cabort-Masson has commented on the philistinism of the caste, stating that *békés* have not "added an atom of cultural creation to the world's vast reservoir." Quoted by Bongie, *Friends and Enemies,* 211.

26. See Traversay, *Les amours,* 206.

27. The contribution of dissidents to the war effort has until recently been relatively neglected, possibly because, as Toureille suggests, contemporary commemorations have privileged Abolition and the struggle for social rights. See "La dissidence dans les Antilles françaises." See also Jennings, *Vichy sous les tropiques* and Childers, *Seeking Imperialism's Embrace,* especially chapter 1, "World War II as a Turning Point in the French Caribbean," 12–45.

28. While the date attributed by Cabort-Masson to the article is incorrect, presumably a typo (it appeared in *La Paix* on 30 August 1943, not 1945) the letter from Hoppenot is accurately reproduced. Despointes was shot as he and his family slept, and the murder was discovered by his daughter Marie-José. Although there is no clear motive, theft alone, according to the journalist, would not explain the brutality of the crime. The article concludes with a letter of condolence from M. Hoppenot, a (real-life) ambassador to whom de Gaulle assigned the task of restoring Republican rule in Antilles in 1943. See Jennings, *Vichy sous les tropiques,* 126. Hoppenot had already left the Antilles for Washington by 18 September 1943. See Barbier, *Henri Hoppenot, diplomate,* 326.

29. See the genealogical website https://gw.geneanet.org/pmchx?lang=fr&m=N&v=HUYGHUES%20DESPOINTES. Robert H. Despointes had six children according to this family tree; the novel refers to four of them. Marie-José is the youngest child. Bruneau-Latouche and Riffaud's history of the Huyghues family records only that he was born in Reunion on 28 October 1894 and was a businessman in Trinité, where he died on 26 August 1943.

30. See the comment by Maurice Domarin in "Brin d'amour à Trinité": "It was he who allowed the Galion workers to build their house on credit." Brin

d'amour (A hint of love), the name of an area in the bourg of Trinité, would become the name of a hotel subsequently established on the site of the chateau. http://vivrauxantilles.canalblog.com/archives/2009/06/29/14244057.html.

31. Cabort-Masson was a strident critic of the mayor of Fort-de-France. See for example his "Lettre ouverte à Aimé Césaire."

32. Loraine, as we see later, is the only remaining daughter of a *béké* "with no male descendants." *Belle créole*, 38.

33. See Simek, *Hunger and Irony*, 140.

34. Fulton, *Signs of Dissent*, 119.

35. The story of a young man's unrequited love for an older, higher-status white woman leads one character to compare the situation to *Lady Chatterley's Lover*, a comparison reprised in the book's blurb and approved by, for example, Dawn Fulton. But Nicole Simek reminds the reader of the happy ending of Lawrence's novel and suggests that *Othello*, also referenced in the novel, is a more appropriate intertext (*Eating Well*, 59). Britton notes that in terms of Lawrence's work, a more apt comparison would be with *Sons and Lovers*. See *Perspectives on Culture*, 136.

36. On the role of dogs in the novel, see Boisseron, "Creole Line of Escape," 209; and Higginson, "Of Dogs and Men."

37. Simek, *Eating Well*, 42.

38. *La belle créole*'s structure mirrors that of the earlier novel; *Traversée* unfolds over a night, *La belle créole* over twenty-four hours. The later novel is divided into three main chapters ("Afternoon," "Dusk," and "Night"), like the temporal mooring points of *Traversée*: "Dusk," "Night," and "Dawn." Both satirize writer characters, while the trio of women romantically involved with Dieudonné (Loraine, Ana, and Dorsica) echoes Sanchez's three lovers, Mira, Dinah, and Vilma.

39. Crosta, "Narrative and Discursive Strategies," 154.

40. Crosta, "Narrative and Discursive Strategies," 147.

41. Coursil, "*Belle créole*," 353.

42. Condé would later become the first president of the Committee for the Memory of Slavery (Comité pour la mémoire de l'esclavage), set up as a response to the Taubira Law of 2001 recognizing slavery as a crime against humanity, a role that she fulfilled between 2004 and 2008.

43. Fulton suggests that "the imbrication of racial essentialism and reparations discourse" that has been critiqued by opponents of the latter might be "usefully examined alongside exoticism and racial stereotyping as an instance of the pitfalls of representativity." The same logic that frames Dieudonné as a "vulgar and dangerous brute" informs the reparations argument that frees him. *Signs of Dissent*, 117, 112.

44. Britton, *Perspectives*, 141.

45. Britton, *Perspectives*, 133.

46. Simek, *Eating Well*, 55.

47. Sullivan, *Revealing Whiteness*, 13.

48. Collins, "'Towards a 'Brave New World,'" 80.
49. Fulton, *Signs of Dissent*, 116.
50. Dyer, *White*, 222.
51. Pearson and Singer, "Introduction," 4.
52. Messent, *Crime Fiction Handbook*, 11–12.

Conclusion

1. Guillaume, "Résistance du pouvoir béké," 292.
2. Walcott, *What the Twilight Says*, 69.
3. Bongie, *Islands and Exiles*, 69.
4. Glissant, *Poetics of Relation*, 64.
5. Bolzinger, *Les derniers maîtres de la Martinique*, https://www.youtube.com/watch?v=FDHItTb-umI. Huyghues Despointes protested that he was misrepresented by the documentary, while Roger de Jaham was quick to distance himself from the elderly *béké*. See https://touscreoles.fr/communique-de-presse/.
6. See McCusker, "All Creoles Now?" 228–30.
7. Herbeck, *Architextural Authenticity*, 141, italics in original.
8. Macey, "Adieu foulard," 20.
9. Guillaume, "Résistance du pouvoir béké," 291.
10. Bonilla, "Guadeloupe Is Ours," 132.
11. *Journal du soir*, RFO, 5 March 2009.
12. See Confiant and Boutrin, *Chronique d'un empoisonnement annoncé*, on the environmental and public health scandal linked to the toxic pesticide.
13. Quoted in Ferdinand, "Ecology, Identity, and Colonialism," 176.
14. Although Guillaume claims that the strikes triggered the foundation of the movement (see "Résistance du pouvoir béké," 299) in fact it was already in existence for two years in 2009.
15. The slick and regularly updated website, http://www.touscreoles.fr/, celebrates the fact that the movement was founded by "Blacks, Mulattoes, Indians, Chinese, Békés, Syro-Lebanese, but also Metropolitans and Africans."
16. Vété-Congolo, "La créolité aujourd'hui," n.p.
17. Vété-Congolo, "La créolité aujourd'hui," n.p.
18. In a radio interview with Harry Eliézer on *L'heure ultramarine*, France Inter, 15 August 2011, Jaham insisted that the *béké*, too, had suffered under slavery, and that an ancestor of his had been worse off than a slave as, unlike the slave, he had no market value. This remarkable statement led to the Mouvement International pour la Réparation (MIR), led by Garcin Malsa, (unsuccessfully) calling for Jaham to be tried for defending crimes against humanity and provoking racial hatred. See also Roger de Jaham, "La place des békés à la Martinique."
19. See Delsham's interview with Patrice Fabre, "Aujourd'hui nous nous sentons persecutés" and Reynal, "Tous Créoles! condamne les dérives racistes anti-békés!"
20. Quoted in Dyer, *White*, 8–9.

21. Marsh, *Narratives,* xiv.
22. Dessalles, *Vie d'un colon: Correspondance,* 29.
23. St-John Perse, "Anabase." *Collected Poems,* 123.
24. Žižek, "Melancholy and the Act," 661.

Bibliography

Primary Sources

Bolzinger, Romain (dir.). *Les derniers maîtres de la Martinique*. TAC Presse. Broadcast Canal +, 6 February 2009.

Brontë, Charlotte. *Jane Eyre* (1847). London: Penguin, 2006.

Cabort-Masson, Guy. *Martinique: Comportements et mentalités*. Saint Joseph, Martinique: La Voix du Peuple, 1998.

———. *Les puissances d'argent en Martinique*. Saint Joseph, Martinique: Laboratoire de recherches de l'AMEP, 1984.

———. *Qui a tué le béké de Trinité?* Saint Joseph, Martinique: La Voix du Peuple, 1991.

Chamoiseau, Patrick. *Chronicle of the Seven Sorrows*. Translated by Linda Coverdale with a foreword by Édouard Glissant. Lincoln: University of Nebraska Press, 1999.

———. *Un dimanche au cachot*. Paris: Gallimard, 2007.

———. *L'esclave vieil homme et le molosse*. Paris: Gallimard, 1997.

———. *Slave Old Man*. Translated by Linda Coverdale. New York: New Press, 2018.

———. *Solibo Magnificent*. Translated by Rose-Myriam Réjouis and Val Vinokurov. London: Granta, 1999.

———. *Solibo Magnifique*. Paris: Gallimard, 1986.

———. *Texaco*. Paris: Gallimard, 1992.

———. *Texaco*. Translated by Rose-Myriam Réjouis and Val Vinokurov. London: Granta, 1997.

Confiant, Raphaël. *Bal masqué à Békéland*. Lamentin, Martinique: Caraïbéditions, 2013.

———. *Eau de café*. Paris: Grasset, 1991.

———. *Le nègre et l'amiral*. Paris: Grasset, 1992.

Condé, Maryse. *La belle créole*. Paris: Folio, 2013.

———. *La belle créole*. Translated by Nicole Simek with an afterword by Dawn Fulton. Charlottesville: University of Virginia Press, 2020.
———. *La colonie du nouveau-monde*. Paris: Laffont, 1993.
———. *Traversée de la mangrove*. Paris: Folio, 1989.
Delsham, Tony. *Dérives*. Schœlcher, Martinique: Editions M.G.G., 1999.
Dessalles, Pierre. *La vie d'un colon à la Martinique au XIX siècle: Correspondance*. Fort-de-France, Martinique: Désormeaux, 1988.
———. *La vie d'un colon à la Martinique au XIX siècle: Journal*. 3 vols. Fort-de-France, Martinique: Désormeaux, 1984–86.
Glissant, Édouard. *La case du commandeur*. Paris: Seuil, 1981.
———. *The Fourth Century*. Translated by Betsy Wing. Lincoln: University of Nebraska Press, 2001.
———. *La lézarde* (1958). Paris: Points, 1995.
———. *Le quatrième siècle*. Paris: Seuil, 1964.
Grandmaison, Daniel de. *Le bal des créoles*. Paris: La Pensée Universelle, 1976.
———. *Rendez-vous au Macouba: Roman de mœurs martiniquaises*. Paris: Littré, 1948.
Houël, Drasta. *Cruautés et tendresses: Vieilles mœurs coloniales martiniquaises* (1925) preceded by *Les vies légères: Évocations antillaises* (1916). Edited with an introduction by Roger Little with Isabelle Gratiant. Paris: L'Harmattan, 2020.
Jaham, Marie-Reine de. *La grande béké*. Paris: Laffont, 1989.
———. *Les héritiers du paradis*. Paris: Laffont, 1998.
———. *Le maître-savane*. Paris: Laffont, 1991.
———. *L'or des îles*. Paris: Laffont, 1996.
———. *Le sang du volcan*. Paris: Laffont, 1997.
Levilloux, Joseph. *Les créoles; ou, La vie aux Antilles* (1835). Edited with an introduction by Christina Kullberg with Roger Little. Paris: L'Harmattan, 2020.
Maline, Alain, dir. *La grande béké*. Broadcast France 3, 14 and 21 March 1998.
Maynard de Queilhe, Louis de. *Outre-mer*. 2 vols. (1835). Edited with an introduction by Maeve McCusker. Paris: L'Harmattan, 2009.
Micaux, Henri. *De nègres et de békés: Une journée de chien*. Paris: Mon Petit Éditeur, 2011.
Parépou, Alfred. *Atipa: Roman guyanais* (1885). Paris: L'Harmattan, 1987.
Placoly, Vincent. *Frères volcans: Chronique de l'abolition de l'esclavage*. Paris: La Brèche, 1983.
Saint-John Perse. *Œuvres complètes*. Paris: Gallimard, 1982.
St.-John Perse. *Collected Poems*. Translated by W. H. Auden, Hugh Chisholm, Denis Devlin, T. S. Eliot, Robert Fitzgerald, Wallace Fowlie, Richard Howard, and Louise Varèse. Princeton, NJ: Princeton University Press, 1971.
Tardon, Raphaël. *La caldeira*. Matoury, Guyana: Ibis Rouge, 2002.
Tous Créoles! *Créoles, tout bonnement!* Paris: Idem, 2019.

Traversay, Auguste Prévost de Sansac de. *Les amours de Zémédare et Carina et description de l'île de la Martinique* (1806). Paris: L'Harmattan, 2017.
Zobel, Joseph. *La rue cases-nègres* (1955). Paris: Présence Africaine, 1974.

Secondary Sources

Adamson, Ginette. "Préface." In *Elles écrivent des Antilles (Haïti, Guadeloupe, Martinique)*, edited by Suzanne Rinne and Joëlle Vitiello, 1. Paris: L'Harmattan, 1997.
"Adresse des planteurs réfugiés dans la ville de Saint-Pierre, aux planteurs des Antilles." Saint-Pierre, Martinique: P. Richard and Le Cadre, 1790. https://gallica.bnf.fr/ark:/12148/bpt6k5457827x/f11.image.r=levilloux?rk=21459;2.
Agence bibliographique de l'enseignement supérieur. Database of doctoral theses defended in France since 1985. https://www.theses.fr/en/?q=blanchite.
Antoine, Régis. *Les écrivains français et les Antilles: Des premiers pères blancs aux surréalistes noirs*. Paris: G.-P. Maisonneuve et Larose, 1978.
———. *La littérature franco-antillaise: Haïti, Guadeloupe et Martinique*. Paris: Karthala, 1992.
Arnold, A. James. "The Gendering of *Créolité*: The Erotics of Colonialism." In *Penser la créolité*, edited by Maryse Condé and Madeleine Cottenet-Hage, 21–40. Paris: Karthala, 1992.
———. "Institution littéraire, discours identitaire, supercherie littéraire." *Cahiers de l'association internationale des études françaises* 55, no. 1 (2003): 123–38.
Aubin, Danielle. "Approche du roman historique antillais." *Présence africaine* 148 (1988): 30–43.
Babb, Valerie. *Whiteness Visible: The Meaning of Whiteness in American Literature and Culture*. New York: New York University Press, 1998.
Bal, Mieke. *Narratology. Introduction to the Theory of Narrative*. Toronto: University of Toronto Press, 2009.
"Bal masqué à Békéland: Entrevue avec l'auteur." *Potomitan*, 21 June 2013. http://www.potomitan.info/confiant/bekeland.php.
Barbier, Colette. *Henri Hoppenot, diplomate (25 octobre 1891–10 août 1977)*. Paris: Direction des archives, Ministère des affaires étrangères, 1999.
Barnes, Natasha. *Cultural Conundrums: Gender, Race, Nation, and the Making of Caribbean Cultural Politics*. Ann Arbor: University of Michigan Press, 2006.
Beattie, Valerie. "The Mystery at Thornfield: Representations of Madness in *Jane Eyre*." *Studies in the Novel* 28, no. 4 (Winter 1996): 493–505.
Benthien, Claudia. *Skin: On the Cultural Border between Self and the World*. New York: Columbia University Press, 2002.
Bernabé, Jean, Patrick Chamoiseau, and Raphaël Confiant. *Éloge de la créolité/ In Praise of Creoleness*. Paris: Gallimard, 1989.
Berthier, Sophie. "La grande béké" (Review). *Télérama* 2513 (11 March 1998): 92.
Bhabha, Homi. *The Location of Culture*. London: Routledge, 1994.

Bishop, Cécile, and Zoë Roth. "Introduction." *L'esprit créateur* 59, no. 2, Special Issue, "Race and the Aesthetic in French and Francophone Cultures" (2019): 1–11.
Bohls, Elizabeth A. *Romantic Literature and Postcolonial Studies*. Edinburgh: Edinburgh University Press, 2013.
Boisseron, Bénédicte. "A Creole Line of Escape: A Story of Becoming-Dog." *Contemporary French and Francophone Studies* 10, no. 2 (2006): 205–16.
Bongie, Chris. *Friends and Enemies: The Scribal Politics of Post/colonial Literature*. Liverpool: Liverpool University Press, 2008.
———. *Islands and Exiles: The Creole Identities of Post/Colonial Literature*. Stanford, CA: Stanford University Press, 1998.
Bonilla, Yarimar. "Guadeloupe Is Ours: The Prefigurative Politics of the Mass Strike in the French Antilles." *Interventions* 12, no. 1 (2010): 125–37.
———. "Guadeloupe on Strike: A New Political Chapter in the French Antilles." *NACLA Report on the Americas* (May/June 2009): 6–10.
———. "Non-Sovereign Futures? French Caribbean Politics in the Wake of Disenchantment." In *Caribbean Sovereignty, Development, and Democracy in an Age of Globalization*, edited by Linden Lewis, 208–27. New York: Routledge, 2013.
Bonniol, Jean-Luc. *La couleur comme maléfice: Une illustration de la généalogie des "Blancs" et des "Noirs."* Paris: Albin Michel, 1992.
"Brin d'amour à Trinité." *Vivrauxantilles*, 29 June 2009. http://vivrauxantilles.canalblog.com/archives/2009/06/29/14244057.html.
Britton, Celia. "Breaking the Rules: Irrelevance/Irreverence in Maryse Condé's *Traversée de la mangrove*." *French Cultural Studies* 15, no. 1 (2004): 35–47.
———. "*Discours* and *histoire*: Magical and Political Discourse in Édouard Glissant's *Le quatrième siècle*." *French Cultural Studies* 5 (1994): 151–62.
———. *Édouard Glissant and Postcolonial Theory: Strategies of Language and Resistance*. Charlottesville: University Press of Virginia, 1999.
———. *Language and Literary Form in French Caribbean Writing*. Liverpool: Liverpool University Press, 2014.
———. *Perspectives on Culture and Politics in the French Antilles*. Oxford: Legenda, 2018.
———. *Race and the Unconscious. Freudianism in French Caribbean Thought*. Oxford: Legenda, 2002.
———. *The Sense of Community in French Caribbean Fiction*. Liverpool: Liverpool University Press, 2008.
———. "Vincent Placoly." *Literary Encyclopedia*. 2013. http://litencyc.com/php/speople.php?rec=true&UID=13251.
Brown, Laurence. "Creole Bonapartism and Post-Emancipation Society: Martinique's Monument to the Empress Joséphine." *Outre-mers: Revue d'histoire* 94, nos. 350–51 (2006): 39–49.

Browne, Katherine E. *Creole Economics: Caribbean Cunning under the French Flag*. Austin: University of Texas Press, 2004.
Brozgal, Lia. "Seeing through Race in Contemporary French Cinema." *L'esprit créateur* 59, no. 2 (2019): 12–24.
Burrows, Victoria. *Whiteness and Trauma: The Mother-Daughter Knot in the Fiction of Jean Rhys, Jamaica Kincaid, and Toni Morrison*. Basingstoke, UK: Palgrave Macmillan, 2004.
Burton, Richard D. E. "The French West Indies à l'heure de l'Europe." In *French and West Indian*, edited by Richard D. E. Burton and Fred Reno, 1–19. Charlottesville: University Press of Virginia, 1995.
———. *Le roman marron: Études sur la littérature antillaise contemporaine*. Paris: L'Harmattan, 1997.
———. "Trois statues: Le Conquistador, l'Impératrice et le Libérateur: Pour une sémiotique de l'histoire coloniale de la Martinique." *Carbet* 11 (1991): 147–64.
———. "West Indies." In *The New Oxford Companion to Literature in French*, edited by Peter France, 851–54. Oxford: Clarendon Press, 1995.
Burton, Richard D. E., and Fred Reno, eds. *French and West Indian: Martinique, Guadeloupe, and French Guiana Today*. Charlottesville: University Press of Virginia, 1995.
Butler, Judith. *Gender Trouble: Feminism and the Subversion of Identity*. New York: Routledge, 1990.
Cabort-Masson, Guy. "Lettre ouverte à Aimé Césaire." *Peuples noirs-peuples africains* 22 (1981): 30–38.
Cailler, Bernadette. *Conquérants de la nuit nue: Édouard Glissant et l'H(h)istoire antillaise*. Tübingen, Germany: Gunter Narr Verlag, 1988.
———. "Le personnage historique en littérature antillaise: La question du genre." *Études littéraires* 43, no. 1 (2012): 117–33.
Callanan, Laura. *Deciphering Race: White Anxiety, Racial Conflict, and the Turn to Fiction in Mid-Victorian English Prose*. Athens: Ohio University Press, 2006.
Carrez, Jean-Pierre. "La Salpêtrière de Paris sous l'ancien régime: Lieu d'exclusion et de punition pour femmes." *Criminocorpus, revue hypermédia* (2008). https://journals.openedition.org/criminocorpus/264.
Carvigan-Cassin, Laura. "Chronique de l'abolition de l'esclavage chez Vincent Placoly et Lafcadio Hearn." In *Vincent Placoly: Un écrivain de la décolonisation*, edited by Jean-Georges Chali and Axel Arthéron, 101–10. Matoury, Guyana: Ibis Rouge, 2014.
Cervulle, Maxime. *Dans le blanc des yeux: Diversité, racisme et médias*. Paris: Éditions Amsterdam, 2013.
Chalard-Fillaudeau, Anne. "From Cultural Studies to *Études culturelles*, *Études de la culture*, and *Sciences de la culture* in France: Questions of Singularity." *Cultural Studies* 23, nos. 5–6 (2009): 831–54.
Chali, Jean-Georges, and Axel Arthéron, eds. *Vincent Placoly: Un écrivain de la décolonisation*. Matoury, Guyana: Ibis Rouge, 2014.

Chambers, Ross. "The Unexamined." In *Whiteness: A Critical Reader,* edited by Mike Hill, 187–203. New York: New York University Press, 1997.

Chamoiseau, Patrick. *Césaire, Perse, Glissant: Les liaisons magnétiques.* Paris: Philippe Rey, 2013.

Chamoiseau, Patrick, and Raphaël Confiant, *Lettres créoles: Tracées antillaises de la littérature 1635–1975.* Paris: Hatier, 1991.

Chancé, Dominique. *L'auteur en souffrance: Essai sur la position et la représentation de l'auteur dans le roman antillais contemporain (1981–1992).* Paris: Presses Universitaires de France, 2000.

———. *Histoire des littératures antillaises.* Paris: Ellipses, 2005.

Charles, John C. *Abandoning the Black Hero: Sympathy and Privacy in the Postwar African American White-Life Novel.* New Brunswick, NJ: Rutgers University Press, 2012.

Chatenet, Madeleine du. *Traversay: Un français ministre de la marine des Tsars.* Paris: Tallandier, 1996.

Childers, Kristen Stromberg. *Seeking Imperialism's Embrace: National Identity, Decolonization, and Assimilation in the French Caribbean.* Oxford: Oxford University Press, 2016.

Claverie, André. "L'auteur au miroir de l'œuvre: Une poétique de décentrement." In *Vincent Placoly: Un écrivain de la décolonisation,* edited by Jean-Georges Chali and Axel Arthéron, 53–62. Matoury, Guyana: Ibis Rouge, 2014.

Collins, Holly. "'Towards a 'Brave New World': Tracing the Emergence of Creolization in Maryse Condé's Canonical Rewritings." *Women in French Studies* 23 (2015): 69–84.

Condé, Maryse. "Order, Disorder, Freedom, and the West Indian Writer." *Yale French Studies* 83 (1993): 121–35.

Condé, Maryse, and Madeleine Cottenet-Hage, eds. *Penser la créolité.* Paris: Karthala, 1995.

Confiant, Raphaël. "*La grande békée* [sic]: Première analyse et critique." *Antilla* 329 (17–23 April 1989): 15–16.

———. "Quelle est l'origine du mot 'béké'?" http://kapeskreyol.potomitan.info/dissertation1d.html#4.

———. "Trois regards féminins sur la Martinique." *Antilla* 331 (1–7 May 1989): 25–28.

Confiant, Raphaël, and Louis Boutrin. *Chronique d'un empoisonnement annoncé: Le scandale du chlordécone aux Antilles françaises 1972–2002.* Paris: L'Harmattan, 2007.

Corzani, Jack. "L'esclavage et son imaginaire aux sources du roman 'gothique' antillais: Au-delà du réel?" In *Esclavage et abolitions: Mémoires et systèmes de représentations,* edited by Marie-Christine Rochmann, 147–62. Paris: Karthala, 2000.

———. "L'image de l'homme de couleur avant 1848." In *La période révolutionnaire aux Antilles: Images et résonances: littérature, philosophie, histoire sociale, histoire des idées,* edited by Roger Toumson, 181–99. Schœlcher, Martinique: GRELCA, 1989.

———. *La littérature des Antilles-Guyane françaises: La Négritude.* Fort-de-France, Martinique: Desormeaux, 1978.

———. "Poetry before Negritude." In *A History of Literature in the Caribbean,* Vol. 1, edited by A. James Arnold, Julio Rodriguez-Luis, and J. Michael Dash, 465–77. Amsterdam: John Benjamins, 1994.

Corzani, Jack, Léon-François Hoffmann, and Marie-Lyne Piccione. *Littératures francophones II.* Paris: Belin, 1998.

Coursil, Jacques. "*La belle créole* de Maryse Condé: Un art d'écriture." *Romanic Review* 94, nos. 3–4 (2003): 345–59.

———. "Édouard Glissant et *Le discours antillais:* La source et le delta." Plenary Lecture, International Conference on *Le discours antillais,* organized by the Institut du Tout-monde, Maison des Sciences de L'Homme, Paris, 25 April 2019.

Couti, Jacqueline. *Dangerous Creole Liaisons: Sexuality and Nationalism in French Caribbean Discourses from 1806 to 1897.* Liverpool: Liverpool University Press, 2016.

———. "Introduction." In *Les amours de Zémédare et Carina et description de l'île de la Martinique,* by Auguste Prévost de Sansac de Traversay, vii–xli. Paris: L'Harmattan, 2017.

Crane, Ralph, and Lisa Fletcher. *Island Genres, Genre Islands: Conceptualization and Representation in Popular Fiction.* London: Rowman and Littlefield, 2017.

"Le crime de Trinité." *La Paix,* 1 September 1943, 3.

Crosta, Suzanne. *Le marronage créateur: Dynamique textuelle chez Édouard Glissant.* Laval, Canada: GRELCA, 1991.

———. "Narrative and Discursive Strategies in Maryse Condé's *Traversée de la mangrove.*" *Callaloo* 15, no. 1 (1992): 147–55.

Curtius, Anny Dominique. "Of Naked Body and Beheaded Statue: Performing Conflicting History in Fort-de-France." In *Critical Perspectives on Conflict in Caribbean Societies of the Late 20th and Early 21st Centuries,* edited by Patricia Donatien and Rodolphe Solbiac, 9–30. Newcastle upon Tyne: Cambridge Scholars Publishing, 2015.

Cyrille, Dominique. "Imagining an Afro-Creole Nation: Eugène Mona's Music in Martinique of the 1980s." *Latin American Music Review/Revista de Música Latinoamericano* 27, no. 2 (2006): 148–70.

Dash, Michael. *Édouard Glissant.* Cambridge: Cambridge University Press, 1995.

———. *The Other America: Caribbean Literature in a New World Context.* Charlottesville: University Press of Virginia, 1998.

Davis, Lennard J. *Resisting Novels: Ideology and Fiction.* London: Routledge, 1987.

Dayan, Joan. "Codes of Law and Bodies of Color." In *Penser la créolité,* edited by Maryse Condé and Madeleine Cottenet-Hage, 41–67. Paris: Karthala, 1996.

———. *Haiti, History, and the Gods.* Berkeley: University of California Press, 1995.

"Le décolonialisme, une stratégie hégémonique." *Le Point,* 28 November 2018. https://www.lepoint.fr/politique/le-decolonialisme-une-strategie-hegemonique-l-appel-de-80-intellectuels-28-11-2018-2275104_20.php.

Delas, Daniel. "Histoires de békés." *Notre librairie: Nouveaux paysages littéraires, Afrique, Caraïbes, Océan Indien 1996–1998* 136, no. 2 (1999): 124–28.

Delsham, Tony. "Patrice Fabre: Aujourd'hui nous nous sentons persecutés." *Antilla* 1275 (29 November 2007): 12–19.

Desse, Michel. "La récente transformation des acteurs économiques dans les D.O.M.: L'exemple de la Guadeloupe, Martinique et Réunion." *Annales de géographie* 598 (1997): 592–611.

Dillman, Jefferson. *Colonizing Paradise: Landscape and Empire in the British West Indies.* Tuscaloosa: University of Alabama Press, 2015.

Dyer, Richard. *White.* London and New York: Routledge, 1997.

Elizabeth, Léo. "Vichy aux Antilles et en Guyane 1940–1943." *Outre-Mers* 91 nos. 342–43 (2004): 145–74.

Engles, Tim. "Toward a Bibliography of Critical Whiteness Studies." *Faculty Research & Creative Activity* 51 (2006). https://thekeep.eiu.edu/eng_fac/51/.

"Enlever la tête de Joséphine fut très simple." *Journal de 19 heures, Martinique 1,* 25 August 2017. https://la1ere.francetvinfo.fr/martinique/enlever-tete-josephine-fut-tres-simple-505015.html.

Fanon, Frantz. *Black Skin, White Masks.* Translated by Charles Lam Markmann. New York: Grove Press, 1967.

———. *Peau noire, masques blancs.* Paris: Seuil, 1952.

Ferdinand, Malcolm. "Ecology, Identity, and Colonialism in Martinique: The Discourse of an Environmental NGO (1980–2011)." In *The Caribbean: Aesthetics, World-Ecology, Politics,* edited by Chris Campbell and Michael Niblett, 174–88. Liverpool: Liverpool University Press, 2016.

Ferrari, Guillermina de. *Vulnerable States: Bodies of Memory in Contemporary Caribbean Fiction.* Charlottesville: University of Virginia Press, 2007.

Fikes, Robert Jr. "Escaping the Literary Ghetto: African American Authors of White Life Novels 1946–1994." *Western Journal of Black Studies* 19, no. 2 (1995): 105–12.

Foster, Gwendolyn Audrey. *Performing Whiteness: Postmodern Re/constructions in the Cinema.* Albany: State University of New York Press, 2003.

Fouchet, Antoine. "La colère antillaise se déverse sur la minorité blanche." *La Croix,* 17 February 2009. https://www.la-croix.com/Actualite/France/La-colere-antillaise-se-deverse-sur-la-minorite-blanche-_NG_-2009-02-18-599295.

Fraiman, Susan. "Jane Austen and Edward Said: Gender, Culture, and Imperialism." *Critical Inquiry* 21, no. 4 (1995): 805–21.

Fulton, Dawn. *Signs of Dissent: Maryse Condé and Postcolonial Criticism.* Charlottesville: University of Virginia Press, 2008.

Gallagher, Mary. *La créolité de Saint-John Perse*. Paris: Gallimard, 1998.
———. *Soundings in French Caribbean Writing since 1950: The Shock of Space and Time*. Oxford: Oxford University Press, 2002.
———, ed. *Ici-là: Place and Displacement in Caribbean Writing in French*. Amsterdam: Rodopi, 2003.
Garraway, Doris. *The Libertine Colony: Creolization in the Early French Caribbean*. Durham, NC: Duke University Press, 2005.
———. "Toward a Creole Myth of Origin: Narrative, Foundations, and Eschatology in Patrick Chamoiseau's *L'esclave vieil homme et le molosse*." *Callaloo* 29, no. 1 (2006): 151–67.
Giraud, Michel. "Dialectics of Descent and Phenotypes in Racial Classification in Martinique." In *French and West Indian: Martinique, Guadeloupe, and French Guiana Today*, edited by Richard D. E. Burton and Fred Reno, 75–85. Charlottesville: University Press of Virginia, 1995.
Glissant, Édouard. *Caribbean Discourse: Selected Essays*. Translated and edited with an introduction by J. Michael Dash. Charlottesville: University Press of Virginia, 1989.
———. *Le discours antillais*. Paris: Seuil, 1981.
———. *Poetic Intention*. Translated by Nathalie Stephens. Callicoon, NY: Nightboat Books, 2010.
———. *Poetics of Relation*. Translated by Betsy Wing. Ann Arbor: University of Michigan Press, 1997.
Glover, Kaiama. *Haiti Unbound: A Spiralist Challenge to the Postcolonial Canon*. Liverpool: Liverpool University Press, 2010.
Gosson, Renée. "What Lies Beneath? Cultural Excavation in Neocolonial Martinique." In *Echoes from the Poisoned Well: Global Memories of Environmental Injustice*, edited by Sylvia Hood Washington, Paul C. Rosier, and Heather Goodall, 225–43. Lanham, MD: Rowman and Littlefield/Lexington Books, 2006.
"La grande béké" (Review). *Téléloisirs*, 11 March 1998, 41.
Greenblatt, Stephen. *Shakespearean Negotiations: The Circulation of Social Energy in Renaissance England*. Berkeley: University of California Press, 1988.
Gregg, Veronica Marie. *Jean Rhys's Historical Imagination*. Chapel Hill: University of North Carolina Press, 1995.
Grogan Lynch, Molly. "*Frères volcans* de Vincent Placoly: Un document sur l'histoire absente de 1848 à la Martinique." *Études littéraires africaines* 26 (2008): 27–33.
Guillaume, Pierre. "La résistance du pouvoir béké à la démocratisation de la société antillaise." In *Élites et crises du XVI au XXI siècle: Europe et Outremer*, edited by Laurent Coste and Sylvie Guillaume, 291–300. Paris: Armand Colin, 2014.
Guillaumin, Colette. *L'idéologie raciste: Genèse et langage actuel*. Paris: Gallimard, 1972.

Guillermet, Fabrice. "Keen de Kermadec: Du zouc à la comédie." *Télé 7 jours*, 21–27 March 1998, 41.

Haigh, Sam, ed. *An Introduction to Caribbean Francophone Writing: Guadeloupe and Martinique*. Oxford: Berg, 1999.

———. *Mapping a Tradition: Francophone Women's Writing from Guadeloupe*. Leeds: MHRA, 2000.

Hall, Kim F. "'These Bastard Signs of Fair': Literary Whiteness in Shakespeare's Sonnets." In *Post-colonial Shakespeares*, edited by Ania Loomba and Martin Orkin, 64–83. London: Routledge, 1998.

Harrison, Nicholas. "Representativity (with Reference to Chraïbi)." *Paragraph* 24, no. 3 (2001): 30–43.

Henderson, James. "Death in Paradise: Guadeloupe, the Real-Life St Marie." *The Telegraph*, 5 January 2016. https://www.telegraph.co.uk/travel/destinations/caribbean/articles/Death-in-Paradise-Guadeloupe-the-real-life-St-Marie/.

Herbeck, Jason. *Architextural Authenticity: Constructing Literature and Literary Identity in the French Caribbean*. Liverpool: Liverpool University Press, 2017.

———. "Detective Narrative Typology: Going Undercover in the French Caribbean." In *Detective Fiction in a Postcolonial and Transnational World*, edited by Nels Pearson and Marc Singer, 63–80. London: Ashgate, 2009.

———. "Raphaël Confiant's *Le meurtre du samedi-Gloria*: Crime and Testimony." *French Review* 82, no. 2 (2008): 342–51.

Higginson, Pim. "Of Dogs and Men: *La belle créole* and the Global Subject." *Romanic Review* 94, nos. 3–4 (2003): 291–307.

Hoffmann, Léon-François. *Le nègre romantique: Personnage littéraire et obsession collective*. Paris: Payot, 1973.

Ignatiev, Noel. *How the Irish Became White*. New York: Routledge, 1995.

"Interview Dé mó, Kat pawol—Marie-Reine de Jaham." *L'or des îles*, 7 March 2013. https://ordesiles.com/2013/03/interview-de-mo-kat-pawol-marie-reine-de-jaham/.

Jaham, Roger de. "Communiqué de presse." *Tous Créoles!*, 7 February 2009. https://touscreoles.fr/communique-de-presse/.

———. "La place des békés à la Martinique: Mythes et réalités." *Creoleways*, 5 May 2009, updated 2011 and 2012. http://creoleways.com/2009/05/07/la-place-des-bekes-a-la-martinique-mythes-et-realites/.

Jamard, Jean-Luc. "Les békés sont des judokas." *Les temps modernes* 441–42 (1983): 1872–93.

Jameson, Fredric. *The Political Unconscious: Narrative as a Socially Symbolic Act*. London: Routledge, 2002.

Jennings, Eric T. *Escape from Vichy: The Refugee Exodus to the French Caribbean*. Cambridge, MA: Harvard University Press, 2018.

———. *Vichy sous les tropiques: La révolution nationale à Madagascar, en Guadeloupe, en Indochine, 1940–1944*. Paris: Grasset, 2004.

Jenson, Deborah. "Mimetic Mastery and Colonial Mimicry in the First Franco-Antillean Creole Anthology." *Yale Journal of Criticism* 17, no. 1 (2004): 83–106.
Jeune, Simon. "L'année littéraire 1835 et les problèmes de l'esclavage." In *La période révolutionnaire aux Antilles: Images et résonances: littérature, philosophie, histoire sociale, histoire des idées,* edited by Roger Toumson, 355–65. Schœlcher, Martinique: GRELCA, 1989.
Joseph-Gabriel, Annette K. "'Ce pays est un volcan': Saint-Pierre and the Language of Loss in White Creole Women's Narratives." *Women in French* 25 (2017): 13–28.
Joyau, Auguste. "Introduction." In *Les amours de Zémédare et Carina et description de l'île de la Martinique,* by Auguste Prévost de Sansac de Traversay, 7–13. Morne Rouge, Martinique: Éditions des horizons caraïbes, 1977.
———. *Panorama de la littérature antillaise.* Morne-Rouge, Martinique: Éditions des Horizons caraïbes, 1974.
Jugé, Tony S., and Michael P. Perez. "The Modern Colonial Politics of Citizenship and Whiteness in France." *Social Identities* 12, no. 2 (2006): 187–212.
Kiberd, Declan. *Irish Classics.* London: Granta, 2000.
Kinsman, Margaret. "Feminist Crime Fiction." In *The Cambridge Companion to Crime Fiction,* edited by Martin Priestman, 148–62. Cambridge: Cambridge University Press, 2003.
Knepper, Wendy. *Patrick Chamoiseau: A Critical Introduction.* Jackson: University of Mississippi Press, 2012.
———. "Remapping the Crime Novel in the Francophone Caribbean: The Case of Patrick Chamoiseau's *Solibo Magnifique.*" *PMLA* 122, no. 5 (2007): 1431–46.
Kováts Beaudoux, Edith. *Les blancs créoles de la Martinique: Une minorité dominante.* Preface by Michel Giraud. Paris: L'Harmattan, 2002.
Lambillotte, R.P.L. *Cantiques pour toutes les fêtes de l'année.* Tournai, Belgium: Casterman et fils, 1852.
Lamming, George. *Coming, Coming Home: Conversations II: Western Education and the Caribbean Intellectual.* Philipsburg, Saint-Martin: House of Nehesi, 1995.
Lanoë, Catherine. *La poudre et le fard: Une histoire des cosmétiques de la Renaissance aux Lumières.* Seyssel, France: Champ Vallon, 2008.
Laurent, Sylvie, and Thierry Leclère. "Introduction." In *De quelle couleur sont les blancs? Des "petits blancs" des colonies au "racisme anti-blancs,"* edited by Sylvie Laurent and Thierry Leclère, 7–22. Paris: Éditions La Découverte, 2013.
Léauthier, Alain. "*Bal masqué à Békéland* de Raphaël Confiant." *Marianne,* 31 July 2013. https://www.marianne.net/culture/bal-masque-bekeland-de-raphael-confiant.
Levillain, Henriette. "Introduction." In *Mémoires de békées,* by Élodie Dujon-Jourdain and Renée Dormoy-Léger, vii–xxiii. Paris: L'Harmattan, 2002.

Li, Stephanie. *Playing in the White: Black Writers, White Subjects*. Oxford: Oxford University Press, 2015.

Lipsitz, George. "The Possessive Investment in Whiteness: Racialized Social Democracy and the 'White' Problem in American Studies." *American Quarterly* 47, no. 3 (1995): 369–87.

Little, Roger, with Isabelle Gratiant. "Introduction." In *Cruautés et tendresses: Vieilles mœurs coloniales françaises* preceded by *Les vies légères: Évocations antillaises*, by Drasta Houël, vii–xxxviv. Paris: L'Harmattan, 2020.

Loichot, Valérie. "Fort-de-France: Pratiques textuelles et corporelles d'une ville coloniale." *French Cultural Studies* 15, no. 1 (2004): 48–60.

———. *Orphan Narratives: The Postplantation Literature of Faulkner, Glissant, Morrison, and Saint-John Perse*. Charlottesville: University of Virginia Press, 2007.

López, Alfred J. "Introduction: Whiteness after Empire." In *Postcolonial Whiteness: A Critical Reader on Race and Empire*, edited by Alfred J. López, 1–30. Albany: State University of New York Press, 2005.

Lorde, Audre. *The Master's Tools Will Never Dismantle the Master's House*. London: Penguin, 2018.

Louis, Patrice. "Roger de Jaham: le béké dissident." *Le Monde*, 1 August 2006. https://www.lemonde.fr/societe/article/2006/08/01/roger-de-jaham-le-beke-dissident_800103_3224.html.

Macey, David. "'Adieu foulard. Adieu madras.'" In *Frantz Fanon's Black Skin, White Masks: New Interdisciplinary Essays*, edited by Max Silverman, 12–31. Manchester: Manchester University Press, 2005.

———. *Frantz Fanon. A Biography*. London: Granta, 2000.

———. "'I Am My Own Foundation': Frantz Fanon as a Source of Continued Political Embarrassment." *Theory, Culture & Society* 27, nos. 7–8 (2010): 33–51.

Madou, Jean-Pol. *Édouard Glissant: De mémoire d'arbres*. Amsterdam: Rodopi, 1996.

Maignan-Claverie, Chantal. *Le métissage dans la littérature des Antilles françaises: Le complexe d'Ariel*. Paris: Karthala, 2005.

Marsh, Kate. *Narratives of the French Empire: Fiction, Nostalgia, and Imperial Rivalries, 1784 to the Present*. Lanham, MD: Lexington Books, 2013.

McCusker, Maeve. "All Creoles Now? Béké Identity and *Éloge de la créolité*." *Small Axe* 21, no. 1 (2017): 220–32.

———. "The Caribbean Novel in French." In *The Cambridge History of the Novel in French*, edited by Adam Watt, 578–96. Cambridge: Cambridge University Press, 2021.

———. "Figuring Abjection: The Slave Mother in the Early Creole Novel." *French Studies* 67, no. 1 (2013): 61–75.

———. "Introduction." In *Outre-mer*, by Louis de Maynard de Queilhe, 2 vols., 1:vii–xxxix. Paris: L'Harmattan, 2009.

———. *Patrick Chamoiseau: Recovering Memory*. Liverpool: Liverpool University Press, 2007.
———. "'Troubler l'ordre de l'oubli': Memory and Forgetting in French Caribbean Autobiography of the 1990s." *Forum for Modern Language Studies* 40, no. 4 (2004): 438–50.
———. "The 'Unhomely' White Women of Antillean Writing." *Paragraph* 37, no. 2 (2014): 273–89.
McMullan, Terrance. *Habits of Whiteness: A Pragmatist Reconstruction*. Bloomington: Indiana University Press, 2009.
Messent, Peter. *The Crime Fiction Handbook*. Chichester, UK: Wiley-Blackwell, 2013.
Michaux, Paul. Genealogy of families of Guadeloupe and Martinique. https://www.geneanet.org/.
Milne, Lorna. "The *marron* and the *marqueur*: Physical Space and Imaginary Displacements in Patrick Chamoiseau's *L'esclave vieil homme et le molosse*." In *Ici-là: Place and Displacement in Caribbean Writing in French*, edited by Mary Gallagher, 61–82. Amsterdam: Rodopi, 2003.
———. *Patrick Chamoiseau: Espaces d'une écriture antillaise*. Amsterdam: Rodopi, 2006.
———. "Sex, Gender, and the Right to Write: Patrick Chamoiseau and the Erotics of Colonialism." *Paragraph* 24, no. 3 (2001): 59–75.
Moreau de Saint-Méry, Médéric Louis Élie. *Description topographique, physique, civile, politique et historique de la partie française de l'isle Saint-Domingue*. Paris: Société de l'histoire des colonies françaises, 1958.
Morrison, Toni. *Playing in the Dark: Whiteness and the Literary Imagination*. Cambridge, MA: Harvard University Press, 1992.
Moudileno, Lydie. *L'écrivain antillais au miroir de sa littérature: Mises en scène et mise en abyme du roman antillais*. Paris: Karthala, 1997.
Müller, Gesine. *Crossroads of Colonial Cultures: Caribbean Literatures in the Age of Revolution*. Translated and expanded by Marie Deer. Berlin: De Gruyter, 2018.
Munro, Martin. "The French Creoles of Trinidad and the Limits of the Francophone." *French Studies* 63, no. 2 (2009): 174–88.
———. "Rhythms, History, and Memory in Édouard Glissant's *Le quatrième siècle*." *Romanic Review* 101, no. 3 (2010): 409–24.
Murdoch, H. Adlai. *Creole Identity in the French Caribbean Novel*. Gainesville: University Press of Florida, 2001.
———. "Ghosts in the Mirror: Colonialism and Creole Indeterminacy in Brontë and Sand." *College Literature* 29, no. 1 (2002): 1–31.
Ndiaye, Pap. "Gommer le mot 'race' de la constitution française est un recul." https://www.youtube.com/watch?v=hH_5-ilyfWc.
Nesbitt, Nick. *Voicing Memory: History and Subjectivity in French Caribbean Literature*. Charlottesville: University of Virginia Press, 2003.

Ngong, Benjamin. "*Le sang du volcan* de Marie-Reine de Jaham ou la nostalgie du 'paradis perdu.'" *Archipélies* 2 (2011): 183–202.

———. "La société esclavagiste vue par une békée des Antilles: Marie-Reine de Jaham, *Le sang du volcan*." *Chimères* 26 (2002): 71–86.

Nicolas, Armand. *Histoire de la Martinique*. 2 vols. Paris: L'Harmattan, 1996.

Noël-Ferdinand, Malik. "L'homme Guy Cabort-Masson et la religion indépendantiste dans *Biblique des derniers gestes* de Patrick Chamoiseau." *La tortue verte: Revue en ligne des littératures francophones*, Université de Lille, 2014. http://www.latortueverte.com/DOSSIER%205%20Patrick%20Chamoiseau%20nov%202014%20-%20La%20Tortue%20Verte.pdf.

Oberlin, Christophe. *Quelle est la blancheur de vos blancs et la noirceur de vos noirs? Pour en finir avec les "races humaines."* Paris: Édilivre, 2014.

O'Callaghan, Evelyn. "Black Irish, White Jamaican: Real and Imagined Irishness in Caribbean Literature." *Caribbean Quarterly* 64, nos. 3–4 (2018): 392–408.

"Odieux assassinat." *La Paix*, 30 August 1943, 2.

Ormerod, Beverley. *An Introduction to the French Caribbean Novel*. London: Heinemann, 1985.

Oudin-Bastide, Caroline. *Des nègres et des juges: La scandaleuse affaire Spoutourne (1831–1834)*. Paris: Éditions complexe, 2008.

Pearson, Nels, and Marc Singer. "Introduction." In *Detective Fiction in a Postcolonial and Transnational World*, edited by Nels Pearson and Marc Singer, 1–14. Farnham, UK: Ashgate, 2009.

Péroncel-Hugoz, J. P. "La Martinique en mots d'auteurs." *Le Monde*, 19 May 1990, 15–19.

Petitjean Roget, Jacques, and Eugène Bruneau-Latouche. *Personnes et familles à la Martinique au XVII siècle*. Paris: Desormeaux, 2000.

Pinalie-Dracius, Pierre. "Une Amérique dépassée: *La grande békée* de Marie-Reine de Jaham." *Antilla* 329 (April 1989): 17–18.

Rabbitt, Kara M. "History into Story: Suzanne Césaire, Lafcadio Hearn, and Representations of the 1848 Martinique Slave Revolts." *Anthurium: A Caribbean Studies Journal* 12, no. 2 (2015): 1–17.

Raiskin, Judith L. *Snow on the Cane Fields: Women's Writing and Creole Subjectivity*. Minneapolis: University of Minnesota Press, 1996.

Reddy, Maureen T. *Traces, Codes, and Clues: Reading Race in Crime Fiction*. New Brunswick, NJ: Rutgers University Press, 2003.

Régent, Frédéric. "La fabrication des blancs dans les colonies françaises." In *De quelle couleur sont les Blancs? Des "petits blancs" des colonies au "racisme anti-blancs*," edited by Sylvie Laurent and Thierry Leclere, 67–75. Paris: Éditions La Découverte, 2013.

Renard, Rosamund. "A Social History of Guadeloupe and Martinique in the Postemancipation Nineteenth Century: 1848–1902." MPhil thesis, University of the West Indies, 1982.

Reynal, Emmanuel de. "Tous Créoles! condamne les dérives racistes anti-békés!" *Tous Créoles!*, 20 October 2019. https://touscreoles.fr/tous-creoles-condamne-les-derives-racistes-anti-bekes/.
Rochmann, Marie-Christine. *L'esclave fugitif dans la littérature antillaise*. Paris: Karthala, 2000.
Russ, Elizabeth Christine. *The Plantation in the Post-Slavery Imagination*. New York: Oxford University Press, 2010.
Sago, Kylie. "Beyond the Headless Empress: Gabriel Vital Dubray's Statues of Joséphine, Édouard Glissant's *Tout-monde*, and Contested Monuments of French Empire." *Nineteenth-Century Contexts* 41, no. 5 (2019): 501–19.
Said, Edward. *Culture and Imperialism*. London: Vintage, 1993.
Schloss, Rebecca Hartkopf. *Sweet Liberty: The Final Days of Slavery in Martinique*. Philadelphia: University of Pennsylvania Press, 2009.
Seguin-Cadiche, Daniel. *Vincent Placoly: "Une explosion dans la cathédrale" ou regards sur l'œuvre de Vincent Placoly*. Paris: L'Harmattan, 2001.
Sheringham, Olivia. "From Creolization to Relation. An Interview with Patrick Chamoiseau." Oxford Diasporas Programme, 17 April 2012. https://www.migrationinstitute.org/files/news/patrickchamoiseauinterview_f.pdf.
———. "Markers of Identity in Martinique: Being French, Black, Creole." *Ethnic and Racial Studies* 39, no. 2 (2016): 243–62.
Simek, Nicole. *Eating Well, Reading Well: Maryse Condé and the Ethics of Interpretation*. Amsterdam: Rodopi, 2008.
———. *Hunger and Irony in the French Caribbean: Literature, Theory, and Public Life*. New York: Palgrave, 2016.
Sourieau, Marie-Agnès. "*Frères volcans* de Vincent Placoly: Réflexions sur l'abolition de l'esclavage." In *Esclavage, résistances et abolitions*, edited by Marcel Dorigny, 507–17. Paris: Éditions du CTHS, 1999.
Spear, Thomas C. "Marie-Reine de Jaham." *Île-en-Île*, n.d. ile-en-ile.org/jaham/.
Spivak, Gayatri Chakravorty. "Three Women's Texts and a Critique of Imperialism." *Critical Inquiry* 12, no. 1 (1985): 243–61.
St. John, Maria. "'It Ain't Fittin'": Cinematic and Fantasmatic Contours of Mammy in *Gone with the Wind* and Beyond." *Studies in Gender and Sexuality* 2, no. 2 (2001): 129–62.
Stuart, Andrea. *The Rose of Martinique: A Life of Napoleon's Josephine*. London: Macmillan, 2003.
Suga, Keijiro. "*Échos-Monde* and Abrasions: Translation as a Form of Dialogue." *Social Identities* 12, no. 1 (2006): 17–28.
Sullivan, Shannon. *Revealing Whiteness: The Unconscious Habits of Racial Privilege*. Bloomington: Indiana University Press, 2006.
Taffin, Dominique, ed. *Moreau de Saint-Méry ou les ambiguïtés d'un créole des lumières [texte imprimé]: actes du colloque, 10–11 septembre 2004*. Fort-de-France, Martinique: Société des amis des archives et de la recherche sur le patrimoine culturel des Antilles, 2006.

Théodose, Céline. "'Martinique is ours, not theirs!': Framing Conflicting Identities during the 2009 Protests." *Postcolonial Studies* 22, no. 2 (2019): 168–87.

Thomas, Bonnie. *Breadfruit or Chestnut? Gender Construction in the French Caribbean Novel.* Lanham, MD: Lexington Books, 2006.

———. *Connecting Histories: Francophone Caribbean Writers Interrogating Their Past.* Jackson: University of Mississippi Press, 2017.

Tomich, Dale W. *Slavery in the Circuit of Sugar: Martinique and the World Economy, 1830–1848.* Baltimore: Johns Hopkins University Press, 1990.

Toumson, Roger. "Les littératures caribéennes francophones: Problèmes et perspectives." *Cahiers de l'association internationale des études françaises* 55, no. 1 (2003): 103–21.

———. *La transgression des couleurs: Littérature et langage des Antilles.* Paris: Éditions Caribéennes, 1989.

Toureille, Julien. "La dissidence dans les Antilles françaises: Une mémoire à preserver (1945–2011)." *Revue historique des armées* 270 (2013): 68–78.

Tous Créoles! http://www.touscreoles.fr/.

Tuan, Yi-Fu. *Topophilia: A Study of Environmental Perception, Attitudes, and Values.* Englewood Cliffs, NJ: Prentice-Hall, 1974.

Turcotte, Gerry. "Vampiric Decolonization: Fanon, 'Terrorism,' and Mudrooroo's Vampire Trilogy." In *Postcolonial Whiteness: A Critical Reader on Race and Empire,* edited by Alfred J. López, 103–18. Albany: State University of New York Press, 2005.

Twine, France Winddance, and Charles Gallagher. "The Future of Whiteness: A Map of the 'Third Wave.'" *Ethnic and Racial Studies* 31, no.1 (2008): 4–24.

Vété-Congolo, Hanétha. "Créolization, Créolité, Martinique, and the Dangerous Intellectual Deception of Tous Créoles!" *Journal of Black Studies* 45, no. 8 (2014): 769–91.

———. "La créolité aujourd'hui: Entretien avec Raphaël Confiant." *Île-en-Île,* Schœlcher, Martinique, 17 January 2008. http://ile-en-ile.org/raphael-confiant-la-creolite-aujourdhui/.

Walcott, Derek. *What the Twilight Says: Essays.* London: Faber and Faber, 1998.

Warmington, Paul. "Taking Race out of Scare Quotes: Race-Conscious Social Analysis in an Ostensibly Post-Racial World." *Race, Ethnicity, and Education* 12, no. 3 (2009): 281–96.

Watson, Jay, ed. *Faulkner and Whiteness.* Jackson: University Press of Mississippi, 2011.

Watson, Veronica T. "Lillian B. Horace and the Literature of White Estrangement: Rediscovering an African American Intellectual of the Jim Crow Era." *Mississippi Quarterly* 64, nos. 1–2 (2011): 3–24.

———. *The Souls of White Folk: African American Writers Theorize Whiteness.* Jackson: University Press of Mississippi, 2013.

Wood, Marcus. *Black Milk: Imagining Slavery in the Visual Cultures of Brazil and America.* Oxford: Oxford University Press, 2013.

———. *Slavery, Empathy, and Pornography.* Oxford: Oxford University Press, 2002.
Young, Robert J. C. *Colonial Desire: Hybridity in Theory, Culture, and Race.* London: Routledge, 1995.
———. *White Mythologies: Writing History and the West.* London: Routledge, 2004.
Zimmerman, Patricia R. "Good Girls, Bad Women: The Role of Older Women on *Dynasty*." *Journal of Film and Video* 37, no. 2 (1985): 66–74.
Zimra, Clarisse. "Second retour au pays natal: *Frères volcans* de Vincent Placoly." In *Carrefour de cultures: Mélanges offerts à Jacqueline Leiner,* edited by Régis Antoine, 525–40. Tübingen, Germany: Gunter Narr Verlag, 1993.
Žižek, Slavoj. "Melancholy and the Act." *Critical Inquiry* 26, no. 4 (2000): 657–81.

Index

Abolition of 1848, 2, 4, 219n27; as context for Antillean literary production, 17, 28, 47, 50, 76, 107, 138; as fictional motif, 29, 76, 78, 79, 93, 106, 108, 116, 118, 123, 124–25, 134, 182; language and, 7, 115, 123; power of *békés* since, 207n30; sesquicentenary of, 107, 154, 157, 182, 196; and shifting meanings of race, 7, 10
ambivalence: in accounts of *béké* power, 24, 28, 33, 37–38, 41, 49, 54, 60, 65, 86, 159; in colonial discourse, 31, 48; of Joséphine's statue, 5. *See also* Bhabha, Homi
amours de Zémédare et Carina, Les (Traversay): "ambivalence" in, 28, 31, 37–38, 49; Joséphine de Beauharnais in, 40–41, 201n13; erasure of non-whites in, 24, 55; and later *béké* novels, 47–48, 51, 52, 53, 56, 60, 76, 98, 158, 189, 192; in literary historiography, 32; *métissage* in, 36–37; Moreau's influence in, 205n12; proto-environmentalism in, 44, 48; publication history of, 205n3; temporality in, 28, 38–41, 44–47; topographical description in, 33–34, 35, 41–47; treatment of slavery in, 28, 33, 35–37, 47, 55; whiteness in, 37, 47
Antilla (newspaper), 139, 140
Antilles, the: colonial history of, x; contemporary economy of, 12, 200n12; contemporary race relations in, 164, 194–98, 200n14; departmentalization, 12; geography of, 24. *See also* Beauharnais, Joséphine de: attacks on statue of; Guadeloupe; Martinique

Antoine, Régis, 9–10, 32, 205n6; *Les écrivains français et les Antilles*, 19
Arnold, A. James, 141

Baldwin, James, 111, 212n4
Bal masqué à Békéland (Confiant): *béké* names in, 22; *békés* versus other whites in, 24; and crime fiction, 30, 161, 162, 163, 168–69, 187; decline of white patriarchy in, 170–71, 174–75, 189; hermeticism of *béké* society in, 163, 217n11; as popular fiction, 26; representations of women in, 171, 218n18; sociopolitical context of, 163–64; sympathetic *békés* in, 175–76
Bartmann, Sarah, 169
Baudelaire, Charles, 49, 118, 120
Beattie, Valerie, 86
Beaudoux, Edith Kováts, *Les blancs créoles de la Martinique*, 20, 200n5
Beauharnais, Joséphine de, 200n1, 206n24, 213n27; in Antillean fiction, 40–41, 142, 169, 201n13, 216n19; attacks on statue of, 1–2, 3–6, 170–71, 175, 195, 198, 200nn2–4, 201nn18–19; links to Traversay family, 7, 32, 40
béké: etymology of, 10–11; history of the term, 9–10, 52, 187, 202n40, 202n42; near synonyms for, 2–3, 95
békés: in Antillean imaginary, ix–x, 2; and the "circle," 192; and contemporary Black activism, xiii, 1–3, 5–6, 194–95; in contemporary fiction and criticism, 19–21; as decadent, 29–30, 93, 95–96, 143–44, 164–65, 176–77; as dominant minority, 2, 3, 12, 15, 16–17, 149–50;

békés (continued)
and femininity, 22–23, 27, 97, 130–31, 136, 142, 144–45, 157, 158, 164–65, 171, 173, 178, 184–85; in fiction by non-white writers, 76–77, 92, 107–9, 110, 120, 161–65, 171, 176, 187, 189–91; genetic continuity of, 191, 193; *grands* versus *petits*, 23, 55, 58, 142–43, 155–56, 172; and incest, 22–23, 102, 103–4, 192; and language, 120–25, 127–29; literary production by, 17–18, 21, 26–27, 97, 138–42, 189; and *métissage*, 102–5, 156–57, 158–59, 167, 172; and the metropole, 103, 181, 195; and mixed race couples, 176–78, 184–86; names of, 22, 58, 143; and noble status, 58, 71–72, 95, 142; nostalgia of, 22, 24, 95, 197–98; novel form and, 76–77, 92, 100, 110–15, 118–19, 160–63; and patriarchy, 23, 127–29, 171, 174–75; reclusiveness of, 8, 18, 20, 138, 171, 191–92; regeneration of, 99, 151–54, 189; as sexually impotent, 167–68, 170; and slavery, 2, 11, 20, 27, 76, 87–90, 92–93, 96–99, 100–101, 105–6, 108, 116–18, 120–25, 158, 165, 185–86; tensions among, 78, 110, 133, 176; and Tous Créoles! movement, 18, 195–97; versus other white Antilleans, 23–24; and Vichy regime, 138, 171–72, 174; violent fictional deaths of, 30, 161–62, 165–66, 168–69, 173–76, 177–79, 189; wealth of, 30, 187, 197, 200n12; and whiteness, x, 89–91, 92, 97, 102, 144–47, 150–51, 159, 169, 190. See also *métissage*; race; whiteness; white women
belle créole, La (Condé), 214n39, 220n38; *béké* femininity in, 27, 164–65, 177; *béké* persecution complex in, 181; as crime fiction, 30, 162–65, 166; decadence of *békés* in, 176–77, 186–87, 198, 220n32; first-person voice in, 178–81; justice system in, 187; legacy of slavery in, 165, 182–86, 220n42; plantation patriarchy in, 23; societal dysfunction in, 177–78; sociopolitical context of, 163–64
Benthien, Claudia, 8
Bernardin de Saint-Pierre, Jacques-Henri, *Paul et Virginie*, 34, 37, 206n14
Berthier, Sophie, 157–58

Bhabha, Homi, 16, 22, 106; ambivalence, 24, 28, 31, 37–38, 49; *The Location of Culture*, 31; whiteness in, 89–90
Black Lives Matter, xi, xiii, 199n8
Bolzinger, Romain, 193, 198, 200n5
Bonaparte, Joséphine. See Beauharnais, Joséphine de
Bonaparte, Napoléon. See Napoléon I
Bongie, Chris, 120, 191, 209n23, 212n64; on Cabort-Masson, 171; and "creolist discourse," 29; *Friends and Enemies*, 21; on Jaham, 21, 29, 140, 141; on Levilloux, 54, 64, 65; on Maynard, 208; on postcolonial literary studies, 18
Bonilla, Yarimar, 11–12, 30, 194
Britton, Celia, 87, 89, 110, 135, 183, 220n35
Brontë, Charlotte, 29, 85–86, 153
Browne, Kathryn E., 20
Brozgal, Lia, xii, 200n10
Burton, Richard, 53, 54, 78, 83, 208n13
Butler, Judith, xi

Cabort-Masson, Guy: biography of, 218n20; criticism of Fort-de-France mayor, 220n31; *Martinique: Comportements et mentalité*, 163; murder of Despointes, 219n28; philistinism of *békés*, 219n25; *Les puissances d'argent en Martinique*, 163; *Qui a tué le béké de Trinité?*, 26, 30, 78, 131, 138, 162, 164–65, 171–76, 186–87; race and class, 163; ridiculing of *béké* names, 58; setting of novels by, 169. See also *Qui a tué le béké de Trinité?*
Cailler, Bernadette, 83, 91
Capécia, Mayotte, 75; as Fanon case study, 96; *Je suis martiniquaise*, 27; *La négresse blanche*, 27
Cervulle, Maxime, 14; *Dans le blanc des yeux*, 15
Césaire, Aimé, 5, 140, 178, 207n31, 211n50, 214n49, 215n53; and departmentalization, 12, 108; *Ferrements*, 212n3; as fictional intertext, 100, 106, 136, 167, 174; as political figure, 196, 201n10, 201n19, 212n64, 212n66; *Tropiques*, 173
Chambers, Ross, 12–13, 15
Chamoiseau, Patrick, 211n50; *béké* nostalgia, 22; and *béké* philistinism,

120, 199n3; *Biblique des derniers gestes*, 94, 97; *Chronicle of the Seven Sorrows*, 92–93; complex *béké* characters of, 76–77, 93, 100, 107, 111, 213n31; and *créolité*, 107–8, 196; and crime fiction, 161; *Un dimanche au cachot*, 25, 28–29, 76, 92, 94, 95, 97, 99–107, 131, 202n27; historical setting of novels by, 17, 28, 75–76; *Hypérion victimaire*, 161; incest, 29, 104–5, 192, 194, 198; intertextuality with Glissant, 92, 94–95, 97–98; intertextuality with Saint-John Perse, 97, 103; *J'ai toujours aimé la nuit*, 161; *Lettres créoles*, 14, 120; and literary form, 25–26, 100, 101; in postcolonial literary studies, 19; *Slave Old Man*, 25, 28–29, 76, 92, 94–99, 106, 107–8, 215n53; and slavery, ix–x, 76, 92–94, 96–97, 98–99, 101, 105–7, 199nn1–2; *Solibo the Magnificent*, 92, 161; *Texaco*, ix, 93–94, 120, 214n38; whiteness, 93, 96–98, 100, 101–4, 146, 190. See also *dimanche au cachot, Un; Slave Old Man*

Charles, John, 111, 113, 117
chlordecone scandal, 195, 221n12
Christie, Agatha, 160–61
Collins, Holly, 185
Collins, Jackie, 140–41
colonial discourse, 31, 42–43, 48
Condé, Maryse: *La belle créole*, 23, 27, 30, 162, 163, 165, 166, 176–85, 187, 198, 214n39, 220n32, 220n38, 220n43; *La colonie du nouveau monde*, 23; and crime fiction, 161–62, 164–65, 185, 187; decadence of *békés* in, 176–77; as female writer, 27; as Guadeloupean writer, 27; incest in, 23; legacy of slavery in, 165, 182–85, 199n2, 220n42; literary status of, 140, 162; *métissage*, 23, 177; in postcolonial literary studies, 19; *Traversée de la mangrove*, 161, 180, 220n38; whiteness, 24, 165. See also *belle créole, La*

Confiant, Raphaël, 75, 200n14; *Bal masqué à Békéland*, 22, 24, 26, 30, 161, 162, 163, 164, 168–71, 175, 187, 189, 218n15, 218n18; *béké* decadence, 170–71, 186–87; and crime fiction, 161–62, 164, 169, 217n3, 217n11; criticism of *béké* literary production, 120; criticism of Tous Créoles! movement, 196; on etymology of *"béké,"* 11; *In Praise of Creoleness*, 107–8; on Marie-Reine de Jaham, 139, 140, 216n17; *métissage*, 175; ridiculing of *béké* names, 22, 58, 218n15; whiteness, 24, 169. See also *Bal masqué à Békéland*

Corzani, Jack, 17, 19, 32, 42, 54, 75, 107, 208nn13–14, 212n60
Coursil, Jacques, xiii, 1, 180
Couti, Jacqueline, 19, 22; *Dangerous Creole Liaisons*, 21; on Levilloux's *Les créoles*, 63, 64, 65; on Traversay's *Les amours*, 32, 34, 52, 206n17
créoles, Les (Levilloux), 206n16, 208n11; ambivalent whiteness in, 53, 61–64, 65–66; British role in, 50–51, 173; Creole hermeticism, 192; and *Frères volcans*, 127, 132; Gothic themes in, 32, 52, 63; as historical fiction, 25, 54–55; mixed-race characters in, 49, 52–53, 54, 60–61, 64, 208n13; and *Outre-mer*, 72, 73, 76; as quasi-ethnography, 55–57, 60; revolutionary ideals in, 54, 57, 60; ridiculing of white Creoles, 58–60, 62–63, 65–66, 71; white Creole naming, 22, 58
créolité, 119; and attitudes toward *béké* literary production, 199; *békés* in theories of, 19; and critical whiteness studies, 14; and French Caribbean literary theory, 191; masculinist aesthetics of, 136–37; parallels with early Creole fiction, 48; and *Slave Old Man*, 107; and the Tous Créoles! movement, 18, 196
crime fiction: *béké* self-destructiveness in, 30, 165; *béké* world in, 163; and Black Antillean literary production, 25, 30, 75, 160–61, 163, 190; and Caribbean settings, 160; the justice system in, 187; sociopolitical context for, 163–64; subversion of codes of, 161, 162, 164, 170; violent *béké* deaths in, 111, 161–62, 163, 189
critical whiteness studies: in Anglophone scholarship, 12–14; in Francophone Caribbean studies, 14–16; patriarchy, 69; and "white-life" novel, 24, 110–11; whiteness as default in, 9. See also whiteness

Dallas (soap opera), 140, 154
Davis, Lennard, 42

244   Index

Dayan, Joan, 7, 62
Delsham, Tony, 140–41, 194, 221n19; *Dérives*, 189, 217n8
De nègres et de békés (Micaux), 168; as crime fiction, 30, 166; decline of white patriarchy in, 165, 167–68, 174–75, 186–87; depiction of *béké* world in, 163; justice system in, 166; sociopolitical context of, 163–64; sympathetic *békés* in, 175–76; violent *béké* death in, 30, 162, 165–66, 174–75, 186; worker conditions in, 147, 166
departmentalization, 108; and *béké* economic dominance, 12, 30; as fictional context, 27, 75, 92, 150, 166
derniers maîtres de la Martinique, Les (documentary), 9, 20, 192–93, 198, 200n12, 200n5, 221n5
Desbordes-Valmore, Marceline, 10, 202n41
Description topographique (Moreau de Saint-Méry), 7–8, 33, 206n16
Despointes, Alain Huyghues, 9, 192–93, 194, 198, 219n29, 221n5
Despointes, Robert Huyghues, 219n29; murder of, 173–74, 176, 219n28
Dessalles, Pierre, 10, 197, 213n30
dimanche au cachot, Un (Chamoiseau), 92, 95; complex *béké* characters in, 76–77, 99–100, 105–6, 107, 108–9; decadence of the plantation in, 101–2, 105–7, 192; historical setting of, 76; incest in, 29, 102, 104, 192, 193–94; intertextuality with Saint-John Perse, 97, 103–4, 106; legacy of slavery in, 76, 100–101, 106–7; literary form, 25–26, 100, 213n32; *métissage* in, 102–5, 131; pessimism of, 108; references to Moreau de Saint-Méry, 100–101, 202n27; resonances with Glissant, 94; Schœlcher as character in, 101–2, 103, 106, 108, 213n31; skin color in, 100–101, 102, 104–5; white patriarchy in, 101, 103
Domota, Élie, 164, 194
Dracius, Suzanne, 27, 140
Dyer, Richard, x, 9, 70; *White*, 13, 186
Dynasty (soap opera), 140, 145, 154

Fanon, Frantz: and the *béké* figure, 20; fictional allusions to, 106, 136, 156, 178; lexicon of whiteness, 14; in postcolonial studies, 16; white masks, 89–90, 96

Faulkner, William, in Chamoiseau works, 26, 100, 106
Fikes, Robert, 110–12
Floyd, George, xiii, 1, 199n8, 201n7
Fourth Century, The (Glissant), 76; allusions to *Jane Eyre*, 85–86, 91, 95, 210n20; ambiguous racial identity in, 28–29, 86–87, 89–91; bifurcation of *béké* world, 77–78; "communication" in, 83, 125; complex *béké* characters in, 76–77; decadence of the plantation in, 84–86, 102, 190, 198; historical setting of, 28, 77; interdependence of characters in, 87–89, 91–92; the master's gaze in, 81–82, 103; matriarchy in, 83–84; names in, 78–81, 95; optimism of, 108, 125; performative whiteness, 96; resonances with Chamoiseau novels, 92, 94–95; white female identity in, 83–92, 95, 102, 198
free indirect discourse: in Chamoiseau novels, 29, 76–77, 95, 109; in Condé's *La belle créole*, 178, 179, 180, 182; in popular fiction, 26
French Revolution: as context for literary works, 38, 50, 205n13; decapitation, 3; as motif in fictional works, 40, 41, 55, 72, 133, 205n6
Frères volcans (Placoly), 78, 215n53; Abolition as motif in, 118, 123, 134; complex *béké* characters in, 113, 135–36, 190; criticism of white Creole literature in, 120–22, 125–26; decadence of the plantation in, 112–13, 129, 144; firmness of color line in, 133–35; as historical fiction, 25, 114, 115–16, 127; intertextuality of, 118, 136; language in, 119, 121–25, 133; legacy of slavery in, 112, 121; literary form, 29, 109, 114, 115–18, 135, 190, 213n30, 213n32, 214n49; masculinism of, 115, 126–30, 135, 136–37; Schœlcher as character in, 109, 118–19, 213n30; treatment of women in, 119, 126, 130–32, 134, 168; as "white-life writing," 110–14, 117, 134
Fulton, Dawn, xi, 182, 185, 220n35, 220n43

Gallagher, Mary, 9, 33, 46; *Soundings in French Caribbean Literature*, 21
Garraway, Doris, 7–8, 96, 105; *The Libertine Colony*, 131–32

Giraud, Michael, 11
Glissant, Édouard, 29, 111, 125, 190, 196, 207n31, 212n60; ambiguous racial identity in, 28–29; and attack on Joséphine's statue, 5; as character in Chamoiseau, 94–95, 100, 106; decadence of the plantation in, 102, 167, 190, 198; *The Fourth Century*, 28–29, 77–92, 95; hermeticism of the plantation, 192–93; historical instability of *"béké,"* 10; historical settings in works by, 17, 28–29, 75–76; *La lézarde*, 75, 217n6; *L'intention poétique*, 94; and literary form, 25; literary status of, 140; *Malemort*, 108; as mentor to Chamoiseau, 94; *Le monde incréé*, 94; nostalgia of *békés* in, 22; *The Overseer's Hut*, 94, 108, 191; pessimism in works by, 108; and postcolonial theory, 191; and post-war *béké* economic dominance, 12; resonances with Chamoiseau works, 97, 103; "sympathetic" portrayals of *békés*, 107, 111; the white gaze, 21. See also *Fourth Century, The*
Gone with the Wind (Mitchell), 24, 148, 216n22
grande béké, La (Jaham), 213n13, 215n6, 217n10; *"béké"* in, 11; *béké* decadence in, 29, 143–44, 191; *béké* endogamy, 170, 191; depiction of Black characters in, 147–50; family regeneration in, 144, 151–54, 190; *grands* versus *petits békés* in, 142–43, 153; incest in, 23, 29; legacy of slavery in, 138; mammy stereotype in, 147–49; *métissage* in, 23, 153, 216n30; parallels with soap operas, 140, 145, 154, 215n16; performative whiteness in, 24; as popular fiction, 26, 140; privileging of female experience in, 142; racial contamination in, 159; reception of, 29, 142, 216n17; reclusiveness of *békés*, 138; white femininity in, 142, 144–47, 216n18, 216n22; yellowness, 159
grande béké, La (Maline), 216n29; Abolition sesquicentenary as context for, 157; exoticism of, 155; liberties taken by, 30, 154; *métissage* in, 156–57; white femininity in, 157
Grandmaison, Daniel de, 131; *Le bal des créoles*, 131, 161, 213n13; as minor author, 18; and novel of manners, 74–75; *Rendez-vous au Macouba*, 74, 161, 213n13; use of *"colon,"* 10
Guadeloupe: attack on Schœlcher memorials in, 201n7; *"béké"* in, 11; as *département d'outre mer*, 9; as fictional setting, 54, 68, 164, 176, 182; French Revolutionary violence in, 3; historical meanings of "white" in, 6; insecticide contamination of, 195; sesquicentenary of Abolition in, 154; status of *békés* in, 11, 27; 2009 strikes in, 133, 164, 165, 194; versus Haiti, 24; visibility of white Creoles in, 15
Guillaume, Pierre, 190, 194, 221n14

habitation (plantation): as dwelling, 9, 45; intercaste mixing on, 6. See also plantation, the
Haiti: as cautionary case, 50, 143; versus Martinique and Guadeloupe, x, 24
Haitian Revolution, x, 10, 38, 49–50, 207n3, 207n5
Harrison, Nicholas, 139
Herbeck, Jason, 161, 164, 193, 217n6
Hoffmann, Léon-François, 32, 50
Houël, Drasta, 18; *béké* names in, 22, 58; *Cruautés et tendresses*, 74, 131, 204n93, 210n16, 211n41, 214n39; and the novel of manners, 74–75
Hugo, Victor, 32; *Bug-Jargal*, 208n11, 209n22; friendship with Maynard, 66; as intertext, 118, 136
Hurston, Zora Neale, 111, 212n4

incest: in *béké* genealogies, 193–94; and legacy of slavery, 101, 105, 183, 190; and *métissage*, 23, 73, 102–3, 104, 192; in soap operas, 154; as theme in *béké* novels, 22–23, 28–29, 47, 69, 176, 218n24; and white femininity, 72

Jaham, Marie-Reine de, 27, 204n91; as *béké*, 31, 139–40, 141, 215n6; *béké* nostalgia in, 22, 141, 197; *Bwa Bandé*, 142, 217n8; as female writer, 27, 142; genealogy of, 215n2; *La grande béké*, 11, 23, 26, 29–30, 138–59, 170, 190–91, 213n13, 215n6, 215–16nn16–18, 216n22, 216n30, 217n10; legacy of slavery in, xiii; literary status, 17–18, 140–41; *Le maître-savane*, 139, 153, 154;

Jaham, Marie-Reine de (*continued*)
L'or des îles, 142; as popular writer, 75; reaction to TV adaptation of *La grande béké*, 158; representativity of, 139–40, 142; *Le sang du volcan*, 141, 142, 158, 201n13, 202n27, 206n22, 213n27, 215n16, 216n19, 216n26, 216n30, 217n37; status in literary studies, 20–21; use of *"béké,"* 11. See also *grande béké, La* (Jaham)

Jaham, Roger de, 108, 221n5, 221n18; on *béké* land ownership, 200n11; family relation to Marie-Reine de Jaham, 139, 215n2; and Tous Créoles! movement, 18, 195–97, 212n64

Jameson, Fredric, 25, 29, 204n99

Jane Eyre (Brontë), 29, 85–86, 95, 153, 170, 210nn19–20

Jenson, Deborah, 10–11, 202nn40–41

Joséphine (empress). See Beauharnais, Joséphine de

Joyau, Auguste, 19, 32, 47

Jugé, Tony, xii–xiii

Kiberd, Declan, 74

Lacrosil, Michèle, 75; *Cajou*, 27; *Sapotille et le serein d'argile*, 27

Lamming, George, ix

Lanoë, Catherine, 90

Laurent, Sylvie, 14; *De quelle couleur sont les blancs?*, 16

Leclère, Thierry, *De quelle couleur sont les blancs?*, 16

Léry, Loïc, *Le gang des Antillais*, 161

Levilloux, Joseph, 74; biography of, 53–54, 204n93, 208n14; *Les créoles*, 22, 25, 32, 49, 52–66, 71–73, 76, 127, 132, 173, 192, 206n16, 208n11, 208n13; literary status, 18; sociohistorical context of, 49–50; status in literary studies, 21; versus *Les amours*, 35, 47. See also *créoles, Les*

Lipsitz, George, 111

Loichot, Valérie, 73, 96–97, 98

López, Alfred, xiii, 16

Lorde, Audre, 121–22

Macey, David, 18, 23, 138, 194, 210n16

Maignan, Chantal, 11, 208n13

Malsa, Garcin, 195, 221n18

Manicom, Jacqueline, 75

Marsh, Kate, 197

Martinique: attacks on Schœlcher monument in, 201n7; *"béké"* in, 11; as *département d'outre mer*, 9; economic dominance of *béké* in, 11–12, 200n12; as fictional setting, 31, 38–39, 44–47, 54, 68–69, 77, 91–92, 99, 115–16, 141, 144, 149, 163–64, 171–72, 189, 217n11; and the Haitian Revolution, 50; insecticide contamination of, 195; legacy of slavery in, 20; post-war race relations in, 99, 108, 186; sesquicentenary of Abolition in, 154; site of Joséphine de Beauharnais monument, 1–6; status of *békés* in, 23, 194; topographical descriptions of, 33, 35, 42; 2009 strikes in, 218n15; versus Haiti, 24; white Creoles as hypervisible minority in, 15; as writers' birthplace, 27, 53–54, 66, 110, 139, 162. See also Beauharnais, Joséphine de: attacks on statue of; Guadeloupe

Mas-Camille, Laurette, *Quand je serais béké*, 8–9

Maynard de Queilhe, Louis de: *béké* nostalgia in, 22; biography of, 66; literary status of, 18, 49–50; *Outre-mer*, 10, 22–23, 25, 32, 49, 51–52, 60–61, 66–73, 76, 103, 127, 132, 171, 173, 176, 192, 198, 206n16, 208n11, 208n13; status in literary studies, 21, 53, 208n13; use of *"béquet,"* 10; use of *"colon,"* 10; versus *Les amours*, 35, 47. See also *Outre-mer*

Messent, Peter, 187

métissage, xii, 209n24; and Creole regeneration, 134–35, 151–53; and crime, 165–66, 177; as family secret, 54, 66–67, 103–6; *hommes de couleur*, 56, 64; and incest, 23, 102, 104–5, 201; and intercaste liaisons, 64–65, 153–54, 155–57, 167, 176–77, 183, 184–86, 191–92; and the "one-drop rule," 159; passing, 54, 60, 72; in postcolonial literary studies, 20; and racial ambiguity, 54, 61–65, 86–87, 90–91, 159, 172; and racial taxonomies, 6–8, 100–101; and semiotics of skin color, 60; as threat to white ethnocaste, 28, 49, 53, 72, 92, 150, 168, 193; white jealousy of mixed-race characters, 57–58. See also *békés*; *métissage*; race; whiteness

Micaux, Henri, 23; biography of, 218n14; *De nègres et de békés*, 23, 30, 162, 163–68, 169, 175, 186–87, 214; as Guadeloupean writer, 27; as popular writer, 75. See also *De nègres et de békés*

Milne, Lorna, 99, 107, 108, 136–37

Moreau de Saint-Méry, Médéric Louis Élie, 158; in Antillean fiction, 202n27, 205n12, 206n16, 208n11; *Description topographique*, 7–8, 33; racial typology of, x, 7–8, 100, 105

Morrison, Toni, 92; *Playing in the Dark*, 13, 14

Müller, Gésine, 55, 56, 64, 65

Munro, Martin, 18, 91, 212n7

Murdoch, H. Adlai, 86

Napoléon I (emperor), 1, 3, 41, 201n19, 207n3

Napoléon III (emperor), 4

Ndiaye, Pap, xii

Négritude, 14, 75, 111, 115, 189

Ngong, Benjamin, 140, 141

Outre-mer (Maynard), 76, 208n13; Black femininity, 132, 206n16; British role in, 50–51, 173; decadence of the plantocracy in, 49, 51–52, 67, 71–72, 73, 198; Gothic themes in, 32, 171; historical context for, 49–51; as historical fiction, 25; incest in, 22–23, 69, 73, 192; mixed-race characters in, 49, 52–53, 61, 66–67, 72; as "mulattophobic," 53; passing, 72; physiognomy in, 60; racial classification, 208n11; semiotics of skin color in, 60; use of *"béké"* in, 10, 66; white femininity, 71, 73, 176; white masculinity, 70–71, 73; white patriarchy in, 67–70, 103, 127

Paix, La (newspaper), 173, 219n28

Parépou, Édouard, *Atipa roman guyanais*, 3

Paul et Virginie (Bernardin de Saint-Pierre), 34, 37, 206n14

Perez, Michael, xii–xiii

pieds noirs, 23, 143

Pineau, Gisèle, 27; *Le parfum des sirènes*, 161

Placoly, Vincent: biography of, 110; *La fin douloureuse et tragique*, 110; *Frères volcans*, 24, 25, 29, 78, 109, 110, 111–37, 144, 168, 186, 190, 213nn30–32, 214n49, 215n53; *Scènes de la vie de Joséphine-Rose Tascher de la Pagerie*, 110. See also *Frères volcans*

plantation, the, xiii, 210n10, 216n18; Joséphine de Beauharnais as emblem of, 3; binary logic of, 91–92, 114–15, 169, 172; as crime scene, 165–66; decadence of, 51–52, 66, 67, 70–71, 79, 84–85, 95–96, 101, 143–44, 167–68, 170–71; economic decline of, 12; economic legacy of, 125, 158, 207n30; as embattled space, 22, 55, 143; and family regeneration, 151–54; as *habitation*, 6, 9–10, 45; hermeticism of, 153, 159, 170, 192–93; historical context, 38–39, 50–51, 76; incest on, 73, 102–6, 192; internal caste hierarchies, 133–34, 143; language and, 121; and the master figure, 81–82, 96–97, 98–99, 101–2, 103–6, 117, 127–28; matriarchy and, 83–84, 183; nostalgia for, 142; physical brutality of, 147, 149; and the plantation house, 93, 106–7; racial classification on, 54; sexual violence on, x, 6, 101, 190; as site of *métissage*, x, 6, 36–37, 60, 63, 72–73, 102–6, 134–35, 153–54, 159, 206n16; slavery on, 33, 35–36, 51, 81, 190; space-time of, 19, 33, 39–48, 76, 97–98; symbolic order of, 88; white patriarchy and, 67–70, 115, 128–29, 165, 175; women on, 107, 126, 130, 132, 142, 143–44, 157, 167

postcolonial studies: race in, 16; white Creole writing in, 18, 19–20, 21

Qui a tué le béké de Trinité? (Cabort-Masson): ambiguity of racial boundaries in, 172; England as source of liberal values in, 51, 173; intercaste tensions in, 171–72, 175, 176, 186–87; mixed-race liaisons, 131–32; as popular fiction, 26; portrayal of *béké* caste in, 78, 174; race and class, 163; Vichy regime in, 138, 171–72, 174; violent *béké* death in, 30, 162, 173–74, 175; white women in, 173, 174–75

race, 203n72, 208n14, 220n43; ambiguous racial identity, 86–87, 90–91; and Antillean geography, 115–16; Antilles as laboratory of, x, 6–8, 10; and Black

248 Index

race (continued)
  femininity, 131–32, 169; and "color-blindness," xii, 184, 199n6, 200n10; disavowal of, 89–90; diverse phenotypes of, x, 169; and economic exploitation, 150, 153–54, 166; and family genealogy, 9, 191, 192–94; in *La grande béké* television adaptation, 155–58; and the justice system, 166, 185–86, 187, 200n14; and language, 119–20, 122–23; and legacies of slavery, 106–7, 165, 169, 182, 184; mixed race liaisons, 64–65, 153–54, 155–57, 167, 168, 176–77, 183, 184–86, 191–92; as performance, xi; in postcolonial studies, 16; raced women's experience, 75; racial discourse in France, xii–xiii; representations of Black bodies, 147–50; and skin color, x, 6–8, 37, 61, 64; taxonomies of, 7, 55–57; in twentieth and twenty-first century Antillean society, 2, 8–9, 165, 184, 194–95; viability as analytical category, xii–xiii. See also *békés; métissage;* whiteness; white women
Régent, Frédéric, 6–7, 202n25
Rhys, Jean, 18, 201n6
Rochmann, Marie-Christine, 107, 108
rue cases-nègres, La (Zobel), 19, 88, 129, 147, 166; adaptation of, 155

Sago, Kylie, 5, 201n19
Said, Edward, 31, 48
Saint-John Perse (Alexis Saint-Léger Léger): in Chamoiseau, 97, 98, 100, 103–4, 103, 106, 211n50, 211n54; construction of whiteness in, 25, 96–97; *Éloges*, 98, 128–29; as intertext for Placoly, 128–29, 214n40; literary status, 17; nostalgia in, 197; status in Antillean literary studies, 20–21
Schœlcher, Victor: attacks on statues of, 3, 195, 201n7; as Chamoiseau character, 100, 101, 102, 103, 106, 108–9, 212n66, 213n31; champion of Maynard, 66; in *Frères volcans*, 118, 119, 136, 213n31; and racial classification, 6
Schloss, Rebecca Hartkopf, 103; *Sweet Liberty*, 20
Slave Old Man (Chamoiseau): béké decadence in, 97–98; construction of whiteness in, 97; and *créolité*, 107; as historical fiction, 28; identification with the racial other in, 98–99; intertextuality with Saint-John Perse in, 97, 98, 211n47; literary form, 25–26, 94–95; optimism of, 108; parallels with *Un dimanche au cachot*, 100, 106, 108; performative whiteness in, 96–97; plantation setting of, 76, 94, 97–98; precolonial period in, 76, 96, 207n31; resonances with Glissant, 92, 94; slavery in, 96, 99; sympathetic portrayal of *békés* in, 29; white femininity in, 95
slavery: and Joséphine de Beauharnais, 1, 3, 5, 206n24; in Black Antillean literary production, 19, 48, 76, 111, 139; British abolition of, 50; construction of race under, xiii, 7–8, 100; contemporary societal legacies of, 5, 20, 92–93, 118, 149–50, 157, 163–64, 165, 191, 201n7, 201n10, 207n36; as crime against humanity, 108, 195–96, 220n42; defenses of, 33, 36, 51–52, 66, 214n36; and dress codes, 62, 209nn22–23; elisions of, 28, 35–37, 48, 55, 158; escaping from, 96, 98; French abolitions of, 4, 17, 29, 41, 75, 116–18, 124–25, 207n4; and the Haitian Revolution, 17, 50; and humiliation, 80, 181; and incest, 101, 104–5; indifference to, 158–59, 182–83, 221n18; and the justice system, 177, 178; and language, 116, 120–24, 214n38; in literary studies, 19; and *métissage*, 61, 66–67, 72, 101, 134, 192; and naming, 22, 78, 81; nostalgia for, 141; and plantation patriarchy, 126–30; and post-Abolition status of white Creoles, 11, 138, 194, 195, 207n30; and psychosexual dynamics, 180–81, 182–86; and racial reconciliation, 107–8, 134; and racial taxonomies, 56–57; reparations for, 182, 220n43; scopic dynamics of, 21, 81–83; and sexual pathology, 85; and sexual violence, 69, 81, 101, 104, 106, 113, 190; slave insurrections, 50; transgenerational trauma of, 27, 101, 112, 158; and twentieth and twenty-first century economic exploitation, 148, 149, 166; in the United States, 13–14; "un-remembering" of, ix, 199nn1–2; and white identity, 87–90, 99
Sourieau, Marie-Agnès, 115, 214n49
Spivak, Gayatri, 86

Suga, Keijiro, 83
Sullivan, Shannon, 15, 184

Tardon, Raphaël, *La caldeira*, 9
Taubira Law, 108, 182, 220n42
Texaco (Chamoiseau), ix, 93–94, 95, 120, 214n38
Toumson, Roger, 17, 32, 37, 52; *Le nègre romantique*, 19
Tous Créoles! movement, 18, 195–97, 212n64; *Créoles, tout bonnement!*, 197; versus *créolité*, 196
Traversay, August-Jean Prévost de Sansac, comte de, 206n22; *Les amours de Zémédare et Carina*, 24, 27, 31–48, 49, 51, 52–53, 55, 56, 76, 98, 158, 189, 192, 201n13, 202n42; biography of, 205n4, 205n13; on the English, 173, 205n6; family history of, 31–32, 40, 206n29; historical context of, 49–50, 52; as Jaham character, 217n37; literary status, 18; status in literary studies, 18, 21, 32; use of *"colon,"* 9–10. See also *amours de Zémédare et Carina, Les*

Walcott, Derek, 48, 191, 194
Warner-Vieira, Myriam, *Le quimboiseur l'avait dit*, 27
Watson, Veronica, 112, 134
white-life novel: and *béké* subjectivity, 29, 134, 135; and creolization, 134; critical whiteness theory, 24; *Frères volcan* as, 110–14, 117, 134–35; and language, 115; U.S. origins of, 110–12, 212n4
whiteness: ambivalence of, 5, 22, 24, 28, 33, 37, 60–61, 65, 78, 86, 89, 126, 130; as beauty ideal, 8–9; and *béké* identity, x, 8, 9–10, 53, 92, 102–3, 190, 192–93, 201n6; and caste decadence, 71–73, 85, 93, 98, 112–13, 129, 143, 165, 174–75, 186, 190, 198; construction of, xi, xii, 4–5, 6–8, 13, 15–16, 25, 33, 53, 96–97, 112, 186; critical study of, 9, 12–16, 24, 69, 111–12; as default norm, 111, 112; in French academic discourse, 14–16, 204n72; under French republican universalism, x, xi–xiii, 9, 14, 199n6; inception as racial marker, 7, 52, 202nn25–26; innocence of, 30, 145–46, 166, 187; and justice, 30, 166, 178, 187; language and, 7, 10, 14, 52, 115, 119, 120–21, 123, 125–26, 202nn25–26, 202n40, 203n66; and masculinity, 12, 70–71, 73, 97, 113, 164–65, 167–68, 169–70, 186; mimicry of, 209n26; nobility of, 57–58, 68–69, 71; and passing, 28, 53, 54, 60, 72; and patriarchy, 68–70, 97, 113, 164–65, 167–68, 170–71, 174–75; as performance, x, 4, 5, 24, 90–91, 96, 134; and privilege, x, xiii, 8, 9, 15–16, 67, 74, 150–51, 163, 169, 173, 184–85, 187, 193, 197; "purity" of, x, 13, 15, 37, 60–61, 70, 102, 158, 192–93, 198; and racial mixing, x, 6–8, 36, 53, 56, 60–66, 72–73, 103, 105, 148, 153, 159; in racial typologies, x, 7–8, 55–56, 100–101, 105, 189–90; and sickliness, 61, 62, 63–64, 93–94, 102–3, 112–13, 176–77; transvaluations of, 186; virtue and, 3, 34, 37, 68–70, 146–47, 151, 158; yellowness and, 61, 62–63, 102–4, 159. See also *békés*; white women
white women: as beautiful, 3, 37, 41; and *béké* identity, 139–48, 150–51, 156–57, 158–59, 175–76, 181, 191; and Creole degeneracy, 85–86, 176–77; and crime, 164–65, 166, 168–69, 172, 177, 180–81; denigration of, 119, 125–26, 130–32, 136–37, 173; incest and, 23, 101, 102, 103–5; incompatibility with colonial life, 72; as mentally infirm, 85–86, 95, 102, 171; and mixed race liaisons, 52, 65, 67, 167–68, 177, 181, 183, 185–86, 191–92; and patriarchy, 1, 23, 97, 174–75; as racially ambiguous, 28–29, 61–62, 63–64, 86–87, 89–91, 102–3, 172; and reproductivity, 79, 83–85, 130, 151–53, 167; as sexually promiscuous, 93–94, 173, 177, 191; sexual violence against, 101, 106, 176, 184–85; and slavery, 1, 87–89, 182, 184–86; as virtuous, 3, 34, 216n22
Wood, Marcus, 86, 149

Young, Robert, 31, 134

Zimmerman, Patricia, 154
Žižek, Slavoj, 197, 198
Zobel, Joseph: laborers' bodies, 129, 214n41; *La rue cases-nègres*, 19, 88, 129, 147, 155, 166

Recent books in the series
New World Studies

Haitian Revolutionary Fictions: An Anthology
Edited and with translations by Marlene L. Daut, Grégory Pierrot, and Marion C. Rohrleitner

Rum Histories: Drinking in Atlantic Literature and Culture
Jennifer Poulos Nesbitt

Imperial Educación: Race and Republican Motherhood in the Nineteenth-Century Americas
Thomas Genova

Fellow Travelers: How Road Stories Shaped the Idea of the Americas
John Ochoa

The Quebec Connection: A Poetics of Solidarity in Global Francophone Literatures
Julie-Françoise Tolliver

Comrade Sister: Caribbean Feminist Revisions of the Grenada Revolution
Laurie R. Lambert

Cultural Entanglements: Langston Hughes and the Rise of African and Caribbean Literature
Shane Graham

Water Graves: The Art of the Unritual in the Greater Caribbean
Valérie Loichot

The Sacred Act of Reading: Spirituality, Performance, and Power in Afro-Diasporic Literature
Anne Margaret Castro

Caribbean Jewish Crossings: Literary History and Creative Practice
Sarah Phillips Casteel and Heidi Kaufman, editors

Mapping Hispaniola: Third Space in Dominican and Haitian Literature
Megan Jeanette Myers

Mourning El Dorado: Literature and Extractivism in the Contemporary American Tropics
Charlotte Rogers

www.ingramcontent.com/pod-product-compliance
Lightning Source LLC
Chambersburg PA
CBHW020113010526
44115CB00008B/817